Loving Our Enemies Through Seasons of Bitterness

Loving Our Enemies Through Seasons of Bitterness

How Christians Can Weather the Culture War

Lex Kohn

WIPF & STOCK · Eugene, Oregon

LOVING OUR ENEMIES THROUGH SEASONS OF BITTERNESS
How Christians Can Weather the Culture War

Copyright © 2025 Lex Kohn. All rights reserved. Except for brief quotations in critical publications or reviews, no part of this book may be reproduced in any manner without prior written permission from the publisher. Write: Permissions, Wipf and Stock Publishers, 199 W. 8th Ave., Suite 3, Eugene, OR 97401.

Wipf & Stock
An Imprint of Wipf and Stock Publishers
199 W. 8th Ave., Suite 3
Eugene, OR 97401

www.wipfandstock.com

PAPERBACK ISBN: 979-8-3852-4563-5
HARDCOVER ISBN: 979-8-3852-4564-2
EBOOK ISBN: 979-8-3852-4565-9

VERSION NUMBER 06/26/25

Old Testament Scripture quotations taken from the (NASB®) New American Standard Bible®, Copyright © 2020 by The Lockman Foundation. Used by permission. All rights reserved. lockman.org

New Testament Scripture quotations from New Revised Standard Version Bible: Anglicized Edition, copyright © 1995 National Council of the Churches of Christ in the United States of America. Used by permission. All rights reserved worldwide.

Where noted Scripture quotations are from the ESV®Bible (The Holy Bible, English Standard Version®), copyright© 2001 by Crossway Bibles, a publishing ministry of Good News Publishers. Used by permission. All rights reserved.

*For everyone who ever held the high ground
despite the urge to give in to bitterness.
Wrestling with a pig might leave one in a muddy heap,
. . . but it sure looks fun sometimes.*

All that most maddens and torments; all that stirs up the lees of things; all truth with malice in it; all that cracks the sinews and cakes the brain; all the subtle demonisms of life and thought; all evil, to crazy Ahab, were visibly personified, and made practically assailable in Moby Dick. He piled upon the whale's white hump the sum of all the general rage and hate felt by his whole race from Adam down; and then, as if his chest had been a mortar, he burst his hot heart's shell upon it.—Herman Melville, *Moby-Dick*

Contents

Acknowledgments | ix
Introduction | xi

Chapter 1: The Media Is the Malefactor? | 1
Chapter 2: The Self and the Cosmos | 31
Chapter 3: Patterns of Bitterness | 58
Chapter 4: No One to Comfort Them (But Me) | 89
Chapter 5: I Pardon You | 115
Chapter 6: To Whisper a Doxology in the Darkness | 146
Chapter 7: The Art of Losing Well | 167
Chapter 8: No Man Is an Island | 192

Conclusion | 213

Appendix | 215
Bibliography | 217
General Index | 253
Ancient Document Index | 261

Acknowledgments

As might become apparent in the following pages, the fruit of the Spirit in my life is typically short on the charisms of love and joy. Ironically, these frequently become themes of my work; clearly I need the experience, and I suspect God (the original practical joker) is having a go at me. Nevertheless, this five-year project is nothing if not a labor of love, mine for the content and love of those who have supported me.

I want to thank my family for their love, emotional support, and (financial) support during the years I have worked on this project. I also want to thank my close friends and companions who have walked with me and taught me, especially Fr. Rob Collis, Fr. Rob Gardener, Fr. Harman Thomas, Fr. Josh and Emily Misner, Jubi Silva, Dr. Matthew Nelson, Tom Douce, Fr. Kyle McKenny, Raphael Donkor, Brandon Daley, Dan Kusbit, Josh Momaney, Isaac Miller, Alexei Listvinski, and Derek Cummins. A three-braided cord is not easily broken.

I also need to thank the many scholars and thinkers who have known which directions to nudge me and when to tell me gently, "That's a bad idea." Thanks to everyone who contributed to my education, especially Drs. Craig Gay, Rikk Watts, Jason Lepojärvi, Iain Provan, Phil Long, Ross Hastings, Hans Boersma, Jack Gabig, Donna Martsolf, John Burgess, and especially Edith Humphrey. Similarly, I must give thanks to Kenneth Bailey of blessed memory, Erik Irvuzumugabe, the various scholars who make their appearance in this text, and my fellow classmates from Dr. Craig Gay's seminar on Christian Political Engagement—all for their contributions from a distance but no less critical. Each of you gave me something that I continue to use to this day, and I will forever owe you a debt of gratitude; this project would not have happened without your input. I must especially single out Jack Gabig,

Donna Martsolf, and Edith Humphrey, who have given me hands-on assistance even without my tuition dollars. I might come to regret not granting you three the dedication.

My thanks to Fr. Thomas Soraka and the community at St. Nicholas Orthodox Church. You have been my family and shelter in some of the very hardest times of my life. Fr. Brian Vanderwel, for your thoughtful nudges and words of wisdom, you have my thanks. I also want to thank Ted and Shahnaz Denlinger, Rob and Donna Martsolf, Chris and Edith Humphrey, Rusty and Mel Magby (of blessed memory), John and Kathy Barnard, Sheldon and Kathy Lenz, Alden and Beth Phelps, and Roger and Amy Maddelena. All of you "adopted" me into your family and taught me that people can grow into more than who they are. Despite the tensions in my biological family, I see that the family of God is rich and kind. Thanks to Ardath and Renee Smith, who taught me the value of forgiveness and helped introduce me to my demons so they might be excised (literally). Thanks also to Honey Badger Radio and contributors, especially Brian Martinez—while we might not always agree on matters of faith and culture, there is no question that this book would not exist without your influence and wisdom. I would be remiss if I did not thank my grandmother for her extraordinarily generous financial support over the past ten years. Without her, I would not have been able to pretend to be a college student . . . I mean to *pursue a formative education* for quite as long as I have. Lastly, my thanks to my Lord Jesus. Trite as it is, when I have forgotten you, yet you never forget me, for you made my being from un-being. With the Saint Johann Sebastian Bach, *Soli Deo Gloria*.

Introduction

Call me Ishmael.—Herman Melville, *Moby-Dick*[1]

WHAT BEGAN AS THE simple task of trying to understand my seminary student community culminated in the book before you. I set out to learn why some of my peers were living with deep bitterness toward others and found myself as Alice down the rabbit hole. I completed three deep dives. The first was into social psychology to investigate how social media influences us and how persons are formed. The second was into the ethics of Friedrich Nietzsche. The third was into holy Scripture, looking for a cure of sorts. If you are concerned with the direction of Western society—particularly with American society—then this text will offer guidance.

I first encountered this problem when I took a short course on theological terminology wherein we encountered "complementarianism" and "egalitarianism." The instructor defined the first as "the belief that the sexes have complementary strengths and weaknesses requiring both to work together in community. Particularly, only men are permitted to lead." The second, she defined as "the belief that there are no differences between the sexes." Given my background in a fairly liberal diocese within the Anglican Communion (ACNA), I disliked both definitions. I grew up with women who were ordained and held leadership positions but who also rejected the idea that the sexes are the same. Thus occurred to me a question, and being something of a rebel, I raised my hand and asked, "Those sound a little lean to me; has there ever been a door 'C?'" Immediately the women demanded an acceptable explanation in exchange for my head. Somewhat cowed, I quickly explained my position and thus appeased my

1. Melville, *Moby-Dick*, 11.

angered sisters. I filed the memory away as it clarified some of the strange culture I had entered into as an American in Canada.

This experience caused my first turn and colored my social experience as a seminary student. As a single man in a community whose sex balance was nearly 50:50, wherein most students were unmarried and that remained substantially self-segregated by sex, I was hardly the only person to recognize that something unhealthy was afoot. One of my professors even publicly admonished all the men in the class for their failure to pursue romantic relationships with the women. Concern about this dynamic led to a semester-long discussion among the student body in the form of a series of articles in the school newspaper. The presence of Joshua Harris in the student body—author of *I Kissed Dating Goodbye* and a prominent figure in the sexual purity movement—also garnered discussion.[2]

Yet I digress. Given the volatile reaction of my female peers, it seemed prudent to educate myself to avoid such antagonism in the future. Much of my focus was on the various current events of feminism. Though I am rather sheepish about the poor quality of my so-called "research" (little more than a series of Google searches and reading of articles on various ".coms"), I gradually concluded that, although women in the Western world have not enjoyed *historical* equality with men, the concerns of feminism were as much as twenty to thirty years out of date and now moot. Arguments about reproductive health care did not reflect the reality that women have multiple options that men lack. Puritanical views about sexual interactions died their last major death with Joshua Harris's renunciation of his writings, which I had the opportunity to observe in real time. Pay inequalities had begun to reverse themselves, with young women's earnings outstripping young men's in 2014. Concerns about violence against women were gently challenged in light of the lack of information regarding men's experience of domestic abuse. Women's educational achievements have outstripped men's, with current college enrollment favoring women over men at nearly two-to-one.[3] As an added bonus, living in Canada meant that I had ample exposure to communities such as MTGOW (Men Going Their Own Way)—similar to the Japanese *hikikomori*, men who intentionally avoid

---

2. For example: Harris, "Strong Enough to be Wrong."

3. For more on this I recommend the writings of Dr. Warren Farrell: Farrell, *Myth of Male Power*; Farrell and Gray, *The Boy Crisis*. See also Goldberg, *The Hazards of Being Male*; Hoff Sommers, *The War Against Boys*; Jaye, *The Red Pill*; and Kates, *Incel Podcast*.

attachment to women—and the Men's Rights Movement. Consequently, my somewhat liberal perspective began to shift.

As my perspective shifted away from a predominantly feminist frame, I noticed something else taking place. While I continued to find the bitter rudeness of my female peers distasteful at best, I found myself slowly beginning to harbor similar emotions toward them. This was compounded by my past experience with a gaslighting lover and mild sexual abuse as a middle-schooler—all of which left me an older man, hurting and facing scorn and accusations of "patriarchy" because it was inconvenient for others when I shared my pain. Whether or not it was justified, I was becoming what I hated. Thus I made a second turn in search of my own door "C."

This second turn was timely in several ways. My concerns regarding interactions between men and women were both confirmed and exacerbated by the rise of the #MeToo movement in 2016—a movement that accomplished the positive end of raising awareness for victims of sexual abuse (especially for women in the wretched hive of sin and avarice that is Hollywood) but also began a crusade of hatred against men rather than offering an invitation to solidarity. Archetypal of this crusade would be the Twitter hashtag #KillAllMen. This also took place during the second rise in popularity of the Black Lives Matter movement in all its controversy, the election of Donald Trump as president of the United States in 2016, and titanic shifts in the LGBTQIA debate as a consequence of the Obergefell v. Hodges ruling in 2015. Since that time, events such as the Charlottesville riot of 2017, the COVID-19 Pandemic, George Floyd's murder and the attack on the White House and St. John's Church on June 1, 2020, the Capitol riots of January 6, 2021, and far more than I can recount here all demonstrate that something is desperately wrong in American society. Behind the curtain lies an ever-present bitterness.

Concern with bitterness has been further driven by my gradual journey *away* from evangelical Christianity to Orthodox Christianity—I am an "exvangelical." For me, the theological draw *towards* Orthodoxy is the greater emphasis on a soteriology of transformation and community.[4] However, the primary *impetus* for this move in my life was the abusive

4. Where Western theology emphasizes a salvation of the individual because of Jesus' death and resurrection, the Eastern tradition emphasizes a salvation of the community because of the whole of our corporate participation in the whole of Jesus' life—including a greater emphasis on his incarnation, baptism, trials in the desert, ascension, and the gift of the Holy Spirit on Pentecost. Western Christendom meditates on Good Friday while Eastern Christendom lives on Resurrection Sunday.

treatment I received in nearly every ministry in which I served throughout the twenty years prior, culminating in the withdrawal of my membership from the church wherein I was raised, on account of abuses of power and pastoral neglect. While no one there celebrated my departure (so far as I know), few grieved it. In fact, while my cultural experiences with feminism and women's issues caused me to look for answers to the problems of bitterness and injustice, I would have little cause to put these principles into practice were it not for my myriad and painful experiences of evangelical Christianity—especially painful given my deep love for the tradition and my desire that it should continue to flourish and bless the world in which it participates.

I began to find some clarity about the issue of bitterness as I cast my mind back to a course that I audited under Kenneth Bailey in 2008, wherein he looked at some of the underlying problems of bitterness in his dealing with Zacchaeus in Luke 19:1–10. I received further food for thought thanks to a timely visit to my seminary by Erik Irvuzumugabe—a survivor of the 1995 Rwandan Genocide. My final breakthrough came about during a seminar I enrolled in during the fall semester of 2017. While I was excited to complete an overview of James K. A. Smith's cultural liturgies trilogy and compare his book *Awaiting the King* to Rod Dreher's publication *The Benedict Option*, it was another student's presentation on James Davison Hunter's *To Change the World* that gave me the final insight that truly inspired the writing of this book.

Okay, so what? A grief of mine for many years has been the cornucopia of Christian literature containing little external support and garnering a popular readership, often (though not always) written by individuals without theological training.[5] Indeed, my reason for seeking a seminary education in the first place was to answer a question that such literature obscured for me: "What is worship? Why do we sing? How shall we make music together?" Given my distaste for cheap answers, this text is not written for anyone who wants quick and easy solutions in the form of trite cliches or memorable slogans (though I try to keep it interesting). The joy of the gospel is partly that there is a feasible way of life presented for anyone who needs immediate reassurance, but it does not shy away from addressing the complexity of life in the process. Thus, my first priority is to provide a level of academic

---

5. See Kruger and Dunning, "Unskilled and Unaware," 1121–34; Constantinou, *Thinking Orthodox*, 17–22. This is especially common among the Orthodox "Ortho-Bros."

rigor that complies with the expectations of basic graduate studies. The text is grounded in authoritative scholarship accompanied by footnote citations. I will make very few unique claims of my own, and where I do so, I will acknowledge it as such. I hope that scholars will benefit from the content herein, being able to verify my claims and address the whole scope of my argument but also to investigate more deeply some topics that I do not have space to address. There are a handful of topics that I found which obviously have been neglected.

However, academic literature often assumes that only the most relevant details are necessary to convey the main idea—terms are undefined, and authors often assume their reader *already knows* enough about entire fields of study that they need not explain further what "Platonism" or "Marxism" are. That is, if you are not smart enough to already know what these things are and what I mean by their invocation, then you are probably not smart enough to read my book, and you should go read someone else's! While invaluable for teaching scholars, this should not be so. Nobody should be denied the opportunity to learn because of their educational level. Therefore, this book will be more thorough and less grandiloquent than a typical scholar might prefer in order to present each topic as simply and directly as possible—just ignore the footnotes if they do not benefit you, as they are meant to assist and not hobble.

Simply, if you will forgive my pride, this will be most useful for people "like me." It is for people tired of political and cultural polarization, social media arguments, and vacuous spirituality. It is for people who long for deeper engagement and the tools to think critically for themselves, even if encountering something for the first time. It is for scholars concerned with matters of suffering or theodicy, with justice, salvation, and living life in a Christlike manner. However, I also wrote this book for myself as these issues cannot be solved overnight. I do not mean to present my ideas from a podium of holier-than-thou spiritualism or the vantage point of someone who has this all figured out. These are not past ideas for me but present realities and ongoing struggles. Lord knows I do not live by these principles well, meaning that this book is an act of self-encouragement—having preached a message, I should do well to live by it, lest I brand myself a hypocrite! Books, by their nature, make it difficult for readers to reply directly and immediately to the author (making them similar to a monologue), but I hope that this book is for anyone who would rather *dialogue*.

Lastly, it should also be evident by now that I have written this book from a distinctly *Christian* worldview. As a result, the rationale and arguments behind my ultimate conclusion might seem weak or irrelevant to anyone who does not share this worldview. However, I hope that the simple practice of drawing wisdom from an ancient text (that is, the Bible) will still prove informative for people of *all* worldviews. I certainly hope to spark discussion among Christians of all stripes—evangelical, Catholic, and Orthodox alike—but I will also consider this work a success if it contributes to the discussion of these issues from a secular perspective. Nevertheless, this text is meant for Christian readers in particular, especially given that some principles here make no sense without the Christian narrative. So, what you are holding is a book for young intellectuals seeking deeper engagement than a Reddit forum, for scholars studying the subjects herein, for priests looking for insight into possible directions to take Christian formation, and especially for Christ-followers who want a better way of living in peace with their neighbors.

My structure for this book is formed into six sections. The first section asks, "Is the rise of bitterness in Western societies caused by social media?" This answer is obscured by the methodology of contemporary studies in media, which includes four broad methods: studying how information technology (IT) works—that is, the *technological*; theorizing about how IT works—*psychological*; documentation of *historical* events and cultural shifts; and mapping trends or the *anthropological* (especially trends, behaviors, and symbols).[6] Unfortunately, these four disciplines are meant to work *together*, yet most studies focus on one. While some studies indicate social media as the cause of the modern rise in bitterness, there is no strong consensus yet. Human nature and the collapse of religious identities are the most likely sources of our bitterness. I will argue that our *politics* has become our *religion*.

The second section looks for a model we can use to understand the current widespread nature of bitterness. I argue for Friedrich Nietzsche's *The Genealogy of Morals* as the best available model. I contend that Nietzsche's explanation is politically bipartisan; it satisfies the demands of justice, addresses the involvement of technology, and adequately explains recent trends in violence and hatred in many parts of modern society. Most significantly, his model is comparatively simple to understand and lends itself to a simple breakdown of how society came

---

6. Vorderer et al., "History of Media Effects Research," 3.

to be controlled by bitterness. In Nietzsche's view, bitterness comes with three prerequisites: acts of injustice, identifiable perpetrators of injustice, and a sensation of impotence (though I have slightly simplified his perspective). The tension in society today results from people identifying a cause to fight for, an enemy to fight against, and a sense that the enemy cannot be defeated. In response, I conclude that Scripture provides answers to all three. The most helpful of these answers is the commandment to *love* our enemies and not fight them.

The remaining four sections of the book highlight attitudes and practices of love that are invaluable for loving our enemies. These four practices are compassion or mercy, forgiveness, gratitude, and hope (or what I call "The Art of Losing Well"). The first two involve our perspectives towards one another—mercy focuses out towards others, and forgiveness focuses in towards ourselves—and the second two involve our perspectives in history—gratitude looks backwards, and hope looks forwards. In each case I answer objections and offer insight into what the practice entails and how it is demonstrated in Scripture. (Each section begins with a list of the Scripture passages in view, and further supporting passages are cited in footnotes.) I also offer examples of recent and contemporary saints who have lived out these practices. I make a point to emphasize minority voices.

Finally, I offer some practical suggestions for how to live and avoid becoming embittered. These are drawn from suggestions in section one from psychologists about mitigating the effects of social media and IT on mood and outlook and from Church practices. In the end, what James K. A. Smith called "The Godfather Problem" remains relevant here—we may talk about these practices, we may encourage others to participate in them, and we may even live our lives as pious churchgoers and readers of Scripture, but *so long as our lives remain unchanged*, the ideas alone are of little value.[7]

It is critical to remember that, setting aside contemporary issues of technology, the problems of suffering, injustice, and godliness have been with us for millennia. These are questions that predate the time of the apostles. These are topics that the ancient sages contemplated. These are the consequences that have reverberated ever since the first Adam took the fruit and ate. The coming of the *second* Adam, Jesus, assures us that there *are* answers, and his gracious gift of wisdom throughout the

---

7. Smith, *Awaiting the King*, 160–61.

ages has allowed us *some* ability to pick at the surface of the solution, but it has never done more than offer a means of living with a temporary peace. Humanity has suffered through millennia of disagreement and conflict, and we shall continue to do so for the foreseeable future in fallenness. The value of the answers we receive from Jesus is that they are *sufficient* and offer *a means of improvement*—even if they do not satisfy us entirely or if we fail to implement them perfectly. As someone with an artistic background, I learned long ago that practice does NOT make perfect, but practice DOES make *progress*. The hope of progress is the reason this book exists—hope that I may progress in love through writing about it, hope that you may progress by reading about it, and hope that by discussing and putting it into practice, *we* may learn to live well in the face of bitterness and injustice as fellow pilgrims in Christ's one, holy, and apostolic Church.

Chapter 1: The Media Is the Malefactor?

Communications Technologies and Social Decline

You are right. Our writing equipment takes part in the forming of our thoughts.—Friedrich Nietzsche[1]

I: Introduction

A TYPICAL FIRST-YEAR PROBLEM for philosophy students is the question, "How do we know we are not just brains in a vat hooked up to a computer?"[2] This haunting question has become particularly salient in recent years, especially following the Watchowski film, *The Matrix*.[3] Fortunately, the answer to this problem is rather simple—though not, perhaps, on the internet. Is it possible that we have been trapped in a sort of virtual reality that only exists on social media, and which is accessed through the phone?

This chapter will break down into several "vignettes": pictures that might help us trace some of the internal patterns of our contemporary social breakdown. I will evaluate several sociological phenomena to determine their ability to influence our affections towards bitterness and the degree to which social media drives them. However, where these

---

1. Nietzsche, quoted in Carr, *Shallows*, 19. See also Kittler, *Gramophone, Film, Typewriter*, 200–203; Nyíri, "Thinking with a Word Processor," 63–74; Emden, *Nietzsche on Language*, 27–29; and Cate, *Friedrich Nietzsche*, 315–18.
2. Nichols, *Death of Expertise*, 130.
3. Wachowskis, *Matrix*.

phenomena lead is not to a sweeping indictment of our media platforms but ultimately to concepts of the self and the centrality of religion—which I will address later. While I will commit some space to analysis, this is less of an analytical endeavor and more of a "fact-finding mission."

Three important notes before we proceed. First, I would like to answer the question, "Is social media or the internet to blame for social changes, especially increasing levels of bitterness?" In response, I offer a paraphrase from the great British philosophers: not at all . . . well, yes . . . ah, maybe?[4] Our media technology is *one* culprit, but it should not be held solely responsible. Many of the changes we are witnessing result from long-running social trends and should not surprise us. Media should be viewed as an exacerbating influence or perhaps as a primary *medium* of change in Western society. The fact that several of these phenomena exist independently of social media shows this.

Second, while I emphasize media developments as a catalyst of our present circumstance, this is not an exhaustive exploration thereof. Media studies pursues four broad avenues of investigation: cybernetics (looking at communications technology), psychiatry (studying neurological responses to media and social stimuli), culture studies (tracking culture shifts through symbols and trends), and social psychology (mapping and recording specific socio-behavioral changes as they take place).[5] However, the ability to identify a causal connection between a media phenomenon and a culture shift (i.e., is the internet *really* making us stupid?) would require a broad spectrum analysis of all four fields simultaneously. While scholars have recognized the need for a broader view of media effects over the past decade, the sheer scope of such a project is so vast that no such work has been undertaken. Indeed, research in this field slowed considerably in the 2010s partly because of this.[6] I can report on what the experts have accomplished, and with the experts is where I leave it.

Third and lastly, while I have a rather stark outlook on media's influence on society, I do not believe the solution is to eliminate social media use. As tempting as that position might seem, the genie is out of the bottle. For all its dangers, social media has brought significant quality-of-life enhancements and the possibility of global interactions and cultural exchanges. The benefits of social media should not be dismissed lightly in the

---

4. Jones and Gilliam, *Monty Python and the Holy Grail*, 0hr 18min 02sec.

5. Peters, "Institutional Opportunities for Intellectual History," 143–52; Vorderer et al., "History of Media Effects Research," 2.

6. Vorderer et al., "History of Media Effects Research," 11–12.

face of its detriments, nor is it my goal to argue otherwise. Our problems run deeper than our technology. Our solutions must do likewise.

In a text primarily oriented toward Christian discipleship and the current needs of the church, a section dedicated solely to media psychology might seem superfluous. This is perhaps an indulgence on my part, but the process of adjusting our identity is not so simple as setting a broken bone. The art of pastoral care must be patient above all. Merely ordering an addict to cease their addictive behavior is doomed to fail. Before we can correct ourselves, we need to understand and correct our *narrative*, our understanding of who we are, how we work, and how we relate.

II: Mechanics of Media Influence

Before introducing my vignettes, I would like to outline the history of media studies briefly. One of the most famous quotes in recent years comes from Nicholas Carr's *The Shallows*: "Once I was a scuba diver in the sea of words. Now I zip along the surface like a guy on a Jet Ski."[7] For Carr, our internet use has a clear and measurable effect on our thinking—we settle for the mundane rather than the extraordinary, for small and disconnected bits of data rather than rich stories. This is the simplest explanation of how media *as a whole* influences our thinking. It is not the history-altering media stories that have the most significant impact—these tend to shape us less than we wish for them to, and they are published infrequently. Instead, the constant influx of low-impact material shapes us the most. As a result, the *landscape* of this information becomes more important than any one advertisement or article. This is consistent with the central idea of the father of Media Matters, Marshall McLuhan, and with social science in general—in some ways, the *medium* is more significant than its content.[8]

While many scholars would justifiably invest a lot of time praising the power of the printing press or radio, much of social science's focus on social media is on television. Marshall McLuhan's book *Understanding Media: The Extensions of Man* (1964) was indeed the first text to spark significant reflection on the power of television, but it was Walter

---

7. Carr, *Shallows*, 7.

8. McLuhan, *Understanding Media*, 9. Harvey Guthrie argues that this message is central to God's relationship with his people, particularly through *symbolism*: Guthrie, *Theology as Thanksgiving*, 40.

Lippmann who first wrote about media's influence on us.[9] Maxwell McCombs and Amy Reynolds write:

> [Walter Lippman's] thesis [in his book *Public Opinion*] is that the news media, our windows to the vast world beyond our direct experience, determine our cognitive maps of that world. Public opinion, argued Lippmann, responds not to the environment but to the pseudo-environment, the world constructed by the news media (Lippmann, 1922).[10]

While Lippmann was focused on the newspaper, this theory has continued to influence researchers. It has also been found to apply to radio and television media—media paints a "pseudo-environment" that we expect to see reflected in the "real world." This theory was first supported with evidence from studies done on the 1968 presidential election—compiled by Maxwell McCombs and Donald Shaw—reflecting on media use and influence during the election.[11] Since that study, many others have been conducted that further support Lippmann's claim, including more than four hundred clinical studies.[12] With the rise of the internet, recent studies have focused on the kind of pseudo-environments the internet creates and how we engage therewith.

Competing theories about the *specific* nature and extent of media influence are many. An oft-touted view is that of Limited Effects—that media have little influence over consumers.[13] While it is true that some scholars overemphasize media, the Limited Effects model is largely disregarded.[14] Directly opposite the Limited Effects Model is the Direct Effects Model (or "hypodermic"), which argues that media consumption injects behavior and beliefs into consumers.[15] This notion was particularly influ-

---

9. McLuhan, *Understanding Media*, 9. McLuhan's ideas are significant given how they shaped the development of study surrounding media, but these ideas have mostly been abandoned. See Valkenburg and Oliver, "Media Effects Theories," 19, 21.

10. McCombs and Reynolds, "How the News Shapes Our Civic Agenda," 1–16, 2. See also the ur-text: Lippmann, *Public Opinion*. I occasionally cite a book in its entirety as a positive source for further knowledge; in such instances, page numbers are omitted.

11. McCombs and Shaw, "Agenda-Setting Function," 176–87.

12. McCombs and Reynolds, "How the News Shapes Our Civic Agenda," 1–2. See also Tolman, "Cognitive Maps," 189–208.

13. Klapper, *Effects of Mass Communication*; McGuire, "Myth of Massive Media Impact," 173–257. For a complete overview, see: Esser, "History of Media Effects," 2891–96.

14. Shrum, "Media Consumption and Perceptions," 50–73, 50.

15. Doob, *Propaganda*; Lippmann, *Public Opinion*; Sears and Kosterman, "Mass

ential after WWII and the success of Nazi propaganda campaigns under Joseph Goebbels. Harold Lasswell wrote that "propaganda is one of the most powerful instrumentalities in the modern world," and Jacques Ellul was a firm proponent of the Direct Effects Model.[16] As with Limited Effects, Direct Effects has mostly been abandoned.[17]

Two additional models are worth noting: Indirect Effects (Moderate Effects) and the Attitude Construct (Negotiated Effects). The Indirect Effects model suggests that media influence subtly pushes individuals in a particular ideological direction. Because this effect is minimal, changing opinions to match a particular position requires media messages that are more extreme than the target. This suggests that media messaging cannot radically alter but can subtly alter or reinforce pre-existing beliefs.[18] The Attitude Construct model suggests that media influence targets the unconscious rather than the conscious mind, resulting in subtle changes in attitude. Alternatively, this may be understood as the result of an internal "negotiation" between competing ideas (either already in a person's mind or introduced via some form of media) to arrive at a consensus, hence "negotiated effects." Although questions remain about the means and efficacy of measurement and the ideological basis through which they were derived, both models suggest that media influence is minor but present.[19]

I believe some combination of Indirect and Negotiated Effects is likely at work in our engagement with media technology. However, as

---

Media and Political Persuasion," 251–78; Sears and Whitney, *Political Persuasion*; Lohr, "Troubled Banks," A33; Zaller, "Information, Values, and Opinion," 1215–37.

16. Lasswell, *Propaganda Techniques in the World War*, 126; Ellul, *Propaganda*.

17. An example of this can be seen in the development of our understanding of the influence of video games. While the initial assumption was that video games would increase aggression and violent tendencies (a direct-effect media portrayal of violent behavior causes the same to be enacted), this has been largely abandoned. See Williams and Skoric, "Internet Fantasy Violence," 217–233; Lin, "Effects of the Internet," 567–91, 574–75. I suspect that the primary influence of video game consumption lies in the narrative structure of each individual game rather than the material content.

18. Hyman and Sheatsley, "Some Reasons Why Information Campaigns Fail," 412–23; Cartwright, "Some Principles of Mass Persuasion," 253–67; Klapper, *Effects of Mass Communication*; Lord et al., "Biased Assimilation and Attitude Polarization," 2098–2109; Shrum, cited in Morgan et al., "Growing Up With Television," 34–49, 40–41.

19. Devine, "Stereotypes and Prejudice," 5–18; Greenwald and Banaji, "Implicit Social Cognition," 4–27; Wilson et al., "Model of Dual Attitudes," 101–26; Fazio, "Multiple Processes," 75–109; Hovland et al., *Communication and Persuasion*. Additional summary can be found in: Petty et al., "Mass Media Attitude Change," 126–31.

already noted, this is not a position that can be conclusively *proven*—it merely fits available data and theoretical models.

The following sections will highlight social phenomena and evaluate two key questions: (1) How does this phenomenon influence us towards bitterness, and (2) Is social media capable of influencing this phenomenon? The phenomena in order are Cultivation Theory, Polarization, Victimhood, and Echo Chambers.

III: Cultivation Theory

Cultivation Theory—which argues that prolonged exposure to television messages encourages viewers to perceive the real world in terms of the television world and is perhaps the most measurable effect of media influence—was developed by George Gerbner in 1969.[20] Though Framing Theory has recently become more popular as interest in Cultivation has waned, Cultivation has remained a useful tool in the internet era.[21] Cultivation is mapped through a three-pronged research practice: (1) Tracing how policies are developed, (2) Analyzing how these policies are communicated through television messages, and (3) Public opinion surveys to establish the efficacy of these messages to influence viewers.[22] Data on Cultivation suggest that it is remarkably consistent and predictable.[23]

Perhaps the most crucial element of cultivation is that it operates automatically and on a *narrative* basis. The following is worth quoting at length:

> Television is a centralized system of storytelling. . . . television has become the primary common source of socialization and everyday information (usually cloaked in the form of entertainment) of otherwise heterogenous populations. Television provides, perhaps for the first time since preindustrial religion, a daily ritual that elites share with many other publics. As with religion, the social function of television lies in the continual

---

20. Gerbner, "Toward Cultural Indicators," 137–48; McCombs and Shaw, "Agenda-Setting Function," 176–87; Holbrook and Hill, "Agenda-Setting and Priming," 277–95.

21. Valkenburg and Oliver, "Media Effects Theories," 19–21. We assume that Cultivation Theory works through the Internet and television, but to my knowledge, this has not been investigated.

22. Gerbner, "Structure and Process of Television," 386–414; Gerbner and Gross, "Living with Television," 173–99.

23. Shanahan and Morgan, *Television and Its Viewers*; Morgan et al., "Growing Up With Television," 35.

repetition of stories (myths, "facts," lessons, and so on) that serve to define the world and legitimize a particular social order. . . . Cultivation does not depend on whether or not viewers profess a belief in what they see on television or claim to be able to distinguish between factual and fictional presentations. Indeed, most of what we know, or think we know, is a mixture of all the stories and images we have absorbed. The labels of "factual," which may be highly selective, and "fictional," which may be highly realistic, are more questions of style than function.[24]

Put simply, cultivation does not influence how we perceive fact but how we understand *telos*—our purpose, our being-in-the-world.[25] We are less likely to notice changes to the framing of the picture than we are to notice changes to the picture itself. However, while subtle and difficult to see, the effects of such changes can be profound.

In conjunction with this, an emphasis on symbolism becomes extremely important because of a symbol's ability to carry a volume of meaning disproportionate to its size.[26] From a teleological perspective, a symbol of the good or a symbol of the bad will necessarily evoke a strong, perhaps even visceral, reaction. To summarize:

> The repetitive "lessons" we learn from television, beginning with infancy, can become the basis for a broader world view, making television a significant source of general values, *ideologies*, and perspectives as well as specific beliefs. Some of the most interesting and important issues for cultivation analysis involve the symbolic transformation of message system data into more general issues and assumptions, as opposed to the comparison of television and real world "facts"[27]

This means that, according to cultivation theory, media can act on us without our knowledge or consent.

The most common example of cultivation theory in action is a phenomenon called Mean World Syndrome.[28] According to Michael

---

24. Morgan et al., "Growing Up With Television," 35–36. See also Hawkins and Pingree, "Television's Influence on Social Reality," 224–47. Further implications will be discussed in the final section of this chapter. See also Smith, *Desiring the Kingdom*.

25. The significance of this will be more apparent in chapter 2, pp. 34, 40, 43, 55.

26. Bandura, "Social Cognitive Theory," 94–124, 101. See also the Milgram experiment.

27. Hawkins and Pingree, "Television's Influence on Social Reality"; Morgan et al., "Growing Up with Television," 39. Emphasis mine.

28. Gerbner et al., "'Mainstreaming' of America," 10–29; Signorielli, "Television's

Morgan, James Shanahan, and Nancy Signorielli, "Long-term exposure to television tends to cultivate the image of a relatively mean and dangerous world." That is, the most common consequence of television consumption is fear, particularly fear that is incommensurate with real-world crime statistics.[29]

Cultivation theory provokes objections, primarily that viewers can choose what they consume, the media's tendency to confirm rather than change opinions, and whether media influences viewers or media creators cater to viewers. The first objection—that viewers choose for themselves what to watch—is contested on the basis that the degree of choice exercised in choosing what media to consume is not as free as we might otherwise believe.[30] This makes the concern about confirmation bias more serious—if we have limited choices in what content we view, then confirmation bias becomes more likely. However, while the possibility of confirmation bias does weaken the potential of media consumption to influence beliefs, it does not eliminate the possibility entirely.[31] Finally, the question of who (or what) influences who leads to infinite regression. Neither media nor its creator has absolute power over the other, but rather, both exist in a dialectical relationship of mutual influence.[32] Ultimately, these objections serve only to illustrate that it is important not to exaggerate the power of media influence in either direction and that our body of knowledge is still growing. In aggregate, this demonstrates that television *does* influence our "pseudo-environments." This addresses

---

Mean and Dangerous World," 85–106; Gross and Aday, "Scary World," 411–26; Lukianoff and Haidt, *Coddling*, 73.

29. Hawkins and Pingree, "Television's Influence on Social Reality"; Morgan et al., "Growing Up with Television," 39; See also: Van den Bulck, "Research Note," 239–48; Busselle, "Television Exposure," 530–56; Goidel et al., "Impact of Television," 119–39; Holbrook and Hill, "Agenda-Setting and Priming"; Holbert et al., "Fear, Authority, and Justice," 343–63. See also the Cognitive-Neoassociationistic Perspective by Leonard Berkowitz, which demonstrates a tendency towards aggression due to frequent consumption of violent media: Berkowitz, "Aggressive Humors as a Stimulus," 710–17; Berkowitz, "Some Effects of Thoughts," 410–27.

30. Signorielli, "Selective Television Viewing," 64–76. For perspectives that express this objection, see Shrum, "Media Consumption," 59–60.

31. Shanahan and Morgan, *Television and Its Viewers*; Shrum, "Assessing the Social Influence," 402–29; Shrum, "Role of Source Confusion," 349–358; Shrum, "Relationship of Television Viewing," 3–25; Shrum, "Implications for Survey," 64–80.

32. Morgan et al., "Growing Up with Television," 38. See also Shanahan and Morgan, "Television and its Viewers." Recall McLuhan's claim that the media is the message.

my second question: "Does Cultivation demonstrate a means for social media to influence our thinking?"

Martha Nussbaum reveals a possible avenue for Cultivation to influence people towards bitterness—thus addressing my first question. In her analysis of the 2016 presidential election, Martha Nussbaum proposes that the primary basis for resentment (a particular form of bitterness) is not anger but *fear*, particularly fear of the unknown or different.[33] This suggests that Cultivation could promote the development of bitterness in a media-heavy society.

Alternatively, the primary effect of Cultivation—Mean World Syndrome—clashes substantially with the Just-World Hypothesis (also mentioned by Nussbaum). This claims that human beings have an intrinsic *need* to believe that the world is naturally "just." From this notion, we intuit the concept of karma or the biblical notion of "sour grapes"—that good things happen to good people and bad things to bad people because of the moral weight of their actions.[34] From this, we also come to demand retribution for acts of evil. The natural demand for a just world is directly countermanded by the implications of Mean World Syndrome—a state that inevitably results in emotional tension if not answered with appropriate theodicy.[35]

However, Cultivation Theory predicted the recent return of partisan news reporting.[36] News outlets no longer frame the news in neutral terms but cater to a particular political party's outlook. This has been accompanied by a tendency for consumers to seek out news that aligns with their political values. This might be a significant influence, given that the most common use of the internet in the 2000s was for reading the news.[37]

---

33. Nussbaum, *Monarchy of Fear*, 63–64, 84–88. I find her argument specious because of several formal fallacies (including *post hoc, ergo proctor hoc*), but it remains worthy of note.

34. Nussbaum, *Monarchy of Fear*, 82; Lerner, *Belief in a Just World*. For "sour grapes," see Jer 31:29–30; Ezek 18:1–4; or the discussion in chapter 5, pp. 135–9.

35. I will not discuss the justification of God in the face of human suffering—properly called "theodicy"—although Nietzsche's atheism makes this a tempting topic to address. The simplest answer is Flannery O'Connor's comment that theodicy is not "a problem to be solved, but a mystery to be endured." O'Connor, *Mystery and Manners*, 209. Suffice it to say I recommend C. S. Lewis's *The Problem of Pain*, as well as Gottfried Wilhelm Leibniz, *Essays de Théodicée*, as prime sources for thinking about this topic. See also: Kasper, *Mercy*, 122.

36. Tsfati and Walter, "World of News and Politics," 36–40; Bergland, "How Has News Changed."

37. Lin, "Effects of the Internet," 568.

Cultivation does represent an evident means of media influence. However, the arguments I have laid out for Cultivation as a driver of *bitterness* strike me as circumstantial and thin. Nevertheless, as I will demonstrate in chapter 2, the creation of stronger partisan identities is itself capable of creating conflict and grounds for bitterness. It is also important to maintain Cultivation as a possible driver of my next two phenomena: Polarization and Victimhood.

IV: Polarization

Polarization is a means of *describing* bitterness, so my primary purpose here is to define polarization and examine whether social media drives it. Lilliana Mason identifies three characteristics that are universal to any form of polarization. These are (1) "when two groups[38] are in a zero-sum competition, they treat each other with bias and even prejudice," (2) One's individual status is inextricably linked to the status of one's group—thus when the group's social status is threatened, the individual will fight to defend it—and (3) Members of a group "feel emotion" on behalf of their group, especially anger in the face of threats and elation after victory.[39]

There are various forms of Polarization. Affective Polarization is typically attributed to Shanto Iyengar and Sean Westwood, who call it "the tendency of people identifying as Republicans or Democrats to view opposing partisans negatively and co-partisans positively."[40] Additional forms of polarization include (1) Policy Polarization—the value judgment between camps revolving around specific issues, (2) Perceived Polarization—the sense of the degree to which two political parties or positions are divided,[41] and (3) False Polarization—the degree of difference between Perceived Polarization and Affective Polarization.[42] Neta Kligler-Vilenchik, Christian Baden, and Moran Yarchi further clarify that

---

38. Alternative terms may include tribe, faction, party, or others. What is significant here is the ability to identify a collective of individuals who share a common value or goal that leads to a sense of camaraderie.

39. Mason, *Uncivil Agreement*, 23. See also: Tajfel and Turner, "Integrative Theory of Intergroup Conflict," 33–48; Mackie et al., "Intergroup Emotions," 602–16. Additional definition found in: Settle, *Frenemies*, 4–6.

40. Iyengar and Westwood, "Fear and Loathing," 691. This definition makes Affective Polarization exclusive to the United States.

41. Banks et al., "#PolarizedFeeds," 631. On "Affective Polarization" see also: Kearney, "Analyzing Change in Network Polarization," 1380–1402.

42. Levendusky and Malhotra, "(Mis)perceptions of Partisan Polarization," 378–91.

CHAPTER 1: THE MEDIA IS THE MALEFACTOR?

Perceived Polarization involves two separate (though related) debates: Positional Polarization encompasses specific moral value judgments, whereas Interpretive Polarization looks at the moral context.[43]

Affective Polarization is challenging to measure.[44] However, the presence of Perceived Polarization in society is uncontested.[45] Therefore, although the debate surrounding "how much polarization" might never be settled, the question is irrelevant.[46] Perceived Polarization causes the same *effects* as Policy Polarization, regardless of how much we really disagree. This should be particularly concerning, given that scholars disagree on whether we can or cannot become more polarized than we already are. Scholars do agree that political polarization can easily lead to the end of a nation.[47] Therefore, our present circumstances might have room to worsen.

Jamie Settle points out that while polarization is already common in American politics, it appears to be snowballing.[48] There are several theories about why this has taken place. One suggestion is that polarization is a long-running trend that might itself be inherent in our society's development.[49] Alternate theories attempt to be more specific. Nolan McCarty argues that Republican political ideals have been steadily becoming more conservative.[50] Delia Baldassarri and Barum Park disagree, arguing that all American politics are trending towards liberalism but at different rates, thus resulting in Democrats moving

---

43. Klingler-Vilenchik et al., "Interpretive Polarization Across Platforms," 1–13. See also: Valkenburg and Oliver, "Media Effects Theories," 19–21.

44. Mason, *Uncivil Agreement*, 76–77; Settle, *Frenemies*, 4–6.

45. Barnidge, "Role of News," 211–18; Bakshy et al., "Exposure to Ideologically Diverse News," 1130–32; Finkel et al., "Political Sectarianism in America," 533–36; Lelkes, "Mass Polarization," 392–410; Webster and Abramowitz, "Ideological Foundations," 621–47; Iyengar and Krupenkin, "Strengthening of Partisan Affect," 201–18.

46. Mason, *Uncivil Agreement*, 77. This might lead to breaks or cessation of conversation, making polarization harder to address, see: Wells et al., "When We Stop Talking Politics," 131–57.

47. Heltzel and Lauren, "Polarization in America," 179–84; Stroud, *Niche News*; Levitsky and Ziblatt, *How Democracies Die*. At least half a dozen scholars support this conclusion.

48. Settle, *Frenemies*, 4.

49. Iyengar et al., "Origins and Consequences of Affective Polarization," 129–46. This was also the opinion of Alexis de Tocqueville, whose work will be referenced over the next two chapters.

50. McCarty, *Polarization*, cited in Baldassarri and Park, "Was There a Culture War?" 809–27.

much faster than Republicans, thereby widening the gap between the two.[51] Settle lists several possible social cues that could be driving this, including the influence of increasingly partisan news media,[52] the influence of family members,[53] an overwhelming number of competing ideals,[54] and pressure from political elites.[55] However, none of these theories address the role played by social media.

Settle has made a persuasive argument that social media actively contributes to the rise in Affective Polarization. Jane Cronin summarizes Settle's argument by saying:

> Settle builds a convincing case that the affordances of the News-Feed encourage psychological and affective polarization, which leads to greater political polarization. An important aspect of this is the finding that "content does not have to be political to be politically informative" (p. 139), as people can accurately ascertain other user's [sic] political beliefs from politicized and even seemingly apolitical content, not just explicitly political postings. Overall, this leads to a situation where Americans "have come to believe they are more polarized than they are" (p. 163), and the view that America is at its most politically polarized since the Civil War.[56]

Settle argues that Facebook is well-situated to influence *political* ideals in an uncertain social context—ideal circumstances for the development of polarization.[57] Settle's conclusions are supported by other scholars and implicate Twitter in the process.[58]

---

51. Baldassarri and Park, "Was There a Culture War?" In my opinion, this is the more likely situation.

52. Settle, *Frenemies*, 7; Stroud, "Polarization and Partisan Selective Exposure," 556–76; Levendusky, *How Partisan Media Polarize America*; Tsfati and Walter, "World of News and Politics," 36–40; Shehata and Strömbäck, "Not (Yet) a New Era," 234–55. This is disputed in: Wojciezak et al., "No Polarization from Partisan News."

53. Iyengar et al., "Home as a Political Fortress," 1326–38.

54. Garrett et al., "Implications of Pro- and Counterattitudinal Information," 309–32; Lelkes et al., "Hostile Audience," 5–20. This will be discussed in chapter 2, pp. 45–9.

55. Tsfati et al., "Exposure to Ideological News," 3–23.

56. Cronin, "Book Review: Frenemies," 701. See also: González-Bailón, "Book Review: Frenemies," 1178–80; Settle, *Frenemies*, 139, 163.

57. Settle, *Frenemies*, 50, 71–72.

58. Lee, "Social Media," 702–22; Tucker et al., *Social Media*; Yardi and Boyd, "Dynamic Debates," 316–27. I will use "Twitter" rather than "X," given the history of the former and the difficulty of identifying the latter in prose.

Other theories exist too. Cass R. Sunstein has written several texts on social media influence and concludes that the primary means by which social media spread polarization is a consequence of AI algorithms. This is sometimes called "Nudge Theory."[59] Alternatively, Denis Stukal and his associates blame Twitter bot accounts for the increased polarization.[60] The complexity of these algorithms makes this claim difficult to substantiate, but revelations by Elon Musk surrounding censorship by Twitter are sure to cause debate, as they represent direct evidence of social media culpability if true.[61]

Several studies claim that social media increases rates of polarization. (These tend to focus on Echo Chambers, which will be addressed later.)[62] One study came to three conclusions about the effect of social media on public views: (1) Negative tweets lead to negative views of political opposition, (2) Polarization increases as users have more time to process, and (3) Framing or Self-Selection (Echo Chambers) increase Perceived Polarization.[63] Additional studies suggest social media as a source of polarization, but these have been subsequently contested.[64]

Some argue that social media does not affect polarization at all.[65] The most popular argument suggests that social media *might* be linked to increased polarization, but this cannot be definitively proven.[66] In addition, it has been suggested that social media does not automatically cause polarization.[67] Social media's ability to polarize might be depen-

---

59. Sunstein, *#Republic*. See also: Calice, "Polarized Platforms?" 1–22; Sunstein, *Republic.com*; Sunstein, *Republic.com 2.0*. On "Nudge Theory," see: Thaler and Sunstein, *Nudge*. Nudge Theory is contested, so I will largely ignore it for this discussion.

60. Stukal et al., "Detecting Bots on Russian Political Twitter," 310–24.

61. As of writing, this story is still unfolding. The Twitter Files may be accessed here as of March 2023: https://www.racket.news/p/capsule-summaries-of-all-twitter.

62. Bail et al., "Exposure to Opposing Views," 9216–21; Törnberg et al., "Modeling the Emergence of Affective Polarization," 1–17; Quattrociocci et al., "Echo Chambers on Facebook"; Garimella and Weber, "Long-Term Analysis of Polarization on Twitter."

63. Banks et al., "#Polarized Feeds," 609–34.

64. Lelkes et al., "Hostile Audience," 5–20; Alcott et al., "Welfare Effects," 629–76; Tsfati and Walter, "World of News and Politics," 41; Fletcher et al., "How Polarized are Online and Offline," 169–95; Boxell et al., "Greater Internet Use," 10612–17.

65. Wojciezak et al., "No Polarization from Partisan News."

66. Barberá et al., "Social Media"; Beam et al., "Facebook News and (De)Polarization," 1–19; Lansdall-Welfare et al., "Change-point Analysis," 434–39. See above "Limited Effects Model," pp. 4–5.

67. Lee, "Impact of Social Media," 56–71.

dent on personality traits.[68] Alternatively, some scholars claim that we have the causality relationship inverted: polarization affects social media messaging, not vice versa.[69] This is reinforced by the observation that social media experiences Perceived Polarization due to the influence of a small minority of extremists.[70] However, two counterarguments against identifying social media as a catalyst for polarization are compelling. The first is that history is the process of a natural cycle of fluctuation between peaceful politics and polarized politics. The second, proposed by Shanto Iyengar, will be discussed in the next chapter.[71]

Jonathan Haidt proposes another approach to the topic of polarization. Haidt suggests that Affective Polarization is due to a failure to sufficiently account for differences in what he calls "Moral Foundations."[72] (This is helpful to consider in terms of Kligler-Vilenchik, Baden, and Yarchi's division of Perceived Polarization into Positional and Interpretive Polarization.) Moral Foundations Theory holds that everyone develops their moral code based on six categories or foundations. These are Care/Harm (the degree to which one practices extending compassion to others, especially children and infants), Fairness/Cheating (the degree to which relationships in a community fairly apportion responsibility), Loyalty/Betrayal (the degree to which an individual rightly prioritizes responsibility to different communities), Authority/Subversion (respect for social or formal hierarchies and the rule of law), Sanctity/Degradation (appropriate recognition of purity against contamination, primarily measures revulsion), and Liberty/Oppression (safeguarding freedom to ensure no one is treated improperly).[73] Haidt argues convincingly that

---

68. Choi and Shin, "Exploring Political Compromise," 163–71.

69. Nordbrand, "Affective Polarization in the Digital Age," 1–20.

70. Klar et al., "Polarized, or Sick of Politics?" 21. This does not address the *degree* of influence possessed by extremists; see: Brady et al., "Attentional Capture Helps Explain," 746–56; Brady et al., "Emotion Shapes the Diffusion," 7313–18. Neither does this reflect the influence of thought leaders and politicians; see: Mert, "Bipolar Voter," 935–65; Mert and Best, "On the Relationship," 1–19; Suk et al., "More You Know," 40–56. My sense is that many political ideals are held by only 12–15 percent of the population, which (if true) would confirm that minority views have a disproportional effect on public discourse.

71. Iyengar et al., "Origins and Consequences of Affective Polarization," 134. See also: Levendusky, *Partisan Sort*.

72. Haidt, *Righteous Mind*, 144–49. See also: Haidt and Graham, "When Morality Opposes Justice," 98–116; Haidt and Graham, "Planet of the Durkheimians," 371–401; Haidt and Joseph, "Intuitive Ethics," 55–66; Haidt and Joseph, "Moral Mind," 367–91.

73. Haidt, *Righteous Mind*, 146, 197–205.

modern Affective Polarization results from the different prioritization of moral foundations that characterize American political parties.

How different political parties prioritize their moral foundations is easily evaluated. Republicans achieve a relative balance in their morals between all six foundations. In contrast, Democrats focus on Care, Fairness, and Liberty, nearly excluding the remaining three foundations. Libertarians make most of their judgments exclusively through the lens of the Liberty foundation.[74] A critical difference exists between how Democrats and Republicans interpret the Liberty foundation, especially against notions of Authority (fear of tyranny) and Fairness (the elimination of oppression). This difference is that Democrats wish for liberty to reflect in an *equality of outcome*, resulting from their expressed concern that each individual be empowered to flourish measurably.

In contrast, Republicans wish for liberty to reflect in an *equality of opportunity*, resulting from their belief that not all individuals are able to achieve the same degree of flourishing and from greater emphasis on the good of the *group* over the individual. Haidt contends that polarization results from failure to appreciate these differences and to compromise effectively where we disagree.[75] Social media does not factor in.

There are numerous possible solutions under discussion for the problem of Affective Polarization. Most of these involve some degree of effort to generate understanding or *empathy* within polarized individuals for their identified outgroup (a group or groups of people that do not belong to one's own group or ingroup).[76] Several organizations are committed to this work, notably Braver Angels, Unify America, and the One America Movement.[77] These are typically committed to conversations with people experiencing polarization to explain the views of their opposing outgroup and highlight points of agreement or commonality. An alternative model focuses less on "ideas" and more on "action." This involves engaging competing groups in shared social activities to create opportunities to bond in areas that are not sources of contention.[78] Both of these solutions have

---

74. Haidt, *Righteous Mind*, 214. See Haidt, *Righteous Mind*, 180–216, for a complete discussion.

75. Haidt, *Righteous Mind*, 319–21. See also his work with Braver Angels: https://braverangels.org/.

76. See chapter 4, pp. 90–2, 111–3.

77. Druckman and Levy, "Affective Polarization in the American Public." See also: https://braverangels.org; https://www.unifyamerica.org; and https://oneamericamovement.org.

78. Adachi et al., "From Out-groups to Allied Forces," 259–65. See also chapter 8,

the potential to backfire, as empathy with one's *ingroup* can cause the individual to become more entrenched in their polarization.[79] However, ideas surrounding solutions for polarization often coincide with "cross-cutting" and Echo Chambers (addressed later).[80]

To summarize, the arguments surrounding social media's influence on the growth of Affective Polarization in America are ongoing and largely inconclusive. It seems clear that social media plays a role in the *spread* of polarization but not necessarily in its formation; the degree of its effect on the spread is contested—particularly due to questions surrounding the role of Cultivation and AI algorithms. The *source* of polarization could be social or a natural result of the structure of American politics.[81] Although how polarization naturally dovetails with concerns about growing bitterness appears sufficient for my purposes, there is another angle worth pursuing before concluding.

V: Victimhood Complex

Another alternative interpretation of bitterness is as victimhood.[82] We all know what a victim is—someone who has experienced some sort of trauma that has left lasting physical and/or psychological damage. However, the *patterns* of victimhood are what make this field diverse—much as with polarization.[83] Four specific patterns of victimhood will be addressed here, but each share three traits in common: (1) A high sensitivity to slights, (2) A pattern of addressing conflict by complaining to a third party, and (3) Cultivating a self-image of a victim deserving assistance.[84]

Competitive Victimhood is characterized by comparing two persons or groups identifying as victims: i.e., "I am a victim of something,

---

pp. 205–6, on solutions through a Common Enemy or Common Goal methods.

79. Simas et al., "How Empathetic Concern Fuels," 258–69.

80. Cross-cutting refers to exposure to opposing ideals that "cut across" the grain.

81. This is my ultimate conclusion and is addressed more in chapter 2, pp. 37–8, 54–7.

82. Ley, "Culture of Victimhood"; Legge, "Victimhood Is Tearing Us Apart." Miroslav Volf has some excellent comments on the topic of Victimhood; see: Volf, *Exclusion and Embrace*, 103–4.

83. In fact, polarization and victimhood are very similar; see: Northrup, "Dynamic of Identity," 55–82. This will become relevant in chapter 3, pp. 82–3.

84. Lukianoff and Haidt, *Coddling*, 210.

and MY victimhood is *bigger* than YOUR victimhood."[85] Thus it shares one of the three critical elements of polarization—that of zero-sum competition. This is typically coupled with the notion of Exclusive Victimhood, characterized by a focus on the self: i.e., "My victimhood should afford me special status, rights, and opportunities."[86] This fulfills the second half of the first critical element of polarization—a zero-sum competition leads to the treatment of the outgroup with bias and even prejudice. Critically, these two characterizations or forms of victimhood are not mutually exclusive. As we shall see going forward, most forms of victimhood have a great deal of overlap in how they are understood. In this sense, it is typically the case that where one form of victimhood is present, others will be too.

A more particular approach to victimhood is Personal Ingroup Victimhood Outlook or *PIVO*. This is defined as

> the belief that one's group is a constant victim persecuted continually throughout history by different enemies. While it entails an element of intergroup threat, PIVO is unique in linking past and present: The historical injustices incurred by the ingroup may have taken place many centuries in the past but still impact the attitudes, emotions, and behaviors of contemporary group members through the belief that past enemies are reincarnated in current adversaries. Moreover . . . the succession of intentional harms against the group throughout its history turns the state of victimhood into a group disposition: The group is being disposed or even destined to be victimized by others. Historical group trauma spreads both vertically, like a stone dropped into a pond, creating an intertemporal construal of the group as an eternal victim; and horizontally, like the ripples spreading outward on the surface of the pond, leading to a perception of other groups as potentially untrustworthy and malevolent.[87]

Notice again the return of the first component of polarization—two groups in zero-sum competition bearing prejudice and bias towards one another. More significantly, *PIVO* causes various changes in an individual's perception of themselves and the world (Perceived Polarization). In

---

85. Schori-Eyal et al., "Perpetual Ingroup Victimhood," 180–94; Shnabel et al., "Overcoming Competitive Victimhood," 867–77.

86. Schori-Eyal et al., "Perpetual Ingroup Victimhood," 180–94.

87. Schori-Eyal et al., "Perpetual Ingroup Victimhood," 181. See also: Schori-Eyal et al., "Shadows of the Past," 1–17; Klar et al., "'Never Again' State," 125–43; Bar-Tal et al., "Sense of Self-Perceived Collective Victimhood," 229–58.

particular, *PIVO* causes individuals to be reluctant to admit their group of victims is complicit in violent or immoral behavior (particularly towards their identified victimizer),[88] a reduced willingness to pursue the restoration of a broken relationship or to forgive their victimizer,[89] a reduced ability to trust others (especially one's victimizer),[90] a significantly decreased potential for empathy (especially towards one's victimizer),[91] and an automatic reaction towards ones victimizer (or enemy) to perceive them as evil.[92]

Conversely, victimhood may be measured as an *individual* personality trait through the concept of a Tendency for Interpersonal Victimhood (*TIV*). Rahav Gabay, Boaz Hameiri, Tammy Rubel-Lifschitz, and Arie Nadler define this as "an enduring feeling that the self is a victim across different kinds of interpersonal relationships."[93] TIV is identified based on four conceptual components in the mind of the victim: (1) The need for personal recognition, (2) moral elitism, (3) a lack of empathy, and (4) rumination.[94] The critical distinction between *TIV* and *PIVO* is twofold: (1) While *PIVO* requires a group identity, *TIV* is strictly individualistic; and (2) because *TIV* is strictly individualistic, it does not have a component of historical linearity of group identification. However, citing Klar et al. ("'Never Again' State of Israel"), the authors acknowledge that *TIV* is nearly indistinguishable from *PIVO*, at least in its outward manifestations. There are, however, several defining characteristics that are unique to *TIV*. The most obvious is a strong external locus of control and power.[95] Additional characteristics include increased sensitivity to personal or romantic rejection, increased sensitivity to hurt, greater anticipation of pain, greater awareness of current events and sensitivity to current issues, greater likelihood to perceive someone's actions as hostile or to perceive others as "bad," decreased

---

88. Cehajic and Brown, "Silencing the Past," 190–96.

89. Noor et al., "Precursors and Mediators," 481–95; Noor et al., "When Suffering Begets Suffering," 351–74.

90. Vollhardt and Bilali, "Role of Inclusive and Exclusive," 489–506. See above under "Cultivation," "Mean World," and "Just-World Hypothesis," pp. 6–10.

91. Cehajic et al., "Forgive and Forget?" 351–67; Chaitin and Steinberg, "You Should Know Better," 197–226.

92. Schori-Eyal et al., "Three Layers of Collective Victimhood," 778–94. All of these shape the background for chapter 5.

93. Gabay et al., "Tendency for Interpersonal Victimhood," 1–43.

94. Gabay et al., "Tendency for Interpersonal Victimhood," 26.

95. Gabay et al., "Tendency for Interpersonal Victimhood," 6.

ability to trust, greater susceptibility to rumination-depression, a sense of moral superiority to others, and the sense that one has a moral right to pursue vengeance.[96] Again, these characteristics should be recognizable as having much in common with *PIVO*.

It is also interesting to note the frequency with which character traits are listed among victimhood mentality that cross over with cognitive distortions: mental patterns that indicate one is not thinking clearly. These distortions can typically be addressed through cognitive behavioral therapy (CBT), which involves learning to recognize and resist one's own cognitive distortions. Typical distortions that are worth noting are those of Catastrophizing (focusing on the worst possible outcome as the most likely outcome), Dichotomous (or black-and-white) Thinking, Mind Reading (assuming the thoughts or feelings of others), Labeling the self or others (ingroup/outgroup), Negative Filtering (focusing on negative patterns to the exclusion of all else), and Blaming (including "victim-blaming").[97] Thus, victimhood may be considered a form of mental illness or at least a permanent tendency towards particular cognitive distortions.[98] How, then, does victimhood develop?

To date, I have found no arguments suggesting that social media is *not* a cause for the spread of victimhood.[99] Harel, Jameson, and Moaz write, "Participation in comment forums can escalate users to anger, which, when validated by other users, reinforces Echo Chambers, incivility, and discourses of hatred."[100] This emotion would naturally spread across social media, given that rudeness tends to literally "go viral."[101] This is particularly the case in light of Emotional Broadcaster Theory,

---

96. Gabay et al., "Tendency for Interpersonal Victimhood," 1–43. See also pp. 64–5.

97. Lukianoff and Haidt, *Coddling*, 37.

98. A concept adjacent to victimhood is that of intractable conflict; see: Northrup, "Dynamic of Identity," 55–82; Harel et al., "Normalization of Hatred," 1–10; Kelman, "Reconciliation from a Social-Psychological Perspective," 15–37.

99. Possible causes for the creation of a victimhood identity are easily identifiable in various forms of trauma, especially those such as prolonged oppression of one demographic by another, slavery, war crimes, torture, genocide, and eugenics. Adapted from: Volf, *End of Memory*, 6.

100. Harel et al., "Normalization of Hatred," 1–10. They do *not* claim that victimhood is connected to social media, but they *do* identify symptoms of victimhood and trace their spread through social media. See also: Baider, "Go to Hell," 69–92; Ermida, "Get the Snip," 205–47; Muddiman and Stroud, "News Values," 586–609; Wolleback et al., "Anger, Fear, and Echo Chambers," 1–14.

101. Anderson et al., "Nasty Effect," 373–87; Steiglitz and Dang-Xuan, "Emotion and Information Diffusion," 217–48.

which argues that social media is a medium wherein emotions are easily spread (likely out of a desire for relationship or emotional closeness), but the physical absence of another person means that no relationship is built.[102] Furthermore, social media comments have an alarming tendency to employ emotionally charged or profane language—possibly an unconscious choice to encourage others to share the comment. This is particularly common in comment sections of news media outlets.[103] Discussing politics is especially prone to bringing out the worst in us, including profanity or highly charged emotional language.[104] Some examples include the 2013 elections in Germany and the 2016 presidential elections in the US.[105] While these do not suggest social media as an initial source of victimhood, they strongly indicate social media (or the internet in general) as a medium for spreading victimhood and as a mode of solidarity.

What about solutions? The most common solution for victimhood is cross-cutting or exposure to your victimizer in a relatable way.[106] Two studies, in particular, suggest that interactions between Israelis and Arabs or exposure to a drug-addicted single mother help reduce negative stereotypes.[107] This means of building familiarity also extends to encounters with fictional narratives—hearing one another out even when we are mistaken.[108] A more significant take on this method involves intentionally creating common ground. Nurit Shnabel, Samar Halabi, and Masi Noor applied the Common Ingroup Identity Model to compare the efficacy of common victimhood status against common perpetrator status.[109] They discovered that, while victimhood could be

102. Nabi, "Media and Emotion," 170. See also: Harber and Cohen, "Emotional Broadcaster Theory," 382–400. This is particularly clear on the subject of paranormal relationships. It will also become relevant in chapter 3, p. 78.

103. Anderson, "Nasty Effect," 373–87; Ceron, "Internet, News, and Political Trust," 487–503; Muddiman and Stroud, "News Values," 586–609; Rowe, "Deliberation 2.0," 539–55.

104. Ziegele et al., "Linking News Value Theory," 1–31.

105. Trilling, "Two Different Debates?" 259–76; Kenski et al., "Lying, Liars, and Lies," 286–99. President Trump's tweets alone have surely inspired a book or two.

106. Such as Northrup's Model of Identity in Intractable Conflict above, p. 19n98.

107. Cohen et al., "Media Identity and the Self," 184; Tal-Or and Tsfati, "When Arabs and Jews Watch," 646–68; Chung and Slater, "Reducing Stigma." See also the previous discussion of empathy and polarization, p. 15.

108. Cohen et al., "Media Identity and the Self," 185; Mar and Oatley, "Function of Fiction," 173–92.

109. Shnabel et al., "Overcoming Competitive Victimhood." For the "Common

abated by seeking common ground on the basis that both groups were victims, it was counterproductive to argue that both groups had been victimizers. This method of reducing victimhood was further studied in the context of race relations in the US and between Jews and Germans reflecting on the Holocaust. It was found to be effective in both cases.[110] Given the similarities between polarization and victimhood, it is possible that shared activities—particularly mutual work towards a common goal—could also address victimhood.[111]

In summation, victimhood is a mentality that inclines persons to feel like victims and bitter towards those they believe are responsible. It is similar to polarization; however, unlike polarization, victimhood is somewhat easier to attribute to social media. Though again, as with polarization, this probably has more to do with the *spread* of victimhood than its creation.

VI: Echo Chambers

Now I turn to the topic of Echo Chambers. Carlos D. Ruiz and Thomas Nilsson explain the phenomenon, writing:

> An "echo chamber" (Nguyen 2020) is an epistemic environment in which participants encounter beliefs and opinions that coincide with their own; that is, "a self-reinforcing mechanism that moves the entire group toward more extreme positions" (Cinelli et al. 2021).[112]

Chris Bail further clarifies that Echo Chambers were identified as a phenomenon in the 1960s by political scientist V. O. Key.[113] Echo chambers might be created over time by making and breaking network connections, mainly through unfriending, blocking, or other means of censorship afforded to social media users. This indicates that Echo Chambers probably form naturally, but they thrive on sites—such as blogs or

---

Ingroup Identity Model," see: Gaertner and Dovidio, *Reducing Inter-Group Bias*; Gaertner and Dovidio, "Reducing Intergroup Bias," 439–57.

110. Nier et al., "Changing Interracial Evaluations and Behavior," 299–316; Wohl and Branscombe, "Forgiveness and Collective Guilt," 288–303.

111. Pettigrew and Tropp, *When Groups Meet*. See also chapter 8.

112. Ruiz and Nilsson, "Disinformation and Echo Chambers," 1; Nguyen, "Echo Chambers and Epistemic Bubbles," 141–61; Cinelli et al., "Echo Chamber Effect."

113. Bail, *Breaking the Social Media Prism*, 4.

Reddit—that are dedicated to a single topic. People are noticeably more selective when deciding which media they consume and might, therefore, form Echo Chambers naturally.[114] Echo chambers are cause for concern given their potential to act as a concentrated force for Cultivation to influence our affections.

While some have responded to Echo Chambers with alarm, we should be cautious.[115] The human capacity to synthesize and engage new information is not limitless; everyone must regulate their exposure to other people and new ideas.[116] This phenomenon also offers a limited explanation for social media behaviors of unfriending, blocking, or other means of censorship. Two social models expound the need for selective exposure. The first—Mood Management Theory—proposes that people select which media to consume based on what they predict will make them feel good, but this model seems outdated.[117] The second—the Selective Exposure Self- and Affect- Management Model (SESAM)—posits that we select media to regulate our emotional state but also to manage and regulate our concept of self.[118] Echo chambers potentially manipulate us, but they also serve a purpose.

Echo chambers raise two questions: first, whether or not social media creates Echo Chambers, and second whether their existence in any way promotes polarization or victimhood. I will begin with the argument that Echo Chambers are the product of social media.

Some scholars argue outright that social media creates Echo Chambers, including Walter Quattrociocci, Antonio Scala, and Cass Sunstein.[119] Others take a more measured approach, such as Paweł Michał Matuszewski and Gabriella Szabó, who argue that Echo Chambers are not exclusively bastions of unity but also sources of

---

114. Iyengar and Hahn, "Red Media, Blue Media," 19–39.

115. Reed, "Are Echo Chambers a Threat."

116. Barnidge et al., "Networks and Selective Avoidance," 1–22; John and Gal, "He's Got His Own Sea," 2971–88. See chapter 2, pp. 45–9.

117. Knobloch-Westerwick et al., "Media Choice and Selective Exposure," 153; Bryant and Zillman, "Using Television to Alleviate Boredom," 1–20; Zillman, "Mood Management Through Communication Choices," 327–40.

118. Nabi, "Media and Emotion," 164; Knobloch-Westerwick, "Selective Exposure Self- and Affect-Management (SESAM) Model," 959–85. See also: Bandura, *Social Learning Theory*; Bandura, *Social Foundations of Thought and Action*.

119. Quattrociocci et al., "Echo Chambers on Facebook"; Reed, "Are Echo Chambers a Threat?"; Zhang et al., "Political Consequences of Disagreement," 1–14.

fragmentation and promote external aggression.[120] Ruiz and Nillson concur that social media creates Echo Chambers, but like Sunstein, they argue that this results from AI algorithms.[121] Additionally, scholars have argued that the January 6 (2021) insurrection and related polarization directly resulted from Echo Chambers on social media.[122]

Hernando Rojas has a different approach. Rojas describes the rise of what he calls "Egocentric Publics." These are "large groups of geographically dispersed people . . . with common information and enthusiasm" that are not bound through spatial proximity and solidarity or kinship but rather because they happen to interact with each other. These egocentric publics frequently form on social media around any focus.[123] Rojas and associates claim that Egocentric Publics function as Echo Chambers and increase perceived polarization.[124] If so, this may serve as an argument by proxy that social media can promote Echo Chambers *and* that Echo Chambers promote polarization.

It is also worth discussing the concept of "weak ties" in conjunction with Echo Chambers. Strong ties are built between two people who know and trust each other well, are often constructed over a long time, and operate on the concept of high risk/high reward, as someone who knows you intimately can meet your deepest needs or expose your deepest pains. Weak ties are used for temporary bridge building. These are low-risk and low-reward. Social media connections almost exclusively use weak ties.[125] These ties also result from extensive smartphone use, which build Echo Chambers concurrently.[126] However, these weak ties are also useful for connecting with people who stress our capacity for difference; that is, they are necessary for cross-cutting to occur at all and thus would appear to run counter to the nature of Echo Chambers.[127]

120. Matuszewski and Szabó, "Are Echo Chambers Based on Partisanship," 1–14.

121. Ruiz and Nilsson, "Disinformation and Echo Chambers," 1–18.

122. Van Swol et al., "Banality of Extremism," 239–51. See also: Kim, "Contribution of Social Network Sites," 971–77; Kim et al., "Influence of Social Media Use," 498–516.

123. Rojas, "Egocentric Publics and Perceptions," 93–95.

124. Rojas et al., "Patterns of Media Use."

125. Turkle, *Reclaiming Conversation*, 297; Fox and McEwan, "Social Media," 378; Donath and Boyd, "Public Displays of Connection," 71–82; Twenge and Campbell, *Narcissism Epidemic*, 110. It should be noted that weak ties are effectively useless at building long-term connections and alleviating intimacy problems or creating space for shared grief.

126. Campbell and Ling, "Effects of Mobile Communication," 389–403.

127. Bourdieu, "Forms of Capital," 46–58. See "Bridging Social Capital."

Several scholars have also considered how processes like unfriending or blocking (components of the creation of Echo Chambers) are far simpler when they involve weak ties. Given that social media mostly builds and employs weak ties, and given that the option to unfriend or block are mechanics that would not exist if platforms did not include them, it follows that social media expressly provide some means for the creation of Echo Chambers.

Other scholars point out that Echo Chambers are not inevitable. Marko Skoric and associates interject that disagreement does not inevitably lead to acts of censorship.[128] Others, like Pablo Barberá, note the unpredictability of Echo Chambers and warn against overstating their significance.[129] However, Bail points out that, while most social media content posted by Democrats does not reach Republicans (and vice versa), there remains a 25 percent overlap.[130] Thus, the influence of Echo Chambers cannot be discounted, nor should it be seen as apocalyptic.

On to the debated effect of Echo Chambers. Cross-cutting (exposure to opposing opinions) can, under the right circumstances, lower rates of Affective Polarization—that is, Echo Chambers cause polarization to *increase*.[131] Diana Mutz and Jeffery J. Mondak point out that cross-cutting increases tolerance for others.[132] Additionally, when one's regular news source offers a balanced perspective of views, this also lowers polarization—sadly, these studies conclude that insufficient cross-cutting is taking place to alleviate polarization.[133]

Conversely, studies argue that excessive cross-cutting can raise polarization—meaning Echo Chambers *decrease* polarization. Tsfati and Walter write:

128. Skoric et al., "What Predicts Selective Avoidance," 1097–1115.

129. Eady et al., "How Many People," 1–21; Barberá, "Social Media, Echo Chambers, and Political Polarization," 34–55; Barberá et al., "Tweeting from Left to Right," 1531–42; Boulianne et al., "Right Wing Populism," 683–99. This is also important because Echo Chambers merely *influence* us. They do not program us.

130. Bail, *Breaking the Social Media Prism*, 5; Bakshy et al., "Exposure to Ideologically Diverse News," 1130–32.

131. Mason, "I Disrespectfully Agree," 128–45; Kim, "Does Disagreement Mitigate Polarization?" 915–37; Levy, "Social Media, News Consumption, and Polarization," 831–70; Barberá, "How Social Media Reduces"; Lee and Choi, "Effects of Network Heterogeneity," 119–39.

132. Mutz and Mondak, "Workplace as a Context," 140–55.

133. Fletcher and Nielson, "Are News Audiences Increasingly Fragmented," 476–98; Webster, "Myth of Partisan Selective Exposure," 1–13; Webster and Ksiazek, "Dynamics of Audience Fragmentation," 39–56.

Theories of motivated processing (Taber and Lodge, 2006) account for both selection of ideologically congruent news and their effects (Levendusky, 2013). These theories argue that when people are presented with information that challenges their worldview, they are motivated to discount the quality of the arguments, derogate the source of the message, or question the accuracy of the claims. By contrast, information that fits within people's broader belief system is often judged as probative and accepted at face value, even when its validity is called into question by experts and authority figures (Chang, 2015). . . . Contrary to the common belief that quality information in the public domain has the potential to bring people together and encourage prosocial behavior, these studies demonstrate that in a news environment governed by motivated processing, even exposure to accurate information has the potential to polarize the public (Hart, Nisbet, and Myers, 2015).[134]

Chris Bail's argument that Echo Chambers decrease polarization is especially strong.[135] He found that too much cross-cutting causes people to double down on their position. The observation that some people may even perceive *balanced* news as hostile exacerbates his concerns.[136] Essentially, too much information from unfamiliar sources causes us to be less receptive to the idea that our perspective could be biased.[137] The consequence is deeper entrenchment into our pre-existing views.

Some scholars argue that Echo Chambers produce, spread, or amplify polarization.[138] Some have argued that less polarized people are more likely to censor ideas that conflict with their own, thus leading to

---

134. Tsfati and Walter, "World of News and Politics," 40–41; Taber and Lodge, "Motivated Skepticism," 755–69; Levendusky, "Why Do Partisan Media Polarize Viewers," 611–23; Chang, "Motivated Processing," 602–34; Nisbet et al., "Partisan Brain," 36–66; Hart et al., "Public Attention to Science," 541–45; Taber et al., "Motivated Processing of Political Arguments," 137–55.

135. Bail, *Breaking the Social Media Prism*, 20–21.

136. Vallone et al., "Hostile Media Phenomenon," 577–85. This is despite the American tendency to prefer neutral news reporting; see: Gentzkow and Shapiro, "Ideological Segregation Online," 1799–1839.

137. Redlawsk et al., "Affective Tipping Point," 563–93; Taber and Lodge, "Motivated Skepticism," 755–69.

138. Banks et al., "#Polarized Feeds," 609–34; Bhattacharya et al., "Perceptions of Presidential Candidates' Personalities," 249–67; Vicario et al., "Spreading of Misinformation Online," 554–59; Vaccari et al., "Social Media and Political Communication," 381–410; Yardi and Boyd, "Dynamic Debates," 316–27.

greater rates of polarization for people less polarized.[139] Others point out that exposure to like-minded media typically increases pre-existing anger, potentially causing bitterness.[140] However, government censorship of political news is always the wrong response, as it hardens political extremists' resolve, making violence more likely and inevitably worse.[141]

In contrast, the potential of cross-cutting to inflame polarization suggests that Echo Chambers help prevent polarization. This is especially true given that Echo Chambers mostly affect people on the margins.[142] Echo chambers might be a natural consequence of the need for human beings to limit their exposure to discomfort. While the existence of tools for censorship provides the means for this to take place, that does not necessarily mean social media users would not create another method for creating Echo Chambers should these tools be removed.[143]

Given the aspects of marginalization in Echo Chambers, it is also important to consider the possibility that social media reflects only the extremists in society due to the Spiral of Silence model. Accordingly, a desire to "fit in" encourages people with moderate viewpoints to remain silent during heated conversations. To offer a moderated view is like a mouse trying to separate two elephants—neither of them will agree with you and you will probably be trampled. Unfortunately, this means moderate views are hidden and less cross-cutting takes place. Furthermore, K. N. Hampton and company have demonstrated that this effect tends to spill over from social media into the real world. This would be consistent with the argument that Perceived Polarization outweighs Affective Polarization—extremists' influence is disproportionate to their numbers.[144]

While the debate surrounding Echo Chambers continues, I worry that we are dragging our feet.[145] I suspect that Echo Chambers are con-

---

139. Zhang et al., "Political Consequences of Disagreement," 1–14. They recognize that this conclusion is not certain.

140. Wojcieszak et al., "Partisan News and Political Participation," 1–20.

141. Casili and Tubaro, "Social Media Censorship," 5–20; Vries et al., "Like a Bridge Over Troubled Water," 2622–49.

142. Bozdag, "Managing Diverse Online," 1–13; Dubois and Blank, "Echo Chamber Is Overstated," 729–745.

143. Zhang et al., "Political Consequences of Disagreement," 1–14. See above p. 22 "SESAM."

144. Tsfati and Walter, "World of News and Politics," 42; Gearhart and Zhang, "Gay Bullying and Online Opinion," 18–36; Hampton et al., "Social Media and the 'Spiral of Silence.'"

145. Iyengar et al. argue that no firm conclusions around the effects of Echo

tributing to *and reinforcing* society's fragmentation.[146] The 25 percent overlap of cross-cutting ideas demonstrates that we continue to be exposed to new ideas. However, these are often expressed in a context that will not entertain alternatives (i.e., Echo Chambers). Echo chambers then provide the primary means by which an individual *maintains* that viewpoint, employing a learning or reinforcement process like Cultivation.[147] From this perspective, ideals are something of an addiction: once we become addicted to a particular ideal, the Echo Chamber that presented it provides the ongoing fix we require. However, though there are strong arguments that Echo Chambers cause bitterness, I cannot reach that conclusion with confidence. Sadly, this creates new questions.

VII: Conclusions—How Now Shall We Live?

There is a consensus that our worldviews are shifting due to our social media engagement—though not specifically towards bitterness. Jonathan Haidt and Jean Twenge have been particularly engaged in mapping how social media is affecting youths. Perhaps the most distressing changes have been a marked increase in levels of depression (particularly among young girls) and increased rates of suicide.[148] Alternative methods of social media influence on the real world are suggested through changes to interactions on college campuses and our unwillingness to trust others—particularly authorities.[149] Sherry Turkle has offered her own perspectives on the dangers of technology and its effect on how we perceive reality.[150] She has observed that our methods of communica-

---

Chambers may be reached as yet; see: Iyengar et al., "Origins and Consequences of Affective Polarization," 136. Though I find Bail, Settle, and Mason's arguments quite sufficient, this should illustrate the degree to which this topic is contested.

146. I will discuss this concept further in the next chapter, pp. 46–9.

147. Alternative models include Social Cognitive Theory by Albert Bandura, and Agenda Setting Theory by Maxwell McCombs and Donald Shaw. See: Bandura, *Social Foundations of Thought*; McCombs and Shaw, "Agenda Setting Function," 176–87. Cultivation is primarily a means of *influence*, whereas SCT and AST describe the inner mechanics of *how* we learn.

148. Twenge et al., "Underestimating Digital Media Harm," 346–48; Twenge and Campbell, "Media Use is Linked," 311–31; Twenge et al., "Age, Period, and Cohort Trends," 185–99; Twenge et al., "Increases in Depressive Symptoms," 3–17. See also: Twenge, *iGen*; Turkle, *Reclaiming Conversation*, 145.

149. See Lukianoff and Haidt, *Coddling*, 91–121; Nichols, *Death of Expertise*, 100–102, 106–8, 111–12.

150. Turkle, *Alone Together*; Turkle, *Reclaiming Conversation*, 3, 5, 32, 40, 112,

tion are increasingly moving to the internet via our phones (even when conversations could take place in person) and that this trend appears to be crippling children's development of empathy.

Perhaps the real prophet and doomsayer of the dangers of social media is Jaron Lanier. His book *Ten Arguments for Deleting Your Social Media Accounts Right Now* was trendy but generated little social change. However, while Lanier's views should *not* be taken lightly—particularly his warnings about Silicon Valley tech giants in light of Nudge Theory—his ideas are generally not grounded in social science but insider knowledge of the tech industry.[151] Whether he is a prophet or a madman is unclear at this time.

My topic, however, is bitterness, not social media. Reviewing this discussion with that in mind reveals several common conclusions. First, social media clearly plays a role in spreading bitterness and shaping our affections. Lukianoff and Haidt say, "Social media, of course, is perfectly designed to help "consensual hallucinations" spread within connected communities at warp speed— . . . on the left and on the right."[152] However, the question of *how much* varies greatly. The difficulty in measuring this influence is that it is rooted in narratives and emotions rather than raw facts or data.

Second, social media could be responsible for the rise in bitterness, but it is more likely a natural human phenomenon that social media exacerbates and spreads. Although we desire to think well of ourselves and others, the human condition does not inspire optimism—we become entrenched in damaging patterns of thought and behavior all too easily. The more important question is, "Without social media, would feelings of bitterness spread too slowly for a pattern to be noticed?" If the answer to that question is "yes," then social media should be blamed for our present situation. However, although such "what-if" questions provide entertaining debate, they rarely (if ever) produce answers.

162–64, 171.

151. I find Lanier's arguments too grandiose to take seriously and backed by little social evidence, though these are worth noting in light of Sunstein's arguments around AI algorithms. See: Lanier, *You Are Not a Gadget*; Lanier, *Who Owns the Future?*; Lanier, *Dawn of the New Everything*; Lanier, *Ten Arguments for Deleting Your Social Media Accounts*; Geertz, "What is the Social in Social Media?" 109; Bail, *Breaking the Social Media Prism*, 84–89. For further information, see the work of Tristan Harris, including his TED Talks: Harris, "Our Brains Are No Match"; Orlowski, *Social Dilemma*.

152. Lukianoff and Haidt, *Coddling*, 10.

Third, while there is a question of social media obscuring the division between fact and falsehood, this issue is far less influential than the role played by our emotions. When we *feel* a certain way, the facts be damned! Affective Polarization and a history of victimization must invariably submit their influence to Perceived Polarization and victimhood mentality. Moreover, even Perceived Polarization and victimhood complexes are themselves capable of harming society when that harm begins by *breaking down relationships*, as bitterness does. Attempting to limit the spread of inaccurate facts does not cut deeply enough to limit the spread of bitterness, and censorship does more harm than good.

Fourth, the more deeply entrenched we become in our views, the more difficult it is to get "unstuck." The problem is compounding. There might continue to be a large contingency of friendly people who welcome debate, but those who are extremists are backing further into their corners and gaining social influence. Furthermore, through social media, extremists can influence society disproportionately to their numbers. We have genuine cause to hope, but its light is dwindling.

Brian Kaylor proposes we return Marshall McLuhan to the forefront of the debate to evaluate our relationship with social media:

> McLuhan offers four important questions to consider about any given medium in order to understand its strengths and weaknesses. First, what does the medium enhance or amplify? For instance, radio amplifies a focus on the spoken word and music. Second, what does the medium make obsolete or reduce? Radio, for instance, downplays the importance of the visual. Third, what does the medium retrieve or recover that other media made obsolete? Radio returned a focus to the importance of the spoken word, which is often lost in other media. Finally, what does the medium reverse or morph into when pushed to its limits? The danger of radio is that it paves the way for television as an attempt to add more to radio's audio.[153]

Despite their age, these warnings are relevant today. Based on these warnings Kaylor suggests that we should recognize three central aspects of social media that should be concerning for us. First, it balkanizes us. Social media divides us into tribes, not just as a consequence of human behavior but as a result of its inherent nature.[154] We should not be surprised when we are brought into contact with members of a competing

---

153. Kaylor, "Likes, Retweets, and Polarization," 186.
154. Kaylor, "Likes, Retweets, and Polarization," 186–87. See also: Junger, *Tribe*.

tribe and choose carefully whether or not a conversation is beneficial at this time and in this context.

Second, social media urges us to "move faster." The speed at which we communicate through the internet encourages us to *react* rather than take the time to reflect and then *respond*.[155] Ironically, taking a break before replying to an upsetting message might be *more* important online than in person.

Finally, social media depersonalizes. This encourages users to employ *ad hominem* arguments rather than communicate respectfully.[156] This emphasizes the importance of *seeing the person behind the screen* and separating the *argument* from the *person*. Both of these are difficult and require practice—some people would benefit from avoiding such circumstances altogether until said skills are developed.[157]

While helpful tips exist for approaching our engagement with social media, we still have to discuss the real problem behind social media and the rise in bitterness: personal identity. A more in-depth discussion of solutions must wait until later. Before closing, however, I should answer my implicit question: Is the media the enemy? Is it true, as Carr suggests, that "the Internet is making us meaner, shorter-fused, and incapable of conducting discussions where anyone learns anything," or is it a neutral tool that is as good or bad as we make it?[158] In short, not at all . . . well, yes . . . ah, maybe?

---

155. Kaylor, "Likes, Retweets, and Polarization," 187–90. See also: Carr, *Shallows*, 6–9, 94; Turkle, *Reclaiming Conversation*, 128–133, 319.

156. Kaylor, "Likes, Retweets, and Polarization," 190–91; Turkel, *Reclaiming Conversation*, 32.

157. More on this in chapters 4, 7, and 8: pp. 112, 187–8, 209.

158. Nichols, *Death of Expertise*, 111.

Chapter 2: **The Self and the Cosmos**

How a Lack of Purpose and Social Media Create the Perfect Storm

> All animals are equal, but some animals are more equal than others. —George Orwell[1]

I: Introduction

As Moses spoke to Israel in Deuteronomy, he exhorted them repeatedly to *memorize* the words of the law. Write them on your hearts! Teach them to your children! Debate them while you travel! Recall them when you sleep and when you wake! Recite them as you eat (and don't you dare boil a kid in its mother's milk)! Tie them to your foreheads! Bind them to your wrists! Engrave them on your doorposts![2] Whatever you do, *do not forget them*! Either we have not paid sufficient attention, or we might well ask why God did not include "post them to social media." However, particularly when taken along with Paul's commandment to *think* on things that are true, honorable, just, pure, pleasing, commendable, excellent, and praiseworthy, I rather believe that God knew *exactly*

---

1. Orwell, *Animal Farm*, 88.
2. Deut 6:4–10; 11:18–21; 32:45–47.

what he[3] was doing (and why social media was omitted).[4] Having made us social creatures, he knew that what we share in society and treasure in our imaginations are those things that most shape our *selves*. As Benedict Anderson wrote, our society is an *imagined community*—and a fragile one at that.[5]

This chapter begins with the social component of identity and how destabilized social identities are the most likely cause of Affective Polarization. These identities are formed from a dialectic between groups and individuals involving narratives (such as history or parables), liturgies, and symbols.[6] The crucial problem is the fragility of these identities in the modern era.

I will appeal to Peter Berger to describe gradations of our social identity from those components that are ordinary (*nomoi*) to those that are extraordinary (*teloi* and *cosmoi*). Those components that are the most important for solidifying a positive social identity are also those that are most unstable—these should be understood as "religious"— what Berger calls "cosmoi" or our "sacred canopy." These components are breaking down in American culture.

Lastly, I will describe how the practice of formal religion in America is declining. I suggest that formerly "secular" concerns have taken on a "religious" significance and influence—what I call "idol-ologies." I will argue that our *politics* is replacing *religion* and that a lack of robust religious identity is causing affective polarization. Social media is the arena where we argue and the "church" where we worship—the context reinforces and destabilizes our sacred values. Social media might not be

---

3. My choice to use male pronouns for God throughout this text reflects the majority perspective in Scripture and a respect for church tradition. This should not be mistaken for the belief that God is "male"—except for Jesus' maleness through the incarnation. There are examples of feminine imagery for God throughout Scripture, such as Isa 49:15–16; Matt 23:37–39; Luke 19:41–44.

4. Phil 4:8.

5. Anderson, *Imagined Communities*, 6. See also: Guthrie, *Theology as Thanksgiving*, 40.

6. For arguments regarding narrative, see: Taylor, *Sources of the Self*; Taylor, *Secular Age*; Taylor, *Modern Social Imaginaries*; and Boersma, *Heavenly Participation*. For arguments regarding liturgy (the ordering of group events, such as the order of worship in church), see: Smith, *Desiring the Kingdom*; and Smith, *You Are What You Love*. For arguments regarding symbol, see Wright, *New Testament and the People of God*; and Jung, *Archetypes and the Collective Unconscious*.

the criminal mastermind; it is the "middleman" fencing the goods to a culturally fragmented America.[7]

Chapter one focused on describing social media; this chapter will ascribe meaning to the description. To do this, I am invoking a methodology of "sociological imagination."[8] I mean to compare broad cultural trends against known psychological patterns and expectations and attempt to paint a picture that explains both on each other's terms. This is not entirely dissimilar to the practice of exercising "spiritual imagination" for the purpose of theological understanding. Thus, the argument depends on presenting a *plausible* picture of current events more than proving an irrefutable conclusion.

II: Social Identity and Conflict

Social Identity Theory (*SIT*) was developed by Henri Tajfel and John Turner in 1979. *SIT* argues that people identify themselves based on their tribal or group membership.[9] The identity associated with membership is understood and lived out through liturgies, stories, and symbols—such as the pledge of allegiance or the United States flag—plus living and interacting with group members. *SIT* argues further that the formation of identity leads almost inevitably to conflict under specific conditions.[10] This suggests that the social conflict we are witnessing in America is a natural or human phenomenon rather than technological.

The importance of our social identity—that is, how we view ourselves in relation to others—cannot be understated. Jonathan Cohen, Markus Appel, and Michael Slater write:

> An important dimension of the social self is the perception of belonging to a larger group of individuals. When asked about who we are, we might respond with our nationality ("I am

---

7. I do not claim social media to be the *only* "middleman" according to this image, but it is undoubtedly the most wide-reaching and successful.

8. Smith et al., *Lost in Transition*, 4; Mills, *Sociological Imagination*, 3–8, 18.

9. Tajfel and Turner, "Integrative Theory of Intergroup Conflict," 33–48. See also: Volf, *Exclusion and Embrace*, 35–56.

10. *SIT* builds on the foundation of Realistic Group Conflict Theory. The weakness of Realistic Group Conflict Theory was its inability to account for ingroup dynamics. See: Campbell, *Ethnocentric and Other Altruistic Motives*, 287; Sherif and Sherif, *Groups in Harmony and Tension*; and Sherif et al., *Robbers Cave Experiment*. These theories should be seen as complimentary rather than conflicting. Both build on the concept of ingroup bias; see: Sumner, *Folkways*, 12–13.

Israeli/American/German"), an affiliate to a political party, a sports franchise, a religious group, and so on. Social Identity theory (e.g., Tajfel and Turner, 1979) explains the relationships between the self, groups, and society. It suggests that the social categories an individual identifies with provide a crucial framework to define one's self. Individuals have multiple distinct category memberships at the same time and therefore multiple social identities, as these group identities are typically linked to different attributes and behaviors. In a given situation, an individual's experience and behavior depends on the salience [importance of or loyalty to] the social identity that is active.[11]

SIT takes this one step further. Conflict between tribes is the result of our desire for a stronger social identity. George Yancey and Ashlee Quosigk write:

> Our social identity is tied to our membership within ingroups, resulting in a powerful tendency to defend and confirm the rightness of the ingroup.... Such loyalty can lead to distorted evaluations of one's ingroup and willingness to inflate the perceived benefits of the group. Although ingroups play a powerful role in shaping our social identities, out-groups also play important roles in this process.... To reinforce the distance that members of an ingroup perceive between themselves and an out-group, they may develop antipathy toward members of that out-group. Out-group members are perceived to be similar [to each other].[12]

As Appel, Cohen, and Slater demonstrated, we refer to many groups for our identity. Yancey and Quosigk demonstrate that any of these groups—including political affiliations—may lead to conflict.[13] This is *SIT* in a nutshell.

SIT works by the importance of interpersonal relationships to group membership under two rubrics. The first rubric compares the

---

11. Cohen et al., "Media Identity and the Self," 181; Gaertner, "Common In-group Identity Model," 1–26.

12. Yancey and Quosigk, *One Faith No Longer*, 10–11. See also: Volf, *End of Memory*, 102. The term "ingroup" appears to have several acceptable spellings. I will use the term without hyphen except when quoting another author. This does not affect or change its meaning. I apply the same spelling pattern to "outgroup."

13. Rogowski and Sutherland, "How Ideology Fuels Affective Polarization," 485–508—argue that our ideals tend to reinforce our politics. Iyengar et al., "Origins and Consequences of Affective Polarization," 136–39, list how affective polarization affects all other areas of our common life.

importance of tribal identity with the importance of the relationship. An *interpersonal* relationship (e.g., between spouses or old friends) puts the importance of the relationship above group membership. An *intergroup* relationship (e.g., between soldiers in opposing militaries) puts the importance of group membership above the relationship.[14] The second rubric reflects on the degree of stratification within society. A dynamic of *social mobility* describes a society in which people believe they can improve their status through hard work. S*ocial change* describes a society in which hard work does not allow improvement of one's station. Group membership is more important in the latter case. These are theoretical concepts—good for the laboratory, lousy in the field.[15]

These rubrics enable sociologists to describe intergroup conflict. An *intergroup* relationship in a dynamic of *social change*—where competing tribes care more about each other, members of their ingroup, than members of the opposing outgroup and where excellence does not allow advancement, conflict is likely.[16] If tribal membership is flexible, or I have close personal ties with individuals in the opposing group, conflict is unlikely.

SIT reveals three additional insights. First is that group membership is a more important source of our sense of identity than our sense of individuality. Like teenage rebellion movements who all dress the same way as each other in the name of nonconformity. Tajfel and Turner write:

> Social categorizations [such as group membership] are conceived here as cognitive tools that segment, classify, and order the social environment, and thus enable the individual to undertake many forms of social action. But they do not merely systematize the social world; they also provide a system of orientation for self-reference: they create and define the individual's place in society.[17]

It is true that some tribes encourage or coerced membership on others (such as through "othering"), but voluntary self-association is the only necessary condition for group membership.[18] That is, I develop my sense of self *first* in terms of the social groups in which I claim membership,

---

14. See chapter 8, p. 200n44. There I discuss the similar distinction between strong-ties and weak-ties, which is analogous to interpersonal and intergroup relationships.
15. Tajfel and Turner, "Integrative Theory of Intergroup Conflict," 34–35.
16. Tajfel and Turner, "Integrative Theory of Intergroup Conflict," 36.
17. Tajfel and Turner, "Integrative Theory of Intergroup Conflict," 40.
18. Tajfel and Turner, "Integrative Theory of Intergroup Conflict," 39–40, 45.

voluntarily or involuntarily. This is part of why victimhood has such a magnetic draw.

The second insight is that intergroup conflict is less likely if two groups share a *secure* relationship (as opposed to an *insecure* relationship). This is the case between groups that are too disparate from each other for comparison (such as adults and children) or in a society where hierarchies are accepted by both parties and possibly enforced. This is a state of *social change* that is generally accepted by everyone as appropriate. For intergroup relations to be *insecure*, the visible underdog (the group that has fewer resources or less power or prestige and stands potentially to gain from conflict) needs to feel that a state of *social change* exists *and* that it is unjust, or the two groups need to possess similar strength. This latter point is critical because groups that are generally equal can advance by achieving superiority. This becomes more volatile if the groups in question have a history of conflict with one another, meaning the opportunity to develop a superior self-image is more appealing.[19] Furthermore, when a "victim" group seeks to establish a position of superiority through conflict, they force the "oppressor" group to defend their moral integrity.[20]

This is similar to the Tocqueville Effect, or Tocqueville Paradox. Alexis de Tocqueville writes:

> The hatred which men bear to privilege increases in proportion as privileges become fewer and less considerable, so that democratic passions would seem to burn most fiercely just when they have least fuel. . . . When all conditions are unequal, no inequality is so great as to offend the eye; whereas the slightest dissimilarity is odious in the midst of general uniformity: the more complete this uniformity is, the more insupportable does the sight of such a difference become. Hence it is natural that the love of equality should constantly increase together with equality itself, and that it should grow by what it feeds on.[21]

By this, Tocqueville means that the closer a society comes to establishing equality, the more that society values equality and resents its absence.

---

19. Tajfel and Turner, "Integrative Theory of Intergroup Conflict," 45.

20. More on this in chapter 3, pp. 60–1, 64–5, as the moral majority defending its position is indicative of the presence of bitterness among the minority group taking the offensive. This is not, however, a *guarantee* that bitterness is present.

21. Tocqueville, *Democracy in America*, 362; Swedberg, *Tocqueville's Political Commentary*, 259–60.

This makes revolution more likely the closer a society comes to that which it desires or more likely after some significant reform. Tocqueville unknowingly prefigured *SIT*. Conditions of such prosperity would *also* lead to a centralization of power within the state.[22]

The third major insight is that group identity is a more significant factor in promoting conflict than any consideration of the distribution of resources.[23] Executive power or wealth takes a back seat when instigating conflict—except when these cause disparate group formation. This sheds further light on the second insight—the relative security of intergroup relations has little to do with who has formal power or wealth: "The mere awareness of the presence of an out-group is sufficient to provoke intergroup competitive or discriminatory responses on the part of the ingroup."[24] Peter Berger goes so far as to say, "Those who hold conflictive views don't even have to say anything about the disagreement—just sitting together can be upsetting."[25] Moreover, this tendency towards conflict is tinged with patterns of cutthroat behavior. This means that, within intergroup conflict, "making the enemy lose" is more important than "winning." Groups will generally prioritize widening the gap between themselves and the outgroup over maximizing their own profit solely for "the greater good."[26] This is the essence of spite.[27]

Shanto Iyengar and company have explained affective polarization in terms of *SIT*.[28] This is the core of their argument:

> *Homo sapiens* is a social species; group affiliation is essential to our sense of self. Individuals instinctively think of themselves as representing broad socioeconomic and cultural categories rather than as distinctive packages of traits. . . . From a social identity perspective, affective polarization is a natural offshoot of this sense of partisan group identity . . . However, changes in

---

22. Tocqueville, *Democracy in America*, 363.
23. Tajfel and Turner, "Integrative Theory of Intergroup Conflict," 37.
24. Tajfel and Turner, "Integrative Theory of Intergroup Conflict," 38.
25. Berger, *Many Altars of Modernity*, 3.
26. Berger, *Many Altars of Modernity*, 39.
27. Murphy and Hampton, *Forgiveness and Mercy*, 76–78.
28. It may be helpful to recall Mason's three characteristics of polarization: (1) zero-sum competitions lead to bias and prejudice, (2) one's social status is linked to their group's status, (3) individuals "feel" emotion with their group. Mason, *Uncivil Agreement*, 23.

the contemporary political and media environment have exacerbated the divide in recent years.[29]

When we recognize the importance of tribal affiliation, it makes sense that we have naturally become polarized over time. Having a clear group affiliation is invaluable for having a positive social identity; thus we gravitate towards larger political parties—Democrats and Republicans.[30] Increasing social equality, as we have pursued, increases intergroup tension. This means most of our society is poised for conflict and that working to provide materially for the needs of minorities will not release the tension because tribe matters more than property.

SIT also explains victimhood. Many historical instances of victimhood were rooted in a society where *social change* rather than *social mobility* was the rule. Likewise, *social change* tends to lead to conflict and an ingroup bias—characteristics of victimhood. Another argument is that, since *SIT* explains polarization, and since polarization is similar to victimhood, by proxy we may explain victimhood using *SIT*.[31]

I believe it is undeniable that the intergroup relationships in America are in a state that would lead to conflict. Our identities are formed by intergroup dynamics within tribes that have deeply insecure relationships with one another in a society that has pursued increasing social equality. The size, complexity, and history of our nation make conflict inevitable. This is a *human* problem first and a *technology* problem second—the internet merely *connects us* to our tribe. But how deep does the problem really go?

III: Identity, Ideals, and Idol-ology

To understand the full scope of the problem, we must contemplate the different areas of our life affected by our social identity. Our identity crosses epistemological lines, affects our values, influences how we understand history, and ultimately enters the realm of the sacred. I will illustrate several elements of our social identity that expand *SIT* beyond politics.[32]

---

29. Iyengar et al., "Origins and Consequences of Affective Polarization," 130. Further discussed in Iyengar et al., "Affect, not Ideology," 405–31; and Lelkes et al., "Hostile Audience," 5–20. See also: Tajfel, *Differentiation Between Social Groups*; and Brewer, "Social Self," 475–482.

30. Iyengar et al., "Origins and Consequences of Affective Polarization," 134.

31. Kelman, "Reconciliation from a Social-Psychological Perspective," 15–37.

32. Berger, *Many Altars of Modernity*, 60.

CHAPTER 2: THE SELF AND THE COSMOS

Peter Berger's model of social identity is instructive for this purpose. He envisions a sort of "spectrum" of social significance—some issues have little significance and meaning, and others much. Some social expectations, practices, or knowledge are basic and generally universal—such as the social etiquette of tipping your waiter or that a green light indicates you may proceed through an intersection safely. Berger writes:

> The socially constructed world is, above all, an ordering of experience. *A meaningful order, or nomos*, is imposed upon the discrete experiences and meanings of individuals. [... And to] participate in the society is to share its "knowledge," that is, to co-inhabit its nomos.[33]

The critical concept here is that of *nomos* (which does not mean "law" as in Greek) or social mores. This may be considered a pseudo-environment shared and constructed by a social group but including expectations of social behavior—it is a shared imaginary picture of our shared society: what it is, how it operates, and how to navigate it.[34] Without this shared source of identity, society fragments, becoming a complex interweaving of smaller social groups, some at peace and others in conflict.

A similar concept, that of "social imaginary," is described by Charles Taylor. He explains the term, saying:

> By social imaginary, I mean something much broader and deeper than the intellectual schemes people may entertain when they think about social reality in a disengaged mode. I am thinking, rather, of the ways people imagine their social existence, how they fit together with others, how things go on between them and their fellows, the expectations that are normally met, and the deeper normative notions and images that underlie these expectations.[35]

This emphasizes that our social identities are *ordering* identities, bringing peace to chaos. They do not only affect what *is*; they affect *how we perceive* what is and *how we should behave*. However, there are more particular components of our *nomoi* that have a greater effect on our sense of self.

Nomoi are broad social ties that may encompass all of society, but they are historically rooted in one *time* as well as one place. To focus on a group's understanding of its *history*, a new term is needed to account

---

33. Berger, *Sacred Canopy*, 19, 21. Emphasis mine.
34. See chapter 1, pp. 4–5.
35. Taylor, *Modern Social Imaginaries*, 23.

for the narrowing of scope. I will use the Greek word *telos* (τέλος) to describe this. In its simplest state, *telos* refers to an "end" or a "cost," but in theological circles, it has taken on the meaning of "purpose" or "consummation."[36] It is these latter concerns that I am primarily referring to, but I am also using the word to imply a *narrative arc*. To understand one's purpose and consummation is to place oneself within the total narrative arc of history: this is what has happened, this is what will happen, this is the meaning or purpose of these things, and *here is where I fit*. This is the first component of *nomos* to consider.[37]

The relationship between *nomos* and *telos* is important. Our *telos* describes our complete social identity in terms of eternity while our *nomos* describes the *present* segment of our *telos*—that historical period which we inhabit, as well as those events of recent history that still press on our self-understanding and our hopes for our immediate future.[38] Because *teloi* encompass a grander vision, we take greater comfort in them. The trade-off is that it is more difficult to reach a social consensus. Therefore, a society may be interpreted as a small number of *nomoi* and a moderate number of *teloi*. A lack of a *telos* introduces what Taylor called the "Malaises of Modernity"—a society that simply feels . . . empty.[39]

Although *teloi* can imply metaphysical values, we turn to a third category for that purpose. Neither *nomoi* nor *teloi* provide a means of coming to terms with chaotic events, the paragon of which is death.[40] In the face of death, we must conceive of reality in supernatural terms to reach an understanding and restore social order. Berger categorizes such elements as our *cosmos*.

Although all three are distinct, they are inseparable. Berger explains this connection, saying:

---

36. Think "Machiavellian." Also, recall that Cultivation can influence *telos*—see chapter 1, pp. 6–7.

37. Berger does not include this category in his discussion. I include it here to highlight a sense of purpose as a necessary component of our identity.

38. Frankl, *Man's Search for Meaning*. I consider that the average American likely focuses on a roughly 250-year-long period in history: one hundred years before their birth, eighty to one-hundred years for their own life span, and fifty years following their death. This should not be taken as a *precise* time span, merely to illustrate the difference between a focus on a narrow temporal period and eternity.

39. While the Malaises of Modernity are more strongly associated with a society bereft of God, Taylor points out that they arise even in situations lacking purpose, driving individuals to seek an alternative; see: Taylor, *Secular Age*, 338; Smith, *How (Not) to be Secular*, 65.

40. Berger, *Sacred Canopy*, 23.

> Whenever the socially established nomos attains the quality of being taken for granted, there occurs a merging of its meanings with what are considered to be the fundamental meanings inherent in the universe. Nomos and cosmos appear to be *co-extensive*. In archaic societies, nomos appears as a microcosmic reflection, the world of men as expressing meanings inherent in the universe as such. . . . Religion is the human enterprise by which a sacred cosmos is established. . . . Put differently, religion is cosmization in a sacred mode.[41]

Cosmos is the most narrow form of *nomos*—they perform the same social function by creating a sense of social stability, but *cosmos* is the most difficult to craft *convincingly*. Thus, *cosmoi* are many (especially in the modern era) and difficult to maintain.

We may also reach from the *cosmic* towards the *nomic*. Berger does not restrict the category of "cosmos" to explicitly religious categories. The key element of *cosmos* is that its purpose is to silence chaos within our otherwise orderly *nomos*—so *any* ideal that fills this role is categorized as *cosmos*:

> In contemporary society, this archaic cosmization of the social world will likely take the form of "scientific" propositions about the nature of men rather than the nature of the universe. . . . Whatever the historical variations, the tendency is for the meanings of the humanly constructed order to be projected into the universe as such. It may readily be seen how this projection tends to stabilize the tenuous nomic construction. . . . Every human society is engaged in the never completed enterprise of building a humanly meaningful world. Cosmization implies the identification of this humanly meaningful world with the world as such, the former now being grounded in the latter, reflecting it or being derived from it in its fundamental structures. Such a cosmos, as the ultimate ground and validation of human nomoi, need not necessarily be sacred. Particularly in modern times there have been thoroughly secular attempts at cosmization, among which modern science is by far the most important.[42]

This is not an argument that religion is human-made.[43] Berger has argued that even atheists possess elements of their social identity that are religious. Let us consider two examples of this.

---

41. Berger, *Sacred Canopy*, 24–25. Emphasis mine.
42. Berger, *Sacred Canopy*, 25, 27; Berger, *Rumor of Angels*, 6–7.
43. This is an understandable interpretation that Berger does not appear to have

First, consider religion in terms of its broadest form: pluralism. Pluralism is a term that typically has two definitions. The first describes pluralism as a philosophical exercise aiming to unify all world religions into a cohesive whole—*pluralism as philosophy*. The second describes a society where multiple religions coexist peacefully—*pluralism as reality*. In this section, I am discussing *pluralism as philosophy*. Jon Hick argued that all religions have three components, including (1) the Ultimate—a supreme power, person, or force, (2) Dukka—evil or opposition to the Ultimate, and (3) Salvation—a means of obtaining the Ultimate despite Dukka.[44] While Hick clearly intends this to apply to established religions, this structure functions as a recipe for *cosmoi*. If our *cosmoi* are meant as an antidote to chaos, then that chaos would figure as Dukka. The Ultimate would be any conception of the supreme good that should exist in place of chaos, and Salvation would be promoted as any pathway or ideal to reduce or eliminate that chaos and achieve the Ultimate.

The second illustration comes from Yancey and Quosigk. On the importance of religion they write:

> Religion is a valuable source of social identity and group affinity. Some scholars argue that religion is the *primary* source of purpose, meaning, and morality (Geertz 1957; Fry 2000; McAdams and Albaugh 2008a; Preston, Ritter, and Ivan Hernandez 2010; Park Edmondson; and Hale-Smith 2013). Religious individuals can see those of other faiths as proponents of competing systems of meaning. Consequently, individuals from different religions have an incentive to envision each other as out-groups.[45]

Their citations are particularly useful. For example, Clifford Geertz points to the idea that *religion* is merely a component of our ordinary social identities that is typically accorded higher honor. Robert Wuthnow

---

intended, particularly in light of his conclusions. While I disagree, I will not take space here to offer counterarguments.

44. Hick, "Next Step Beyond Dialogue," 3–5. See also: Hick, *Interpretation of Religion*. Miroslav Volf presents a clear counterargument to Hick—that the claim "all roads lead to God" begs the question; see: Volf, *Exclusion and Embrac*, 44. Hick uses the term "Ultimate" rather than "God" or "Deity" to reflect the reality that not all religions have a concept of god. Buddhism is a good example of this.

45. Yancey and Quosigk, *One Faith No Longer*, 20, emphasis mine; Geertz, "Ethos, World-View and the Analysis of Sacred Symbols," 421–37; Fry, "Religious Involvement," 689–718; McAdams and Albaugh, "Redemptive Self," 255–86; Preston et al., "Principles of Religious Prosociality," 574–90; Park et al., "Why Religion? Meaning as Motivation," 157–71.

clarifies: "Religion, we might suppose, is fundamentally a hedge against uncertainty. It offers meaning, as Geertz has observed, where there was no meaning."[46] Wuthnow continues, "Religion gives millions of Americans a sense of their place in the *cosmos*, or at least in their community. An appropriate term for these social and cultural aspects of religion is *moral order*."[47] Moral order, or values, are always *socially constructed or negotiated*. Reinhold Neibuhr concurs, saying:

> In so far as it is impossible to live at all without presupposing a meaningful existence, the life of every person is religious, with the possible exception of the rare skeptic who is more devoted to the observation of life than to living it, and whose interest in detailed facts is more engrossing than his concern for ultimate meaning and coherence. . . . [Such persons construct] a little *cosmos* in a world which they regard as chaos and derive vitality and direction from their faith in the organizing purpose of this cosmos.[48]

Religion is socially constructed. It is not exclusively metaphysical, and it is inextricably intertwined with our *values*.[49]

Therefore, I propose that not only is religion the primary source of purpose, meaning, and morality, but that *the primary source of purpose, meaning, and morality is religion*.[50] In the absence of an explicit faith,

---

46. Wuthnow, *After the Baby Boomers*, 14. See also: Haidt, *Righteous Mind*, 287, 290–91; Durkheim, *Elementary Forms of the Religious Life*, 62.

47. Wuthnow, *America and the Challenges*, 95. See also: Wuthnow, *Meaning and Moral Order*; Orsi, "Introduction," 33, cited in Wuthnow, *America and the Challenges*, 95.

48. Niebuhr, *Interpretation of Christian Ethics*, 6–7, emphasis mine. His use of "cosmos" mirrors Berger's.

49. Again, this should not be mistaken with the claim that religion is *not* a matter of the metaphysical. While I value the insights of treating religion as a sociological phenomenon, these pale in comparison to religion understood theologically.

50. Berger, *Rumor of Angels*, 37–38, 45–46. I am speaking in terms of the *social* component of religion. Theologians might rightly object that *God* or Hick's "Ultimate" is the primary source of purpose, meaning, and morality, but religion, as the collection of practices and teachings associated with God, remains the sole *conduit* of that meaning. The argument that "our source of purpose and morality is religion" has also been proposed by James Lindsey and Archbishop José H. Gomez. See: Lindsey and Nayna, "Postmodern Religion and the Faith"; Jenkins, "Top Catholic Bishop Calls"; Carrette, and Dowley, "Critical Theory and Religion,", 28–31. This is supported by Albert Bandura's SESAM model—see chapter 1, section VI. See also: Schmemann, *For the Life of the World*, 98–99. Schmemann argues that secularism is a kind of religion. Furthermore, while not sufficient evidence in itself, Wuthnow notes that political and religious polarization are increasing together. This is not causation but correlation. It might be due to the frequency with which a person's religious and political values *match*. However, this

or for people whose faith is lackluster, their sense of purpose, meaning, and morality—their *teloi*—can substitute as *cosmoi*, which must be defended as ardently as any religion. The term I have chosen for these *teloi* become *cosmoi* is "idol-ology."

The term has a binary meaning. First, it highlights that the *ideals* or *beliefs* go beyond the *nomic* and approach the *cosmic*. Second, when secular ideologies (such as scholastics, athletics, or politics) take on religious significance, an individual will seek out others to share their newfound values. When sufficient members of a religious community have adopted an ideology in this way, the community must either adjust their religion to accommodate the new values as doctrine or renounce the ideology as incompatible with their religion or heresy.[51] In the latter case, the new "ideals" are better described as "idols"—things set up before the face of God so that God is obscured. Eugene Peterson marvelously described this, saying:

> God and his ways are not what most of us think. Most of what we are told about God and his ways by our friends on the street, or read about him in the papers, or view on television, or think up on our own, is simply wrong. Maybe not dead wrong, but wrong enough to mess up the way we live.[52]

So an idol-ology for the atheist or agnostic is their *cosmos* (such as scientism), but for the *theist*, an idol-ology is heterodoxy at best and heresy

---

relationship is striking and illustrates the plausibility of my claim, see: Wuthnow, *After the Baby Boomers*, 160–63. See also: Taylor, *Secular Age*, 310.

51. Consider, for example, the relationship between feminism and Christianity. For a Christian to adopt feminism with its narratives and values, they must demonstrate that Jesus was a feminist, or that Christians have been (or should have been) feminists all along. However, since feminism is grounded on the narrative that all of history should be understood in terms of patriarchy (Dukka) and proposes a means of changing this (Salvation), it cannot be a mere "idol." Neither can it be a complete "religion," as generally, it makes no metaphysical claims. To be integrated with Christianity, feminism must reconcile Christianity with these objections. Feminism is, therefore, part of Christianity, or it is an "idol-ology." (File under: "Schrödinger's Religion.")

52. Peterson, *Eat This Book*, 34–35. It is also worth considering: "Their idols are silver and gold, the work of human hands. They have mouths, but they cannot speak; they have eyes, but they cannot see; they have ears, but they cannot hear; they have noses, but they cannot smell; they have hands, but they cannot feel; they have feet, but they cannot walk; they cannot make a sound with their throat. Those who make them will become like them, everyone who trusts in them" (Ps 115:4–8 NASB), see p. 194.

at worst.⁵³ Idol-ologies sufficiently conflict with pre-existing religious faith to turn *cosmos* to *chaos*.⁵⁴

Idol-ologies are difficult to distinguish from legitimate religious teachings. They are *also* extremely attractive in the *absence* of religious teachings, and I will argue later that idol-ologies are *replacing* established religions. However, first we must consider the difficulty in maintaining a stable sense of self, especially today.

IV: Maintaining Frame

Our social identity is essential to our individual identity and must be guarded *religiously*. According to Tajfel, our social identities are socially embedded in a tribe or faction. Berger explains how this works:

> Worlds [*nomoi* and/or *cosmoi*] are socially constructed and socially maintained. Their continuing reality, both objective ... and subjective ... depends upon specific social processes, namely those processes that ongoingly reconstruct and maintain the particular worlds in question. ... Thus each world requires a social "base" for its continuing existence as a world that is real to actual human beings. This "base" may be called its *plausibility structure*.⁵⁵

Berger elsewhere clarifies that "a plausibility structure is the social context in which any cognitive or normative definition of reality is plausible."⁵⁶ Plausibility structures are the communities that make up our churches, synagogues, mosques, temples, and "spiritual seekers" Facebook groups.

---

53. It must be acknowledged that idol-ologies are not *always* evil and that the line between acceptable ideals and unacceptable idol-ologies is difficult to discern. C. S. Lewis points out in his *Screwtape Letters* that God ("the enemy") accepts people on the basis of these beliefs, even though he disapproves of them, when the people in question know no better; see: Lewis, *Screwtape Letters*, 27–28. However, even Lewis recognizes that an ideal may become damning when it corrupts one's *prior* religious beliefs—hence the possibility of heterodoxy; see: Lewis, *Screwtape Letters*, 36–37. The process of degradation will be discussed more in chapter 3, pp. 66, 76–7, 84–5.

54. In this context, Douglas Adams's answer to "Great Question of Life, the Universe, and Everything" is a legitimate religious claim. It is silly and blasphemous all at once; see: Adams, "Hitchhiker's Guide to the Galaxy," 119–20.

55. Berger, *Sacred Canopy*, 45. Emphasis mine.

56. Berger, *Many Altars of Modernity*, 31. Note that he does *not* use the term *probable*. Maintaining *cosmoi* is *not* a matter of provability or probability but *plausibility*. The issue is creating a picture that inspires and excites, not necessarily one that is scientifically verifiable.

These plausibility structures support us socially and provide the liturgies, narratives, and symbols that help to keep us grounded.

When our plausibility structure falters—such as through hypocrisy, social delegitimization, or a resource crash—or if we are radically separated from our plausibility structure, we lose the most important tool for maintaining a positive self-identity. Berger calls the resulting state "anomy." Haidt explains:

> Religions are moral exoskeletons. If you live in a religious community, you are enmeshed in a set of norms, relationships, and institutions that work primarily on [your emotions and desires] to influence your behavior. But if you are an atheist living in a looser community with a less binding moral matrix, you might have to rely somewhat more on an internal moral compass, read by the [intellect]. That might sound appealing to rationalists, but it is also a recipe for *anomie*—Durkheim's word for what happens to a society that no longer has a shared moral order. (It means, literally, "normlessness.") We evolved to live, trade, and trust within shared moral matrices. When societies lose their grip on individuals, allowing all to do as they please, the result is often a decrease in happiness and an increase in suicide, as Durkheim showed more than a hundred years ago.[57]

Such is the danger of weakened religious affections, though this is not to say that theocracy is preferable to nihilism. Balancing the demands for religious security against the threat of religious violence is rarely done well.[58] Plausibility structures are fragile.

The difficulty of maintaining frame plus the argument that we have become polarized due to social friction between competing *nomoi* and *cosmoi* allows a return to the topic of social media: social media can destabilize our sense of self and provide an arena for social conflict.[59] Social media can also be a plausibility structure because Echo

---

57. Haidt, *Righteous Mind*, 313; emphasis mine. Although Haidt's spelling of "anomie" is different from Berger's "anomy," the meanings are the same so far as I can discern.

58. See, for example: Weil, "Romanesque Renaissance," 44–54. Consider also the concept of "Social Capital" in Putnam, *Bowling Alone*.

59. Törnberg et al., "Modeling the Emergence." Törnberg et al. build on Iyengar et al., "Origins and Consequences of Affective Polarization," cited earlier, which acknowledges the possibility of media consequences.

Chambers regulate our sense of self.[60] The size and reach of the internet make these possible.[61]

However, the sheer size of the internet suggests destabilization is more likely than not.[62] Too little cross-cutting leads to ignorance and a more polarized society.[63] Too much cross-cutting destabilizes our sense of connection to our plausibility structures and leads to anomy.[64] David Helfand estimates that we create 2.5 quintillion bytes of new internet data every day. This is the equivalent of 5 trillion books, each 600 pages long, or three quadrillion pages per day. Over a year, that amounts to 1.095 quintillion pages: 1,095,000,000,000,000,000.[65] An average person, reading 20 pages an hour and reading non-stop, can read 175,320 pages per year. A global population of about 8 billion people could read a total of 1.402560 quadrillion pages in a year: 1,402,560,000,000,000. That means that the entire population of humanity would only be able to read through 0.1281 percent of the total volume of information the internet *generates* yearly.

Try to visualize that. If a sheet of paper is 0.05mm thick, a printout of that data would be a stack of paper 54,750,000km high: a third of the distance between the earth and the sun. Since this statistic was published (five years), if the rate has remained consistent, the amount of data we have generated equates to a stack of paper that would stretch from the Sun to beyond Mars.

The counterargument points out that this includes all possible kinds of information, so much of this material is interesting for internet

---

60. Cohen et al., "Media Identity and the Self," 186-87; Preston and Wegner, "Ideal Agency," 103-126; Slater et al., "Temporarily Expanding the Boundaries of the Self," 439-55.

61. Ruiz and Nilsson, "Disinformation and Echo Chambers," 1-18; Leung and Lee, "Cultivating an Active Online Counterpublic," 340-59. We also find this in traditional news media; see: Powers and el-Nawawy, "Al-Jazeera English and Global News Networks," 263-84.

62. Kwon et al., "Social Network Influence," 1345-60.

63. For more on False Polarization, see the previous chapter, section IV, as well as Levendusky and Malhotra, "(Mis)perceptions of Partisan Polarization," 378-91; Mason, "I Disrespectfully Agree," 128-45.

64. Tsfati and Walter, "World of News and Politics," 40-41; Taber and Lodge, "Motivated Skepticism," 755-69; Bail, *Breaking the Social Media Prism*, 20-21; Levendusky, "Why Do Partisan Media Polarize Viewers," 611-23; Chang, "Motivated Processing," 602-34.

65. Helfand, *Survival Guide to the Misinformation Age*, cited in Tsfati and Walter, "World of News and Politics," 41.

analysts (such as site traffic data) but useless for anyone else. Even so, this is data being *generated* and does not account for the size of the internet *prior*. The sheer volume of information this suggests is staggering.[66] Even if we *discount* all the books yet to be digitized, the entire *species* cannot *read* 99.9 percent of the data on the internet (let alone mark or inwardly digest it), and most of that data is little more than white noise. Additionally, these numbers do no include the size of the internet prior to 2016, nor the likely increase in the rate of expansion of the internet since then. The internet is naturally overwhelming.[67]

Statistics from social media companies further demonstrate how the internet is destabilizing.[68] It is not just the amount of data that has become overwhelming but the number of people as well. Previously, roughly six degrees of separation stood between the individual and every other person on earth. That number is now four. Combined with population growth, that translates to far more socializing. We can no longer "keep up with the Joneses."

Sherry Turkle further demonstrates how internet socialization affects us. We are gradually *replacing* face-to-face interactions with instant messaging.[69] This includes interactions between family members, who choose to communicate through their phones while sitting together or go to different rooms in the house to avoid seeing each other.[70] Turkle worries that our increasing reliance on digital communication is causing us to lose our ability to empathize—especially among the religiously unaffiliated.[71] She describes her study at an elementary school (which she calls by the pseudonym "Holbrooke"), saying:

> Friendships [at Holbrooke] seem based on what students think someone else can do for them. . . . Reade, the dean . . . asked members of her [groups of student advisees] to list three things they want in a friend. In more than sixty responses she

---

66. Wuthnow identifies information over-saturation as a critical change in young adult culture. Wuthnow, *After the Baby Boomers*, 44–49.

67. Further developments in internet technology, such as AI, also indicate that my statistics are potentially low. They also foreshadow the future of internet technology and the possibilities of media formation beyond human control.

68. Edunov et al., "Three and a Half Degrees of Separation"; Backstrom et al., "Four Degrees of Separation," 33–42; Ugander et al., "Anatomy of the Facebook Social Graph." Recall also some of Lanier's arguments about the problems of tech giants, p. 28.

69. Turkle, "Tethered Self," 28–31.

70. Turkle, *Reclaiming Conversation*, 112.

71. Wuthnow, *After the Baby Boomers*, 149. More on this in the following section.

received, only three students mentioned trust, caring, kindness, or compassion. Most of the students say they are interested in someone who could make them laugh, who could make them happy. . . . Reade sums up her "What do you want in a friend?" exercise: "I feel that these kids have a sense that friendships are one-sided. It is a place for them to broadcast. It is not a place for them to listen. And there isn't an emotional level. You just have to have someone there. There is no investment in another person. It's like they can turn the friendship off." . . . Reade worries that the habits developed with online "friending" have become the habits of friendships in face-to-face, everyday life.[72]

She does not use the term anomy, but it fits. "Real people," Turkle says, "with their unpredictable ways, can seem difficult to contend with after one has spent a stretch in simulation."[73]

The central reality of social media is this: we are making many social connections, but they are mostly *weak* connections. For all the algorithms written to help connect people appropriately, the fundamental *design concept* is nothing more or less than an overwhelming quantity, which is not conducive to maintaining a stable identity.[74] So too is the scope of the internet. This raises one final question: are we maintaining our *religious* identities?

V: The Age of Agnosticism

In 1978 Aleksandr Solzhenitsyn made the following observation about the Western world's sense of moral order:

> The West has finally achieved the rights of mankind even to excess, but man's sense of responsibility to God and society has grown dimmer and dimmer. In the past decades, the legalistic selfishness of the Western approach to the world has reached its peak and the world has found itself in a harsh spiritual crisis and a political impasse. All the celebrated technological achievements of progress, including the conquest of outer space, do not redeem the twentieth century's moral poverty.[75]

---

72. Wuthnow, *After the Baby Boomers*, 163–64. See also: Twenge, *iGen*, 3. For more on media effects on society, see sources cited in chapter 1, especially: Lukianoff and Haidt, *Coddling*; and Carr, *Shallows*. More on this topic in chapter 8, pp. 198–203.

73. Turkel, *Reclaiming Conversation*, 7.

74. Twenge and Campbell, *Narcissism Epidemic*, 110.

75. Solzhenitsyn, *World Split Apart*, 51, cited in Wuthnow, *Meaning and Moral*

Do Solzhenitsyn's concerns for the world apply to modern America? Paul McClure prefigures my answer: although young adults in America are *not* more likely to be pluralists (*pluralism as philosophy*), they *are* more likely to be syncretists.[76] Wuthnow describes religious syncretism in terms of "Spiritual Shopping."[77] He explains:

> Like the farmer rummaging through the junk pile for makeshift parts, the spiritual tinkerer [syncretist] is able to sift through a veritable scrap heap of ideas and practices from childhood, from religious organizations, classes, conversations with friends, books, magazines, television programs, and Web sites.[78]

Thus we freely create new idol-ologies. Additionally, we are more likely to practice syncretism as adults.[79] This section will explore these phenomena more thoroughly.

Young adults are increasingly areligious.[80] Among young adult Protestants, 38 percent never attend church, and the figure is 36 percent among Catholics.[81] These represent persons claiming Christian faith who otherwise ought to qualify as agnostic or atheist. Among young adults, only 5 percent can be considered genuinely committed, and 20 percent participate in religious services.[82] This is especially evident from Twenge's claim that "iGen is, with near certainty, the least religious generation in US history."[83] She continues, "More young Americans are thoroughly secular, disconnecting completely from religion, spirituality, and the

---

Order, 67.

76. McClure, "Faith and Facebook," 818–34. See also: Wuthnow, *After Heaven*; Wuthnow, *American Mythos*; Wuthnow, *America and the Challenges*, 192; Wuthnow, *After the Baby Boomers*.

77. See: Eck, *New Religious America*. Christian Smith directly contradicts this claim. Although there are many religions practiced in America, most of these religions have very few followers. See: Smith and Denton, *Soul Searching*, 32. For Wuthnow's use, see Wuthnow, *America and the Challenges*, 107. See also: Roof, *Spiritual Marketplace*; Cimino and Lattin, *Shopping for Faith*. As we will see, this is most common and destructive amongst "exvangelical" Christians: Constantinou, *Thinking Orthodox*, 39; Newport, "More US Protestants"; and Bullivant, *Nonverts*.

78. Wuthnow, *After the Baby Boomers*, 15.

79. Putnam and Campbell, *American Grace*. Cited McClure, "Faith and Facebook," 819; Smith and Snell, *Souls in Transition*, 137.

80. Smith and Snell, *Souls in Transition*, 86–87.

81. Smith and Snell, *Souls in Transition*, 115–17. See also: Twenge, *iGen*, 123.

82. Smith and Snell, *Souls in Transition*, 259; Wuthnow, *After the Baby Boomers*, 52–53; Twenge et al., "Generational and Time Period."

83. Twenge, *iGen*, 128.

larger questions of life."[84] Most significantly, Christianity forms the most common *starting point* for religious shoppers.[85]

Among young adults, only 30 percent believe one religion to be exclusively true, but this is not the whole story. In the same group, 57 percent believe many religions to be true.[86] People who are comfortable with spiritual shopping make up roughly 50 percent, an increase from teen years to adulthood.[87] Among teens, 51 percent believe practicing multiple religions is acceptable, and 67 percent believe religious communities (our plausibility structures) are unnecessary.[88] Among young adults, 75 percent reject religious community.[89] Among internet searches for information about religions, 72 percent of the population appear to be looking for information about their own beliefs (reinforcing their plausibility structure). However, 51 percent appear to be looking for information about other faiths—either out of a desire to understand at a distance or to imitate.[90] According to Pew Research, nearly one-third of American society identifies as "spiritual but not religious."[91]

These statistics might indicate a breakdown of social identity and a rise in social conflict. Diane Eck worries, "We may find ourselves fragmented and divided with too much *pluribus* and not enough *unum*,"[92] that is, anomy. Christian Smith explains further:

> It is not so much that U.S. Christianity is being secularized. Rather more subtly, Christianity is either degenerating into a pathetic version of itself or, more significantly, Christianity

---

84. Twenge, *iGen*, 132. See also: Kinnaman and Hawkins, *You Lost Me*.

85. Wuthnow, *America and the Challenges*, 123.

86. However, to paraphrase C. S. Lewis, this might only reflect the belief that many religions are true insofar as *all* of them agree with one religion that is *completely* true. Lewis, *Mere Christianity*, 35.

87. Smith and Snell, *Souls in Transition*, 134–37. The extent to which people are willing to go combining religious values can differ significantly.

88. Smith and Denton, *Soul Searching*, 74.

89. Smith and Snell, *Souls in Transition*, 134–37.

90. Wuthnow, *After the Baby Boomers*, 210. The reason for these not adding up to one-hundred percent is that one may search for information about their own faith *and* about other faiths.

91. Lipka and Gecewicz, "More Americans."

92. Eck, *New Religious America*, 65, cited in Wuthnow, *America and the Challenges*, 77.

is actively being colonized and displaced by a quite different religious faith.[93]

This fits our present circumstances. The greatest indicator that our social identities might be crumbling is what Wuthnow has to say about the driving force behind syncretism: "Much of the present spiritual shopping is guided by authors, speakers, artists, healers, and lay individuals who view themselves as spiritual leaders rather than as religious leaders."[94] This means that experts are not driving syncretism but hobbyists—people without the necessary know-how to avoid or prevent anomy.

While these details mostly implicate teens and young adults, older generations are complicit. Smith, noting that many older adults are disinterested in the conditions of younger adults, counters:

> Having studied young Americans for a decade . . . we have clearly seen that, contrary to this well-worn cultural script [young adults cause their own problems], most of the problems in the lives of youth have their origins in the larger adult world into which the youth are being socialized. . . . one way or another, adults and the adult world are almost always complicit in the troubles, suffering, and misguided living of youth, if not the direct source of them.[95]

There is nothing new under the sun. Younger generations *imitate* the older generations, even their admitted failures.

Where have all the previous trends in religiosity come from? According to Twenge, many young adults feel that religious institutions ignore the tension between religion and science. Many young adults feel they cannot share their own views without being criticized. Young adults are especially opposed to Christian views on sexuality.[96] Christianity does not appeal to young adults.

N. J. Demerath III offered a second, and highly convincing, explanation. Smith summarizes Demerath's argument:

> Liberal Protestantism's core values—individualism, pluralism, emancipation, tolerance, free critical inquiry, and the authority of human experience—have come to so permeate broader American culture that its own churches as organizations have

---

93. Smith and Denton, *Soul Searching*, 171.
94. Wuthnow, *America and the Challenges*, 128.
95. Wuthnow, *America and the Challenges*, 11.
96. Twenge, *iGen*, 139–40.

difficulty surviving. One reason for this development is that these very liberal values have a tendency to undermine organizational vitality. The strongest organizations are generally not built on individualism, diversity, autonomy, and criticism. Furthermore, having won the larger battle to shape mainstream culture, it becomes difficult to sustain a strong rationale for maintaining distinctively liberal church organizations to continue to promote those now omnipresent values. Liberal Protestantism increasingly seems redundant to the taken-for-granted mainstream that it has helped to create. Why organize to promote what is already hegemonic?[97]

Why remain a liberal protestant Christian when your faith does nothing to change or improve your life? At the very least, one ought to recoup the lost two hours on Sunday morning.[98]

Smith offers a third explanation. The breakdown in moral understanding appears to stem from two primary sources. The first is a lack of elementary and secondary school education which fails to prepare students for college.[99] Trends on college campuses support this conclusion, such as those illustrated by the incident at Yale College when president Nicholas Christakis asserted that college was about polite and scholarly debate, whereupon the student with whom he was discussing screamed that the purpose of college was *not* about creating a dialogue but about creating a home on campus.[100] As Smith writes, "Many representatives of the adult world who are responsible for socializing youth have in the previous two decades not asked them to [think through their moral assumptions] or shown them how. And why not? Because, we suspect, a lot of them do not know how to do that themselves."[101]

---

97. Smith and Snell, *Souls in Transition*, 134–37, 288. See also: Demerath, "Cultural Victory and Organizational Defeat," 458–69.

98. Craig Gay suggested that Christians are becoming "practical atheists"—Christians who claim all the right doctrinal beliefs but whose lives remain unchanged. It is a short distance from "practical atheism" to actual atheism. This would seem to support Demerath's theory; see: Gay, *Way of the (Modern) World*, 3–5; Berger, *Rumor of Angels*, 5–9, 20–21.

99. Smith et al., *Lost in Transition*, 62–63. These realities also lead to nihilism and a lack of a positive social identity; see Smith et al., *Lost in Transition*, 36–43.

100. Nichols, *Death of Expertise*, 100–102; Twenge, *iGen*, 158–59; Lukianoff and Haidt, *Coddling*, 56. These texts offer additional examples of this phenomenon and draw similar conclusions to Christian Smith's.

101. Smith et al., *Lost in Transition*, 62.

Unfortunately, this is only one half of Smith's explanation. Smith continues:

> Another factor is that, with the advent of globalization, the Internet, digital video, and cable and satellite television, this cohort of young people has exponentially more information, narratives, and political, ideological, and moral claims at its fingertips than any generation before. This mass of information, stories, and claims is also less filtered and evaluated by institutional gatekeepers—book editors and news executives, people who might guarantee some level of accuracy, significance, and value—than it ever was in the past. . . . In short, most emerging adults today are inundated with more competing information, narratives, and truth claims than any person could possibly assimilate, assess, and synthesize. . . . Making good sense of it all can be very difficult, if not impossible.[102]

Thanks to this explanation, the internet returns to the stage as a source of destabilized identity.

Although the possible causes for the rise in syncretism are complicated, the consequences thereof are simple. Smith concludes, "[Young adults] lack larger visions of what is true and real and good, in both the private and the public realms. And so, it seems to us, a small set of predefined default imperatives quickly rush in to fill that normative and moral vacuum."[103] Julian Barnes described this, saying, "I don't believe in God, but I miss him."[104] Smith continues to identify these imperatives: materialism, drugs and alcohol, and sexual hedonism. I suspect, though, as I shall illustrate in the next section, that a fourth imperative has emerged: political activism.

VI: Conclusions—What Is Man That You Would Remember Him?

The existence of social conflict originates in a stratified society with strong intergroup social dynamics. The severity of this conflict may be predicted by the importance of tribe to identity. In Berger's terms, conflicts over *nomoi* are unpleasant but not particularly challenging. Conflicts over *teloi*

102. Smith et al., *Lost in Transition*, 63–64.
103. Smith et al., *Lost in Transition*, 294.
104. Barnes, *Nothing to Be Frightened Of*, cited in Smith, *How (Not) to be Secular*, 65. Recall also the Malaises of Modernity.

CHAPTER 2: THE SELF AND THE COSMOS

can be unpleasant and personally destabilizing. Conflicts over *cosmoi* can be catastrophic. When it is not day-to-day matters but sacred cows being used as weapons in social conflict, the impetus to defeat the enemy is greatest. This is precisely what appears to be occurring. There are two primary reasons for considering this.

First, the formation of a global internet society confronts us with an overwhelming number of *cosmoi*. Taylor calls this "The Nova Effect," a rapid expansion and diversifying of religious experience.[105] This is old news, but the internet has made it more "virulent." Berger describes modernity as a "seed-bed" for religious pluralism that has radically altered the human condition:[106]

> Modernization leads to a huge transformation in the human condition from fate to choice.... But the range of choices increases through history and has increased exponentially since the Industrial Revolution.... This endless array of choices is reinforced by the structures of capitalist systems, with their enormous market for services, products, and even identities, all protected by a democratic state which legitimates these choices, not least the choice of religion.[107]

The reality of *quantity* and *choice* means that we choose not only our vocations but also our *teloi*. One does not simply receive a sense of purpose; one must craft it for oneself.

Second, living in such a pluralistic society (*pluralism as reality*) has revitalized syncretism. Young adults are abandoning their parents's religion, causing social division within the family. Young adults are abandoning their loyalty to the teachings of any one *cosmos* and creating their own unique *cosmoi*; or rather, they are creating idol-ologies.

This twofold pattern of pluralism and syncretism, along with the decline of plausibility structures (religious communities) creates a vacuum of *meaning*, that is, anomy.[108] Though most Americans have submitted to this through apathy and hedonism, it appears that a small minority are transforming their *nomoi* into *cosmoi*.[109] As our religious affections wane,

---

105. Taylor, *Secular Age*, 300–304; Smith, *How (Not) to be Secular*, 60–73; Berger, *Rumor of Angels*, 8.

106. For more thorough arguments of this claim, see: Taylor, *Secular Age*; Boersma, *Heavenly Participation*.

107. Berger, *Many Altars of Modernity*, 5.

108. Or *telos*—recall the Malaises of Modernity.

109. This claim is more plausible than it might first appear. See Lindsey and Nayna,

we turn to idol-ologies to secure a positive self-identity. Starting perhaps with the turbulence of the 2016 presidential election, these idol-ologies more frequently involve or centralize social or political activism. Without an established *cosmos* to provide a sense of meaning, and with a growing sense of *fear* for society's wellbeing, the only meaning that can be found is either in *tikkun olam*—in defending the poor and suffering in society from the threat of social or political oppression—or in quietism.[110] Neither solves the underlying problem of anomy due to the loss of religion.[111]

The sacred/secular divide so hallowed in American society is breaking down. Ergo, we are no longer traditionalist and progressive ideologues arguing over our *nomoi* in government. We are religious zealots crusading for our *cosmoi*, demanding that the government arbitrate while social media steps in as a de-stabilizer and plausibility structure.

Such a conflict as this is not unknown to us. Berger describes both the conflict and its aftermath. He describes the conflict thusly:

> There are reactionary and progressive fundamentalisms. What all these projects have in common is a promise to the potential convert: "Come join us, and you will have the certainty you have long desired. You will understand the world, you will know who you are, and you will know how to live."[112]

About the fallout, Berger writes:

> Both relativism and fundamentalism are dangerous for individuals and much more so for society. Relativism moves individuals toward moral nihilism, fundamentalism toward fanaticism. Neither is attractive as a way of life, but as long as my nihilistic or fanatical neighbors do not seek to impose their views on me, I can live with them and collaborate in taking out the trash. However, the threat to society is harder to manage. If there is no agreement at all on what is permissible behavior (in Emile Durkheim's phrase, no "collective conscience"), the moral basis and consequently the very existence of a society is put in question. It will lack the solidarity that motivates individuals to

---

"Postmodern Religion and the Faith"; and Jenkins, "Top Catholic Bishop." See also: Lindsey, *Race Marxism*; Lindsey and Pluckrose, *Cynical Theories*; Dreher, *Live Not by Lies*, 60.

110. Nouwen, *Wounded Healer*, 13–15.

111. Berger, *Rumor of Angels*, 12.

112. Berger, *Many Altars of Modernity*, 9. I believe Berger uses the term "fundamentalism" for the stereotypical emotional reaction it receives and not for its theological meaning. It is perhaps not the best term here.

make sacrifices for fellow members of the society and ultimately motivates them to risk their lives if the society is attacked. Fundamentalism, even if it is not successful in imposing itself on the entire society (with the above mentioned ensuing costs), will bring about ongoing conflict which, even short of civil war, will undermine social stability.[113]

This is the situation we face now in society. Not merely an argument of ideals, not a war of expansion, but a new sort of holy war with our government as the benevolent god to whom we make sacrifice and offer petition and in which we are soldiers in holy cause to reshape the world in the image of *our* religious teachings.

To conclude, I may now present two hypotheses surrounding social media. First, perhaps God did not exhort us to "post our *nomoi* to social media" because he had no need to. Social media is not the patient, nor even the devil, but Wormwood the junior tempter.[114] We are the patient, and it appears we have posted in error.

Second, our bitterness is the natural product of the American project. The development of American society has followed a natural progression: social groups compete for status. This has led to increasing equality, which leads to increasing levels of conflict and competition. Christians understand this as "sin." To quote Qoheleth, "I have seen everything that is done under the sun, and behold, all is vanity and a striving after wind."[115] We are victims of ourselves. Whether or not this is the end of the American project, I do not know.

This explains how we *became* embittered. In order to solve the problem of our bitterness, we need to understand the bitterness itself. I have already begun this work in describing victimhood, but to find a solution I intend to go somewhat further.

---

113. Berger, *Many Altars of Modernity*, 66. See also: Shriver, *Ethic for Enemies*, 46. Shriver cites John Crossan, claiming that nationalism and globalism are equally destructive. This will be important in the next chapter.

114. Wormwood being the junior tempter from C. S. Lewis's *Screwtape Letters*. Wormwood demonstrates his ineptitude through his correspondence with his uncle and senior tempter, Screwtape; see: Lewis, *Screwtape Letters*.

115. Eccl 1:14 ESV. Qoheleth is the traditional name for the Hebrew sage thought to be the author of Ecclesiastes.

Chapter 3: **Patterns of Bitterness**

Illuminations from the Eighteen-Hundreds for the Twenty-First Century

> Wrath is love of justice perverted to revenge and spite.
> —Dorothy Sayers[1]

I: Introduction

ONE OF MY FAVORITE childhood books is *Follow My Leader* by James Garfield. It tells the story of Jimmy, an athlete, student, and Boy Scout. However, all these are taken from him when he is blinded in a playground accident. The story describes his journey of relearning how to function in a society without his sight.

The subplot that stuck with me the most explains how Jimmy came to terms with the *reason* for his blindness. He was blinded in a childhood prank involving his friend, Mike, who lit an abandoned firecracker found on the playground—despite its dangerously short fuse—and then, in panic, threw the firecracker at Jimmy, whereupon the firecracker exploded in Jimmy's face. Although it was an accident, Jimmy quite understandably blames Mike for his blindness and harbors a deep bitterness against Mike. But when he tries to explain his pain and desire for vengeance to his roommate at The Seeing Eye (the school for the blind), Mack replies with a question that confronts Jimmy with Mike's perspective: "How

---

1. Dorothy Sayers quote from her introduction to Dante Alighieri, *Purgatorio*.

would you like to go through the rest of your life knowing you made someone else go blind?"[2]

Jimmy does not come around immediately, but he eventually forgives Mike and asks if they might continue being friends. Jimmy explains, "I've learned that holding on to anger is like carrying poison around."[3] Mack's wisdom and Jimmy's revelation are the backdrop of this chapter.

In this chapter, I will move the microscope lens away from the inner psychology of bitterness in pursuit of a broader narrative frame (i.e., a particular framing of history that illustrates part of our social identity—*nomos*, *telos*, and *cosmos*). That narrative frame is Friedrich Nietzsche's *The Genealogy of Morals*.

I will begin with an explanation of Nietzsche's theory of the revolution in morals, in particular the psychology of what he calls the "slave mentality"—called *ressentiment*. I will argue that the *ressentiment* is an excellent illustration of Jimmy's experience. Subsequently, this will necessitate answering three questions: (1) "How may Christians comfortably use material from Nietzsche that centralizes strong anti-Christian sentiments?" (2) "Is not bitterness a necessary prerequisite for justice, and given that justice is a core Christian value, why should we identify bitterness as a vice rather than a virtue?" (3) Because vengeance is a critical part of Nietzsche's understanding of bitterness, "Amid the computer age, cannot anyone avenge themselves on their enemy in effigy through Twitter?"[4] Finally, I will argue the value of using Nietzsche as a model for current societal trends of hatred over the obvious alternative, Karl Marx, including specific examples. In so doing, I will demonstrate that polarization, victimhood, and Nietzsche each explain bitterness in the same way. In conclusion, I will propose that the proper Christian response to a society thus interpreted must be a renewed emphasis on our Lord's commandment to love our enemies.

II: Nietzsche's Genealogy: Defining Ressentiment

Although most Christians worry about Nietzsche's ideas about atheism and the Übermensch, it is his *Genealogy of Morals* that introduces the

---

2. Garfield, *Follow My Leader*, 125–26.
3. Garfield, *Follow My Leader*, 174.
4. Although the platform formerly known as Twitter has been renamed "X," I will continue using "Twitter" in this context as the former name had a long history and "Twitter" is more easily recognizable in prose.

debate of ethics and draws both prior concepts into dialogue, eventually forming a framework for how to live.[5] This is the focus of the following discussion.

In the *Genealogy*, Nietzsche presents a theoretical recount of history before the rise of Judeo-Christian values. In this prehistory, moral and legal codes were constructed by the strong and forced on the weak.[6] He calls these codes "aristocratic morality" and "slave morality," respectively.[7] These correspond roughly to social stratification by class: aristocratic morality originates with the wealthy and powerful, while slave morality originates among the peasantry. The aristocrats perceive themselves as naturally good. Conversely, everything unlike the aristocrats is innately bad, so aristocrats spend their lives reshaping society to fit their own image. The slaves find themselves constantly pressured to conform to a different and (for them) foreign way of life. Nietzsche calls the gap between aristocratic morality and slave morality "the pathos of distance."[8] Justice serves the interests of the stronger.[9]

---

5. Alternatively, *Genealogy of Morality*. The German has more than one correct translation. See also Nietzsche's "Parable of the Madman" in Nietzsche, *Gay Science*, 119–20; and Nietzsche, *Thus Spoke Zarathustra*, 104. I am including the German "Übermensch" rather than the usual translation "Superman" for clarity's sake. The notion of the *Übermensch* is introduced in *Also Sprach Zarathustra* and becomes a central theme in all of Nietzsche's subsequent writing. He proposes that the way forward for humanity is for each person to formulate a sense of their own *telos* (purpose) for themselves through a sheer act of will. The ability to determine "good" and "evil" for oneself is the pinnacle of human achievement and a necessity for a good life. The notion of the Aryan race as the true *Übermensch* is not native to Nietzsche's thought but a perversion by Nazism; see: Shapiro, "Translating, Repeating, Naming," 235; Nussbaum, "Pity and Mercy in Nietzsche's Stoicism," 140; Yovel, "Nietzsche, the Jews, and *Ressentiment*," 224; Whyte, "Uses and Abuses," 171–94.

6. I am not making a value judgment through my use of the terms "strong" and "weak." These are typical of Nietzsche in *The Genealogy of Morality*, which I will shorten to *TGM*. I happen to disagree with his application of the terms, particularly in light of Jesus' assertion that "the meek shall inherit the earth," (Ps 37:11; Matt 5:5) and Paul's assertion that God's "strength is made perfect in weakness" (Ps 8:2; 2 Cor 12:5–9).

7. Smith, "Introduction," vii, xv. Smith's introduction includes a comprehensive and accurate interpretation of Nietzsche's work. Nietzsche himself does not use these two terms per se, but his initial comparison of the "masters" with the "slaves," "plebeians," or "herd" occurs: Nietzsche, *TGM*, 21. See also: Hegel, *Phenomenology of Spirit*, cited in Murphy and Hampton, *Forgiveness and Mercy*, 55.

8. Nietzsche, *TGM*, 12–13.

9. Hicks, *Explaining Postmodernism*, 182–83. For a detailed explanation of the interplay between aristocratic morality and slave morality, see: Solomon, "One Hundred Years of *Ressentiment*," 111; Elgat, *Nietzsche's Psychology of Ressentiment*, 38. This is counter-indicated by *SIT* in the previous chapter, pp. 33–6, 38.

CHAPTER 3: PATTERNS OF BITTERNESS

The idea of a class struggle as a moral struggle between the aristocracy and the slaves is clearly reminiscent of Karl Marx's political struggle between the bourgeoisie and the proletariat.[10] There is also a similarity between Charles Darwin's *Origin of the Species* and Nietzsche's eventual conclusion that Western morality is the *product* of the ethical struggle between two social classes, similar to "survival of the fittest."[11] Though Nietzsche is influenced by these two, his unique approach makes his work stand out.[12]

The essential element of Nietzsche's approach is the transformation of slave morality into *ressentiment*—essentially bitterness. The slaves naturally resented the aristocrats, particularly due to the Pathos of Distance.[13] To quote Walter Kaufmann, "The basic distinction which Nietzsche proposes is between two states of being: the 'overfullness of life' and the 'impoverishment of life,' power and impotence."[14] Over time, this dynamic transforms resentment into *ressentiment*, which spawned a revolution in ethics.[15] No longer would good and evil be determined by the strong but rather by the weak: "the meek shall inherit the earth."[16] Because of its centrality in Judeo-Christian ethics, Nietzsche concludes that Judeo-Christian values caused the slave revolt.[17] What, then, is this *ressentiment* so central to Nietzsche's thinking?

Ressentiment has various meanings. The dominant perspective argues that the term originates from the French and has become a *terminus technicus*.[18] *Ressentiment* "is close to the English 'resentment,' but with a more curdled bitterness, more seething and poisoned and bottled up for a long

---

10. Tomelleri, *Ressentiment*, pp. 6/loc. 507. See also: Haidt, *Righteous Mind*, 200, 322.

11. Wilson, "Darwin and Nietzsche," 354–70.

12. These similarities fit most naturally here, and I will return to them later.

13. Solomon, "One Hundred Years of *Ressentiment*," 111.

14. Kaufmann, *Nietzsche*, 323, cited in Scheler, *Ressentiment*, 21. Recall the dichotomy of Social Mobility and Social Change within *SIT* and the requirement that there be something to be gained before conflict is incited, see chapter 2, pp. 33–8.

15. Nietzsche, *TGM*, 22.

16. Matt 5:5.

17. Nietzsche, *TGM*, 19–20, 20–21, 35–36. I do not find Nietzsche's argument convincing here, as it amounts to a tautology.

18. Scheler, *Ressentiment*, 39. See also Solomon, "One Hundred Years of *Ressentiment*," 95; Elgat, *Nietzsche's Psychology of Ressentiment*, 26. Argument for Germanic origin comes from Bittner, "Ressentiment," 128. In my opinion, the argument for a Germanic origin of the term is weak, and even Bittner is not satisfied by the connection.

time."[19] Max Scheler couples *ressentiment* with emotional flavors including "revenge, hatred, malice, envy, the impulse to detract, and spite." He adds, "Thirst for revenge is the most important source of *ressentiment*."[20]

There are other possible emotional roots for this phenomenon. René Girard and Stefano Tomelleri interpret *ressentiment* through mimetic theory,[21] redefining it as extreme envy that is perpetually insatiable.[22] This also emphasizes *repression* within *ressentiment*.[23] There is merit here, but it fits *within* Scheler's definition. Alternatively, Martha Nussbaum suggests *ressentiment* could be the product of fear. She claims that fear causes the individual to lash out to eliminate the perceived cause of their fear. This causes fear to become *ressentiment*.[24] Guy Elgat affirms, "While *ressentiment* is indeed an instinctive reaction to displeasure, when disaster strikes ... [subjects would] be more concerned with avoiding further harm or be struck motionless from fear, in a state of petrifying panic and disbelief."[25] However, though Nussbaum's suggestion is interesting, it appears to describe a *catalyst* for *ressentiment* rather than a core component thereof. Therefore, "hatred" and the desire for revenge are the essential qualifiers of *ressentiment*. We might say it is a sort of *festering bitterness*.

Ressentiment can also be identified by three fixations: (1) an "enemy," (2) a history of oppression, that is, a *prolonged* or *severe* form of suffering forced on the individual,[26] and (3) a feeling of impotence[27]—these create

19. Hicks, *Explaining Postmodernism*, 193.

20. Scheler, *Ressentiment*, 45.

21. Mimetic Theory seeks to understand world history in terms of a sociology of desire. Once basic wants are provided, our desires push us to seek out excess, which inevitably leads to war for material gain and resetting the cycle. *Ressentiment* in this context is the driving emotion behind the cycle.

22. Girard, *Risentimento*, x. Tomelleri, *Ressentiment*, 24/672, 27/699, 76/1116; Scheler, *Ressentiment*, 52–53. This creates a fascinating connection with Jas 4:1–12; 5:1–11, suggesting that Girard and Tomelleri have struck on a point of ancient wisdom. See also Wis. 2 from the Apocrypha.

23. Nietzsche, *TGM*, 22–24; Cosner, "Introduction," 24; Scheler, *Ressentiment*, 48–49. Elgat rejects the idea that repression is central to *ressentiment*, but I will accept it here given its support in other sources and given that the question of its validity is not essential to my argument; see: Elgat, *Nietzsche's Psychology of Ressentiment*, 27.

24. Nussbaum, *Monarchy of Fear*, 63–64, 80–88. Recall the chapter 1, p. 9, section on Cultivation Theory.

25. Elgat, *Nietzsche's Psychology of Ressentiment*, 35.

26. See Nietzsche, *TGM*, 22–25. These first two points are largely implied from the necessary interactions between aristocrats and slaves. Recall victimhood; see chapter 1, pp. 16–8.

27. Scheler, *Ressentiment*, 48. Impotence is also indicative of an internal locus of

a "thirst for revenge." What makes these conditions particularly interesting is that they need not be *tangible*. They can be *imaginary* (mirroring Perceived Polarization, victimhood characteristics, and perception within *SIT*). For example, Nietzsche's description implies the enemy is not necessarily an "individual" but a "class." The enemy could an institution or a social force as well as a person or demographic. The power of imagination does not lessen the power of *ressentiment*.

Scheler argues that *ressentiment* actually increases when it targets a demographic, institution, or social force because such circumstances mean the individual feels permanently dissatisfied with vengeance. Furthermore, the *ressentiment*-afflicted person sees vengeance as a "duty" and makes it their life's mission to seek out and attack everything that can be connected with the object of their anger—even attacking others in circumstances that are otherwise entirely innocent (outgroup bias)[28]—as in cancel culture. However, Elgat warns that we cannot hold the notion of such an enemy for long and will eventually settle on a person or tribe rather than something intangible.[29] Eventually, imaginary enemies are replaced with persons, but imaginary enemies are sufficient for *ressentiment*.

Oppression can be imaginary too. James Davison Hunter writes, "Perception is everything. It is not the weak or aggrieved per se [who suffer from *ressentiment*] though it could be, but rather those that perceive themselves as such."[30] Tomelleri implies this when he describes the actions resulting from *ressentiment* as "playing the victim"—imaginary oppression is implicit in his work.[31] This concurs with the psychology of victimhood.

---

reality; see: Lukianoff and Haidt, *Coddling*, 37, 46.

28. See also: Scheler, *Ressentiment*, 48–49. Recall the power of disagreement to create conflict even in silence; see chapter 2, p. 33.

29. Elgat argues that you cannot take revenge on an enemy unless they can feel pain—though we may sometimes anthropomorphize an inanimate object. Elgat, *Nietzsche's Psychology of Ressentiment*, 30–32, 36–37, 74. In fairness, Scheler does admit that "usually, revenge and envy still have specific objects"; thus the possibility of conceptual enemies is disputed. Scheler, *Ressentiment*, 47. See also: Tomelleri, *Ressentiment*, 92/1244. This reality makes it difficult to take enemies such as patriarchy, white supremacy, socialism, or a "Jewish cabal" with any seriousness—the one hating will likely transfer their hatred to the *individuals* these ideals imply. See also: Bailey, *Cross and the Prodigal*, 69.

30. Hunter, *To Change the World*, 107.

31. Tomelleri, *Ressentiment*, 27/699, 95/1267. Hunter, *To Change the World*, 107–8. Nietzsche, *TGM*, 57; Scheler, *Ressentiment*, 51. Recall chapter 1, pp. 16–8, 28, on victimhood.

Lastly, as Tomelleri argues via Gilles Deleuze, the feeling of impotence need only be imagined to generate *ressentiment*.[32] The initial role of *ressentiment* (according to Nietzsche) is not to exact revenge in reality but "*in effigie*," [sic] or to "find compensation in an imaginary revenge."[33] This does not preclude the possibility of *ressentiment* leading to *actual* acts of vengeance but explains Nietzsche's "revolution" in *morals*. If one felt empowered to exact tangible vengeance, one would not pursue vengeance in effigy.

We must also understand the revolution. At its center, the revolution redefines morality itself. Nietzsche explains,

> The slave revolt in morals begins when *ressentiment* itself becomes creative and ordains value: the *ressentiment* of creatures to whom the real reaction, that of the deed, is denied and who find compensation in an imaginary revenge.[34]

This is the only act of vengeance Nietzsche ascribes to individuals affected by *ressentiment*—the "creative act" that "ordains value." Scheler clarifies:

> *Ressentiment* brings about its most important achievement when it determines a whole "morality," perverting the rules of preference until what was "evil" appears to be "good."[35]

Nietzsche claimed that this was how Christianity changed the world. Whereas in Nietzsche's theoretical prehistory, moral and legal codes were conceived of by the strong and forced on the weak, now the weak and powerless set the standards by which we judge good and evil.

While Nietzsche focuses mainly on this *initial* revolution in morals, that does not discount the possibility of *further revolutions* in morals throughout history and even today. Nietzsche worried that such a revolution was taking place in Industrial Age Europe. This reinforces the image of *ressentiment's* power to drive moral change in a manner akin to the evolutionary drive of "survival of the fittest." All such revolutions creatively reshape society. This creativity elevates the enemy's importance in the eyes of the *ressentiment*-afflicted. The individual moves from perceiving the enemy as irritating or immature to labeling the enemy as morally deficient—giving them the *right* to avenge

---

32. Deleuze, *Nietzsche and Philosophy*, cited in Tomelleri, *Ressentiment*, 17/601.
33. Nietzsche, *TGM*, 22–23.
34. Nietzsche, *TGM*, 22–23.
35. Scheler, Ressentiment, 81. See also: Nietzsche, *TGM*, 25.

themselves—and making it a moral *requirement* to oppose the enemy. "If you aren't 'with us,' then you're against us!"³⁶ Tomelleri hints at this when he points out that "envy tends to make rivals (enemies in *ressentiment*, or the target of *ressentiment*) more uniform."³⁷

However, repressed *ressentiment* does nothing more than rewrite morals. *Ressentiment* necessarily builds in intensity while repressed—what I would call "cold" *ressentiment*. Once it reaches a point of intensity where the individual can no longer forcibly suppress it, there is an inevitable explosion, after which the individual does everything possible to seek vengeance until they are satisfied—I would call this state "hot" *ressentiment*.³⁸ The result is violence. Elgat suggests cold *ressentiment* is purely theoretical and favors the notion of a hot *ressentiment*,³⁹ but must we choose one or the other? Surely both can be observed in our own lives and the lives of others. Both may lead to a change in moral structure but through different means. Cold *ressentiment* influences the enemy through shame to adopt the new values, whereas hot *ressentiment* forces the new values on them through violence.⁴⁰

To summarize, Nietzsche theorized that societal shifts in morals are forced by conflict between two people groups—those with the current and dominant moral values and those who feel oppressed by the dominant group. The oppressed group, or "slave morality," is primarily recognized through the characteristic of *ressentiment*, which is a festering sort of bitterness—though it contains fear and envy.

Ressentiment develops through harboring resentment against an enemy (1) because of their oppressive behavior, (2) in the face of one's own impotence, (3) which ultimately leads to enacting vengeance. The enemy may be an institution, "force," or imagined foe, but theoretical or symbolic enemies must ultimately be replaced with an individual

36. I am paraphrasing the point here, not quoting. See Hunter, *To Change the World*, 107–8; Nietzsche, *TGM*, 30.

37. Tomelleri, *Ressentiment*, 79/1145. This notion should also draw to mind the practice of cognitive behavioral therapy, which addresses the notion of cognitive distortions, or ways of thinking that are fundamentally hurtful or at minimum unproductive. Particularly "overgeneralizing," "dichotomous thinking," and "labeling"; see: Lukianoff and Haidt, *Coddling*, 37–42.

38. Scheler, *Ressentiment*, 50; Dühring, *Cursus der Philosophie*, 224; Hunter, *To Change the World*, 168–169.

39. Elgat, *Nietzsche's Psychology of Ressentiment*, 27–29.

40. Elgat, *Nietzsche's Psychology of Ressentiment*, 38. Dr. Martin Luther King Jr. discusses this more times than I could count. Some examples can be found: King, *Testament of Hope*, 7, 10, 12, 17, 58, 80–81, 82–83, 140, 230.

or group. Oppression may also be imaginary (or, more likely, an exaggeration) but most often, the source of oppression will involve some real conflict between the individual and their enemy. The sense of impotence may result from a simple need for therapy (such as cognitive behavioral therapy for an external locus of power) or a sort of tyrannical oppression—both causes can lead to self-victimization.[41] *Ressentiment* can remain cold and force a shift in morals through influence, but it can become hot and lash out seeking vengeance.

Now we turn to three questions this material raises: (1) "How may Christians comfortably use material from Nietzsche that centralizes strong anti-Christian sentiments?" (2) "Is not bitterness a necessary prerequisite for justice, and given that justice is a core Christian value, why should we identify bitterness as a vice rather than a virtue?" (3) Because vengeance is a critical part of Nietzsche's understanding of *ressentiment*, "Amid the computer age, cannot anyone avenge themselves on their enemy in effigy through Twitter?"

III: Contra Nietzsche

Christians might oppose studying Nietzsche given his strong anti-theistic views. We should first consider three points: first, we need not accept Nietzsche's assumption that "God is dead"—often the first point of concern for Christians. Second, we need not accept Nietzsche's claim that Christian morals are rooted in hatred. Third, if the practice of our faith becomes corrupted by *ressentiment*, it would behoove us to be able to recognize, understand, and reverse that corruption.[42]

Let us begin with Nietzsche's *The Gay Science* and his parable of the madman. While his claim that "God is dead" is distressing, it is often misunderstood. The irony of Nietzsche's parable of the madman is that the central character—the madman who claims that we have killed God—is *not* pleased about the idea of God's death. Rather than declaring triumphantly that we have thrown off the chains of repressive religion, the madman fears the consequences of the end of religion, crying, "I'm looking for God! I'm looking for God!"[43]

---

41. See chapter 1, p. 35, for an overview of CBT.
42. See chapter 1, p. 9n35.
43. The relevant paragraph reads: "Haven't you heard of that madman who in the bright morning lit a lantern and ran around the marketplace crying incessantly, 'I'm looking for God! I'm looking for God!' Since many of those who did not believe in God

The madman reveals two concerns: (1) How are we to make sense of ourselves without God? (2) If we have killed God, how can we possibly atone? The first concern is easier to understand with a quote from *Also Sprach Zarathustra*, wherein Nietzsche says: "Away with *such* a god! Better no god, better to produce destiny on one's own account, better to be a fool, better to be god oneself!"[44] This is what the madman *fears* most.[45] As for his second fear, the madman says,

> God is dead! God remains dead! And we have killed him! How can we console ourselves, the murderers of all murderers! The holiest and the mightiest thing the world has ever possessed has bled to death under our knives: who will wipe this blood from us? With what water could we clean ourselves? What festivals of atonement, what holy games will we have to invent for ourselves? Is the magnitude of this deed not too great for us? Do we not ourselves have to become gods merely to appear worthy of it?[46]

Nietzsche was under no illusion that the death of God was cause for joy. He understood the death of God as an unavoidable problem that demanded a solution.

In contrast, consider the apostle Paul. Even he admitted the danger inherent to our faith. In 1 Corinthians, he wrote that if Jesus was truly dead, then we are above all most to be pitied—our faith and all the labor of our lives are futile (1 Cor 15:12–19). Nietzsche demonstrates that Paul's concern works both ways: if God is *not* dead—if he, in fact, "got better"—then surely it is Nietzsche who is most to be pitied, for *both* of the madman's fears are realized. If Jesus is alive, then this so-called enemy of Christendom needs *our* compassion. Not we his. Christians need not accept Nietzsche's premise for atheism. Any subsequent arguments are likewise dismissible.

Second, even if we need not accept Nitzsche's premise of anti-theism, one of the claims of his internal argument in the *Genealogy* is itself open to criticism. Nietzsche argues that Judeo-Christian morals are themselves

---

were standing around together just then, he caused great laughter. Has he been lost, then? Asked one. Did he lose his way like a child? Asked another. Or is he hiding? Is he afraid of us? Has he gone to sea? Emigrated?—Thus they shouted and laughed, one interrupting the other. The madman jumped into their midst and pierced them with his eyes. 'Where is God?' He cried; 'I'll tell you! We *have killed him*—you and I!'" Nietzsche, *Gay Science*, 119–20.

44. Nietzsche, *Thus Spoke Zarathustra*, 274.
45. Recall the difficulty of maintaining a social identity; see chapter 2, pp. 45–9.
46. Nietzsche, *Gay Science*, 120.

rooted in *ressentiment*. In other words, Christian values of love are really hatred in disguise.[47] This also means that the source of Christian love is *weakness* rather than strength. This creates two contradictions.

The first contradiction is Nietzsche's claim that Christian love is disguised hatred while also claiming that Christ was "the pinnacle of love." Elgat says Nietzsche viewed Jesus as the only human ever to live and be free of *ressentiment*.[48] Essentially, Nietzsche claims that Jesus transformed Jewish hatred into love, but this never caught on.[49] How can we know Jesus as the pinnacle of love if no one passed on his teachings correctly? Furthermore, Nietzsche's claim that Judeo-Christian morals are rooted in *ressentiment* is unsubstantiated, and his anti-Christian prejudices obviously influence him. Both of these claims are purely speculative—one should not judge the intentions or emotions of the dead so flippantly—thus, we need not accept them.

As for the second contradiction, René Girard wrote in response, "Nietzsche sees *ressentiment* not only as Christianity's child, which is certainly true, but also as its father, which is certainly false."[50] If we take both of these contradictions together, the resulting conclusion is rather striking. Consider James's description of the tongue:

> With it we bless the Lord and Father, and with it we curse those who are made in the likeness of God. From the same mouth come blessing and cursing. My brothers and sisters, this ought not to be so. Does a spring pour forth from the same opening both fresh and brackish water? Can a fig tree, my brothers and sisters, yield olives, or a grapevine figs? No more can salt water yield fresh. (Jas 3:9–12, NRSVA)

In this same spirit, Nietzsche is arguing either that the mouth of Christianity is not Jesus—fresh water—or that a source of fresh water yields not fresh and brackish water but brackish water *alone*. In rejecting the divinity of Jesus, Nietzsche necessarily rejects the miracle at the wedding in Cana, where Jesus turned water into wine. Nietzsche immediately recreates and reverses this same miracle with the claim that the wine that was the life of Jesus yielded only plain water—hate-filled Christianity. To deny the first miracle only to reenact it is absurd.

---

47. Nietzsche, *TGM*, 30.
48. Elgat, *Nietzsche's Psychology of Ressentiment*, 47.
49. Nietzsche, *TGM*, 20–21. Nietzsche's "anti-Semitism" is debated and contested.
50. Girard, "Dionysius Versus the Crucified," 825. See also: Scheler, *Ressentiment*, 82–88; Tomelleri, *Ressentiment*, 13/567.

CHAPTER 3: PATTERNS OF BITTERNESS

As for the notion that Christian love is rooted in weakness, Scheler counters that Christian love *must* be rooted in strength, life, and goodness.[51] He writes:

> The Christian view [of love] boldly denies the Greek axiom that love is an aspiration of the lower towards the higher. On the contrary, now the criterion of love is that the nobler stoops to the vulgar, the healthy to the sick, the rich to the poor, the handsome to the ugly, the good and saintly to the bad and common, the Messiah to the sinners and Publicans. The Christian is not afraid, like the ancient, that he might lose something by doing so, that he might impair his own nobility. . . . God spontaneously "descended" to man, became a servant, and died the bad servant's death on the cross! Now the precept of loving good and hating evil, loving one's friend and hating one's enemy, becomes meaningless. There is no longer any "highest good" independent of and beyond the *act* and movement of love! Love itself is the highest of all goods.[52]

This is hardly the description of weakness as Nietzsche understood it. This redefines strength (1 Cor 1:25). Strength is not removed from or indifferent to the suffering of others but seeks to uplift them.[53] Scheler's explanation of the connection between *ressentiment* and love, between weakness and strength, is correct: "I realized that the root of Christian love is entirely *free* of *ressentiment*, but that *ressentiment* can very easily use it for its own purposes."[54]

If we consider both of these problems—Nietzsche's failure to address the connection between Christ and Christianity and his improper association of Christian love with hatred—we have sufficient grounds on which to reject Nietzsche's anti-Christian stance in the *Genealogy*.

Third, given that Nietzsche's theory of *ressentiment* and the dynamics between aristocratic and slave moralities are not unique to Nietzsche, there is good reason for us to take his warning seriously.[55] Should we notice *ressentiment* creeping into our communal walk of faith, faithful

---

51. Cosner, "Introduction," 22.
52. Scheler, *Ressentiment*, 86–87.
53. See chapter 4, pp. 94–6, on God suffering without being weakened.
54. Scheler, *Ressentiment*, 88.
55. See, for example: Haidt, *Righteous Mind*, 198–203, 322; Lukianoff and Haidt, *Coddling*, 14–15, 37–43, 53, 57, 60, 66, 101–102; Nichols, *Death of Expertise*, 59, 64, 101–2. See also Scheler's warning above that *ressentiment* can easily take advantage of Christian love.

Christians must act! Scripture is replete with warnings that idolatry is easy to fall into.[56] Moreover, Tomelleri warns that *ressentiment* is characterized by the way it blurs the line between a Christian's love for the neighbor and a desire for their flourishing, and the subversive desire for vengeance found within *ressentiment*:

> *Ressentiment* is the emotional reaction, the revolt of the "sufferers against the sound and the victorious": it clothes itself in compassion, love, and the thirst for justice, but behind these vestments of Christian goodness there is the *reaction* of the weakest, their desire for revenge that has been buried over time.[57]

We must keep alert (1 Pet 5:8)! Remembering Tomelleri's proposal that *ressentiment* is a sort of blunted desire, consider Jas 4:1–2, 7–8:

> Those conflicts and disputes among you, where do they come from? Do they not come from your cravings that are at war within you? You want something and do not have it; so you commit murder. And you covet something and cannot obtain it; so you engage in disputes and conflicts. . . . Submit yourselves therefore to God. Resist the devil, and he will flee from you. Draw near to God, and he will draw near to you. Cleanse your hands, you sinners, and purify your hearts, you double-minded. (NRSVA)

While I cannot say whether or not James was speaking of *ressentiment*, I cannot dismiss the similarities: acting violently out of a desire you cannot satisfy and double-mindedness or self-deception. James Hunter argues that *ressentiment* has already infiltrated some corners of Christian practice today.[58] While Christians should be careful when contemplating Nietzsche, we should not throw out ideas that could be valuable for fear of his bad ideas. Furthermore, if we can lay aside his core failures in the *Genealogy*—the claim that *ressentiment* is both the father and offspring of our faith and the premise of anti-theism—surely we can (and should) consider his other proposals without fear.

---

56. This perspective is common throughout the prophetic writings. Some examples include Deut 4:25–26; 8:19–20; 31:20; Jer 25:5–6; 35:15; and 1 Pet 5:8. The need to watch out least we fall into idolatry is also common to Hosea and Revelation. Recall also the slippery character of "idol-ology," 44–5, 55–6, 135–38.

57. Tomelleri, *Ressentiment*, pp. 13/loc. 567.

58. Hunter, *To Change the World*, 133–34, 141–43, 168–69. Examples to follow.

IV: On the Pursuit of Justice

Now we turn to the topic of justice and whether or not it depends on *Ressentiment* for its achievement. This raises a particularly challenging issue—how to argue against the myriad forms of hatred in our justice activism without arguing against activism itself. The need for real justice cannot be denied and is a personal concern for me. Therefore, be it crystal clear that justice advocacy is a Christian value![59] However, justice advocacy *must* be free of hatred and victimhood.[60] This section explains the tension between hatred and justice.

We begin with the quintessential argument that *ressentiment* is necessary for justice to be achieved. Robert Solomon writes:

> This is the crux of my doubts about Nietzsche's thesis—his refusal to acknowledge resentment as an essential ingredient in our sense of justice (and his corresponding restriction of "justice" to a dearth of the powerful and privileged.) ... An ethics of resentment is not just a matter of good character/bad character or good emotions and bad emotions. It is also ... a question of justification, of the political and social context and legitimacy of motives and emotions.[61]

Without bitterness there would be no justice; therefore the ends justify the means.[62] Machiavelli is relentless. While Solomon's criticism of Nietzsche is justified—justice is *not* restricted to a dearth of the powerful and privileged—Solomon's claim that resentment is necessary for justice is dubious.

---

59. I have already cited the epistle of James, not to mention admonishments throughout Hosea, Amos (which deserves more space than I have), Joel, and Jesus' sharp words on this topic in Matt 25:31–46.

60. Tomelleri, *Ressentiment*, 101/1326.

61. Solomon, "One Hundred Years," 112, 124. Solomon uses "resentment" in place of *ressentiment*. Solomon's full argument appears in: Solomon, *Passion for Justice*.

62. In support of this claim, Solomon cites John Rawls as a primary source. In his view, justice becomes doubly important when it is no longer a matter restricted to individuals, but a matter of institutions and communities. Here it would be prudent to recall Scheler's words about the nature of imaginary enemies and the character of *ressentiment* that follows. See above footnote 27. See also Solomon, "One Hundred Years," 117–18. Although Rawls has significantly affected our contemporary view of ethics, I find myself typically skeptical that his ideas fit within a Christian framework. An alternative take on this notion is cited by Haidt, who cites John Stuart Mill as the originator of what he called the "harm principle"—the idea that morality is rooted in harm—in 1859, arguing that the only excuse for the exercise of power over another in civilized community is to prevent harm to others: Haidt, *Righteous Mind*, 112.

First, Solomon's argument is an example of the logical fallacy *post hoc, ergo proctor hoc*—that is, "after it, therefore because of it."[63] This assumes that because *ressentiment* often precedes action taken to correct injustice, the subsequent action happened because of *ressentiment*.[64] While justice sometimes follows acts of *ressentiment*, that does not demonstrate a *causal relationship* between the two. Neither does it account for instances in which justice may be achieved *without* a preceding act of revenge or cases in which acts of revenge lead to *injustice*. We should always be grateful for every victory in the name of justice, but we should never justify acts of gross injustice—such as character assassination, vandalism, rioting, and murder—assuming that they necessarily precede justice. It is impossible to demonstrate that any historical victory of justice over injustice is somehow *dependent* upon prior acts of injustice. Solomon's argument that *ressentiment* is essential for justice is purely speculative.

Second, we should challenge the claim that justice begins in *hurt*. According Jonathan Haidt's Moral Foundations Theory,[65] a complete understanding of morality—and thereby what constitutes a breach of morality, an act of injustice—must be built on more than the question of hurt.[66] Given Haidt's proposed foundations, justice has broader roots than the experience of pain, as Solomon implies.[67] According to Haidt, while social justice issues are primarily rooted in the Liberty/Oppression category, this is notably separate from the foundation of Care/Harm—the foundation that Solomon invokes.[68] Moreover, Solomon almost entirely disregards the categories of Authority/Obedience and Sanctity/Degradation, which cannot be discarded from a Christian worldview. This suggests that Solomon's understanding of justice as a response to hurt is too narrow and that resentment might be insufficient

---

63. Content Team, "Post Hoc Ergo Propter Hoc."

64. It is worth considering four possible models of relationship: Causation (A causes B), Reverse Causation (where B causes A afterwards), "Counterpoint" (where an external cause C affects A and B, causing A and B to demonstrate a relationship), and Spurious Correlation (where A and B are entirely unrelated but appear connected). See: Lukianoff and Haidt, *Coddling*, 227–229. Solomon appears to be appealing either to reverse causation or spurious causation, either of which are suspect. This claim is supported in Niebuhr, *Interpretation of Christian Ethics*, 12.

65. See chapter 1, p. 14n72.

66. Haidt, *Righteous Mind*, 146, 197–205.

67. The six foundations are Care/Harm, Fairness/Cheating, Loyalty/Betrayal, Authority/Obedience, Sanctity/Degradation, and Liberty/Oppression. See chapter 1, p. 19.

68. Haidt, *Righteous Mind*, 203.

CHAPTER 3: PATTERNS OF BITTERNESS

as the point of origin of justice. But what standard might suffice if Solomon's interpretation of justice falls short?

Third, Nietzsche offers a formal rebuttal to the argument that *ressentiment* is the origin of justice. He associates Solomon's arguments with the idea that "justice [is] at bottom merely an extension of the feeling of injury—and with revenge to bring all the *reactive* feelings retroactively to a position of honor."[69] In other words, the primary reason for associating *ressentiment* with justice is *really* an association of justice with *hurt*. Nietzsche continues:

> The ground of reactive feeling is the *last* ground occupied by the spirit of justice! ... There is no doubt that on average just a tiny amount of aggression, malice, and insinuation is sufficient to make even the most honest people see red and to deprive them of an impartial eye.[70]

The issue of "seeing red" is the critical flaw in Solomon's argument. Justice is always objective (ideally), whereas vengeance is always emotional.[71]

Elgat warns that the innate nature of *ressentiment* to "see red" causes an individual to be substantially impaired, inhibiting their ability to follow these standards. *Ressentiment* refuses to be introspective and tends to lash out at people adjacent to the perpetrator, thus limiting the ability to identify the perpetrator correctly. *Ressentiment* does not discriminate between acts committed with knowledge and accidents, thus failing to acknowledge the intent of an action. *Ressentiment* can respond to situations that include pain but not wrongdoing, or it can ignore situations of genuine injustice out of disinterest, thus failing to acknowledge the nature of the act. Perhaps most importantly, *ressentiment* is driven by rage—this can only impair one's ability to act with proportionality or mercy. Furthermore, as the levels of rage increase, *ressentiment*'s ability to seek justice decreases. These qualities indicate that *ressentiment* both perverts the pursuit of justice and only produces vengeance.[72]

---

69. Nietzsche, *TGM*, 54. This may also be considered in light of John Rawls's claims.

70. Nietzsche, *TGM*, 55, citing Eugen Dühring. See also: Unknown, "You Tear Yourself Apart," 120.

71. See also: Elgat, *Nietzsche's Psychology of Ressentiment*, 64; Scheler, *Ressentiment*, 46.

72. Also, recall cognitive behavior therapy from the discussion of Moral Foundations Theory in chapter 1, p. 19.

Tomelleri warns, "We need to be critical of our desire for justice and constantly interrogate it to be sure it is not disguised ressentiment."[73] How are we to do this? Elgat provides a handy tool for this: a summary of the components necessary for justice, including five essential qualities. These are as follows: (1) Identification of the correct perpetrator of the injustice, (2) Identifying the action in question as unjust, or the legal concept of *actus reus* or "guilty act," (3) Recognizing that the perpetrator of this action intended to commit the act; it was not an accident—known in law as *mens rea* or "guilty mind," (4) Responding to the unjust action with appropriate proportionality; someone who failed to repair a crack in their sidewalk leading to a bad fall doesn't "get the chair;"[74] and (5) an element of mercy in the judgment—that is, taking the circumstances of the perpetrator into account when pronouncing sentence.[75]

Although Elgat's list is excellent, recent events demand a sixth quality be added to it: for justice to be pursued, a specific injustice must have occurred prior. In this lies the distinction between justice and utopia—the kingdom of Earth and the kingdom of God.[76] Although justice is a biblical good, the kingdom of God is far greater, for the kingship of Jesus eliminates all injustice.[77] This echoes C. S. Lewis's argument that our dissatisfaction with this world should indicate that we are not *made* for this world.[78]

Here is why the sixth point is needed. After the conviction of Derek Chauvin in the death of George Floyd, House Representative Alexandria

73. Tomelleri, *Ressentiment*, 161/1836.

74. This arguably originates in the Christian teaching of *Lex Talionis*, or "eye for an eye" (Exod 21:24). God insists on appropriate limits to how we address injustice. In this case corrective justice cannot be more severe than the injustice it corrects.

75. Elgat, *Nietzsche's Psychology of Ressentiment*, 53–62. See also: Elgat, "How Smart (and Just) is *Ressentiment?*" 247–55; Elgat, "Slave Revolt, Deflated Self-Deception," 524–44; and Elgat, "Nietzsche on the Genealogy," 155–77. See also: Lukianoff and Haidt, *Coddling*, 217–30. Especially notions of fairness, the superiority of the process of justice over the outcome of justice, and the danger involved in "Equal-Outcomes Social Justice."

76. Boris Bobrinskoy, *Compassion of the Father*, 42–43.

77. God consistently identifies himself as the final arbiter of Justice and agent of vengeance: Lev 19:18; Deut 32:35; Ps 149:6–9; Prov 20:22; Rom 12:19. It is also critical to note the expected perfection of the culmination of the kingdom of God: Isa 65:17–25; Rev 21–22, especially 21:4. In a society where God has delivered vengeance and nothing remains to grieve, justice is complete. This will be discussed further in chapter 5, pp. 123–4. See also: Kasper, *Mercy*, 18, 58; Leithart, *Gratitude*, 141; Volf, *Free of Charge*, 160.

78. Lewis, *Mere Christianity*, 136–37. See chapter 7, pp. 167–8, 181–5, 189–191.

Ocasio-Cortez issued this statement: "That a family had to lose a son, brother and father; that a teenage girl had to film and post a murder, that millions across the country had to organize and march just for George Floyd to be seen and valued is not justice."[79] On Instagram she clarified, "It's not justice, and I'll explain to you why it's not justice. It's not justice, because justice is George Floyd going home tonight to be with his family. Justice is Adam Toledo getting tucked in by his mom tonight."[80] Senator Bernie Sanders and former Secretary of State Hillary Clinton echoed this sentiment.[81] There is no denying the suffering that millions of Americans experienced over the murder of George Floyd, nor the sense of relief felt over Chauvin's conviction. However, responses such as Ocasio-Cortez's are dangerous. For Floyd and Chauvin, there can *only* be justice. To wish that he had not died—to wish away *any* murder—is to yearn for utopia and to sit on the fence between godly desires for justice and *ressentiment*.[82] We should be careful not to be tempted into adopting this inappropriate belief, but we should also guard against injustice.

Tomelleri offers three criteria for identifying an unjust society: (1) Democratisms—misplaced concepts of equality conceal *ressentiment*,[83] (2) Utility over Vitality—that people should be treated as resources to exploit and not as creatures to be loved,[84] (3) Negation of Solidarity—your neighbor is not someone for whom you are personally responsible but a potential competitor, especially tempting when your neighbor has wealth that you want to exploit.[85] These offer another

---

79. Polus, "Ocasio-Cortez"; Ocasio-Cortez, "That a family had to lose."

80. Polus, "Ocasio-Cortez"; Ocasio-Cortez, "That a family had to lose."

81. Pesce, "'Accountability . . . but Not justice,'" Polus, "Ocasio-Cortez"; Sanders, "Jury's Verdict Delivers"; Hillary Clinton, "George Floyd's family and community." I find it interesting that these perspectives flatly disagree with the national statement put out by the NAACP on the subject.

82. This is typical of Marxism. Berger, *Rumor of Angels*, 25; Niebuhr, *Interpretation of Christian Ethics*, 16–19.

83. Recall the Tocqueville Paradox, chapter 2, pp. 36–7.

84. This point is further reinforced by the work of Sherry Turkle on social trends in conversation. In her book *Reclaiming Conversation*, she talks at length about the collapse of conversation as the heart of friendships. In a particularly chilling account, she describes the situation at Holbrooke Elementary School (name changed to protect the community) wherein children are no longer forming effective relationships. In particular, school officials note a distinct lack of empathy among the children coupled with *an attitude towards one another that sees other students as tools to be manipulated rather than persons to be cared for*. Turkle, *Reclaiming Conversation*, 63–65, 293. See chapter 2. This will be further addressed in chapter 8, pp. 198–203.

85. Tomelleri, *Ressentiment*, 21/645. Recall chapter 2, pp. 33–8, and the claims of

means for us to judge whether we are acting in the service of justice or *ressentiment*, and they illustrate how justice is opposed to *ressentiment*. I conclude that justice is a goal that cannot be rooted in *ressentiment* but must be something greater and nobler.

The notion that a sort of bitterness or resentment is necessary for justice is a flawed one. Understandable, even sympathetic at times, but flawed. We all long for the coming of the kingdom of God and to live in a world that is not merely just but free of injustice. That can make it very tempting for Christians to pursue justice at any cost, even corrupt justice. As Tomelleri writes:

> The destructive Force of *ressentiment* is nothing other than a desire for revenge nurtured by these weak people against the strong people: an "evil" desire for revenge hidden even to themselves that in their arguments and moral justification usurps the name of "good" justice.[86]

I believe that God has given us leave to be neither pragmatists nor quietists. We cannot pursue a Machiavellian notion of justice wherein the ends justify the means, nor can we throw up our hands in surrender with the realization that what we want cannot be accomplished in this life. Instead, God calls us to be idealists—to never be fully satisfied with incomplete or corrupt justice, but to relentlessly work to be a total reflection of God's desire for a healthy, loving society.[87]

Therefore, we ought to be aware of the qualities of justice—finding the correct perpetrator(s), identifying specific unjust actions, discerning whether or not an action was accidental, and responding with proportionality and mercy—and we ought to look for them in our justice activism, and worry if they are absent. We should also scrutinize our actions to discern whether we *truly* see one another as human beings—worthy of dignity and love—and we should worry if we are not doing so.[88] Lastly, we should always be aware that the longing for justice is

---

SIT regarding social climbing.

86. Tomelleri, *Ressentiment*, 9/530.

87. Pragmatism vs. idealism is my own interpretation of Jerry Hwang's summation of a critical problem in the book of Hosea: realpolitik vs. theopolitik. In the face of the concrete political tension between Assyria and Egypt, God exhorts Israel *not* to take sides (immediate and pragmatic solution to the problem) but to trust in God (far more frightening but idealistic solution that puts God's plans before all practical considerations). See Hwang, *Hosea*, 29–31, 200–206. See also Kasper, *Mercy*, 18; Niebuhr, *Interpretation of Christian Ethics*, 51. I will return to this in chapter 7.

88. Concepts of hope, and the kingdom of God, will be addressed in chapter 7.

innately tied to our desire for the kingdom of God. Should we confuse one for the other, we either end up believing that we live in a world that is utterly devoid of justice, or our desire for the kingdom of God is perverted into a yearning for a lesser idol. As both justice and God's kingdom are things of extraordinary worth, we should make every effort to ensure they are prized as they ought to be—and not replace a holiday at sea with making mockeries in the mud.[89]

V: For a Bird of the Heavens Shall Carry Your Voice[90]

Most fans of Aerosmith will recognize the not-so-ancient pseudo-wisdom, "Don't get mad, get even." Very little typifies this old chestnut more than Twitter, the modern-day incarnation of wrath itself.[91] In this context, Twitter also provides the third challenge to my adoption of Nietzsche, "How can *ressentiment* possibly develop in a world where Twitter—or any online forum really—empowers everyone to take vengeance if a key requirement for *ressentiment* is power*less*ness?" If everyone has the opportunity to "get even" with their enemies, then why are people still so angry?

The first indication that this might not be quite so simple is the fact that this is not a new problem. In the 1910s, Scheler wrote, "The desire for revenge disappears when vengeance has been taken, when the person against whom it was directed has been punished or has punished himself, or when one truly forgives him."[92] Scheler did not have the benefit of Twitter, but he *did* have the benefit of the press.

Scheler suggests that discharging *ressentiment* by acting through the press is ineffective. The result is only a mild relief of the pressure to seek

---

Further qualities and virtues we should seek to cultivate in order to renounce *ressentiment* will be the focus of the remainder of the book following this chapter.

89. Lewis, "Weight of Glory," 3–4; Bonhoeffer, "Thy Kingdom Come," 341, 347.

90. Ecclesiastes 10:20—"Revile not the king, no, not in thy thought; and revile not the rich in thy bedchamber: for a bird of the heavens shall carry the voice, and that which hath wings shall tell the matter" (NASB).

91. In this section I am not so much concerned with Twitter specifically but with the influence of all social media platforms. I use "Twitter" here to refer colloquially to social media at large, not to criticize the corporation.

92. Scheler, *Ressentiment*, 47. More on this in chapter 5. See also Solomon, "One Hundred Years," 105; Elgat, *Nietzsche's Psychology of Ressentiment*, 37.

vengeance, but even more importantly, *it is likely to spread*.⁹³ Rather than discharging *ressentiment* like a short-circuited battery, you have "shared" some of the emotion with others like a contagion. Elgat elaborates, saying vengeance often does less to assuage *ressentiment* than we might like it to—though this applies to *all* situations, not just to those involving media.⁹⁴ However, given his earlier claim that *ressentiment* needs an enemy to *suffer*, this would suggest that media is a poor substitute for vengeance *in person*, if only because you cannot see the pain on the face of your enemy when you deliver your chosen stinging remark through cyberspace.⁹⁵

There is another point to consider regarding media use and *ressentiment*. Elgat argues that:

> It would . . . be imprecise to assert . . . that every act motivated by *ressentiment* is an act of revenge. This is because *ressentiment*, while indeed a desire to retaliate, a desire to take revenge, might or might not be consummated in real or imaginary acts of revenge.⁹⁶

Given that comments on the internet are typically *reactions*, and given that they are typically responding to a particular stimulus unique to that specific page (i.e., replying to *this* article that I have just read), it seems appropriate to question whether the average tweet is a calculated act of revenge or "a crime of passion." While this point does not address all instances of media use involving *ressentiment*, it does suggest that some angry comments in cyberspace are not examples of vengeance served cold.

The final possibility is perhaps the most convincing of the three. In his book *Democracy in America*, Alexis de Tocqueville observed that the nature of the American government meant that it would function with decreasing efficiency the larger it became and the more people it attempted to govern—essentially, the larger a society becomes, the more difficult it is for a democracy to govern it effectively. This is a sensible observation, as anyone will have experienced at any holiday feast involving that critical mass of family size wherein nobody can agree on who should wash the dishes; thus, the dishes are not washed at all. This is consonant with the

---

93. Scheler, *Ressentiment*, 68–69. Recall Emotional Broadcaster Theory, chapter 1, p. 20.

94. Elgat, *Nietzsche's Psychology of Ressentiment*, 67.

95. Although seeing the pain on the face of your enemy could also be part of the solution to the broader problem of bitterness, as I will explore in chapter 8. See also: Bandura, "Social Cognitive Theory," 107–8.

96. Elgat, *Nietzsche's Psychology of Ressentiment*, 36.

theory of "Mass Society."[97] Sherry Turkle describes a similar effect at work in our online conversations. In response to Stephen Colbert's question regarding Twitter, "Don't all those little tweets, don't all those little sips of online communication, add up to one big gulp of real conversation?" Turkle responds with a resounding "no." She further clarifies, "A National Conversation is a fantasy."[98] With such a large volume of material, the content of Twitter sounds more like white noise than a setting in which to take vengeance. There is further evidence supporting this.

In her book *iGen*, Jean Twenge points out that a growing number of young people feel completely powerless to influence the direction of the American government. She takes this one step further and identifies the root of their sense of apathy as political polarization on the internet.[99] Again, referencing Tocqueville, Tom Nichols writes that a key aspect of American politics is our distrust of one another.[100] While these two suggest the internet as a *source* of *ressentiment* (note Twenge's use of the term "powerless"), they also demonstrate that the internet might not be the best place to address *ressentiment* by seeking some sort of corrective solution to underlying problems. Indeed, if Twenge is correct about the source of discontent being experienced by young Americans, Twitter is not the *solution* to the problem but a possible *cause*.

For these reasons, I am not convinced that Twitter—or any social media platform—is an effective tool for discharging *ressentiment*. Instead, Twitter is "muddying the waters" at best and spreading the problem at worst.[101] However, this does not mean we ought to abandon our use of the platform entirely.[102] The classic problem of media development is the twofold reality that (A) we cannot put the genie back in the bottle, and (B) despite the real downsides of social media, there are some extraordinary positives. In the case of the internet, the greatest

---

97. Mass Society is a complex theory with multiple components. Here, I am referring to the tendency for larger societies to become increasingly dysfunctional—similar to concepts of bureaucracy or "red tape." It is not restricted to America and may be easily applied to Soviet Russia or Communist China. See: Tocqueville, *Democracy in America*, 324–45, 360–64; Macionis, *Society*, 496–98; Mills, "Mass Society," 300–303. See also: Nichols, *Death of Expertise*, 17–18; Lukianoff and Haidt, *Coddling*, 191.

98. Turkle, *Reclaiming Conversation*, 15.

99. Twenge, *iGen*, 283.

100. Nichols, *Death of Expertise*, 17–18.

101. This is consistent with my conclusions from chapters 1 and 2.

102. Recall chapter 1, pp. 2–3. The two reasons I give here for keeping social media are repetitions.

positive is how information is made universally available and the means through which to have potentially *global* conversations (for example via Zoom or email). While Twitter might be an agent of chaos, it is ironically a potential agent of peace too. Whether social media platforms are a cause or cure for *ressentiment*, we need to remember that our core desire is for the coming kingdom of God—because *ressentiment* will not just disappear on its own.

VI: Conclusions—Jimmy, Nietzsche, and Ourselves

Thus we return full circle to Jimmy trying to figure out what to do about his feelings toward Mike. In a sense, Jimmy's response demonstrates *ressentiment*. He has identified Mike as his enemy, Jimmy is powerless to correct his blindness, and he has resigned himself to a sort of revenge in effigy by withholding his friendship from Mike and maintaining a sense of righteous and self-entitled anger. All that remains is to demonstrate that Jimmy's problem is our problem.

Initially, *ressentiment* appeared to me as a way to explain the rise in popularity of "critical theory" and its application to critical feminist theory.[103] However, critical theory is typically associated with Karl Marx and subsequent academic schools.[104] This would seem to suggest that the appropriate course would be to study cultural trends through the lens of critical theory and Marx rather than *ressentiment* and Nietzsche.

However, using Marx has serious drawbacks. Critical theory is almost entirely restricted to thinkers on the political Left in America,

---

103. I began this project with an interest in critical gender theory. However, critical race theory has become more popular in the intermediate years.

104. Subsequent schools include the Frankfurt School in the 1920s (Theodor Adorno, Walter Benjamin, Max Horkheimer, and Herbert Marcuse), mid-twentieth century French postmodernists (Gilles Deleuze, Michel Foucault, Jacques Derrida, and François Lyotard), and finally critical theory, including critical feminist theory (bell hooks, Deborah Rhode, and Andrea Dworkin), and critical race theory (David Bell and Kimberlé Crenshaw). For more on this history see: Shapiro, "Translating, Repeating, Naming," 233–35; Macdonald, "Critical Theory," 1; Pecora, "Nietzsche, Genealogy, Critical Theory," 104–30, 104–5; Rhode, "Feminist Critical Theories," 617–38. For more on the topic of critical theory, see: Andersen and Collins, *Race, Class, and Gender*; Levinson, *Beyond Critique*; Crenshaw et al., *Critical Race Theory*, especially the first essay by David Bell; and bell hooks, *Feminism is for Everybody*. For criticism of critical theory, see: Lindsey, *Race Marxism*; Lindsey and Pluckrose, *Cynical Theories*; Trueman, *Rise and Triumph of the Modern Self*, 204–56. For arguments on the relevance of Nietzsche as an alternative to critical theory as a lens for social analysis, see: Payne and Roberts, *Nietzsche and Critical Social Theory*.

yet similar patterns of *ressentiment* appear on the political Right.[105] Furthermore, the volume of literature on Marx and critical theory is daunting, making any thorough study of the topic difficult. Lastly, while the Frankfurt School took Marx's ideas and applied them to the field of ethics, Marx's original framework was economic. Using Nietzsche as a lens to evaluate current social trends is far more appealing, given that (A) his work and scholarly studies of *ressentiment* can be covered in a chapter, (B) he begins with ethics, (C) this approach is politically bipartisan, and (D) Nietzsche is not Marx.[106]

Fortunately, Nietzsche also addresses critical theory, given his own oblique connection to the field while remaining independent from Marx. Nancy S. Love points out that Theodor Adorno (another scholar in the genealogy of critical theory) solidified his own theories by complementing "Marx's economic with Nietzsche's psychological critique of exchange."[107] Nietzsche was also popular with the scholars Derrida and Foucault (and probably Marcuse) *independently* of Marx.[108] Thus, Nietzsche may be used to address our cultural issues of bitterness without deferring to Marx.

Nietzsche is also an appealing alternative to Marx, given Nietzsche's political bipartisanship. Despite Nietzsche's frequent association with the political Right, scholars have demonstrated that his ideas defy restriction to a single political ideology.[109] *Ressentiment* may be observed anywhere, regardless of politics. Furthermore, Marx's connection to the Southern Strategy as a sort of boogyman makes any expression of concern regarding Marx a subtle indicator of anti-Semitism, an association Nietzsche avoids.[110]

---

105. I will look at specific examples later in this chapter.
106. See also: Polanyi and Prosch, *Meaning*, 12.
107. Love, "Epistemology and Exchange," 72.
108. Macdonald, "Critical Theory," 104-5; Hicks, *Explaining Postmodernism*, 67, 81, 83, 192-98; Shapiro, "Translating, Repeating, Naming," 233-44; Scheler, *Ressentiment*, 95-96; Love, "Epistemology and Exchange," 71-94; Pecora, "Nietzsche, Genealogy, Critical Theory," 104-30; Carrette and Dowley, "Critical Theory and Religion," 28-31; Miller, "Some Implications of Nietzsche's Thought"; Pütz, "Nietzsche and Critical Theory," 103-14.
109. Smith, "Introduction," xvi; Yovel, "Nietzsche, the Jews, and *Ressentiment*," 225, 234-35; Humble, "Heinrich Mann and Arold Zweig," 40-52; Foot, "Nietzsche's Immoralism," 7.
110. See: Boyd, "Nixon's Southern Strategy"; Murphy, *Southern Strategy*.

The best reason to revisit Nietzsche's work is the possibility of his predictions coming to fruition. Elgat explains:

> It seems we are living in an age of resentment, rage, and anger: from politics to economics, from morality to religion, strong and negative emotions tend vociferously to dominate our public discourse in their protestations against what is considered to be perverse, unjust, corrupt, or plain evil.[111]

We should vigilantly strive to recognize and critique *ressentiment* at work today. This is more manageable given the similarities between *ressentiment* and victimhood.[112]

Victimhood and *ressentiment* share fixation on an enemy responsible for inflicting pain on the individual or the group. Robert Horwitz makes this connection explicit: "In the abstract, [victimhood] is closer to what Friedrich Nietzsche spoke of as resentment, or *ressentiment* as he labeled it in *On the Genealogy of Morals* [than to any other potential source]."[113] Horwitz also observes that victimhood is integral to modern American politics:

> The victim has become among the most important identity positions in American politics. Victimhood is now a pivotal means by which individuals and groups see themselves and constitute themselves as political actors. Indeed, victimhood seems to have become a status that must be established before political claims can be advanced.[114]

This coincides with the previous discussion of *SIT* and religious trends in America. The similarities are too close to be ignored.[115]

Polarization also coincides with *ressentiment*. Polarization, victimhood, and *ressentiment* all share the notion of a zero-sum game, an

---

111. Elgat, *Nietzsche's Psychology of Ressentiment*, 1. René Girard wrote that unchecked *ressentiment* could destroy humanity (though I suspect this is hyperbole): Girard, "Dionysius Versus the Crucified," 826–27. See also: Tomelleri, *Ressentiment*, 50/888; Foot, "Nietzsche's Immoralism," 13.

112. Refer to the relevant sections from chapter 1, pp. 10–1, 16–8, for a refresher.

113. Horwitz, "Politics as Victimhood," 554.

114. Horwitz, "Politics as Victimhood," 553.

115. Horwitz makes this connection explicit with a quotation from Charles Taylor. For a society that holds equality as an ultimate good (recall Haidt's "Moral Foundations Theory"), we must inevitably include equality for *tribes* as a goal, not just individuals. This makes the sort of tribal conflict we are currently witnessing almost inevitable. Horwitz, "Politics as Victimhood," 556.

identifiable outgroup, and prejudice. Polarization and *ressentiment* view others with distaste, and given the pressure of identity, both groups are prone to dehumanizing behavior (which is a seedbed for insult and injury)—thus, polarization can produce *ressentiment*.

This argument also works in reverse. So preeminent is victimhood identity in Horwitz's understanding of modern politics that it would necessarily *precede* polarization. If no victimhood identity has been established, says Horwitz, no political claims may be advanced, and if no political claims have been advanced, then no political tribe may be claimed. He also furthers his earlier comment on the connection with Nietzsche, saying:

> [Following Nietzsche, suffering] became constitutive of self-understanding and produced a moral code validating hatred of the evil enemies who caused the suffering. In Nietzsche's view, ressentiment is a generalizable cultural/psychological phenomenon. The resentful are no longer actors per se; rather they are defined passively by their victimhood.[116]

If all politics is built on victimhood, then both polarization and *ressentiment* are implicated.

Given the direct connection between *ressentiment* and victimhood, and the interconnection of victimhood and polarization, I suggest that these three are nearly indistinguishable.[117] Therefore, because victimhood and polarization are demonstrably present in America, *ressentiment* is too.[118] This also implies that *ressentiment* is being *spread* through the internet via Cultivation Theory or some similar mechanism. We can see explicit examples of this in recent history.

The op-ed "Why Can't We Hate Men?" by Suzanna Danuta Walters, published in the Washington Post in 2018, is an undeniable example of *ressentiment*. The following excerpt summarizes the piece:

> So men, if you really are #WithUs and would like us to not hate you for all the millennia of woe you have produced and benefited from, start with this: Lean out so we can actually just stand up without being beaten down. Pledge to vote for feminist women only. Don't run for office. Don't be in charge of anything. Step away from the power. We got this. And please

116. Horwitz, "Politics as Victimhood," 554.
117. Lukianoff and Haidt, *Coddling*, 127.
118. See also: Gharib and Boler, "Narratives in America."

know that your crocodile tears won't be wiped away by us anymore. We have every right to hate you. You have done us wrong. #BecausePatriarchy. It is long past time to play hard for Team Feminism. And win.[119]

As Charles Sykes comments, "The new culture reflects a readiness not merely to feel sorry for oneself but to wield one's *resentments* as weapons of social advantage and to regard deficiencies as entitlements to society's deference."[120] Walters's op-ed demonstrates bitterness and a desire for vengeance. The enemy is explicitly identified as "men" or "patriarchy." There is an explicit demand for power, suggesting some degree of envy. This demand for power implies a sense of impotence. The concept of "millennia of woe" indicates a victim mentality, not to mention a prolonged period of suffering.[121]

Consider also the controversy caused following a lecture given by Dr. Aruna Khilanani wherein she stated:

> I had fantasies of unloading a revolver into the head of any white person that got in my way, burying their body and wiping my bloody hands as I walked away relatively guiltless with a bounce in my step. Like I did the world a . . . favor.[122]

In a later interview with Black News Tonight, she clarified further that she believes white people to be "psychopathic."[123] Her original lecture described fantasies of taking revenge on her oppressor class and feeling morally justified in doing so.[124] This is unmistakably *ressentiment*.

Hunter describes his observations of similar phenomena within liberal activism in the evangelical church, particularly those he describes as "Politically Progressive," and offers a warning of religious syncretism between the Christian Left and the secular Left.[125] He highlights the work of Randall Balmer, writing:

---

119. Walters, "Why Can't We Hate Men?"

120. Sykes, *Nation of Victims*, 12, emphasis mine. See also: Murphy, *Getting Even*, 40.

121. A similar example may be seen in Mary Wakefield's article, "Dangerous Pleasure of Hating Men."

122. Levenson, "Psychiatrist Invited to Yale." Profanity removed.

123. Video footage can be found here: https://www.youtube.com/watch?v=o2otk-QrZiE.

124. For similar comments see also: Martinez, "Your DNA Is an Abomination," cited in Lukianoff and Haidt, *Coddling*, 63–64.

125. Hunter, *To Change the World*, 133–34. Recall the chapter 2, pp. 49–54, discussion

> [*Thy Kingdom Come: An Evangelical's Lament*] is a curious book, for it reflects most of the problems [Balmer] attributes to the Religious Right. His disdain for the Christian Right leads him to engage in name-calling that is as one-dimensional and dehumanizing as the most extreme voices of the Christian Right, labeling his opponents "right-wing zealots" and "bullies" and their followers "minions," who together are "intolerant," "vicious," "militaristic," "bloviating," and theocratic.... the Christian Right is monolithic and it is bad. Liberals, by contrast, are good. The sum of his *ressentiment* is found in an anticipatory sense of personal injury."[126]

This indicates that trends of *ressentiment* among the Left are not limited to secular spheres.

Hunter continues to criticize the Christian Right as well. In the 2018 Laing Lectures at Regent College, Stanley Hauerwas repeatedly expressed shock and concern that evangelical Christians had voted for a man like Donald Trump.[127] His concerns also apply to Christian Nationalism, as conceived by Andrew L. Whitehead and Samuel L. Perry. This ideology pushes the view that Christian values ought to have a privileged position in society over all others, particularly when Christianity appears to be declining, and that it is acceptable to achieve this position by force.[128] While examples of Christian Nationalism vary significantly in terms of their levels of bitterness, there should be little question that this pocket of conservative Christians is struggling with *ressentiment* and must repent.

---

of syncretism in America.

126. Hunter, *To Change the World*, 141–43.

127. I attended the lecture series. Recordings are available for purchase at Regent Audio: https://www.regentaudio.com/products/the-laing-lectures-2018-santley-hauerwas-theological-existence-today.

128. Whitehead and Perry, *Taking America Back for God*; Miller, *Religion of American Greatness*; Miller, "What Is Christian Nationalism?"; Lee, "Christian Nationalism is Worse"; Warren, "We Worship with the Magi." These fears are supported by Rod Dreher's claim that the most significant element of the 2016 election was Donald Trump's choice to largely ignore Christian values in his campaign. Dreher argues this should be a signal to all Christians that they should view neither political party as an ally. See: Dreher, *Benedict Option*, 3, 79–82. I believe the concern surrounding Christian Nationalism is valid, albeit overstated. The problem at the heart of Christian Nationalism, in my opinion, is a tendency to confuse nationalism with jingoism. Jingoism is always wrong. Nationalism is circumstantially wrong; see: Moule, *Forgiveness and Reconciliation*, 25. It is also important to recognize that both extremes of exclusivism and inclusivism—nationalism and globalism—can bear catastrophic consequences; see: Shriver, *Ethic for Enemies*, 46, citing John Crossan.

The MAGA movement is another example. In his essay "Why Friedrich Nietzsche Is the Darling of the Far Left and the Far Right," Elgat identified the Trump era as a period of resurgent Nietzscheanism for both the political Left and the political Right. He explains:

> To the radical right, it is [Nietzsche's] rejection of equality and the democratic ideas that are based on it that is scintillating and rings true (besides his often and—as I have argued—misunderstood flirtations with the concept of race); to the left, it is his anti-essentialism with its emphasis on the plastic nature of identity that promises liberation from societal oppression.[129]

Douglas Kelly argues in his essay "The Trump Horror Show Through Nietzschean Perspectives" that the entirety of the Trump era must be understood in terms of *ressentiment*.[130] Casey Ryan Kelley echoed this sentiment in a detailed investigation of Trump's leadership through the lens of *ressentiment*—particularly how Trump evokes a sense of powerlessness, fear, and hurt in his supporters before submitting himself as the only available defender of their values.[131]

That Trump evokes *ressentiment* can be seen in the Charlottesville rally turned riot in August 2017. This includes the use of the slogan "Jews will not replace us," the violent beating of a black man, and the murder of Heather Heyer. Furthermore, President Trump's statement that there were "very fine people on both sides," though *not* a statement in support of neo-Nazis and the Ku Klux Klan as often depicted, at the very least shows he was sympathetic to the men who staged the event.[132] Trump's speech on January 6 and the subsequent violent acts should be understood as examples of this *ressentiment* in action, both that of President Trump and a minority of his supporters. There is a widespread sense among conservatives that their needs and wants are being *ignored* if not rejected by liberals. This is a natural gateway to bitterness.

---

129. Elgat, "Why Friedrich Nietzsche."

130. Kellner, "Trump Horror Show," 60–72. See also: Nussbaum, *Monarchy of Fear*; Ott and Dickinson, *Twitter Presidency*; Remley, *Philosophical Foundation*.

131. Kelly, "Donald J. Trump and the Rhetoric of *Ressentiment*," 2–24.

132. Lukianoff and Haidt, *Coddling*, 90–92, 139. This event was especially difficult for me after a close friend from high school—a black man and Baptist Pastor—posted his grief to social media. Particularly so because I recall no other time when he was so emotionally transparent. This is not a strong example of *ressentiment* but should evoke sympathy from conservatives towards liberals despite media obfuscation.

Reinhold Niebuhr offers this helpful observation: "Modern communism and modern nationalism are both religions, both modern, and both maintained by a demonic fervor in which partial perspectives and devotion to a high ideal are compounded." We may even conclude that communism and fascism are fruits of the same tree.[133] Both groups share the responsibility for our present cultural state of bitterness.

Where do we go from here? While these are only a handful of recent examples of *ressentiment*, they should be sufficient to establish that *ressentiment* is a current problem for everyone in America regardless of religious or political affiliation. The three main foundations of *ressentiment*—powerlessness, oppression, and an enemy—might indicate a Christian solution, specifically a biblical solution.

The Bible has very little to offer on the subject of powerlessness. We might adopt the teachings around "resist the devil and he will flee from you," or "put on the whole armor of God that you may be able to stand against the wiles of the devil" (Jas 4:7; Eph 6:10–13 NRSVA). Yet, in the entire Psalter, there is only one example of a psalm in which it is *not* God who ultimately resolves the pain of oppression.[134] Furthermore, this one exception makes it absolutely clear that, while Israel (as representative of the whole people of God) must keep a sword in their hand to execute vengeance on the enemies of God, this vengeance is done in the service of God *exclusively*: acting under God's authority and in his power. The Bible affirms that we are indeed powerless. This does not solve the problem of *ressentiment*.

On the subject of oppression, the Bible is somewhat mixed. The ideal of acting justly in the world for the sake of the poor and the hurting is a common theme throughout the Law, the wisdom literature, and the Prophets and is one of Jesus' frequent concerns. However, we have disagreed for nearly two millennia on *how* this should be accomplished.[135] We agree that the Bible calls us to action, and we agree that the

---

133. Niebuhr, *Interpretation of Christian Ethics*, 224–25. See also: Shriver, *Ethic for Enemies*, 46; Polanyi and Prosch, "Meaning," 12. As Gregory of Nyssa warned, "All virtue is found in moderation, and . . . any declension to either side of it becomes a vice." Gregory of Nyssa, *On Virginity*, 22.

134. "Let the high praises of God be in their mouth, and a two-edged sword in their hand; to execute vengeance upon the nations, and punishments upon the peoples" (Ps 149:6–7).

135. The nature of democratic governance and the freedom to take an active role in setting policy for society have, if anything, made this problem significantly more difficult.

essential lifestyle and emotion within this action is the love of God, but we *disagree* on precisely which actions to take. I would argue further that our own disagreements and confusions about the biblical message surrounding justice are part of the cause of *ressentiment* in the church in the first place. I do *not* believe Christians should stop discussing ways to improve society, but neither do I believe these discussions will lead to a solution for *ressentiment*.[136]

This leaves the topic of the "enemy," and it is here that I see a solution. Here, we find a surprising but unambiguous commandment: we must *love* our enemies. We must recover this practice to undo bitterness. This is also the solution for how we may continue to persevere in the pursuit of justice while remaining uncorrupted. Scripture contains four behavior patterns essential to loving our enemies: compassion, forgiveness, gratitude, and hope. The remainder of the book will explore these four themes, beginning with compassion.

---

136. See also chapter 2, pp. 36–7, on cultural division due to relative equality and the Tocqueville Paradox. It is *possible* that some of the cultural issues currently debated are already in balance and that our division is actually a consequence of this balance. Specific issues surrounding oppression might not have a solution at present.

Chapter 4: **No One to Comfort Them (But Me)**

Loving Our Enemies Through Compassion

> Then must the Jew be merciful. . . . The quality of mercy is not strain'd, it droppeth as the gentle rain from heaven upon the place beneath: it is twice blest, it blesses him that gives, and him that takes . . . It is an attribute to God himself; and earthly power doth then show likest God's when mercy seasons justice . . . in the course of justice, none of us should see salvation: [therefore] we do pray for mercy, and that same prayer, doth teach us all to render the deeds of mercy.—William Shakespeare[1]

I: Introduction

MY FAMILY HAS LONG enjoyed the Warner Bros. series *The West Wing*. This political drama tells the story of the fictional eight-year presidency of Jebediah Bartlet (Dem). Season seven includes the story of Bartlet's anticipated replacement, Matthew Santos (Dem), campaigning for the presidential election. During this campaign, a social crisis occurs when a Hispanic police officer shoots an unarmed black child. Himself Hispanic, Santos goes to visit with the grieving black community and asks to speak at their church the following Sunday. His speech inspired this chapter, but as it is rather lengthy I will paraphrase.

---

1. Shakespeare, *Merchant of Venice*, 111–12.

Santos expresses his sense of victimhood in such painful social crises and the desire to identify an outgroup to fight. Then he tries to express compassion for the people he wants to blame. This leads to a critical reference to a speech by Dr. Martin Luther King in 1968, wherein King called his listeners to be compassionate. Not to express a false emotion but to act compassionately. Not out of some exhortation to "do the right thing" but because even faking compassion was better than vengeance. Even so, the practice of compassion is tiring, and slow progress is demoralizing. Yet, lacking an alternative other than bitterness, we need to endure in compassion.[2] I have been particularly haunted by Santos's reference to King's 1968 speech, so I invested a lot of time reading King's work trying to find it.

Sadly, it looks as if Santos made up the speech on the spot; none of King's speeches call for compassion quite this explicitly. The only quote from King that *directly* invokes compassion reads:

> Here is the true meaning and value of *compassion* and nonviolence, when they help us to see the enemy's point of view, to hear his questions, to know his assessment of ourselves. For from his view we may indeed see the basic weaknesses of our own condition, and if we are mature, we may learn to grow and profit from the wisdom of the brothers who are called the opposition.[3]

This is valuable insight, but it does not match Santos's description. The date is wrong, and while Santos assumes compassion is a balm for *both* sides, this quote assumes that compassion benefits only me. The most likely source is Dr. King's speech "I've Been to the Mountaintop."[4] King models compassion through this speech and through his lifelong refusal hate the white community. He consistently called for *love* over violence and that the white man be seen as a *brother* rather than an obstacle.[5] Santos's speech embellishes the details, but the premise is appropriate.

---

2. Misiano, West Wing, "Undecideds."

3. King, "Trumpet of Conscience." Emphasis mine. All essays and sermons by Dr. King come from *A Testament of Hope*, the definitive anthology of his work, unless otherwise noted.

4. King, *Call to Conscience*, 217–19. From his last speech, often referred to as his "mountaintop" speech.

5. Examples of this within King's writings are so common as to defy citation. See examples in King, *Testament of Hope*, 7, 10, 12, 17, 58, 80–83, 87, 110, 118, 139–40, 144, 215, 230, 256–57, 365.

Dr. King absolutely believed *compassion* was essential to the creation of a better nation. I think we have forgotten this.

In this chapter, I will argue that we must practice *compassion* or *mercy* if we are to weather the current storm of bitterness. I will address specific issues related to mercy, then I will highlight several examples of compassion in Scripture. These will include Kenneth Bailey's argument that we ought to read Luke 19:1–10 (Jesus' visit to Jericho and his encounters with Bartimaeus and Zacchaeus) alongside Eccl 4:1—particularly that compassion is for everyone, even our enemies. I will look more deeply at the parable of the good Samaritan in Dr. King's speeches and in the history of Israel. Lastly, I will consider *why* we ought to have compassion for our enemies as revealed in Ps 73. I will conclude with suggestions for praxis.

This chapter and the three that follow are extraordinarily challenging. Let us be under no illusion. This is the path of the cross. We choose this path because Jesus has the words of life, and in him we see the richness of life that we desire for ourselves (John 6:68). We choose it despite its inherent suffering because there is no other path by which we may find joy.

II: Why Compassion?

Before looking at specific examples from Scripture, I must answer three essential questions. (1) Why is compassion important for the task of reducing one's bitterness? (2) Are not demons our only enemies? (3) How can God be compassionate without being diminished? These will be addressed in turn.

First, why do I deem compassion essential for the task of reducing one's bitterness? I am following the road map laid out by Orson Scott Card's novels *Ender's Game* and *Speaker for the Dead*. The main character describes the choice between love and destruction, saying:

> In the moment when I truly understand my enemy, understand him well enough to defeat him, then in that very moment I also love him. I think it's impossible to really *understand* somebody, what they want, what they believe, and not love them the way they love themselves.[6]

---

6. Card, *Ender's Game*, 238, emphasis mine. See also: Card, "Introduction," in *Speaker for the Dead*.

To have compassion for one's enemies is to empathize with them. Empathy breeds understanding, understanding breeds love, and love reduces fear (1 John 4:18). At the very least, this requires us to "engage in debate with the opponents of the gospel, who are as many today as there were in the past, firm in our cause, but not foaming at the mouth polemically, nor should we repay evil with evil."[7]

Theologians understand this as well. Walter Kasper describes compassion as "having a heart for the poor," where "poor" means those who are in need of God's saving grace and not those who lack money. This leads in turn to actions on behalf of the poor in order to meet their needs.[8] As for compassion's ability to empower us to *love* our enemies, Kasper explains:

> [Compassion] is direct participation in the suffering of another being. Through such compassionate feeling, the previously insurmountable wall between "I" and "You" is dismantled more and more. [It is] finding what is one's own in the other.[9]

Kasper is invoking Martin Buber here. Boris Bobrinskoy makes the same point, writing: "The Holy Spirit teaches that one should love one's enemies so much that one will have compassion on them as one would on one's own children."[10] To love in this way makes bitterness impossible.

Second, why not only demonic enemies? Surely Eph 6:12, "For our struggle is not against enemies of blood and flesh, but against the rulers, against the authorities, against the cosmic powers of this present darkness, against the spiritual forces of evil in the heavenly places," (NRSVA) is authoritative in this instance? I do not dispute this. Indeed, Bobrinskoy writes:

---

7. Kasper, *Mercy*, 161–62. See also chapter 1, pp. 19–20.

8. Kasper, *Mercy*, 21, 23. Note that Kasper does *not* conflate mercy and compassion—see: Kasper, *Mercy*, 16—in line with Rogers, "Empathie-eine unterschätzte Seinsweise," cited in Kasper, *Mercy*, 16. I do not draw such a clear distinction, though my emphasis is on the term "compassion" rather than on "mercy" due to the *emotional* engagement of "compassion." If any distinction is to be made, I would describe compassion and mercy as having affective and active components but mercy as having an element of leniency in the face of injustice, which compassion does not require. See: Volf, *End of Memory*, 113.

9. Kasper, *Mercy*, 26. Schopenhauer, *Basis of Morality*, 2:1198. This is also reminiscent of Martin Buber: Buber, *I and Thou*, 56–61, 69, 84, 89–95.

10. Bobrinskoy, *Compassion of the Father*, 71–72, quoting Sophrony, *Starets Silouan*, 260. See also: Catherine of Sienne, cited in Kasper, *Mercy*, 110.

> Behind the mystery of evil and hatred, the profile of the Adversary stands out, of Satan—which means "adversary" in Hebrew. He is the one who personifies hatred, who is the preeminent enemy, the enemy of people and the enemy of God, the one who spreads evil in the hearts [of men].[11]

However, I suspect that the church has fallen into a trap here. Rather than pretending the demonic does not exist, we would rather pretend that demons (not human persons) are our *only* enemies. By way of illustration, one of my fellow students in seminary was an ardent opponent of Donald Trump. One day, I asked him, "If Donald Trump were to knock on your front door and ask to share a meal with you, how would you respond?" He replied, "I'd slam the door in his face. I don't want that asshole in my home!" I should have asked this follow-up question: "If Donald Trump is your enemy, would that reaction be consistent with Jesus' behavior in the Gospels? If Donald Trump is *not* your enemy, how do you justify your reaction?" Nelson Mandela warned us about this trap: "When we dehumanize and demonize our opponents, we abandon the possibility of peacefully resolving our differences, and seek to justify violence against them."[12]

I suspect American culture contains a vestige of the Christian commandment to love our enemies.[13] I suspect further that, because of this vestige, we are reluctant to admit that we even have enemies—if a person is not merely someone I disagree with but my enemy, then specific behaviors are expected of me.[14] However, if that same person is not my enemy but merely "someone I dislike or disagree with," then I have greater freedom to treat them with disdain—so runs our unconscious logic. However, we must read Ps 127:5 as referring to flesh and blood enemies when the psalmist writes, "They shall not be put to shame, when they speak with their enemies in the gate" (NASB); otherwise, we assume that the demons are somehow constrained by brick and mortar. We must read Matt 5:38 and 44 the same way: "You have heard that it was said, 'An eye for an eye and a tooth for a tooth.' . . . But I say to you,

---

11. Bobrinskoy, *Compassion of the Father*, 69–70. "Satan" can also mean "accuser" in Hebrew.

12. Cited in Lukianoff and Haidt, *Coddling*, 81.

13. Berger, *Rumor of Angels*, 9. See also: Taylor, *Secular Age*; Boersma, *Heavenly Participation*.

14. Leithart, *Traces of the Trinity*, 99.

Love your enemies and pray for those who persecute you." (NRSVA)[15] Surely the demons have no physical eyes or teeth that we may put out in retaliation. Jesus means for us to have this kind of compassion for our earthly enemies, meaning we *have* earthly enemies. To focus on demons while ignoring human enemies makes us spiritually emaciated. As our bitterness is directed towards flesh-and-blood enemies (and here I mean both those who seek our downfall and those we hate—though the latter is an affront to God),[16] we must first admit that we *have* flesh-and-blood enemies so that we may approach our relationships with them in love.

Moreover, failure to hold people responsible cheapens the reality of sin. Give the devil his due responsibility for the world's brokenness, but we cannot call sinners to repentance if they have nothing to repent from! As Jesus said, "I have not come to call the righteous but sinners to repentance," and, "I take no pleasure in the death of the wicked, but rather that they turn from their ways and live." (Luke 5:32 NRSVA; Ezek 18:23; 33:11)

Third, how may we say that compassion "is an attribute to God himself"[17] without requiring that God be "diminished" somehow? Unfortunately, this requires us to speak of the immanent Trinity—of God as he is fully in himself—which is precisely that which we cannot know.[18] Agonizing human suffering typically changes us or reduces us in some way. This is perhaps most apparent in circumstances where a loved one has died or a limb has been amputated—there used to be a blessing in life, but no more. To "suffer with" someone is to enter into that suffering and to risk being changed by it yourself—perhaps even diminished. Yet we

---

15. The value of verse 38 will be revisited in chapter 7, pp. 168–170. I am choosing to combine these two verses for the sake of clarity. Jesus addresses two topics here—*lex talionis* and hating our enemies. To the first, he counters by commanding peaceful defiance and in the second by commanding genuine love. While these two topics are separate, they are clearly related, given their subject matter. I would even suggest this is an example of parallelism by synthesis—two statements in which the second is related to *and* strengthened over the first. For commentary on this passage of Matthew, see also: Bonhoeffer, *Cost of Discipleship*, 131–38.

16. Bonhoeffer, *Cost of Discipleship*, 132.

17. Shakespeare, *Merchant of Venice*, 112.

18. Orthodox Christians prefer apophatic systematics (negative statements identifying what God is not) over cataphatic systematics (affirmative statements identifying what God is) for precisely this reason. We can say that in God "there is no darkness at all" (1 John 1:5) and be perfectly confident that this is true and that we understand it. Saying that "God is love" (1 John 4:7–8), although true, is beyond our ability to understand completely.

find in Scripture that God is "unchanging" throughout eternity; neither past nor present (as we understand them) but an eternal "now." How can we speak of God "suffering with" us yet remaining unchanged?

We must first recognize that God does indeed suffer with us. Moreover, God suffers for us. Bobrinskoy writes:

> God is not indifferent, impassable, or insensitive when faced with evil, human suffering, and degradation. Origen wrote an extraordinary text on the subject of a God who suffers before he becomes incarnate, a God whose bowels of mercy are destroyed, crushed, by the very sight of the creature's degradation. The suffering of a loving God compels him to leap into the abyss where man is about to perish. The book of Genesis visualizes the blood of Abel crying out to God (Gen 4:10) regarding the iniquity that gradually covers the earth.[19]

Here, Bobrinskoy invokes the incarnation and the cross. Kasper explains further that compassion of any kind is not merely an act but a feeling of great potency:

> One must understand the word *compassion* not only as compassionate behavior. Rather, we must also hear in "compassion" the word "passion." This means discerning the cry for justice as well as making a passionate response to the appalling unjust relationships existing in our world.[20]

This reveals a significant part of the answer: God not only suffers *passionately*[21] with us but has acted by becoming incarnate and dying on our behalf—God's passionate response to injustice in the world. Were it not for the resurrection, we would have an unsolvable contradiction with God having suffered the ultimate change—passing from life to death. So we may say with Kasper, "The Bible does not know a God, who, in his majesty and blessedness, sits enthroned over a world full of terror and is apathetic to it.... he [God] was not *overpowered* by suffering."[22]

The remainder of the answer lies in recognizing that we have not a contradiction but a paradox. We cannot understand suffering except while adjacent to loss. However, we have a God who suffers—indeed,

19. Bobrinskoy, *Compassion of the Father*, 54.

20. Kasper, *Mercy*, 17.

21. I mean here "intensely," not with "earthly passions," as understood within Orthodox Christianity.

22. Kasper, *Mercy*, 118–19, emphasis mine. See also: Kasper, *Mercy*, 113; Volf, *Free of Charge*, 162–165.

who suffered death—yet is not overpowered or diminished thereby. This is not a paradox to be solved but a mystery to be contemplated—albeit with trepidation and (at times) confusion.[23]

With these questions answered—"Why Compassion?" "Are not demons our only enemies?" and "How is God compassionate yet undiminished?"—I now turn to my three meditations on Scripture.

III: Bartimaeus and Zacchaeus

Eccl 4:1–12; Luke 18:35–19:10

Kenneth Bailey, while arguing that Jesus is a savior for all who are sinners, makes a peculiar observation:

> This perspective is present as early as Eccl 4:1, which reads:
>
>> Again I saw all the oppressions that are practiced under the sun
>>
>>> And behold, the tears of the oppressed,
>>>
>>>> And they had no one to comfort them!
>>>
>>> On the side of the oppressors there was power
>>>
>>>> And there was no one to comfort them.
>
> In such a text both the oppressors and the oppressed are trapped in prisons from which they cannot escape. Each needs grace from outside the prison. The text in Luke [1:77–78] speaks of salvation from "our enemies" and of the internal problem of "our sins."[24]

Bailey is interpreting this as an example of *direct parallelism* rather than *synthesis*. Instead of contrasting the rich and poor, Bailey demonstrates their mutual similarity.[25]

---

23. The paradox of God's suffering will be revisited in chapter 7, pp. 177–9.
24. Bailey, *Jesus Through Middle Eastern Eyes*, 51.
25. By way of explanation: reading this in terms of parallelism by synthesis focuses the entire passage on the oppressed. "Behold the tears of the oppressed, and they have no comforter"—that's bad. "And in the hand of their oppressors was power, *and they STILL have no comfort!*" That's *really* bad. Direct parallelism compares two things that might not otherwise be related—in this case, "behold the tears of the oppressed, and they have no comforter," then, "in the hand of their oppressors was power, and *they have no comforter either.*"

CHAPTER 4: NO ONE TO COMFORT THEM (BUT ME)

There are problems with this approach. The Targum has a more pessimistic perspective:

> And I further observed all the violence which was done to the righteous and how they were oppressed in this world under the sun by the hand of their oppressors and there is none to speak to them comforting words, and there is none to redeem them from the hand of their attackers with a strong hand and with power and there is none to comfort them.[26]

This is a typical interpretation: the rich are absolutely evil and oppress the poor. A related problem is a word variant in the *Biblia Hebraica Stuttgartensia* (BHS)—do the oppressors have no "comforter" (*nāḥam* נָחַם) or no "avenger" (*nāqam* נָקַם)?[27] The BHS clearly favors the first, but the variant would not exist if no documents used the second.

On the other hand, Iain Provan focuses on the centrality of *relationship* within Eccl 4. He writes:

> In pursuing out of envy the neighbor above us on the ladder, we inevitably step on the head of the neighbor below us. As disastrous as this is for the people who are trampled on, it is also futile for the person who is upwardly mobile at their expense.... It is not surprising, then, that in 4:7–12 we find material that first focuses on the loneliness of the striving individual and then moves on to offer a stirring and uplifting commendation of community.[28]

This affirms that oppressors need compassion too.[29] Moreover, if the *real* enemy in this passage is the community that *stands by and does nothing*, then the structure of the chapter makes more sense.[30] The chapter's principle claims then are that life is meaningless toil, we will witness and lament oppression and suffering, and the *solution* to these ills is to invest

---

26. Knobel, "Targum of Qohelet," 30. The Targums are Aramaic translations of the Bible from the first century BC. These translations significantly differ in some ways from the Hebrew and provide interpretive insight into how the first-century Jews understood their Scriptures. See also: Pinker, "Oppressed in Qohelet 4:1," 393–405.

27. Elliger and Rudolph, *Biblia Hebraica Stuttgartensia*, 1341. The BHS is a critical companion to the Old Testament and contains a copy of the Leningrad Codex—the most complete Hebrew copy of the Scriptures available. It also includes commentary on disputed words along with the alternatives and arguments in favor. See also: Jastrow, *Gentle Cynic*, 213. The pronunciation of these two words in Hebrew is nearly identical.

28. Provan, *NIV Application Commentary*, 105–6; Basil, *On Social Justice*, 50.

29. Bollhagen, *Ecclesiastes*, 164–65.

30. Krueger, *Qoheleth*, 95; Bailey, *Jesus Through Middle-Eastern Eyes*, 51.

in community.³¹ This supports Bailey's interpretation. Even so, I cannot conclude that Bailey has found the *primary* meaning of this passage. This is a *secondary* interpretation or a hidden meaning—one that fits the book and reflects the heart of Jesus.³²

For Bailey to apply this interpretation of Ecclesiastes to Luke 18:35–19:10 (Jesus' visit to Jericho) is a natural step.³³ The two stories form a literary *inclusio*: Jesus restores blind Bartimaeus's sight and fellowships with Zacchaeus.³⁴ In both chapters, *the crowd* is the enemy. They obstruct access to Jesus for both Bartimaeus and Zacchaeus.³⁵ In both chapters, Jesus interposes himself between the crowd and their target—thereby diverting the crowd's anger onto himself. In both chapters, there is a reversal of wealth due to the character's encounter with Jesus—Bartimaeus gives up his trade, and Zacchaeus gives away his money.³⁶ A poor man and a wealthy man seek comfort from God while the community tries to prevent them.

Jesus' treatment of Zacchaeus is crucial. Zacchaeus climbs a tree for two reasons: his height and safety. As a Roman collaborator, he is despised

---

31. Ogden, *Qoheleth* (1st ed.), 65–66.

32. Ogden, *Qoheleth* (1st ed.), 13–15; Jastrow, *Gentle Cynic*, 8–9. That this is a secondary interpretation weakens my position somewhat but does not eliminate it.

33. Kenneth Bailey does not include this claim in his book, though it is strongly implied. He *did* include it in his teachings on 1 Corinthians for the all-parish retreat of the Church of the Ascension. See: Bailey, "Dr. Ken Bailey (4) 10.01.11 October 1, 2011." Contact the Church of the Ascension Music Director for recordings.

34. An inclusio is a literary style in which the beginning and end are identical, but the content in the middle is free-form. The most obvious example is Psalm 8. In this case, the visit to Jericho has these two very similar stories, but nothing in the middle. This may also be interpreted as a simple example of long-form parallelism. See also: Bailey, *Jesus Through Middle Eastern Eyes*, 173.

35. Bailey, *Jesus Through Middle Eastern Eyes*, 174–77. The injunctions against the mistreatment of the disabled are especially poignant as such behavior is seen as exceptional cruelty. See Philo, *Works of Philo*, 633–34 (XXXIV. 176–82).

36. As Bailey explains, beggars in the Middle East are not as poor as we might believe because both Judaism and Islam command giving to the poor as a spiritual duty. However, to live as a beggar, one must have a visible *reason* to beg. Without his blindness, Bartimaeus will need to find a "real job." See Bailey, *Jesus Through Middle Eastern Eyes*, 158–59, 173–74. Guy Nave argues from Luke 3:13–14 that Zacchaeus must abandon his profession entirely as he cannot be faithful to Jesus and do otherwise. See: Nave, "Repent, for the Kingdom of God Is at Hand," 96; Nave, *Role and Function of Repentance*, 155–58. I find it difficult to believe that Zacchaeus will be wealthy after following through with his promise to give up half of his property and repay his debts fourfold (though this is likely an exaggeration to prove his intent) *and* give up his profession.

CHAPTER 4: NO ONE TO COMFORT THEM (BUT ME)   99

by everyone as a traitor and thief—this is how he obtained his wealth (Luke 19:2-3). It could be dangerous for Zacchaeus to enter the crowd. If one of the people he has defrauded notices him and decides to stick a knife in his back, the perpetrator will remain a mystery. Who will notice the knifing of this half-height? Neither the Roman nor the Jewish authorities will do anything because you cannot arrest an entire crowd. Moreover, Zacchaeus is immanently replaceable to the Romans (many a traitor has been made by the promise of money), and both a traitor and a financial drain on the Jews.[37] Zacchaeus is threatened by the crowd.

When he *is* noticed up a sycamore tree (an excellent place to hide and see), the crowd gets rowdy.[38] Zacchaeus is safe from knives, but his circumstances are embarrassing (grown men do not climb trees), and the crowd is free to mock him. Although Jesus can probably deduce Zacchaeus's profession from the catcalling, and clearly Zacchaeus is a wicked man, Jesus does not rally the crowd by chastising Zacchaeus and demanding he repent. Instead, Jesus breaks tradition by declaring Zacchaeus his *host*, offers to ceremonially defile himself by coming under the roof of an outcast, and presents his sole attention to the oppressor.[39] Thereby Jesus brings upon himself the ire of the crowd and extends the same compassion to Zacchaeus as he did previously for Bartimaeus (Luke 18:40-43).[40] Furthermore, Jesus does not speak again until the end of the chapter. Jesus never demands that Zacchaeus repent of his sin, nor mentions sin in any capacity. Rather, Jesus' *compassion* for Zacchaeus causes Zacchaeus to repent.[41]

This raises an important point on the topic of liberation theology.[42] Let me preface this by saying again that serving the poor and liberat-

37. Bailey, *Jesus Through Middle Eastern Eyes*, 177.
38. Bailey, *Jesus Through Middle Eastern Eyes*, 179.
39. Bailey, *Jesus Through Middle Eastern Eyes*, 180.
40. See also: Bailey, *Jesus Through Middle Eastern Eyes*, 256. Jesus acts in this way on more than one occasion.
41. Bailey, *Jesus Through Middle Eastern Eyes*, 180-84; Brueggemann, "Summons to New Life," 335. Notice that Zacchaeus is declaring that he will go *beyond* the demands of the law in this. It is also worth noting that Jesus' compassion for Zacchaeus does not extend to reintegrating him into the community—calling Zacchaeus a "Son of Abraham"—until *after* Zacchaeus declares his intention to repent. See also: Battle, "Penitence as Practiced," 335; Peterson, *Engaging with God*, 119.
42. A theological school primarily associated with South American thought that places the utmost emphasis on liberating the oppressed as the essential message of the Gospel. See: Gutiérrez, *Theology of Liberation*. Note that the origins of liberation theology demand that the goal is a society built on *love* and NOT a just or equal society. My

ing the oppressed are essential components of the gospel. I would go so far as to say that certain forms of political actions to oppose oppression are a Christian *responsibility*.[43] However, liberation theology has a severe Achilles' heel.[44] Good liberation theology can make significant positive differences in the world. However, it usually makes *minor* differences and is extraordinarily costly to do well. When liberation theology is done poorly, it becomes an "idol-ology." It turns people away from God and sometimes creates more oppression. It is easy to do poorly. Sadly, Zacchaeus is frequently misused as a polemic against oppressors and not as an example of God's compassion.

The most potent indictment of this problem in liberation theology was made by Leslie Newbigen, who writes:

> If, in effect, we identify the cause of the oppressed with the cause of God so completely that we bring forward the last judgment into today, do we not cut ourselves off from grace and pave the way for a new tyranny that acknowledges nothing higher than its own judgment?[45]

This declares that we must never allow ourselves behave as if our enemies—even monstrous oppressors—are hopelessly damned. Newbigen gives three reasons for this: (1) Because *God* is the arbiter of justice, not us, (2) Because we tend to overestimate the wrong our neighbors do to us while underestimating the wrong we do to our neighbors, and (3) Because it is too easy for the oppressed, once they gain power, to flip the tables and become oppressors themselves.[46] This last part is crucial. Dr. King even wrote:

---

criticism here is of incomplete or unhealthy liberation theology, not liberation theology at its core. See: Volf, *Exclusion and Embrace*, 105.

43. The first exodus being from physical slavery to freedom, the second being from slavery in *sin* to life. See Rom 6. See also: Newbigen, *Open Secret*, 106–7; Philo, *Works of Philo*, 639 (XLII. 231), 695 (XIX. 136), 704 (IX. 70).

44. Schmemann, *For the Life of the World*, 23, 44–45.

45. Newbigen, *Open Secret*, 110.

46. Newbigen, *Open Secret*, 110–11. Newbigen's primary concern is that no one who has been baptized be refused access to the Eucharist on account of being an oppressor. I agree insofar as we are discussing an issue that is disputed and difficult to determine, as is often the case with forms of oppression, given that human nature is itself oppressive. I disagree only slightly in that *some* violations of Scripture—such as violations of the decalogue—should warrant temporary withholding of the Eucharist pending the repentance of the *Christian*. But this is also an issue exclusively for clergy to determine. Judgment should be made after great deliberation *with* the person in question and only with the compassionate desire for the betterment of the sinner at

> There is the danger that those of us who have lived so long under the yoke of oppression, those of us who have been exploited and trampled over, those of us who have had to stand amid the tragic midnight of injustice and indignities will enter the new age with *hate and bitterness*. . . . We must blot out the hate and injustice of the old age with the love and justice of the new.[47]

A lack of compassion undermines liberation theology.

Newbigen also points out the danger within liberation theology of it becoming no longer Christian, but an idol-ology:

> The community of Christians in Christ allows and requires the mutual acknowledgment of these opposing political decisions [Marxism vs. Capitalism], and I therefore reject the liberation theologians' view that their judgment about the nature of Christian obedience requires them to treat their opponents not as sinners to be corrected, but as heretics to be excluded.[48]

This problem is *ongoing*, as Kaspar notes:

> Tolerance can then very easily be converted into intolerance against anyone who dares to hold a conviction that departs from the mainstream. Indications of going in this dangerous direction are multiplying.[49]

---

heart. See also: Aleksandr Solzhenitsyn—"The line separating good and evil passes not through states, nor between classes, nor between political parties either—but right through every human heart—and through all human hearts. This line shifts. Inside us, it oscillates with the years. And even within hearts overwhelmed by evil, one small bridgehead of good is retained. And even in the best of all hearts, there remains . . . an unuprooted small corner of evil." Solzhenitsyn, *Gulag Archipelago*, 312. Lastly, see: Basil, *On Social Justice*, 51.

47. King, "Facing the Challenge of a New Age," 139–40. Emphasis mine. King's most common exhortation was, "Our aim must never be to defeat or to humiliate the white man, but to win his friendship and understanding, and thereby create a society in which all men will be able to live together as brothers." King, "Give Us the Ballot," 200. See also: Klar et al., "In the Aftermath of Historical Trauma," 212–13, 221. They address the Jewish commandment to care for our enemies in Deut 23:7 and the sociological phenomenon of "Fear of Victimizing"—the possibility of a "victim-to-victimizer" cycle. It is especially noteworthy that much of the research into "victimhood" has been done at Israeli universities. See also: Volf, *End of Memory*, 33, 94, 105; Kasper *Mercy*, 172.

48. Newbigen, *Open Secret*, 117. While rather liberal-leaning and firmly against materialism, King and Kasper both reject Marxism; see: King, *Testament of Hope*, 45, 96, 109, 214, 250; Kasper, *Mercy*, 13–15, 183. Note that this problem affects anyone anywhere on the political spectrum, as with *ressentiment*.

49. Kasper, *Mercy*, 201–2.

Compassion for the oppressed is a biblical mandate, but it should *never* be accompanied by withholding compassion from our enemies. We should *not* reject liberation theology whole cloth, but we must treat it with the utmost care and criticism, "[for] Christ did not die only in solidarity with sufferers but also as a *substitute for offenders*."[50]

Returning to Zacchaeus, there is a second point to consider. Jesus' act of costly love for Zacchaeus itself *becomes* an act of compassion for the poor. Zacchaeus's repentance ends the oppressive taxation system in Jericho (removing the chief tax collector and having him return his ill-gotten gains) and wins the oppressor over to the kingdom.[51] This is at the center of the life and ministry of Jesus, for "without disregarding justice, Christ's death pointed beyond the struggle for retributive justice for victims to the wonder of transforming grace for perpetrators and reconciliation of the two."[52] We must take seriously Walter Kasper's claim that "the call for mercy surpasses the cry for justice in the Bible. The Bible understands mercy as God's own justice. Mercy is the heart of the biblical message, not by undercutting justice, but by surpassing it."[53]

In conclusion, our compassion must be extended to all, oppressors as well as the oppressed. This undergirds rather than undermines justice. Moving on, we will see just how extreme God's compassion—our paragon—really is.

IV: Israel and Samaria: The "Bloody Pass"

Luke 10:25–37

In his 2017 TED talk, His Holiness Pope Francis raised the topic of the good Samaritan. He described the Samaritans as "a very much despised ethnicity at the time."[54] Although accurate, this description is unclear. Were the Samaritans seen in the same vein as drug addicts? Gang members? IRS representatives? Politicians? How about evangelical Christians?

50. Volf, *End of Memory*, 115–16.
51. Volf, *End of Memory*, 184.
52. Volf, *End of Memory*, 111. See also: Niebuhr, *Interpretation of Christian Ethics*, 46–47.
53. Kasper, *Mercy*, 18. See also Jas 2:13.
54. Segarra, "Read What Pope Francis Said." Find the original video by Pope Francis, "Why the Only Future Worth Building Includes Everyone," at: https://www.ted.com/talks/his_holiness_pope_francis_why_the_only_future_worth_building_includes_everyone,

CHAPTER 4: NO ONE TO COMFORT THEM (BUT ME) 103

This section will reveal the history *behind* Israel's relationship with Samaria and how this colors our reading of Jesus' parable on compassion.

Samaria was founded just before the time of the prophet Elijah (1 Kgs 16:24).[55] In the 700s BC, King Shalmaneser of Assyria conquered the city (2 Kgs 17:24-41).[56] The Assyrian army conquered Samaria, removed many Israelites living there, and took them to Nineveh as slaves.[57] Shalmanezer decided to bolster the numbers of those who remained, so he brought the nation of the Cutheans from their native Persia and transplanted them into the Northern Kingdom to supplement the remaining Israelites—these are the ancestors of the Samaritans. However, the Cutheans brought their own religious practices with them and found (to their surprise) that they experienced extraordinary plagues of bears and lions.

Given that divine authority in the Ancient Near East was geographically limited, they concluded that their gods had no authority in Israel. Therefore, they requested that a Jewish priest come and teach them the Jewish faith.[58] The Samaritans are briefly mentioned in Josephus when Nebuchadnezzar defeats Assyria *and* Judah and takes most Jewish people into exile in Babylon during the 600s (2 Kgs 25:1-26).

Josephus claims that the Samaritans were the only people left in the land of Israel until Israel's return under King Cyrus—one hundred and thirty years, six months, and ten days.[59] However, this is likely an exaggeration on his part.[60] The Jewish priests brought from Nineveh would have intermarried with the Samaritans. Furthermore, some of the peasantry would probably have remained in Israel while the intelligentsia and royalty were taken into slavery.[61] Since the Cutheans came

---

55. Josephus, *Works of Josephus*, 236 (8.12.5): "Now it was in the thirtieth year of the reign of Asa that Omri reigned for twelve years; six of these years he reigned in the city of Tirzah, and the rest in the city called Semareon, but named by the Greeks Samaria; but he himself called it Semareon, from Semer, who sold him the mountain whereon he built it."

56. Josephus, *Works of Josephus*, 264-65 (9.14.1-3)

57. Recall Jonah's message of repentance to Nineveh (Jonah 3:4). This may also serve as an excellent reminder of the appropriate answer to the question, "Which city is the capital of Assyria?" (Once again, recalling the British Pythons of humor).

58. Bailey, *Jesus Through Middle Eastern Eyes*, 164.

59. Josephus, *Works of Josephus*, 278 (10.9.7).

60. Penwell, "Josephus on Samaritan Origins."

61. The exaggeration of "total defeat" was typical at this time. Joshua recorded that *all* the gentiles were removed from the land of Israel (Josh 21:43-45), yet these gentiles had been resurrected somehow in the time of the Judges (Jdg 1:2). More likely, the

from the same area of the Middle East as Abram, they would have been racially indiscernible from the Israelites. These would not lessen the tensions between Jews and Samaritans because the Jews would have higher religious expectations of the Samaritans than if the Samaritans were a group of gentiles.[62]

When the Babylonian Empire fell to Alexander the Great, there was a great scandal in the priesthood at Jerusalem. The high priest, Jaddua, had a brother named Manaseh, who had married a foreign woman in defiance of Scripture yet continued practicing his priestly duties—very scandalous. The people demanded that Manaseh either divorce Nicaso, his wife, or never again approach the altar. Manaseh promptly went to his father-in-law, Sanballat, and announced he was unwilling to divorce Nicaso or abandon his "sacerdotal dignity." Sanballat, being a shady character, declared that he would ensure Manaseh lost none of his wealth or authority and further, "that he [Sanballat] would build him [Manaseh] a temple like that at Jerusalem upon Mount Gerizzim, which is the highest of all the mountains that are in Samaria [over which Manaseh would be High Priest]."[63] This declaration led to a major revolt among the priesthood over which high priest to follow. Sanballat later made good on his promises by pledging his loyalty to Alexander the Great when Jaddua *withheld* his allegiance from Alexander until King Darius was killed.[64] This secured funds from Alexander for Sanballat's Temple and allowed an unauthorized temple to God to be established on Mt. Gerezzim.[65]

Although some additional scandals took place over the years, none of them were especially significant until shortly before Jesus' birth.[66]

---

gentiles were *not* completely eradicated, but Joshua claims they were both to prove a point and inflate the reader's view of Joshua's military feats.

62. I will skip over the Samaritans' encounter with the Jews immediately following the return from exile. For more, see: Josephus, *Works of Josephus*, 291–92 (11.4.3); Ezra 4.

63. Josephus, *Works of Josephus*, 305–6 (11.8.2–3).

64. Josephus, *Works of Josephus*, 306 (11.8.3–4).

65. Josephus, *Works of Josephus*, 306–7 (11.8.5)

66. Josephus, *Works of Josephus*, 324 (12.5.5), 323–24 (12.5.3–4), 340 (13.3.4). These incidents represent the disputed nature of the temple, and Samaria's response to Antiochus Epiphanies, a brutal dictator who sparked the Maccabean rebellion under Judas, "the Hammer." Not only did Antiochus Epiphanies plunder the temple for all of its wealth and kill many of the inhabitants, but he also offered pigs on the temple altar, thereby ceremonially defiling it—See 1 Macc 1:10–53. The only other significant example of this behavior was when Pompey conquered Jerusalem and entered the holy of holies, thereby defiling it, for as a gentile he was prohibited from so much as entering the temple. Pompey, however, required the priests to immediately sanctify the temple

The last incident Josephus recorded was the most brazenly insulting to Israel. During the Passover (within a decade of Jesus' birth), it was the Jewish custom to open the gates of the Jerusalem temple at midnight. After that, Josephus records:

> Some of the Samaritans came privately into Jerusalem, and threw about dead men's bodies in the cloisters; on which account the Jews afterward excluded them out of the temple, which they had not used to do at such festivals; and on other accounts also they watched the temple more carefully than they had formerly done.[67]

This extraordinary insult ceremonially defiled the temple—the only place where the Jews are permitted to offer sacrifices to God and thereby secure his presence with them—during one of the holiest festivals of the Jewish year.[68]

Although the average Jew likely had little knowledge of these events, they left a lasting stain on relations between Samaria and Israel. The religious fury resulting from the Samaritans' defiling of the temple lasted at least until the time of Jesus. This desecration numbered the Samaritans among the worst enemies in Israel's history and resulted in them being banned from the temple. However, this does not suffice to explain the religious conflict between these two groups.

According to N. T. Wright, to understand the life of a first-century Jew requires understanding their shared social narrative.[69] This narrative is structured around four primary symbols: (1) Temple, (2) Torah, (3) Land, and (4) Racial Identity.[70] For the first-century Jew, salvation "[had] to do with rescue from the national enemies, restoration of the national symbols, and a state of *shalom* in which every man [would] sit under his vine or fig-tree."[71] But this goal of salvation was impossible so long as foreign oppressors ruled the land *and* the national symbols remained defiled. As Torah was the most stable of the four symbols at this time, it was heavily emphasized, particularly by the Pharisees—but

---

so that worship could continue; see: Josephus, *Works of Josephus*, 369–70 (14.4.2–4). See also: Wright, *New Testament and the People of God*, 158–59.

67. Josephus, *Works of Josephus*, 478 (18.2.2).
68. Lev 5:2; Num 5:2, 19:11–16.
69. Recall chapter 2, pp. 42–3, 45–6.
70. Wright, *New Testament and the People of God*, 224–32.
71. Wright, *New Testament and the People of God*, 300.

in truth, all four symbols were contested.⁷² Indeed, the first century was an extraordinarily frightening time to be a Jew in Israel: culture war with Rome was constant, right religious practice was obscured and debated, and oppressive rulers existed on both sides.⁷³

Here is how this involves the Samaritans. By their possession of a competing temple and their history of defiling Solomon's temple, the Samaritans represented a direct threat to the restoration of Israel's temple. By improper use and alteration of Torah, the Samaritans represented a threat to the restoration of Torah.⁷⁴ As gentiles in the land, the Samaritans represented a threat to racial purity. Through association with Shalmaneser, they threatened Israelite control of the land. The Samaritans' existence threatened Israel's salvation. Politically, they represented foreign oppression and political enmity—they were duplicitous, aligned themselves with Israel's enemies, and occasionally raided Israel to steal and enslave. Simply, the Samaritans symbolized everything that had caused pain in David's kingdom for over seven hundred years—religiously, politically, and socially.

This degree of social unrest is far beyond what we know today. Israel was a small country with numerous sects vying for control, and right in the middle of it all (geographically and culturally) were the Samaritans.⁷⁵ They were impossible to ignore.⁷⁶

When Jesus told this story of a Jewish man being ambushed on the road to Jericho, everyone listening recognized this as a common occurrence. Martin Luther King identified the road in question as the "Bloody Pass"—a "winding, meandering road conducive for ambushing."⁷⁷ Jesus invoked an image of fear and danger with this setting. It is not surprising

---

72. Wright, *New Testament and the People of God*, 160, 224–32.

73. Wright, *New Testament and the People of God*, 157–67.

74. See, for example, Exod 20:17 in the Samaritan Pentateuch, where the Samaritans *add* a commandment to build an altar on Mt. Gerizzim upon entering the land of Israel. This is intended to legitimate the temple on Mt. Gerizzim against Jerusalem. Compare this against the Old Testament Josh 4:20, where the stones are set up at Gilgal. See the Samaritan scriptures: https://www.stepbible.org/version.jsp?version=SPE.

75. The presence of Rome and the competition of various religious sects was likely more immediately pressing for the average citizen, but we still see in the Gospels that Samaria was a recurring topic and geographic barrier. See John 4:1–42; Luke 17:11–19.

76. We will see evidence of this in chapter 6, pp. 154–6, where I will look at the tale of the ten lepers. In this story, Jesus and his disciples have to make a long loop on their way north from Jerusalem in order to *avoid* going through Samaritan territory.

77. King, *Call to Conscience*, 218. See also: Kasper, *Mercy*, 21; King, "Draft of Chapter III."

that the priest and Levite were cautious. However, for a Samaritan—a man who represents everything the Jewish people despise, a man who is barred from worshipping in the temple, who has endured insults and scorn, who is confined to Samaria, and who is associated with the bandits—to stop and offer his assistance beggars belief.[78]

Jesus' word choice in verse 33 makes the story even more implausible. Jesus says that the man was ἐσπλαγχνίσθη (es-planch-nis-thē)—he was *moved in his guts*.[79] He was filled with compassion. As King puts it:

> We see men as Jews or Gentiles, Catholics or Protestants, Chinese or American, Negroes or whites. We fail to see them as fellow human beings made out of the same basic stuff as we are, molded by the same divine image. The Priest and the Levite saw only a bleeding body, not a human being made in their own likeness.[80]

But the Samaritan not only saw past the "bleeding body" to the fellow human being: he also made a choice. King continues:

> The first question that the priest asked, the first question that the Levite asked was, "If I stop to help this man, what will happen to me?" But then the Good Samaritan came by, and he reversed the question: "If I do not stop to help this man, what will happen to him?". . . [The Samaritan] got down with him, administered first aid, and helped the man in need. Jesus ended up saying this was the good man, this was the great man because he had the capacity to project the "I" into the "thou," and to be concerned about his brother.[81]

Whereas the lawyer who challenges Jesus asks, "Whom may I legally exclude from the category of my 'neighbors,'" Jesus responds with the challenge, "Whom must you include?" In a final scandalous indictment, Jesus holds up the Samaritan, the *intractable enemy of Israel* as a paragon of Jewish virtue and commands his listeners to imitate *their enemy* (Luke 10:37). In this, we see just how far Jesus intends us to go. We are commanded to extend compassion to the most hated enemies imaginable.

---

78. Bailey, *Jesus Through Middle Eastern Eyes*, 289–94.

79. Louw and Nida, *Greek-English Lexicon of the New Testament*, 101, 295; Wigram, *Englishman's Greek Concordance*, 696.

80. King, "Draft of Chapter III."

81. King, *Call to Conscience*, 218–19. See also Buber, *I and Thou*. Notice that King does not describe the relationship between these two as antagonistic but filial. Not "enemy" but "brother."

V: You Set Them in Slippery Places

Pss 1; 2; 35; 73; 149

This raises one final question: how are we to drum up compassion within ourselves? I want to address the answer given by Asaph, the Psalmist—for he addresses this question head-on and gives an unusual answer.

Derek Kidner summarizes this psalm marvelously:

> This great psalm is the story of a bitter and despairing search, which has now been rewarded beyond all expectation. It recalls the kind of questions that distracted Job and Jeremiah; but at the end they no longer seem unanswerable, and the psalmist has a confession and a supreme discovery to share.[82]

Asaph asks an age-old question: why do the wicked prosper?[83] In verses 3–12, Asaph lays out a detailed description of the wicked. They die painless deaths, they are physically fit, they do not experience hardship, they are well-fed, they oppress their neighbors, curse God with their lips, and get away with it, all while profiting—not unlike the oppressors in Eccl 4:1. In contrast, Asaph labors to be obedient to God, and it all seems to be vanity and striving after the wind.

The turning point of the psalm comes in verses 16–19:

> When I thought of understanding this, it was troublesome in my sight until I entered the sanctuary of God; *then* I perceived their end. You indeed put them on slippery ground; you dropped them into ruin. How they are destroyed in a moment! They are utterly swept away by sudden terrors! (NASB)

So Asaph's perspective is reshaped when he recognizes that the current state of his enemies is an illusion. In reality, they will eventually make a mistake and fall to their ruin.[84] My favorite example of this is Ps 37:35–36—"I have seen a wicked, violent person spreading himself like a luxuriant tree in its native soil. Then he passed away, and behold, he was no more; I searched for him, but he could not be found" (NASB). It is as if this wicked person literally vanished overnight without a trace! This is in keeping with the first two lines of Ps 37: "Do not get upset because of

---

82. Kidner, *Psalms 73–150*, 259.

83. Jer 12:1. This also bears significant echoes from the book of Job. See Kidner, *Psalms 73–150*, 259.

84. Recall Provan's comment on the impossibility of social climbing by stepping on the heads of those below you. In this instance, Ps 3 is also relevant.

CHAPTER 4: NO ONE TO COMFORT THEM (BUT ME) 109

evildoers, do not be envious of wrongdoers. For they will wither quickly like the grass, and decay like the green plants" (NASB). The wicked might continue to hurt us far longer than we think we can bear, but in the end, they disappear.[85] When asked, God assures Jeremiah of this: their end is inevitable because God has sworn to take vengeance on the wicked (Jer 12:7–17).[86] God's inevitable vengeance is also present as an eschatological promise in Pss 1:6; 2:9; and 149:6–9. These texts bookend the Psalter as a sure guarantee that no matter how painful life appears for the psalmist (and if Pss 41, 88, and 137 are any measure, life becomes unbearably painful), it is not the end until God passes judgment. Asaph has learned, as Wolfgang Amadeus Mozart's titular character Don Giovanni, that God's judgment *will* come, and it will be inescapable.[87]

Asaph does not remain in this place of obsession over his enemy's downfall. He continues by describing his *own* actions leading up to his moment of clarity in the temple. Verse 21 clarifies that he was *embittered*, not merely jealous.[88] This understanding is perhaps an understanding gifted to Asaph following his revelation in worship. It nearly had dire consequences for him. He continues: "So brutish was I, and ignorant; I was as a beast before thee" (vs. 22). Asaph is confessing to *ressentiment*. Asaph confesses that his *ressentiment* has damaged his relationship with God. However, God has mercifully grabbed Asaph by the scruff of the neck and dragged him back from the brink.

We cannot simply let Asaph off the hook for his *ressentiment*;[89] it is not merely a human reaction to oppression. As John Goldingay writes, "The verbs [embittered and pierced] express the paradox that our embitteredness and pain is both something that comes upon us and also something we are responsible for."[90] The bitterness that has such power

---

85. See also 2 Esd/4 Esd 15:4–5, 22–25.

86. Once again, we need to be careful here, as the Jeremiah passage makes it very clear that this end is not reserved for "our enemies" only. It is possible that we can ourselves become the enemies that God will punish justly. If you have the fortitude, the descriptions of this vengeance in Pss 109 and 137 are particularly gruesome.

87. Tate, *Psalms 51–100*, 238.

88. There is some debate among scholars as to whether the Hebrew "יִתְחַמֵּץ" (*yithamets*) ought to be translated as "embittered" or as "grieved." Given the connotations of this word and based on an argument by John Goldingay, I prefer the use of "embittered" rather than the simpler "grieved." See: Goldingay, *Psalms*, 412.

89. By this, I do not mean that we have no compassion for the one riddled with *ressentiment*, but rather that we must hold everyone to account for their actions.

90. Goldingay, *Psalms*, 412. We may insert "*ressentiment*" in the place of "bitterness."

to separate us from God is something that Asaph must take responsibility for, and so he does.

At the end of the psalm, Asaph has turned his gaze solely upon God and received a reality check. His heart was cleansed, and the bitterness melted away.[91] Thanks be to God, we are not left fully enslaved to bitterness. The pious Israelites suffered at the hands of the wicked, but where the wicked will suffer judgment, the end of the righteous is fellowship with God.[92] This is true prosperity—true *Shalom*—not "equated with health, wealth and prosperity but with "being near to God.""[93] In a surprising reversal, the roles of the wealthy and the hurting are flipped!

Asaph has offered us several insights on how to find compassion for our enemies. First, shedding our bitterness and extending compassion go hand in hand. They both begin by recognizing that our highest loyalty is due to God and not ourselves. Asaph only has his revelation when he turns his gaze to God.[94] Second, we must recognize that our enemies might be suffering even now; if not, they will be in the future. We may not use this as leverage against them or to fuel our anger. Instead, we should recognize *their pain* and do what we can to empathize with them. Third, we acknowledge that were it not for God's extraordinary love for us, we might end up in just as bad a situation as our enemies—cut off from God's love by our own hard-heartedness. Fourth, we recognize that if we are in Christ, we have already found a small measure of our *shalom*. In Jesus, we are truly invited to encounter "the life of the world" (John 1:4).

Thus we come to the end of my focus on Ps 73, but by a strange mystery, we have also arrived at the beginning. Izak Spangenberg argues that multiple hermeneutical connections may be made between Ps 73 and the book of Ecclesiastes, specifically chapter 7. Graham Ogden further argues that Eccl 7 must be interpreted in conjunction with Eccl 4.[95] Thus

---

91. I think it further worthy of note that this Psalm begins book III of the Psalter, the book that, on the whole, reaches the lowest point of the whole given its conclusion with the only Psalm that lacks a sense of redemption at the end. Is this a forerunner of this end point for us to hold onto?

92. I understand Worship as "entrance" or "fellowship with God" according to Edith Humphrey: Humphrey, *Grand Entrance*, 3–4. Thus we must understand that the center of the psalm—Asaph entering into the temple—is an act of worship and fellowship with God. This topic will return in chapter 6, pp. 150–2. See also: Guthrie, *Theology as Thanksgiving*, 18; Pao, *Thanksgiving*, 33. See also: Carson, "Worship the Lord Your God," 13; Ross, *Recalling the Hope of Glory*, 197–98.

93. Spangenberg, "Psalm 73 and the Book of Qoheleth," 161.

94. Kidner, *Psalms 73–150*, 261–62.

95. Ogden, *Qoheleth* (2nd ed.), 113.

we find that interpreting Ps 73 should recognize a link with the oppressor and oppressed of Qoheleth, the Sage. We have come full circle.

VI: Conclusions and Testimony—What Did King See?

In an interview with *Playboy*, Martin Luther King perfectly explained our situation:

> Those fighting for independence have the purpose to *drive out* the oppressors. But here in America, we've got to live together. We've got to find a way to reconcile ourselves to living in community, one group with the other.[96]

King had a clear vision of the end of *ressentiment*. Like Asaph, we all end up like brute beasts, cut off from God and bereft of dignity. However, King saw more than this:

> Black supremacy is as dangerous as white supremacy, and God is not interested merely in the freedom of black men and brown men and yellow men. God is interested in the freedom of the whole human race and in the creation of a society where all men can live together as brothers, where every man will respect the dignity and the worth of human personality.[97]

King recognized that there is a higher goal than justice, and that is *mercy*. Though King did not speak of this explicitly, as Santos claims, there should be no question that King understood the value and necessity of being merciful.

So before we move on to the next posture for Christian love for our enemies, let me draw some conclusions. The value of compassion is threefold. First, as King pointed out, it allows us to understand ourselves better. Choosing to listen carefully to our enemies tells us where we are weak and where we need to repent. This is necessarily coupled with one of the key elements of compassion—being willing to accept responsibility for our own wrongdoing or at least refusing to belittle or discount our enemies' concerns. Second, compassion helps us reframe our enemy from an "it" into a "thou," from a horror into a person.

---

96. King, "Interview with *Playboy*," 365. As I will show in the next chapter, p. 138, this sentiment was echoed by Desmond Tutu about the end of apartheid South Africa.

97. King, "American Dream," 215. See also: King, "Current Crisis in Race Relations," 87; King, "Ethical Demands for Integration," 118-19.

Looking to see their joys and pains humanizes them and staves off bitterness.[98] Third, compassion reduces the pressure on our enemies. Not unlike Newton's third law of motion, if we escalate a conflict, our enemy escalates in response. We must ensure that conflict remains in the realm of "I-Thou" so that we do not permanently eliminate the possibility of reconciliation after the dust settles. As with Zacchaeus, there is also the possibility that offering greater compassion to our enemies may even grant relief to the oppressed. Most of all, however, we must strive to extend mercy to our enemies because it is an attribute of God and an essential work of the church.[99] We cannot imitate the life of Jesus while ignoring his acts of compassion and mercy—for while we were yet sinners, Christ died for us (Rom 5:8).

How are we to accomplish something so difficult? Yechiel Klar, Noa Schori-Eyal, and Lior Yom Tov cite Mina Cikara and Jay Van Bavel to argue that our ability to empathize with the suffering of an outgroup is limited.[100] For this reason, I will suggest that *only some are adequately equipped to interact with their enemies!* Many of us would benefit from simply *avoiding them altogether* rather than having our bitterness towards them agitated further.

However, when avoidance is impossible, there are two essential foci: live in the presence and likeness of God, and remember that our enemies' suffering is inevitable.[101] Engaging in healthy conversation with our enemies begins with a right recognition of who God is, who we are before him, and what is happening in the lives of our enemies.

Next, we have to remember King's recommendation. We must ask, "What will happen to my enemy if I do *not* show them compassion?" To this end, one question must be asked: *What is my enemy afraid of, or why are they hurting?*[102] I think the five stages of grieving can be reduced to three. In theory, the five stages are (1) denial, (2) anger, (3) bargaining, (4) grief, and (5) acceptance. I believe that denial, anger, and bargaining are all a means of *avoiding* grief—they are all a form of *denial*. Western

---

98. Simas et al., "How Empathetic Concern Fuels Political Polarization," 258–269. Remember Card's *Speaker for the Dead*.

99. Bobrinskoy, *Compassion of the Father*, 63.

100. Klar et al., "In the Aftermath of Historical Trauma," 213; Cikara and Bavel, "Neuroscience of Intergroup Relations," 245–74.

101. This will return during chapter 7, pp. 67, 176–7.

102. Refer to *SIT* in chapter 2, pp. 33–8. While conflict can be understood in terms of competition, it can also be understood in terms of *protection*. It is as much a defensive act as an offensive one.

societies, particularly America, society, are very allergic to *pain*.[103] Given a choice, we prefer the comfort of anger to the agony of grief because we *feel* as if we are empowered. But as Asaph demonstrates in Ps 73:22, this empowerment is an illusion. So when conversing with our enemies, we need to patiently and gently peel back the layers of their anger to find what *pain* or *fear* lies beneath it. Sometimes it is a *very personal* memory, and other times it is ingroup loyalty—ultimately, they typically are concerned for someone's wellbeing. We will only be able to *progress* towards a solution in cooperation with our enemies when we demonstrate our sincerity in being compassionate towards those they are trying to protect.

Likewise, we must be willing to acknowledge and take responsibility for our own failures. Even if your group has the moral high ground, that does not mean you or your group are wholly innocent. Merely acknowledging our failures without defending them can build bridges. It is an act of compassion in itself to recognize that you or your group are responsible for another's hurt.[104] This can be eased by choosing not to identify yourself with a particular group explicitly. If it is not necessary to "fly the flag," it will insulate you and your enemy. Remember that merely identifying two groups currently in conflict is sufficient to make your enemy "see red." This has another benefit: though you might feel you are on trial yourself, this is only if your enemy *knows* you are a part of their outgroup. You need not take full responsibility for your group or your values in every conversation; you *do* need to take responsibility for how you treat your enemy every time you interact with them.

It might also help to recall that Echo Chambers have the potential to *lower* bitterness by insulating us from our enemies, essentially "giving us a break."[105] There is another way to accomplish this too. We can also practice empathy through *reading*.[106] C. S. Lewis even goes so far as to write:

> We want to see with other eyes, to imagine with other imaginations, to feel with other hearts, as well as with our own. We are not content to be Leibnitzian monads. We demand windows.

---

103. Recall Christian Smith's notion of Moral Therapeutic Deism: Smith and Denton, *Soul Searching*, 162–63. See also: Lukianoff and Haidt, *Coddling*, 6–7, 19–32; Twenge, *iGen*, 161, 166.

104. See Volf, *End of Memory*, 28–30.

105. Bail, *Breaking the Social Media Prism*, 20–21; Bail et al., "Exposure to Opposing Views," 9216–21.

106. Mar et al., "Exploring the Link Between Reading Fiction and Empathy," 407–28. See also: Oatley, "Fiction," 618–28; Mar and Oatley, "Function of Fiction," 173–92.

> Literature as Logos is a series of windows, even of doors. One of the things we feel after reading a great work is "I have got out." Or from another point of view, "*I have got in*"; pierced the shell of some other monad and discovered what it is like inside. Good reading, therefore, though it is not essentially an affectional or moral or intellectual activity, has something in common with all three. In love we escape from our self into one other. In the moral sphere, every act of justice or charity involves putting ourselves in the other person's place and thus transcending our own competitive particularity.[107]

So "taking a break" from the pressure of constant crises or immanent enemies—even if only closing social media and picking up a book—can help us "recharge" *and* practice for the work of showing our enemies compassion. Being compassionate is difficult enough, but being compassionate towards our enemies is a completely different matter.

King's hope for us was that we might show compassion to one another—to our enemies and our allies alike. If we can manage this, then we might be ready to endure the slow process of healing our sad divisions and eventually find peace. I hope—indeed, I *believe*—that this is true. We have only to reach out and try. Yet there is more reason to hope that things can improve, for there are still three more patterns of love to consider and learn. With that, we turn to the difficult topic of forgiveness.

---

107. Lewis, *Reading Life*, 4, emphasis mine. Notice also that Lewis sees a parallel between this kind of compassion and *justice advocacy*.

Chapter 5: **I Pardon You**

Loving Our Enemies by Forgiving

> Forgiveness is the key that unlocks the door of resentment and the handcuffs of hatred. It is a power that breaks the chains of bitterness and the shackles of selfishness.... Forgiveness is an act of the will, and the will can function regardless of the temperature of the heart.
> —Corrie Ten Boom[1]

I: Introduction

IN STEVEN SPIELBERG'S FAMOUS work *Schindler's List*, we find Oskar Schindler suggesting to the monstrous Nazi commandant Amon Goeth (head of the Kraków-Płaszów concentration camp during WWII) that forgiveness reflects greater strength than vengefulness. Goeth tests Schindler's claim, and it appears momentarily that he might choose to show mercy to his Jewish prisoners—but after releasing a boy who has spilled tea on him, giving forgiveness a test run, Goeth thinks differently and shoots the boy from behind. The historical Goeth was executed for crimes against humanity, and Schindler is remembered as one of the "righteous among the nations" for preserving the lives of over one thousand Jews during the Holocaust. Goeth was incapable of even the most superficial act of forgiveness; he paid the price for this and his barbarism. I can confidently say that learning forgiveness would have been insufficient

---

1. Ten Boom, *Clippings from My Notebook*, 19, 94.

to make a righteous man out of Goeth, but it would have been a step in the right direction—a critical step we too must take.

I now turn to the complicated and sensitive topic of forgiveness.[2] This is a profoundly challenging topic for two main reasons: (1) forgiveness appears to invalidate justice—particularly in the face of the worst atrocities, it takes characteristics of both action and emotion—and, (2) it carries the veiled threat of damnation if ignored. Perhaps these challenges help explain the extraordinary lack of literature on the subject following Constantine's era—another challenge.[3]

Indeed, most authors brave enough to address the topic appear to be writing self-help psychology or popular theology, so a comprehensive overview of forgiveness theology is desperately needed. However, as one chapter cannot fill that lacuna, I will focus on five issues. First, I will outline the problem, including the primary passages in Scripture, the standard definition of forgiveness, and a discussion about bitterness, or nursing a grudge. Second, I will offer a more detailed description of forgiveness. This will divide forgiveness into its constituent parts—what I have chosen to call repentance, release, and reconciliation. I will argue that all three of these must occur in order for us to say someone has been "forgiven." Though this way of understanding forgiveness aids in clarifying what is expected of each participant in forgiveness, these three components cannot be separated cleanly as they are deeply interlocked. Third, I will address the importance of the cross and how it models the component of release in forgiveness. Fourth, I will offer some thoughts on the contentious topic of reparations and the process of reconciliation. I will conclude with practical suggestions for learning forgiveness and the paradigm of forgiveness provided by African theology.

Because this chapter alone demands a greater emphasis on the New Testament than on the Old, and because of the sheer number of passages that engage with the subject of forgiveness, this chapter is difficult to arrange by chapter and verse. For the record, the four passages that have the greatest bearing on this topic are the story of Joseph's reconciliation with his brothers (Gen 50:15–21), the parable of the unforgiving servant (Matt 18:15–35), the Lord's Prayer (Matt 6:9–15 and Luke 11:2–4), and Jesus' prayer for his enemies (Luke 23:34).

---

2. Murphy, *Getting Even*, 5.
3. Shriver, *Ethic for Enemies*, 46, 58.

Additionally, we must all build our practice of forgiveness on a foundation of compassion—for as we saw in the previous chapter, without compassion, our enemies remain demons in our eyes.[4] Because only humans can be forgiven, we must recognize the humanity of our enemies *before* they can be forgiven.[5] By contrast, we must also acknowledge that forgiveness is *itself* an act of compassion—thus, compassion undergirds and surrounds forgiveness.[6] We must further acknowledge that, while forgiveness has a way of blessing *individuals*, it is also an act of compassion that must be extended to our enemies *corporately* (see for example Luke 23:34 and Rom 5:6–8).

Lastly, we must be aware that while compassion looks *outwardly* toward our enemies, forgiveness begins by looking *inwardly* at ourselves. Also, while compassion is typically grounded in the *present*, forgiveness looks both to the *past* and the *future*. Desmond Tutu writes:

> True forgiveness deals with the past, all of the past, to make the future possible. We cannot go on nursing grudges even vicariously for those who cannot speak for themselves any longer. We have to accept that what we do we do for generations past, present, and yet to come. That is what makes a community a community or a people a people—for better or for worse.[7]

This is the center of why forgiveness matters—the pressure of the moment distracts us from the reality that forgiveness has eternal consequences for us, our enemies, our ancestors, and those yet unborn.

II: Forgiveness Overview

Except for the story of Joseph and his brothers, forgiveness in the Old Testament is dealt with only tangentially and typically focuses on God's forgiveness. The Epistles offer commentary on forgiveness and its components but do not clearly define it. Thus, a focus on the Synoptic Gospels will dominate this section. We may divide the Gospel teachings in this manner:[8]

---

4. Shriver, *Ethic for Enemies*, 8.
5. This does not include literal demons.
6. Kasper, *Mercy*, 142.
7. Tutu, *No Future Without Forgiveness*, 279.
8. Taylor, *Forgiveness and Reconciliation*, 11; Mayo, *Limits of Forgiveness*, 7–8. It will become apparent that I find much of Mayo's analysis distasteful and inaccurate, but her

The Lord's Prayer:	Matt 6:9–15; Luke 11:2–4
Forgive That You May Be Forgiven:	Matt 5:38–46; Mark 11:25; Luke 6:37–38
Forgive Seventy-times-Seven:	Matt 18:15–17, Luke 17:3–4
The Unforgiving Servant:	Matt 18:18–35
The Healing of the Paralytic:	Matt 9:2–8; Mark 2:2–12; Luke 5:17–26
The Woman's Sins Forgiven:	Luke 7:36–59
The Unforgivable Sin:	Matt 12:32; Mark 3:28–30; Luke 12:8–10
Jesus' Prayer for Forgiveness:	Luke 23:34[9]

That the list of Scripture passages on this topic can be so briefly stated is both an asset and an impediment. On the one hand, there is little to read and interpret, so it can be covered quickly. On the other hand, the lack of detail leaves much to be intuited.

Consequently, while there is consensus on the *meaning* of forgiveness, the simple explanation typically breaks down quickly when applied to practice or when we ask *why forgive*. Jean Hampton outlines the Hebrew and Greek words and their definitions. In Hebrew, there are three—*Kāphār* (כָּפַר)—meaning "to cover," *Nāśā* (נָשָׂא)—meaning "to carry off," and *Shālāch* (שָׁלַח) "to loose." In Greek, there is *Aphiēmi* (ἀφίημι), meaning "to remit, send away, or liberate."[10] To the Greek meaning, Maria Mayo adds that this may be seen as both an emotional stance and an action.[11]

These raise the question, "*What* exactly is being covered, released, or banished?" I want to stress first what forgiveness is *not*. Forgiveness does *not* remove, hide, or ignore the sin that precedes forgiveness—for

---

analysis makes some significant points. She is also deeply thorough in her research, making it an excellent structure.

9. Because of the sheer number of Scripture passages this chapter covers, it will not always be possible to list "chief passages" at the start of each section. This list should be taken as the selection of key Scripture passages.

10. Murphy and Hampton, *Forgiveness and Mercy*, 37.

11. Mayo, *Limits of Forgiveness*, 15.

we should remember that if there were no wrongdoing, there would be nothing to forgive![12] Forgiveness neither excuses nor condones the act that needs to be forgiven. Forgiveness also does not address the possibility that there could be *legal* ramifications of the sinful action, nor does it entail forgetting the act that prompted it.[13] What then does forgiveness dismiss?

Typically scholars argue that forgiveness dismisses *barriers to relationship, despite the sin*. Joseph Butler describes forgiveness as "forswearing resentment," Tutu says forgiveness is "abandoning your right to pay back the perpetrator in his own coin," and Vincent Taylor calls it "the canceling of obstacles to reconciliation."[14] Tutu further clarifies that forgiveness's primary purpose is to benefit the person forgiving, but this should not be accepted so quickly. Miroslav Volf agrees in principle that forgiveness is the release of a sort of "legal claim" against the one who has sinned, but clarifies that forgiveness is primarily for the benefit of the *perpetrator* and not the *aggrieved*.[15] This should not be to say that there are no benefits for the aggrieved in forgiveness but to emphasize that the primary beneficiary is the perpetrator.[16] In this, I agree with Volf.

Thus, forgiveness is commonly described as the act of releasing our entitlement to revenge when we have been wronged and the choice to forswear bitterness. While this involves elements of both emotional

---

12. Enright and Coyle, "Researching the Process Model," 141; Volf, *End of Memory*, 28–30; Lewis, *Mere Christianity*, 117; and Shriver, *Ethic for Enemies*, 7. Though I cannot address the argument in detail, it is my contention that only God can choose to forget sin—see, for example, Jer 31:34; Ps 130:8, 12; Mic 7:18–19; Heb 8:12. See also: Bobrinskoy, *Compassion of the Father*, 78. Though as we will see in chapter 7, pp. 180–1, there is a possibility that we will forget sin *by God's grace.*

13. Enright and Coyle, "Researching the Process Model," 141. Legal consequences will be addressed further in section V of this chapter; forgetting will be discussed in chapter 7. These are supported by Murphy, *Getting Even*, 13–16.

14. Butler, "Sermon IX," 96–102; Mayo, *Limits of Forgiveness*, 22; Murphy, *Getting Even*, 58; Tutu, *No Future*, 272; Taylor, *Forgiveness and Reconciliation*, 11. See also: Moule, *Forgiveness and Reconciliation*, 22. Tutu's interpretation is nearly identical to that of Smedes, *Forgive and Forget*, cited in Mayo, *Limits of Forgiveness*, 25–30. Smedes wrote the popular quote, "To forgive is to set a prisoner free and discover that the prisoner was you."

15. Volf, *Free of Charge*, 168–69. In this chapter, I will use the terms "aggrieved" and "perpetrator" rather than "victim" and "oppressor" as is typical today to avoid suggesting any sense of victimhood identity (see chapter 1, pp. 16–8).

16. See for example: Anonymous, "You Tear Yourself Apart by Hating," 120; Freedman and Enright, "Forgiveness as Intervention," 983–92; and McCullough et al., "Interpersonal Forgiving in Close Relationships," 321–36.

self-control and action (or inaction), it should also be understood as a stance or ethos rather than a simple one-off.[17] This leaves a lot to be explained—particularly the question of *how*—but provides a basic understanding on which to build.

Next we come to the question of *why*. While there are theological dimensions to the purpose of forgiveness (especially that no evil may present itself to God, thus we *must* receive forgiveness to share fellowship with him),[18] the most crucial concern is practical: the contrast between "grudge theory" and "forgiveness theory."[19] It is the prevailing view that when we have suffered an injury, we may either hold a grudge or forgive—that is, release. Let us explore this contrast.

Robert Enright reveals the nature of this contrast with his own definition of forgiveness:

> The forgiveness process properly understood and used, can free those bound by anger and resentment. It does not require accepting injustice or remaining in an abusive situation. It opens the door to reconciliation, but it does not require trusting someone who has proven untrustworthy. Even if the offender remains unrepentant, you can forgive and restore a sense of peace and well-being to your life.[20]

This affirms that we may follow either "grudge theory" or "forgiveness theory." Though Jeffrie Murphy describes Enright as the "guru of forgiveness," Maria Mayo is unconvinced by Enright's argument.[21] She counters, "Enright pits forgiveness against a seemingly necessary negative opposite, in this case, being "bound by anger and resentment" or not just *feeling* anger, but being *controlled* by it."[22] However, the only alternative Mayo proposes is "apathy."[23] She suggests that the aggrieved may request that the perpetrator be incapacitated so they cannot cause further harm—such as through a restraining order. Unfortunately, this strikes me as inadequate for two reasons. First, there is the danger of apathy leading to a sort of ethical nihilism or total indifference—such as in chapter 2.

---

17. Marty, "Ethos of Christian Forgiveness," 15.
18. Mayo, *Limits of Forgiveness*, 15.
19. Baumeister et al., "Victim Role," 80, 90–99.
20. Enright, *Forgiveness Is a Choice*, 43, cited in Mayo, *Limits of Forgiveness*, 22.
21. Murphy, *Forgiveness and Its Limits*, 74.
22. Mayo, *Limits of Forgiveness*, 22.
23. Mayo, *Limits of Forgiveness*, 91. See also: Griswold, *Forgiveness*, 19–37.

Second, I find it unlikely that an individual could arrive at and maintain a state of apathy except by a Herculean effort. As described in chapter 3, we are most likely to "see red,"[24] and as I explained in chapter 4, I am not convinced we can escape the pain of grief for any appreciable length of time through denial or some other *neutral* stance.[25]

Regardless, we should consider what merit may lie in holding a grudge. Roy Baumeister, Julie Exline, and Kristin Sommer argue that holding a grudge gives the aggrieved a claim to reparations. It acts as a deterrent against recurrence and offers the illusion of maintaining justice.[26] However, they also note that the cost of holding a grudge is prolonged pain, a debilitating sense of victimhood, and damaged relationships (particularly within families) leading to isolation.[27] Volf explains this in terms of his own experience of suffering, saying:

> I sensed—maybe more subconsciously than consciously—that if I gave in to [my enduring anger that even vengeance would not alter], I would not be responding as a free human being but reacting as a wounded animal.[28]

We should also consider the wisdom that we should "not let the sun go down on [our] anger" (Eph 4:26). This is not to say that anger is wrong, but that we should *do something* with anger so that it does not become a grudge. Therefore, I conclude that, although Mayo's warning against overstating the power of anger is well-taken, forgiveness still provides the only viable alternative to holding a grudge, and that forgiveness is the superior option.

---

24. Furthermore, I find her argument unconvincing, given that she begins her book by revealing that she has a history of deep bitterness—I find it odd that she would suggest an alternative to bitterness that, while theoretically *possible*, is counter-indicated by her own testimony, see: Mayo, *Limits of Forgiveness*, 2, 4. See chapter 3, p. 73.

25. Mayo's argument for a third way strongly implies that she is less interested in providing a third alternative to bitterness and forgiveness than in arguing that promoting forgiveness is a sort of violence against "survivors," see: Mayo, *Limits of Forgiveness*, 91. In support, she cites: Herman, "Justice from the Victim's Perspective," 578; Minow, *Between Vengeance and Forgiveness*, 17. See also: Mayo, *Limits of Forgiveness*, 186–98. See above chapter 4, pp. 112–113.

26. Baumeister et al., "Victim Role," 90–96.

27. Baumeister et al., "Victim Role," 98–99.

28. Volf, *End of Memory*, 8. See also: Nussbaum, *Anger and Forgiveness*, 5; Nussbaum, *Monarchy of Fear*, 80–81; and Murphy and Hampton, *Forgiveness and Mercy*, 48, 64–65. Recall Asaph as a "brute beast," chapter 4, p. 109.

III: Repentance, Release, and Reconciliation

Gen 50:15—21

This still paints a cheap and simplistic view of forgiveness. Assuming that forgiveness is an ethos or a process (and not a one-off event),[29] how do we understand the inner workings of forgiveness?[30] Furthermore, how is it that we can expect the aggrieved to simply "release" their bitterness without the participation of the perpetrator? These are the questions I will consider in this section. I will begin by breaking down forgiveness into "chunks" that can be more easily studied.

I believe that forgiveness describes the completed state of a process between two parties that involves (1) the act of *repentance* by the perpetrator of a wrong, (2) the *release* of the perpetrator from the threat of retaliation by the aggrieved,[31] and (3) *reconciliation*, or the repair of their relationship.[32] All three components—repentance, release, and reconciliation—must be present for us to describe their efforts as forgiveness.

Typically, the term "forgiveness" has two potential meanings. It can refer to the act of the afflicted *releasing* the perpetrator (à la Butler or Tutu), or it can refer to the whole completed process of forgiveness—including repentance and reconciliation as well as release. To avoid this confusion, I will *only* use the term "forgiveness" when I mean the completed process, and I will attempt to interpret whether a scholar means to speak of "forgiveness" or merely "release." In this frame, "release" is the most critical component of loving our enemies.

Perhaps the most significant scholarship suggesting forgiveness be divided into components is the work of Stephanie van de Loo. Van de Loo distinguishes between *Vergebung* (forgiveness, what I call release)

---

29. I am assuming here that the specific component of forgiveness I will shortly call "release" can sometimes need to be accomplished more than once or as an ongoing activity. This will be discussed in more detail at the end of the chapter in terms of Process Forgiveness (gradually processing our emotions and releasing our desire for retribution) or Decision Forgiveness (deciding once to release the aggrieved and then working through our feelings over time). This can also be accompanied by prayer, especially through praying Ps 22.

30. Countryman, *Forgiven and Forgiving*, 43; Shriver, *Ethic for Enemies*, 8.

31. Ernesto Verdeja proposes a similar term, what he calls "partial pardon." See: Verdeja, *Unchopping a Tree*, cited in Mayo, *Limits of Forgiveness*, 154.

32. Forgiveness in this sense may involve two individuals or *groups*. However, as group forgiveness differs somewhat and is less common, much of this chapter will assume individual forgiveness—one person releasing, one person repenting.

and *Versöhnung* (reconciliation). The first is a change of attitude on the part of the afflicted only, the second includes the first as well as repentance and the mutual decision of both parties to improve their relationship in future.[33] Practically, this makes sense. The act of releasing the perpetrator from the threat of revenge (whether the perpetrator is informed of this or not) is insufficient to restore, repair, or rebuild the broken relationship. Particularly in instances of abuse (of any kind) or crime, it is appropriate for boundaries to be put in place to maintain the safety of the afflicted.[34] As Donald Shriver puts it, reconciliation is "the end of a process that forgiveness [release] begins."[35] However, given the nature of reconciliation, it should be clear that reconciliation depends on some degree of repentance.

Partitioning forgiveness like this is theologically tricky. Martin Marty writes, "In the New Testament, while each has its nuances, forgiveness [release] always leads to reconciliation, and reconciliation results from mutual experiences of forgiveness. They cannot, finally, be separated."[36] Ideally, release and reconciliation should be interdependent. The distinction between repentance and reconciliation is also blurred. Mayo reluctantly acknowledges that the Bible demands that repentance be answered by release.[37] Therefore, reconciliation—the act of deciding what the new boundaries of the relationship ought to be, and ideally, the restoration of the relationship—is practically inevitable even if that reconciliation is tacitly accepted.[38]

Similarly, reconciliation theoretically does not need to lead to a restored relationship but a clean ending of the relationship.[39] Examples of

---

33. Mayo, *Limits of Forgiveness*, 68–69. See also: van de Loo, *Versöhnungsarbeit*; and Martin, "Moving Beyond Just Forgive."

34. Mayo, *Limits of Forgiveness*, 16–21, 186; see also Arendt, *Eichmann in Jerusalem*, 269, 279. The issue of boundaries is critical to the subject of reconciliation, but it goes slightly beyond the scope of this work. Regarding boundaries, I recommend: Cloud and Townsend, *Boundaries*.

35. Shriver, *Ethic for Enemies*, 8.

36. Marty, "Ethos of Christian Forgiveness," 11. See also: Mayo, *Limits of Forgiveness*, 12, 68–69.

37. Mayo, *Limits of Forgiveness*, 33. The primary basis for this, Matt 18, will be discussed later. However, she later recants this claim and argues that afflicted persons should never be required even to *release* the perpetrator from guilt, (p. 189).

38. Shriver, *Ethic for Enemies*, 28.

39. Shriver uses the phrase "co-existence" for this conclusion. The distinction has semantic use but little ethical value, in my opinion, see: Shriver, *Ethic for Enemies*, 8–9. Lewis Smedes also supports this, see: Smedes, *Forgive and Forget*, 30.

this include criminal cases that end in incarceration, execution, the issuance of a restraining order, or the afflicted moving to avoid the perpetrator. Insofar as such ends restore *order*, they can surely be described as a form of reconciliation—both with reality and one another—and this reconciliation operates *regardless* of the perpetrator's feelings.[40] What remains is for the aggrieved to *release* their bitterness towards the perpetrator and for both to begin learning to structure their lives within the boundaries that have been established. This is an imperfect solution, but attempting to force a reconciliation is trying to manifest the kingdom of God without the King.[41] Sadly, we must settle for "what resources we need to live in peace in the absence of the final reconciliation."[42]

If the relationships between release and reconciliation, and repentance and reconciliation are blurred, this leaves only the relationship between repentance and release to address. This raises two questions: is repentance *required* for forgiveness (the whole process), and is repentance a *prerequisite* of release? I will conclude that repentance and release are not *competitors* but *companions* on the road to forgiveness. Perpetrators are commanded to repent. Afflicted persons are required to release. Both are dependent upon each other, but neither is preeminent.

Mayo argues that requiring perpetrators to repent and the afflicted to release are mutually exclusive demands.[43] Furthermore, she holds that it is abusive to require the afflicted to release their perpetrator, and we should allow the afflicted to choose whether or not to release.[44] Yet, such exclusivism implies a victimhood outlook and ignores the possibility that both desires for release and repentance are good and proper. I want to challenge her position gently.

To begin, I should define what repentance is. The Hebrew word *šûb* (שׁוּב) is typically used to explain repentance. *Šûb* means "to turn back" or "to return," which illustrates that repentance is more than an apology. Instead, repentance requires a change of direction, and

---

40. Similarly, Athanasius argues that repentance is insufficient to satisfy the needs of sin because repentance *only* causes sin to cease. Athanasius, *On the Incarnation*, 56–57.

41. See chapter 3, pp. 73–7, on justice.

42. Volf, *Exclusion and Embrace*, 109–10. See chapter 3, pp. 73–7. This also demonstrates the need for an eschatological frame, to be discussed in chapter 7, pp. 181–6. See also: Volf, *End of Memory*, 78.

43. Mayo, *Limits of Forgiveness*, 37–43, 185–198.

44. Mayo, *Limits of Forgiveness*, 198. In this instance, she is concerned that requiring battered women to forgive their abuser is a further act of abuse.

sometimes working to repair what has been damaged because of one's actions.[45] Murphy writes:

> Repentance is the remorseful acceptance of responsibility for one's wrongful and harmful actions, the repudiation of the aspects of one's character that generated the actions, the resolve to do one's best to extirpate those aspects of one's character, and the resolve to atone or make amends for the harm that one has done.[46]

This is most often applied to our relationship with God—and is, therefore, a matter of *obedience* as well as of love—but the definition applies to all circumstances.

Notice the conditional nature of this definition. To repent from a minor accident requires no making of amends. Determining the requirements of the amends would be more trouble than the value of the amends themselves, and therefore a waste. In yet other circumstances, making amends might not be possible at all, such as in the parable of the prodigal son (Luke 15:11–32).[47] We can always express sorrow at our sins, but we cannot always measure or offer appropriate repayment.

There might not always be a clear path to repentance, but it remains biblically required.[48] Mayo's insistence that we emphasize repentance over release is easily understandable given the Levitical distinction between the "sin offering" and "reparation offering" (See Lev 4–7). Every time an Israelite sinned, he or she was *required* to make a sin offering (הַחַטָּאת *Hā khattā't*) in an act of contrition; otherwise no one was permitted to enter the presence of God. For known sins that incurred significant cost to the aggrieved, a further reparation offering (אָשָׁם *āshām*) was *required*, as well as restoring the cost of the damage plus 20 percent interest. Repentance is not optional.[49]

This is a practical requirement as well. An unrepentant sinner compounds the pain they have already inflicted by making it nigh impossible to restore the broken relationship. Volf writes, "Bound in a perverse bond with wrongdoers by having suffered at their hands, victims

---

45. Fretheim, "Repentance in the Former Prophets," 40.
46. Murphy, *Getting Even*, 41.
47. Bailey, *Cross and the Prodigal*, 70.
48. Porter, "Penitence and Repentance in the Epistles," 133; Nave, "Repent, for the Kingdom of God," 100.
49. Ross, *Recalling the Hope of Glory*, 200. For more on these forms of sacrifice, see pp. 198–203.

can be fully liberated and healed from the wounds of wrongdoing only if the perpetrators genuinely repent and the two parties are reconciled to each other."[50] Dietrich Bonhoeffer further illustrates how a lack of repentance creates further theological challenges, writing, "Cheap grace is the preaching of forgiveness without requiring repentance; baptism without church discipline; communion without acknowledging sin; absolution without personal confession."[51]

However, while it is desirable that the perpetrator should repent before the aggrieved can release, repentance is not a *pre*-requisite of release. Michael Battle writes, "Theologians sometimes debate whether one can forgive another if that other does not repent. But we should also ask if one can repent without the prospect of forgiveness."[52] This need for *release* as a possible consequence of repentance is signified by the *third* sacrifice in Israel's worship: the whole-burnt offering or *ʿōlāh* (עֹלָה). The whole burnt offering simultaneously symbolized the worshiper's intention to live a new life *and* the truth of God's *release*. Thereby the worshiper was assured that their repentance was efficacious.[53] This suggests that the relationship between release and repentance is *not* unidirectional.

There is also the reality that no amends can be made for some sins, as their cost has been irredeemably high. Volf writes:

> Important as political liberation is on its own, however, it leaves forever in captivity the unvindicated oppressed who have died, with the possible consolation that their suffering has contributed to the well-being of future generations and that their story will live on in the memory of posterity.... Faith in "progress"—a conviction that future generations will live more fulfilled and more humane lives than past generations—is no more than a modern superstition.[54]

In such situations, the demand for complete repentance—including a total restoration of what has been lost—is actually an *injustice*. It risks undercutting the severity of the wrong that has been done and risks saddling the perpetrator with a burden that no one could be expected

---

50. Volf, *End of Memory*, 119.

51. Bonhoeffer, *Cost of Discipleship*, 47.

52. Battle, "Penitence as Practiced," 335. See also: Chryssavgis, "Life in Abundance," 217–19; Kasper, *Mercy*, 141.

53. Ross, *Recalling the Hope of Glory*, 200–201.

54. Volf, *End of Memory*, 114.

to bear.⁵⁵ To assume repentance as a prerequisite of release, in situations where repentance is impossible, risks permanently trapping the aggrieved person in their bitterness.⁵⁶

We should also consider the story of Joseph. In Gen 37:28, his brothers sell Joseph into slavery. Over the following nine years, Joseph's suffering reaches rock bottom, but in a miraculous reversal of fortune, he is elevated from imprisoned slave to personal advisor to Pharoah. Eventually, he finds himself uneasily reunited with his father and brothers (Gen 43–45).⁵⁷ During this time, and over the next seventeen years (a total of twenty-six years), there is no mention of forgiveness.

Forgiveness only comes into the story after Jacob (Joseph's father) dies in chapter 49. The text reads:

> When Joseph's brothers had seen that their father was dead, they said, "What if Joseph holds a grudge against us and pays us back in full for all the wrong which we did to him!" So they sent instructions to Joseph, saying, "Your father commanded *us* before he died, saying, "This is what you shall say to Joseph: "Please *forgive*, I beg you, the offense of your brothers and their sin, for they did you wrong."" And now, please forgive the offense of the servants of the God of your father." And Joseph wept when they spoke to him. Then his brothers also came and fell down before him and said, "Behold, we are your servants." But Joseph said to them, "*Do not be afraid*, for am I in God's place? As for you, you meant evil against me, *but* God meant it for good in order to bring about this present result, to keep many people alive. So therefore, *do not be afraid* [of my wrath]; I will provide for you and your little ones." So he *comforted* them and spoke kindly to them. (Gen 50:15–21 NASB, emphasis mine)

Here is the *first* time the word "forgive" (*nāšā* or "offer up") appears in the entire story. This passage reveals four things to us.

First, so far as we know, the brothers have not repented. Despite the severity of having sold Joseph into slavery, they do not apologize themselves. Instead, they take advantage of their Father's death to try to coerce Joseph into releasing them. Despite this, Joseph releases them anyway and even comforts them. Release *precedes* repentance.

---

55. The Treaty of Versailles is one example.
56. Bailey, *Cross and the Prodigal*, 84, 86.
57. Shriver, *Ethic For Enemies*, 24–27.

Second, Joseph weeps when confronted by his family (privately in Gen 43:30, publicly and shamefully in 45:2), which shows that he is emotionally distraught. Who could blame him, given their family history? However, his ability to *release* his brothers from fear of retaliation is not dependent on his (precarious) emotional state *or* his perception of his brothers's sense of guilt. He does not release because he "feels" like it, but because it is right to do so.

Third, Joseph's brothers are wary of retaliation. We are reminded again that the roles of victim and oppressor are fluid—one can go from the first to the second far too easily.[58] The brothers's self-interest leads them to at least feign repentance out of fear of reprisal.[59] Joseph forgives and thereby preemptively ends a potential cycle of violence.[60] Ensuring that his family can live together peacefully is more important than reprisal.

Lastly is that twenty-six years elapsed during the tale. Joseph's ability to recognize the hand of God at work is essential to his explanation of how he came to forgive his brothers (to "offer up" their sin to God), but this recognition took a long time. However it happened, we must thank God that Joseph could release his brothers, or the nation of Israel might have been divided from its inception! Time might not heal, but it can lessen the pain.

Repentance need not precede release. Release may be offered regardless of the emotional state of the afflicted. Release is critical to forestalling violence, and time makes release easier. Volf summarizes this, writing:

> Forgivers' forgiving is not conditioned by repentance. The offenders' [sic] being forgiven, however, is conditioned by repentance. Without repentance the forgivers will keep forgiving but the offenders will remain unforgiven, in that they are untouched by that forgiveness. . . . Repentance is important, even indispensable, and it is indispensable because forgiveness is an event *between* people, not just an individual's change of feelings, attitudes, or actions. Instead of being a *condition* of forgiveness, however, repentance is its necessary *consequence*.[61]

---

58. Volf, *End of Memory*, 33; Volf, *Exclusion and Embrace*, 103; Bobrinskoy, *Compassion of the Father*, 68. See chapter 3, pp. 73–4.

59. There is not enough information in the passage to discern the brothers's intent. I see two possibilities. First, that they are genuinely distraught over their actions and too ashamed to ask forgiveness for themselves. Second, that their primary motive is fear of reprisal. The second is clearly evident, but the first can only be inferred.

60. See also: Baumeister et al., "Victim Role," 79–80.

61. Volf, *Free of Charge*, 83, 183.

D. A. Carson reinforces this, saying, "sometimes the forgiveness of which the New Testament speaks presupposes repentance on the part of the offender and sometimes not." We see an expectation of repentance *first* in Luke 17:3-4. We see an expectation of release regardless of repentance in Rom 5:6-8.[62] "For while we were still weak, at the right time Christ died for the ungodly. . . . God proves his love for us in that while we still were sinners Christ died for us." (NRSVA) God's gracious gift of release is available to *all* because of the cross *before* we have repented.[63] This suggests that Jesus' followers should at least be *open* to offering release to those who have yet to repent.

I can also conclude that repentance, in some form, is a *requirement* for the conclusion of forgiveness. However, this leaves the question of *release* still unanswered. We agree that sinners *must* repent of their sins, but *must* the rest of us *release* them? This is the question I will consider in the next section.

IV: They are New Every Morning—The Cross and the Mercies of God

Matt 18:15–35; Matt 6:9–15; Luke 11:2–4; 23:34

Nietzsche believed that all forms of forgiveness are the pinnacle of human arrogance—who are we to assume that anyone else *needs* to be released from the weight of *our* morals?[64] However, with the possible exception of wartime sins (which Volf rightly points out require a declaration of *peace* to make forgiveness even remotely feasible),[65] I will be taking the position that Christians are *required* to release our enemies from the threat of retribution in all circumstances. Although Mayo argues against this idea, I hope to demonstrate that "the imperative to forgive is not just a moral issue; it is a soteriological necessity."[66] To this end, I will look at Mayo's

---

62. Carson, *Love in Hard Places*, 81; Bobrinskoy, *Compassion of the Father*, 56. Carson also includes Col 3:12-14.

63. Bailey, *Cross and the Prodigal*, 67, 69-70, 82-83, 87.

64. Murphy and Hampton, *Forgiveness and Mercy*, 40. Remember that we need not accept all of Nietzsche's claims at face value. I certainly do not in this instance. See chapter 3, pp. 67-9.

65. Volf, *Exclusion and Embrace*, 304.

66. Mayo, *Limits of Forgiveness*, 15. Ironically, Mayo ultimately rejects this claim.

interpretation of three narrative threads in the Gospels: the Lord's Prayer, the parable of the unforgiving servant, and Jesus' prayer from the cross.

The Lord's prayer appears in Matthew and Luke with little difference between the two in the Greek.[67] In Matt 6:12 we find, "Forgive us our debts as we forgive our debtors" (NRSVA), and in Luke 11:4, the parallel: "Forgive us our sins as we forgive everyone indebted to us" (NRSVA). Here, of course, "forgive" is "*aphiēmi*"—"to remit, send away, or liberate"—thus indicating "release." (The image of the creditor and the debtor is biblical "code" for God and sinners—our debts are those things owed to God *because* of our sins.[68]) Because recognizing *our* need for forgiveness is paramount in both verses, Mayo interprets this as instruction that repentance *must* precede release.[69] However, this is a reversal of logic. She has transformed "forgive *me my* sin" into "repent *thou of thy* sin."[70] Cyril of Alexandria demonstrates the proper approach here: "We must ask God for the forgiveness of the sins that we have committed. First, we must have forgiven [released] whoever has offended us in anything."[71] We cannot ask God to release us if we refuse to release others.

The same pattern continues in Matt 18, including the parable of the unforgiving servant. Beginning with Peter's question of how often we should forgive (vs. 21), Mayo emphasizes that in Peter's example, the fellow believer repents before release is required. However, she omits the rest of the passage from her interpretation (Matt 18:23-35). A king has a servant who owes an impossible and unpayable debt that the king mercifully releases. The servant subsequently refuses to offer the same merciful release to a coworker. Upon hearing the story, the king reasserts his claim on the debt because of the servants' refusal to release another. Mayo insists this is not a model of forgiveness because it cannot be applied to the circumstances of abuse victims. However, in doing so, she fails to recognize the presence of *three* parties involved in the second debt and the true identity of the King, that is, God.[72] Further-

---

67. Matt 6:9-15 and Luke 11:2-4.

68. Keck et al., *New Interpreter's Bible*, 381-82; Bailey, *Jesus Through Middle Eastern Eyes*, 252. See also: Lewis, *Four Loves*, 111.

69. Mayo, *Limits of Forgiveness*, 10.

70. We cannot take a request for forgiveness as coercion to repentance. See: Murphy, *Getting Even*, 37. See also: Cyprian, "Asking Pardon Daily," 136.

71. Cyril, "To Forgive Sins Is to Imitate God," 188. See also: Shriver, *Ethic for Enemies*, 39.

72. Lewis, *Mere Christianity*, 51-52; Volf, *Free of Charge*, 131; Bobrinskoy, *Compassion of the Father*, 16, 28, 75.

more, she does not support her argument from within the text.[73] Mayo fails to account for the whole passage and again shifts the focus from *my* responsibility to *your* responsibility.

There is also the cultural context to consider. Leander Keck offers an excellent overview of forgiveness in Jewish tradition:

> Forgiveness was one of the expected blessings on the day of salvation (Jer 31:34; Ezek 36:25–32; Isa 40:2, 55:6–7), and the sixth of the eighteen benedictions was a prayer for forgiveness.... As surely and desperately as we need bread, we need forgiveness. Jewish teachings, moreover, had already linked the necessity of [releasing] others to one's ability to receive forgiveness: "Forgive your neighbor the wrong he has done, and then your sins will be pardoned when you pray" (Sir 28:2). One who will not [release] cannot receive forgiveness; mercy flows through the same channel, whether being given or received. There is no *quid pro quo* here; however, the ability to [release] and to be [released] is part of the same gift. We stand in need not only of daily sustenance but also of continual forgiveness.[74]

Carson summarizes this sentiment by saying "people disqualify themselves from being forgiven if they are so hardened in their own *bitterness* that they cannot or will not [release] others."[75]

The crux of the matter—of repentance and release as *parallel* commandments—is the cross (Rom 5:6–8). This demands that I briefly address my understanding of the purpose of the cross for our salvation. I believe that the cross simultaneously fulfills the demands of the law concerning sin while offering an undeniable demonstration of God's love for creation and the length to which he is willing to go to free us from sin and death.[76] It does not mean we no longer take responsibility for our sins, but it does *release* us from fear of God's retribution. It is,

---

73. Carson, *Love in Hard Places*, 79.

74. Keck, *Gospel of Luke*, 235. Keck's comparison to our need for bread is especially poignant because bread was standard fare in the Middle East during this time and absolutely essential in daily life. According to Bailey, "A man does not work to "make a living." Rather he works to 'eat bread.'" See Bailey, *Cross and the Prodigal*, 60.

75. Carson, *Love in Hard Places*, 79, emphasis mine. See also: Cyprian, "Asking Pardon Daily," 136; Chrysostom, "Praying Daily for Forgiveness," 136.

76. Athanasius, *On the Incarnation*, 57. This should *not* be seen as a rejection of the cross's role in subverting and destroying death—a role I joyfully affirm—but rather a focus on the cross as the instrument to defeat sin. I am here speaking of the purpose of the cross *solely* on Good Friday, not as it extends into the weekend and into the resurrection.

in a word, God's assurance that in Jesus we will find forgiveness for our sins *and* freedom from death.[77]

Mayo likewise sees the answer to the significance of release in the cross. In Luke 23:34, Jesus prays, "Father forgive them, they do not know what they are doing."[78] She sees this as absolute proof that we are not required to release our enemies. Rather than releasing his executioners himself, Jesus instead asks the Father to release them.[79] However, this demonstrates an inability to apply a consistent theology of Jesus' hypostatic union—that is, Jesus' identity as both human and God. When discussing the "unforgivable sin," she identifies Jesus as one with the Holy Spirit—to blaspheme against the Holy Spirit is to sin against *Jesus* as well.[80] However, when Jesus asks that the *Father* release, Jesus is nothing more than a man. His divinity and humanity are interchangeable within her argument.[81] Unfortunately, to understand Jesus' prayer to the Father for our forgiveness, we must assume *both* his humanity and his divinity.

Let us first consider the implications of Jesus' divinity.[82] If, as Mayo suggests, "the prayer is a cry, a *demand*, even, for God the Father to do what Jesus either cannot or is not willing to do in that moment," then Jesus cannot be fully God. If Jesus is divine, then he must submit to the Father's will.[83] Jesus himself confirms this through his prayer in the garden of Gethsemane (Matt 26:38, 42; Mark 14:36; Luke 22:43).[84] If we accept Jesus' divinity, it follows that if Jesus petitions his Father to release his enemies *and* the Father does, then Jesus *must* release them too. Following

---

77. Moule, *Forgiveness and Reconciliation*, 15–17.

78. Because of the wording of Luke 23:34, I am using the term "forgive" in this paragraph instead of "release." In this case, the latter is the meaning I intend.

79. Mayo, *Limits of Forgiveness*, 66, 184–85, 199–201, 211. This *appears* consistent with Bobrinskoy, *Compassion of the Father*, 69; Ambrose, "On the Cross," 108.

80. Mayo, *Limits of Forgiveness*, 8, 12, 16, 35, 211.

81. In fairness, Jesus' twofold nature is challenging even to the church fathers, who occasionally focus on *one* aspect of Jesus' nature for didactic purposes—often to emphasize how listeners should respond to the text *in action*. This should not be taken as a license to *ignore* one side of Jesus' essence for convenience. This is how I interpret Bobrinksoy and Ambrose in this instance.

82. Here we may consider numerous Scripture passages, including John 8:58 and 10:10, which Novatian confirms are claims to divinity; see: Novatian, "One with the Father," 358. See also Kasper, *Mercy*, 51.

83. Mayo, *Limits of Forgiveness*, 184–85.

84. Jesus' union with and submission to the Father is also present all throughout the book of John, including 5:19, 30; 6:38; 8:28; 9:4; 12:49, 50; and 14:10.

John Chrysostom, we are compelled to recognize that Jesus' prayer obtains for us release from our sins against God.[85]

If we understand Jesus' prayer in his humanity, we ought to connect his words with the sayings of the Maccabean martyrs, executed by Antiochus Epiphanes (2 Macc 7). Most notably, the Maccabean martyrs appealed to God to punish their executioners and to show mercy (release) to Israel because of their suffering. Jesus' prayer reinterprets the martyrs in two ways: (1) where the youngest martyr damned his executioners, Jesus did not, and (2) where the youngest martyr prayed for the *nation* (admittedly experiencing God's just wrath), Jesus prayed *for his enemies*. This implicates his executioners—the corrupt temple authorities and the Roman soldiers—Jews and gentiles.

I believe Jesus' prayer and the purpose of the cross are not merely extended to his executioners (as we see in the context of the Maccabean martyrs) but to *everyone*.[86] In his book, *On the Incarnation*, Athanasius argues that Jesus' ministry must offer release from sin to all.[87] So too does John Chrysostom, who further indicates the cross as the instrument of our release.[88] Bobrinskoy affirms this interpretation when he exhorts our prayer lives to imitate Jesus:

> In this way, the most secret, solitary prayer becomes a fervent intercession for the entire world and *imitates Jesus*. . . . Concerns for this world are laid at the feet of the Savior, in his heart of compassion.[89]

In the words of John the theologian, "Behold the Lamb of God who takes away the sins *of the world*" (John 1:29 NRSVA).[90] Volf even goes so far as to write, "Before the dawn of creation God, having seen all the evil humankind would commit, had to [release] the world before

---

85. Chrysostom, "*In Ascensionem Christi*," 435–36. I cannot commend this sermon highly enough.

86. Schmemann, *For the Life of the World*, 23; Ross, *Recalling the Hope of Glory*, 397.

87. Athanasius, *On the Incarnation*, 90–91. See also Isa 53; Heb 2:17, 4:14–16, 7:25–26, and Chrysostom, "*In Ascensionem Christi*."

88. Chrysostom, "*In Ascensionem Christi*." To identify the presence of the cross in this homily, one needs to read the whole of Galatians chapter 3 to understand Chrysostom's reference

89. Bobrinskoy, *Compassion of the Father*, 113–14. Emphasis mine. This could be an echo of Schmemann's claim from *For the Life of the World*; see above footnote 86.

90. Bobrinskoy, *Compassion of the Father*, 51. See also Shriver, *Ethic for Enemies*, 41.

creating it. Between the complete disregard of justice and the relentless pursuit of justice lies [*release*]."[91]

For me, the penny finally dropped as I meditated on the cross. If the cross puts to death our corruption by sin and reconciles us to God, then I must recognize that God has offered release *to the world*.[92] This places me in a quandary. Assuming that, while walking the streets, a stranger approaches me and punches me in the face, this person has *already* been released of that sin by God, through the cross.[93] Subsequently, if I refuse to release this person, I am acting on the conviction that God is somehow in the wrong: God forgives, but I do *not* forgive. I can interpret this no other way than to conclude that, as my position opposes God, I have become an *enemy* of God. The act of releasing our enemies from their sins—i.e., forgiveness—is not merely a commandment but a "soteriological necessity," lest I become an enemy of the cross of Christ (Phil 3:18–19).[94]

Thus, I arrive at my conclusion about the proper ordering of repentance and release. Rather than granting precedence to one, we must recognize both as parallel and related requirements.[95] It is not that the perpetrator must repent first nor that the afflicted must release first: the perpetrator must repent, and the afflicted must release. We do not offer release simply because we feel like it but because God has commanded us to do so, because God has done so himself on the cross, because to fail to do so risks voiding our salvation, and because this is a way we give up our bitterness. I cannot help but recall the hymn text:

> How can your pardon reach and bless the unforgiving heart
>
> that broods on wrongs and will not let old bitterness depart?
>
> In blazing light your cross reveals the truth we dimly knew:
>
> how small the debts men owe to us, how great our debt to you.[96]

---

91. Volf, *End of Memory*, 110–111.

92. Pao, *Thanksgiving*, 71–74.

93. Notice that I say here *release*, not *forgiveness*. The fact that God offers assurance of forgiveness to all who seek it—which requires repentance and reconciliation—does not provide universal salvation.

94. Mayo, *Limits of Forgiveness*, 15; Kasper, *Mercy*, 139; Chrysostom, "Homily 61.4," 87–88.

95. Battle, "Penitence as Practiced," 339; Volf, *Free of Charge*, 166.

96. Herklus, "Forgive Our Sins as We Forgive,"

V: Until He Pay All His Debt—Reparations and Reconciliation

This brings me to the last component of forgiveness: reconciliation. We have already seen that ideal reconciliation restores the broken relationship to its previous state or, at the very least, forcibly settles the chaos created by the broken relationship. Furthermore, we have seen that the Bible tends to assume that reconciliation and forgiveness are coupled—that two people having repented and released should subsequently reconcile. However, this still leaves two questions unanswered: what are we to make of *corporate* sin, and what are we to make of *intergenerational* sin? Given their connection to reconciliation, it makes sense to discuss them here.

Although I have hitherto assumed that forgiveness is *primarily* interpersonal, this does not mean forgiveness is *exclusively* interpersonal. Indeed, if Jesus' forgiveness is for the *world*, then surely humanity is guilty of sin collectively![97] It is unsurprising, therefore, that the overwhelming perspective of Scripture treats sin as a *corporate* phenomenon first.[98] The reason for the focus on interpersonal forgiveness in literature is a matter of simplicity and because most circumstances of forgiveness are interpersonal.[99]

Because the Western world is *individualistic*, such societies struggle to understand *communal* sin in ways that second- and third-world societies often do not.[100] Westerners understand that when part of the community suffers, the whole suffers in solidarity. We can even acknowledge that a community might be held responsible for a sin that is rampant and unchecked. Where Westerners begin to struggle is the question of how to *respond* to corporate sin. Scripture contains three patterns for this response.

The first pattern is the punishment of the whole community by God. This is clear from Exod 32: God promises that a plague will come upon the people as punishment for creating an idol in Moses' absence— the golden calf. This is also clear when God exiles the whole nation

---

97. Dempsey, "Turn Back, O People," 61.

98. Pope John Paul II, "Dives in Misericordia"; Battle, "Penitence as Practiced," 331; Bautch, "May Your Eyes Be Open," 82–85; Boda, "Renewal in Heart, Word, and Deed," 22; Tutu, *No Future*, 279.

99. Murphy, *Getting Even*, 5.

100. Tutu, *No Future*, 31. South African identity—ubuntu—argues that a person is a person insofar as they are part of a *community*. This, or a similar concept, is nearly universal to all African cultures.

of Israel (2 Kgs 17:18; 23:27). However, in each instance where God punishes the entire community for corporate sin, Scripture is clear that it is *God alone* who punishes.

The second pattern involves separating the sinners from the righteous. In Josh 7, Achan, son of Karmi, disobediently takes the spoils of the "sacred things" following Israel's victory over Jericho, but God's wrath burns against *Israel*. The nation loses its subsequent battle because of Achan. When Joshua asks why they were defeated, God instructs him to find and destroy what Achan has secretly taken. The nation casts lots, discovers Achan's treachery, and stones him to death. In the end, though the whole suffers because of Achan's sin, only Achan pays the price.[101]

The last pattern of response to communal sin is to see the responsibility fall on a community representative—typically the prophet, high priest, or king—though this often doubles with the second example, as the King is frequently the leading cause of Israel's sin. Typical examples of this are Ezra 10 and Dan 9, wherein a representative repents on behalf of the nation and insists that the nation follow suit. This is also apparent in Israel's idolatry with the golden calf, when Moses intercedes on behalf of the nation and God appoints him "the one in charge" of the people by God (Exod 32:7, 11–14, 30–32).[102] However, the quintessential example of this is Jesus—the true prophet, priest, and king—taking responsibility for the sin of the world and asking forgiveness from the Father on our behalf.

However, the contemporary Western disposition appears to combine these patterns when it comes to communal sin. If a community is guilty of sin, then *each individual* within that community is held responsible as a representative of the whole. The community is seen not as a cohesive whole but as the sum of its parts. Consequently, though an individual may be innocent of wrongdoing, they are held personally responsible for their tribe. This is inappropriate.

Intergenerational sin is also confusing. Mark Boda confirms that sin has an intergenerational element.[103] Daniel and Ezra take responsibility

---

101. Similarly, in Num 25, "the men" indulge in sexual immorality, bringing a plague on the nation. However, when Phineas kills an Israelite who brought a Midianite woman to his tent in broad daylight, God announces that this act has turned away his anger from Israel. Both instances (Num 25 and Josh 7) are referenced in Josh 22 when three tribes rebel by building an unauthorized altar.

102. Ross, *Recalling the Hope of Glory*, 182.

103. Boda, "Renewal in Heart, Word, and Deed," 22.

not only for the nation's present sins but also for the burden of sin that has built up throughout the past. The sin of king Manasseh was so severe that not even the righteousness of Josiah and his program of repentance was enough to sate God's anger (2 Kgs 23:26-27). However, there are mitigating factors to consider on this topic as well.

When we recount the law, we find warnings against idolatry—probably the most common sin in Israel's history.[104] Moses elaborates on the danger of idolatry in Deut 5 and says this:

> You shall not worship them nor serve them; for I, the Lord your God, am a jealous God, inflicting the punishment of the fathers on the children, even on the third and fourth generations of those who hate Me, but showing favor to thousands, to those who love Me and keep My commandments." (Deut 5:9-10 NASB)

On the one hand, this affirms that there *is* generational punishment for idolatry. On the other hand, it *suggests* that the sin most likely to incur divine punishment generationally is idolatry. It also clarifies that God's *mercy* is greater than God's punishment: his punishment extends unto the third or fourth generation, but his mercy to thousands.[105] This is also significant considering the life of Josiah (2 Kgs 22-23:30; 2 Chr 34-35). Though his extraordinary repentance was insufficient to permanently ward off God's wrath, God chose delay the destruction of Israel because of Josiah.

There are also what I call the "sour grapes" passages. Jeremiah prophesies, "In those days they shall no longer say: 'The fathers have eaten sour grapes, and the children's teeth are set on edge.' But everyone shall die for his own iniquity. Each man who eats sour grapes, his teeth shall be set on edge." (Jer 31:29-30 ESV; see also Ezek 18:1-4) This refutes the heretical notion that, if someone is experiencing great hardship, it *must* be due to their actions or the actions of their parents (such as in John 9:2). Hardship is not necessarily a sign of sinfulness (like Job). However, the clarification that punishment falls only on the sinner and not on their children suggests a shift in the Christian understanding of intergenerational sin that begins during the exilic period and

---

104. Boda, "Renewal in Heart, Word, and Deed," 22.

105. This sentiment is echoed in parallel passages including Exod 20:5-6, 34:6-7; Num 14:18-19; Deut 4:31, 7:9-10; Jer 32:18; Joel 2:13; Jonah 4:2; Mic 7:18-19; and Pss 30:5, 86:5, 15, 103:8-9.

culminates in the new covenant.[106] This does not mean reparations are irrelevant—Zacchaeus promised to make reparations, and reparations can still be an act of *mercy* and *love*—but it emphasizes responsibility *now* is more important than a model of "rolling punishments."

In a culture of victimhood such as ours, it is hardly surprising that a renewed zeal for punishing the children for the sins of the ancestors would surface—that is, the question of whether the descendants of sinners ought to pay the reparations required of their ancestors.[107] The challenge is to remember that the goal of reconciliation should never be to *punish* the offender but rather to restore what has been broken as much as possible.[108] Tutu recognized this when he wrote, "While the Allies could pack up and go home after Nuremberg, we in South Africa had to live with one another."[109] This is especially relevant for Americans as well. It is in situations like this—where two groups have a history of abuse towards each other (such as whites and blacks or men and women)—where compassion for our enemies leads to reconciliation more effectively than reparations.[110] The goal of reconciliation, after all, is to *close* the matter, not continue it.[111]

VI: Conclusions—Many Now Live as Enemies of the Cross of Christ

Allow me to summarize. Forgiveness is the culmination of a process wherein perpetrators are called to repent, aggrieved persons to mercifully release the perpetrator, and both to seek reconciliation together. Forgiveness is a process, but it is also an ethos. It engages individuals but also communities. It operates primarily on the agents involved but carries consequences that can last for generations. Forgiveness can require long-suffering, as it did for Joseph. *All* forgiveness stems from the preeminent mercy of God supremely demonstrated by Jesus through the cross. What remains is to set forth a practical model for how to *do* forgiveness.

---

106. I am uncomfortable either asserting or denying such a shift.
107. For example: Tisby, *Color of Compromise*, 197–200.
108. See section III above as well as chapter 3, pp. 74–7.
109. Tutu, *No Future*, 21.
110. Carson, *Love in Hard Places*, 93.
111. It is also critical to avoid the pitfall of the oppressed becoming the oppressor. See the section on liberation theology from chapter 4, pp. 100–2.

Psychological models to facilitate forgiveness (that is, release) involve treating forgiveness as a decision or as a process.[112] Decision forgiveness can be accomplished immediately from a therapeutic perspective but takes more time and effort on the part of the afflicted to take hold. Process forgiveness is not instantaneous but instead addresses the emotional, behavioral, and cognitive elements of the underlying hurt *in situ*. The typical examples are the REACH Model (decision forgiveness) and the Enright Model (process forgiveness).

REACH is an acronym standing for [R]ecall the hurt, [E]mpathize with the one who hurt you, [A]ltruism—practice empathy by offering forgiveness, [C]ommit to Forgive, [H]old on to forgiveness.[113] In contrast, the Enright model focuses on reframing the wrongdoer by contextualizing their behavior—thus allowing for the development of empathy for them. This allows the afflicted to separate the wrong from the wrongdoer and address the remaining pain through a normal grieving process—thus leading to release.[114] Both models require the gradual integration of our painful memories into our psyches—a task therapists should be prepared to assist with.[115]

We should also consider theological suggestions including boundary setting, remembering our own sins, focus on God's example, and forgiveness as a gradual process. First is the importance of boundary setting. Mayo rightly insists that many circumstances involving severe physical or emotional abuse should result in separating the perpetrator from the afflicted.[116] It is also critical for pastors and community members to work *simultaneously* for the good of the perpetrator as for the afflicted—repentance is as vital to the process of forgiveness as release, and a period of separation allows both persons to be supported.[117]

---

112. Because these models deal exclusively with the afflicted person, "forgiveness" should be understood as "release."

113. Worthington, "Pyramid Model of Forgiveness," 108.

114. Enright and Coyle, "Researching the Process Model," 145. See also: Bergin, "Three Contributions of a Spiritual Perspective," 21–32; Cunningham, "Will to Forgive," 141–49; North, "Wrongdoing and Forgiveness," 499–508.

115. Volf, *End of Memory*, 27–28, 76–78. For psychological help, I highly recommend finding a good therapist. The American Psychological Association offers a locator tool for this purpose: <locator.apa.org>.

116. Mayo, *Limits of Forgiveness*, 189; Volf, *Free of Charge*, 186.

117. Mayo, *Limits of Forgiveness*, 185, 198.

Building up the afflicted person's sense of self-worth during this separation period is also critical. Volf lists five points to consider that assist this process:

> First, we don't just happen to be in the world as products of chance or necessity; the God of love created each one of us, together with our world. Second, we are not in the world just to fend for ourselves while pursuing lives filled with as little pain and as much pleasure as possible; God has created us to live with God and one another in a communion of justice and love. Third, humanity has not been left by itself to deal with the divisive results of our deadly failures to love God and neighbor—a fissure of antagonism and suffering that taints all human history and scars individual lives; in Christ, God entered human history and through his death on the cross unalterably reconciled human beings to God and one another. Fourth, notwithstanding all appearances, rapacious time will not swallow us into nothingness; at the end of history God, who took on our finitude in Jesus Christ, will make our fragile flesh imperishable and restore true life to the redeemed, so that forever we may enjoy God, and each other in God. Fifth, the irreversibility of time will not chisel the wrongs we have suffered into the unchangeable reality of our past, the evildoer will not ultimately triumph over the victim, and suffering will not have the final word; God will expose the truth about wrongs, condemn each evil deed, and redeem both the repentant perpetrators and their victims, thus reconciling them to God and to each other.[118]

We are of infinite value to the God who suffers with us.[119] By living into these truths, we are using our time well during periods of separation and allowing boundary setting to prepare us to be reconciled with the perpetrator.

Second, whether we are the afflicted or the perpetrator, it is critical to remember our own sins (Matt 7:1-5). Even the mythopoetic "perfect victim" is a sinner in need of forgiveness. Desmond Tutu recognized this: "As I listened in the TRC to the stories of perpetrators of human rights violations, I realized how each of us has this capacity for the most awful evil—every one of us."[120] This is particularly difficult for evan-

---

118. Volf, *End of Memory*, 43–44.

119. Murphy and Hampton, *Forgiveness and Mercy*, 44; Battle, "Penitence as Practiced," 339.

120. Tutu, *No Future Without Forgiveness*, 85, 107. See especially his recounting of the murder of Stompie: Tutu, *No Future Without Forgiveness*, 134–35. See also:

gelical Protestants, given the general *lack* of teaching on "sin, judgment, and confession" and the absence of confession as a sacrament.[121] There are a few ways to do this.

For Roman Catholic and Orthodox Christians, confession (or reconciliation) is required for a healthy spiritual life.[122] Walter Kasper suggests that this has become unpopular because "younger Christians have reservations because they [do not believe they commit sins] that require confession. In addition, many contemporaries have a virtually pathological delusion of innocence. Only others or 'the system' are guilty."[123] The stigma around formal confession suggests it is misunderstood. We should not fear confession for the priest's primary role is to offer aid in *healing* what is broken—and God's forgiveness is not predicated on how badly we feel but on our ability to recognize our *need* for forgiveness.[124] I find the practice of confession also encourages me to *stop sinning!* Fundamentally, we cannot release others until we have been released, and we learn repentance in the assurance of God's forgiveness.[125]

Another practice of confession in the Orthodox tradition occurs on Reconciliation Sunday—the service that formally begins Lent. This tradition requires everyone to repent and forgive everyone else verbally and *publicly*. This has made me aware that I prefer to pretend an offense has not happened (whether against me or by my own fault) rather than practice forgiveness. Therefore, Reconciliation Sunday is essential because it reveals an important truth about the kingdom of God: God is not as interested in creating a sinless community as he is in creating a community that forgives. Surely, we have all had the experience of accidentally hurting someone by sharing an opinion that they are uncomfortable

---

Solzhenitsyn, *Gulag Archipelago*, 312. TRC is an acronym for "Truth and Reconciliation Commission."

121. Smith, "Penitential," 268, 285. While not all Protestants offer a form of confession before a priest, *some* (such as Anglicans) do. However, this is not often discussed openly, and many are unaware of this gift.

122. Chryssavgis, "Life in Abundance," 211–12; Bobrinskoy, *Compassion of the Father*, 127.

123. Kasper, *Mercy*, 165. Recall chapters 2–3, pp. 33–8, 60–1, 64–5, on how we treat others in defense of our own tribe.

124. Jesus gives authority to extend forgiveness to others in John 20:23. An interesting aspect of this passage is that Jesus further gives them authority to *retain* sins, which is another origin for the concept of "release." We might interpret this passage, "If you release the sins of any, they are released. If you retain the sins of any, they are retained." See: Cyril, "Jesus Gives to His Church," 93–94.

125. Chryssavgis, "Life in Abundance," 217, 219.

with: I express my distaste for a book, and my brother replies that it is his favorite. Though I have not *sinned* in this action, I have still wounded my brother. In situations like this, we express our sadness to the other out of love for him or her. This is only speculation, but I suspect such things might continue even in the restored kingdom of God. So, even if we *are* perfect as our heavenly Father is perfect, we *still* might need to practice forgiveness to some degree.[126] Forgiveness is not a stopgap measure on the road to perfection but an essential component thereof.

Third, we must continually mediate on the forgiveness we have received from God by the cross.[127] Volf shares how the cross allowed his mother to endure the death of one of her sons:

> The pain of [my mother's] terrible loss still lingers on, but bitterness and resentment against those who were responsible are gone. It was healed at the foot of the cross as my mother gazed on the Son who was killed and reflected about the God who forgave.[128]

The cross demonstrates God's love and concern for us amid our suffering and the reminder that nothing can separate us from God.[129] The cross is the instrument of forgiveness that in turn teaches us to forgive others even the most painful of losses.[130]

Lastly, we learn forgiveness gradually. C. S. Lewis recommends that we begin by forgiving mild sins before moving to weightier ones.[131] We must also have a healthy prayer life: partly for our own well-being and partly to practice release. We need to recognize that our *pain* and *rage*

---

126. I recognize this claim requires a concept of pain without pain, the ability to "hurt" without that sensation being damaging or unpleasant—our pain, not Gods as above, p. 94–6. Both this concept and the possibility of forgiveness in the kingdom of God are wholly theoretical, and defending either lies outside the scope of this work. The important point I am making here is that forgiveness reflects the life of the immanent Trinity—three persons engaged in selfless and sacrificial self-giving to one another for eternity—even as it is a necessary response to the fall.

127. Volf, *Free of Charge*, 180.

128. Volf, *Free of Charge*, 122.

129. The only unforgivable sin is apostasy, that is, active and continuous rejection of God. Even this may be forgiven once the sinner ceases their rejection and returns to God, see: Humphrey, "And I Shall Heal Them," 116; Keck, *Gospel of Luke*, 253–54; Lewis, *Mere Christianity*, 56; Volf, *Free of Charge*, 179.

130. Lewis, *Mere Christianity*, 45; Cryssavgis, "Life in Abundance," 217.

131. Lewis, *Mere Christianity*, 116.

belong at the feet of God (recall Ps 73).[132] I have prayed Ps 22 to share my pain with God. The Orthodox Prayer Book contains several prayers I have found helpful in this endeavor—I pray these daily.[133] Some days the prayers are no more than recitations. Other days, when the hurt has resurfaced, I must pray intentionally. Over time I have improved my ability to release my rage even in the moment of being hurt, and though my memory of the hurt has diminished little, I find the memories surface less often. In many of these cases, I cannot be "reconciled" with my enemies, but I *can* commit them to God and remember that the hurts will be addressed and the wrongs righted.

When hurts resurface, it can be tempting to believe the original act of forgiveness was false. The fact that I have to release my enemy *again* does not mean I have returned to God and snatched back what was already given to him. Rather, all of my pain needs to be laid at the feet of God, and it can take time for this pain to surface. Ultimately, the challenge is to persevere with patience for however long forgiveness takes.

VII: Testimony from Eric Irvuzumugabe

To close, let me offer a practical example of forgiveness. Battle claims, "When enticed to respond violently, African Christian spirituality has instead given the world the 'best practices' of learning how to stop abusive historical cycles all together."[134] I agree. Battle summarizes these practices:

> Instead of allowing negative circumstances to define human worth, black Christians maintained hope and a benign perspective on life. Those outside the black Christian experience can learn from the black experience that suffering is not the final definition of humanity for God's creation. . . . True reconciliation begins when victims abandon revenge and perpetrators abandon professions of innocence.[135]

This is evident in the life of Desmond Tutu and his work with the TRC in South Africa.

---

132. Bobrinskoy, *Compassion of the Father*, 85–87; Volf, *Exclusion and Embrace*, 124.
133. See appendix A for the texts of these prayers.
134. Battle, "Penitence as Practiced," 330.
135. Battle, "Penitence as Practiced," 339. See chapter 7, pp. 181–5.

One of the most extraordinary exemplars of these "best practices" is Eric Irvuzumugabe. In 1994 over seventy members of his family were murdered over three months for a single reason—they were Tutsis. The Rwandan Genocide remains a source of horror more than twenty years later, not because of the number of people killed (one-sixth that of the Holocaust) but because of the *rate* at which they were killed—at least 10,000 per day. Eric, then a teenager, survived by hiding in cypress trees with his uncles during the day—but he was lucky to survive. After the horror was ended and he returned home, Eric found himself the head of his family as the eldest survivor; a child yet responsible for his eight siblings. He did not know Jesus yet.

Bitterness consumed him in the years that followed. To support his family in their grief, he forced himself to smother his own. He became responsible for their financial well-being, and though the extended clan drew together for mutual comfort, he felt constantly cut off from his family. In his twenties, however, Eric found a church where the life of the community gave him hope that there might be healing for him. In that place, Hutus and Tutsis came together to form a *new* community before the face of God, and in that place, he encountered Jesus.

First on Jesus' agenda with Eric was *requiring him* to release the Hutus from their sin. For Erik, this was an excruciating journey. He writes, "Bitterness felt like my right as a survivor. I savored its flavor, and though I thought it was nourishing my broken heart, it was a kind of poison that God had to expel."[136] God was not always especially gentle with Eric either. He writes:

> I kept reminding God that even Hutu Christians were killers during the genocide. How could he expect me to pursue a relationship with someone who might kill me? But then I heard God speak to me in a way that silenced my rebuttals. God said, "Eric, I did speak to the Christian Hutus during the genocide, but they would not listen to me. That is why Christians acted the same as those who did not know me. If you do not listen to me, you are just like the Christian Hutus of the genocide.[137]

Today Eric works as a cabbie in Kigali, and he is the founder of Humura Ministries Rwanda, working to serve those who lived through

---

136. Irvuzumugabe and Lawrence, *My Father, Maker of the Trees*, 158. Sounds a lot like Jimmy; see pp. 16–18, 58–9.

137. Irvuzumugabe and Lawrence, *My Father, Maker of the Trees*, 160–61.

the genocide and to teach them to seek peace with one another through forgiveness.

That Eric would rise out of the horrors of Rwanda with *forgiveness* for his enemies should be both encouragement and a warning to all. We should be encouraged that anyone could learn to forgive such *unimaginable* horrors as he experienced. We should also be warned, knowing that if even genocide may be forgiven, there is no forgiveness for the one who steadfastly refuses to forgive—something that has become all too common in our relentless pursuit of justice.[138] Amon Goeth's failure need not be ours.

Even so, the challenges involved in forgiving our enemies remain daunting. Is there nothing else that can be done to ease that difficulty? In the following chapter, I will suggest one option: practicing gratitude.

---

138. Tisby, "White Christians, Do Not Cheapen the Hug." Tisby's commentary here is entirely appropriate *only if* he is addressing black Americans who are *not* Christian. His choice to omit this clarification tacitly extends permission to black Christians to *withhold* release based on their emotional state, which is antithetical to Jesus' teachings. His conclusion also follows the improper understanding of justice that seeks a utopian society free from sin and pain discussed in chapter 3, pp. 74–7.

Chapter 6: **To Whisper a Doxology in the Darkness**

Loving Our Enemies by Practicing Gratitude

> How sharper than a serpent's tooth it is to have a thankless child!—William Shakespeare[1]

I: Introduction

ON THE SIXTH SUNDAY of Easter, Anglicans celebrate Rogation Sunday. Though occasionally a day of prayer and fasting for God's mercy, Rogation Sunday celebrates the harvest. The collect for Rogation Sunday reads:

> Almighty God, Lord of heaven and earth: We humbly pray that thy gracious providence may give and preserve to our use the harvests of the land and of the seas, and may prosper all who labor to gather them, that we, *who constantly receive good things from thy hand, may always give thee thanks*; through Jesus Christ our Lord, who liveth and reigneth with thee and the Holy Spirit, one God, forever and ever. Amen.[2]

For urban people, such a practice might seem odd. Why thank God for something that happens naturally?

Moreover, what does gratitude have to do with loving our enemies? Surely our enemies give us very little for which we should be grateful! Gratitude might not be a component of loving our enemies, but the two are intimately connected. Gratitude looks *backward* into our past to find

---

1. Shakespeare, *King Lear*, 64.
2. Episcopal Church, *Book of Common Prayer*, 207, emphasis mine.

CHAPTER 6: TO WHISPER A DOXOLOGY IN THE DARKNESS   147

something to look *forward* to in our future. This in turn generates hope, and hope undergirds compassion and forgiveness. Additionally, though scholars have bemoaned our failure to lament, giving thanks is a *commandment* that we have sorely neglected (Phil 4:4–6; 1 Thess 5:16–18). Most importantly, gratitude is a counteragent to many sins, especially bitterness (Rom 1:21, 28–32).[3] Thus, to love our enemies and stave off bitterness, we must practice gratitude.

This topic requires me to address two questions: "Is gratitude an action or an emotion?" and, "Is gratitude a matter of repaying a debt or merely recognition of an unmerited gift?" Afterwards, I will discuss the role of gratitude in the Torah, and how this is developed in the New Testament—particularly through the Eucharist. Lastly, I will illustrate how gratitude aided Corrie and Betsie ten Boom while incarcerated in Ravensbrück concentration camp.

First, it should be clear that we live in a society that struggles with gratitude. Assuming gratitude to be a matter of *emotion*, we are hesitant to go beyond superficial statements of "thanks, dude" upon receiving something unexpected; otherwise, we risk being inauthentic.[4] We can experience resentfulness upon receiving an unsolicited gift, concerned that the gift obligates us to some future action.[5] Gifts have symbolic value, so we expect gifts to incorporate something of the giver, but this demands greater thought from the giver.[6] If we become too used to gifts,

---

3. Leithart, *Gratitude*, 136. See also: Hannah Arendt, cited in DeCort, *Bonhoeffer's New Beginning*, 28. The Romans passage reads: "For though they knew God, they did not honor him as God or give thanks to him, but they became futile in their thinking, and their senseless minds were darkened . . . . and since they did not see fit to acknowledge God, God gave them up to a debased mind and to things that should not be done. They were filled with every kind of wickedness, evil, covetousness, malice. Full of envy, murder, strife, deceit, craftiness, they are gossips, slanderers, God-haters, insolent, haughty, boastful, inventors of evil, rebellious toward parents, foolish, faithless, heartless, ruthless. They know God's decree, that those who practice such things deserve to die—yet they not only do them but even applaud others who practice them" (NRSVA). Although bitterness is not mentioned explicitly, it is implied through the descriptors, which are consistent with Nietzsche's description of *ressentiment* (see chapter 3). See further the possible connection to Asaph as a "brute beast" (Ps 73:22) in Rom 1:23—"they exchanged the glory of the immortal God for images resembling a mortal human being or *birds or four-footed animals or reptiles*" (NRSVA, possibly referring to animals that were ceremonially unclean).

4. Pao, *Thanksgiving*, 19; Leithart, *Gratitude*, 2, 4, 120.

5. Leithart, *Gratitude*, 45–47, 121. Cicero went so far as to insist that a *return* gift should be more valuable than the first, representing a cycle of escalating extravagance that was morally required.

6. Leithart, *Gratitude*, 16, 219. See also: Gasset, *Revolt of the Masses*, 36–39.

we may develop a sense of entitlement. However, because Scripture does *not* prioritize the emotional component of gratitude, these emotional concerns should be irrelevant to us.

Modern society typically presumes that our feelings dictate our actions. The Bible assumes that our actions *train* our emotions: fake it 'til you make it. Therefore, gratitude functions regardless of our emotions.[7] David Pao summarizes this well:

> When thanksgiving is grounded on salvation history, the call to give thanks is no longer understood primarily in psychological terms. In an age when spirituality is defined primarily through the lens of subjective sentimentalism, and, even more fundamentally, of postmodern epistemology, the Pauline call to thanksgiving as an act of remembering God through his mighty acts provides a much needed correction in our understanding of the development of our lives in the Spirit.[8]

Therefore, gratitude requires that we do more than reverse our emotional equation, we must redirect all gratitude to an external third party.[9] Gratitude teaches us to recognize that God is the ultimate source of all good and our rightful sovereign, and to respond appropriately.[10]

Second is the issue of reciprocity. Greek culture required all gifts to be reciprocated. This is also reflected in Pagan worship—sacrifices were made to the gods to secure their favor, notably rain. Such a system only leaves the recipient free to choose *when* they reciprocate.[11] This we might describe as a sort of "economy of giving." Gifts are a form of currency, given to obligate someone to give me something in the future. From this perspective, gifts are manipulative rather than loving.[12]

Christian gratitude differs in that it is tempered by a sort of outside interference: that of our creator (Jas 1:17). For the Christian, *all* gifts ultimately come from God—everything that we give to others or even to God is a sort of *regifting* of something that we have received from God (Ps 50:9–13). Thus, every instance of gift-giving is triangular: both the giver and the recipient owe thanks to God in recognition that even the

---

7. Notice the similarity with forgiveness—it is something that we do because it is right and we are commanded to do so, not because we *feel* like it.

8. Pao, *Thanksgiving*, 85.

9. O'Donovan, *Entering into Rest*, 80.

10. Pao, *Thanksgiving*, 88.

11. Leithart, *Gratitude*, 20–25.

12. This is one possible reason for modern societies' discomfort with giving.

gift being given is already a gift.¹³ This also means that the only gift we can offer to God is a verbal expression of thanks.¹⁴

This is not to say that Christianity has never recognized an economy of giving but that Christian giving has typically been understood as totally unmerited.¹⁵ To give a gift brought with it no obligations for the future. Instead, Scripture instructs us to give from unrestrained generosity (Ps 112:9; Acts 4:32–35). This kind of free giving was so alien to Greek culture that the emperor Diocletian accused Christians of being wholly *un*grateful, "an odd charge to level against a faith that places almost supreme value on thankfulness."¹⁶ Although the concept of unmerited giving is difficult, it is essential. It demonstrates a culture that views gratitude (and generosity) with the highest regard.

For these reasons, Christian giving can be somewhat puzzling. Gifts are unmerited, so *regifting* is not an obligation. Moreover, regifting does not discharge our gratitude. Therefore, gratitude to others is a call to humility and acceptance, like a child to their parents or citizens to a benevolent ruler. A simple "thanks" will suffice because no gift can repay God, the true giver. Generosity is a separate commandment meaning that the tightwad who *never* gives *is* failing in their obligation. However, gratitude for *all* gifts is due to God, meaning we can only regift what we receive. No wonder Diocletian perceived Christians to be ungrateful!¹⁷

---

13. Leithart, *Gratitude*, 7, 68; Pao, *Thanksgiving*, 19–21.

14. Leithart, *Gratitude*, 42; DeSilva, *Hebrews*, 12; Volf, *Free of Charge*, 45, 62; Pao, *Thanksgiving*, 16–17. Leithart cites the work of Paul Boobyer, who (inappropriately) argues that praising and thanking God somehow increases his glory. All of this comes with a caveat, as will be seen later; God has even gifted us with the gift of being able to regift to God in a display of gratitude—the "thank offering" first and now our participation in the Eucharist. It is also worth noting that this display of gratitude is both sign and substance of the ultimate gift we give to God: ourselves. Even this is fundamentally a regifting, for we receive our lives from God as a gift. "No one can by any means redeem another or give God a ransom for him—for the redemption of his soul is priceless, and he should cease imagining forever . . . But God will redeem my soul from the power of Sheol, for he will receive me" (Ps 49:7–8, 15 NASB).

15. Leithart, *Gratitude*, 65–68, 92–94. Early Judaism experienced difficulty understanding giving as wholly unmerited, and Thomas Aquinas embraced an economy of giving. Leithart criticizes Aquinas for presenting a view of gratitude and gift-giving that is not especially "Christian."

16. Leithart, *Gratitude*, 58.

17. Particularly understandable, seeing as he would not have been the recipient of many gifts beyond the gift of prayer (significant on its own) given his persecution of the church.

II: I Will Raise Up the Cup of Salvation

Lev 2–7; Deut 26; Pss 30; 73; 75; 92; 116; 136

We now turn from an overview of gratitude to specific requirements of gratitude in Scripture. Pao writes, "As a covenant people, we are to look to God as the source of all power and goodness, and we need to "practice" acts of remembering as we move our attention away from our "self" as the criterion of truth to what God did for us through his beloved son."[18] Both testaments include instructions on how to do this.

The Torah offered specific instructions on how to thank God correctly. This was to be done in worship.[19] The worshiper would offer further sacrifices after the sin, guilt, and whole burnt sacrifices. The two relevant offerings are the dedication offering or *minḥâ* (מִנְחָה) and the peace offering or *šelem* (שֶׁלֶם)—as well as an elaborate ceremony involving elements of both, called the *tôḏâ* (תּוֹדָה).[20] I will discuss these in order.

Allen Ross explains the dedication offering: "All who received [God's] gracious provision of atonement realized that they belonged to God and owed him a debt of gratitude they could never repay. But God also opened a way for worshippers to pay that gratitude in token by the "dedication offering" (*minḥâ*; Lev. 2)."[21] The peace offering was typically the capstone of worship. The sacrifice was made to signify and celebrate God's forgiveness, whereby the worshiper achieved *peace* with God. Therefore, a portion of the sacrifice was returned to the worshiper to eat. God played host to the worshiper at a banquet.[22] The *tôḏâ* offering combined elements of *both*. Therefore, while the dedication and peace offerings could be made anytime, more elaborate preparations were necessary for the *tôḏâ*.[23]

---

18. Pao, *Thanksgiving*, 85.

19. See chapter 4, p. 110. See also: Guthrie, *Theology as Thanksgiving*, 18, 41–43. Review chapter 4, p. 112n100; and chapter 5, pp. 124–5n44 and 49 for a review on the nature of worship. See also: Ross, *Recalling the Hope of Glory*, 198–201; Guthrie, *Theology as Thanksgiving*, 18, 41–43.

20. Ross, *Recalling the Hope of Glory*, 201–4; Lindsay, "*Tôḏâ* and Eucharist," 83–100; Löhr, "Eucharist and Jewish Ritual Meals," 468–83; Gese, "Origin of the Lord's Supper," 117. See also: Longman III, *Immanuel in Our Place*, 77–92.

21. Ross, *Recalling the Hope of Glory*, 201.

22. Ross, *Recalling the Hope of Glory*, 202–4; Longman, *Immanuel in Our Place*, 90–91; Bailey, *Jesus Through Middle Eastern Eyes*, 256–57. See also: Gen 18:1–16; Exod 22:21; Lev 19:17–18, 34; Deut 10:19; Luke 7:36–50.

23. Longman, *Immanuel in Our Place*, 86–89.

The *tôḏâ* was the proper response to delivery from hardship. When suffering, the worshiper was expected to entreat God's deliverance. This constituted a vow before God that would have to be repaid.²⁴ Once God had delivered them, the worshiper would come to the temple or tabernacle and make a *peace offering*. While the sacrifice was being offered, the worshiper would tell the rest of the community (in elaborate detail) what their hardship had been, how God had rescued them, and would declare that they had come to the temple to fulfill their vow to God—it was not uncommon for them to exaggerate by describing their travails in terms of life and death.²⁵ Afterward, the entire community would share in the peace offering. This was no mere "self-help" ritual or means of maintaining "positive vibes"—it was a biblical *requirement* and a source of *identity*.²⁶

Gratitude was also practiced in Israel's festival celebrations, particularly Pentecost and Sukkoth (the festival of booths or harvest festival, sometimes called the festival of "ingathering").²⁷ On Pentecost, when the crops were harvested, the worshiper would travel to Jerusalem to present their first fruits.²⁸ Deuteronomy 26 instructs the worshiper to bring a basket of their first crops and offer them to the priest with the declaration that God had fulfilled his promise to bring the children of Israel into the land promised them and proceed by telling the story:

> My father was a wandering Aramean, and he went down to Egypt and resided there, few in number; but there he became a great, mighty, and populous nation. And the Egyptians treated

---

24. Psalm 7 might be an example of this, see: Ps 7:17—"I will give thanks to the Lord according to his righteousness and will sing praise to the name of the Lord Most High," following a list of laments. See also: Ps 28, which might be a vow (vs. 1–5) and a response (vs. 6–9).

25. Guthrie, *Theology as Thanksgiving*, 8. For example, Ps 118 pits the psalmist against all the nations they defeated.

26. Ross, *Recalling the Hope of Glory*, 271–75; Rowley, *Worship in Ancient Israel*, 123; Lindsay, "*Tôḏâ* and Eucharist," 86–87.

27. Ross, *Recalling the Hope of Glory*, 229, 231–34, 237–38; Longman, *Immanuel in Our Place*, 191–92, 196–98; see: Exod 34:22; Lev 23:9–14; Num 29:12–40.

28. I have found conflicting arguments about the precise timing of this. Some suggest that this occurred at the end of Passover, while others that it occurred during Pentecost. This is not the most significant distinction, given that the two feasts were closely related. Still, I am inclined to see the connection between Deut 26 and Lev 23 as indicating that the first fruits ceremony would have been celebrated on Pentecost. Longman, *Immanuel in Our Place* 190–92; Ross, *Recalling the Hope of Glory*, 231–34; Block, *For the Glory of God*, 290.

us badly and oppressed us, and imposed hard labor on us. Then we cried out to the Lord, the God of our fathers, and the Lord heard our voice and saw our wretched condition, our trouble, and our oppression; and the Lord brought us out of Egypt with a mighty hand, an outstretched arm, and with great terror, and with signs and wonders; and he has brought us to this place, and has given us this land, a land flowing with milk and honey. And now behold, I have brought the first of the produce of the ground which You, Lord have given me. (Deut 26:5-10 NASB)

This story was not just an annual ceremony; it was a "pledge of allegiance," a symbol of shared identity.[29] It was a sort of *tôḏâ* that was both personal and corporate.

Every three years additional giving was required: to the Levites (the priestly caste), sojourners, widows, and orphans—the stereotypical poor in Scripture (Deut 26:12).[30] The celebration would conclude with a double peace offering and the associated feast. To express gratitude together was insufficient—the community was required to be charitable.[31]

Sukkoth was the celebration of the *end* of the harvest season. It doubled as a celebration of all they had received from God and a reminder of their years wandering in the desert. As Sukkoth signaled the beginning of the dry season, this reminder was meant to be carried through the coming months that God had personally cared for the Israelites by giving them mana and quail when there was *no* harvest to gather (Exod 16). Sukkoth was also an excellent opportunity to celebrate *tôḏâ*.

Through these, the Israelites were taught the correct posture for worship, and they were *reminded* how to prepare their hearts for worship. Whether or not you felt grateful was irrelevant—the choice to submit to God in obedience through submitting to the ceremony (which would cost the value of the animal to be sacrificed) was a start.[32]

Gratitude is reflected in the Psalms, particularly Ps 30.[33] Psalm 30 begins with a declaration that God has saved the psalmist from their

---

29. Recall chapter 2, pp. 33-6, 45-6.

30. This was part of a broader list of practices to care for the poor, such as leaving the corners of your field untouched for gleaning; see: Lev 23:22.

31. Ross, *Recalling the Hope of Glory*, 231-34; Longman, *Immanuel in Our Place*, 191-92. Though the *date* is the same as the Christian celebration, this was a somewhat different holiday—more on this later.

32. See also O'Donovan, *Entering into Rest*, 73-75.

33. Sigmund Mowinckel points out that there is little distinction between "praise" and "thanksgiving" in Hebrew. As there is no word for "thanks" in Hebrew, the word

CHAPTER 6: TO WHISPER A DOXOLOGY IN THE DARKNESS   153

enemies and brought healing. It exhorts the surrounding assembly to give praise to God due his name. It then describes a wholly self-centered person: "As for me, I had said in my prosperity 'I shall never be moved'" (vs. 6 NASB). God responded by removing this security from them (vs. 7). Finally, it concludes with a restatement of gratitude to God for having brought the psalmist through this season of God's absence. The psalmist has learned to put their trust more fully in God (contrast vs. 6 and 10).[34] The psalmist has received the healing of their *soul* and deliverance from material hardship (vs. 1). Psalm 30 holds this similarity with Ps 73: although he was *his own* enemy, God delivered Asaph from his bitterness and restored him to a life of fullness, and the psalmist recognizes this *in worship*.

It is also worth noting a shared image in Pss 75 and 116—a cup raised. While both of these are psalms of Thanksgiving, the imagery of the cup plays two different roles. In Ps 75:8, God holds a cup of spiced wine that he pours out on the wicked in punishment.[35] This act is connected with the wicked "lifting up their horn" in verses 5 and 10.[36] In these verses, the psalmist (or perhaps God) warns the wicked *not* to raise up their horn—this as a symbol of arrogant defiance against God.[37] However, in verse 10, the psalmist has a *double* parallel—"He [God] will

---

"*tôdâ*" combines both praise and thanksgiving. See: Mowinckel, *Psalms in Israel's Worship*, 26; Guthrie, *Theology as Thanksgiving*, 13–14; Pao, *Thanksgiving*, 25–27; Brueggemann, *David's Truth in Israel's Imagination*. With this in mind, psalms of thanksgiving typically begin with the word "*tôdâ*" or "give thanks!" Note that the special grain offering (*minḥâ*), called the "thank offering," carries the same name in Hebrew. Second, psalms of thanksgiving tend to rely on the perfect verbal tense (always past tense) or consecutive, whereas the songs of praise rely on the imperfect tense (present or future) and the imperative tense. This illustrates the nature of thanksgiving as past-oriented. Lastly, psalms that are meant to be used with the tôdâ offering will likely include reference to repaying of vows (in Hebrew נֶדֶר *nadār*). Guthrie, *Theology as Thanksgiving*, 6–7. Psalms that I am comfortable classifying as thanksgiving include 18, 30, 32, 37, 40, 65, 66, 67, 73, 75, 92, 107, 116, 118, 136, and 138. Psalm 75 is a stretch but should at least be recognized as a *corporate* psalm of thanksgiving. See Mowinckel, *Psalms in Israel's Worship*, 26–43.

34. "Now as for me, I said in my prosperity, "I will never be moved."" (vs. 6) against "Hear, Lord, and be gracious to me; Lord, be my helper." (vs. 10)

35. See also Jer 49:12.

36. The Hebrew word for horn, "*qeren*" (קֶרֶן) does not just mean a literal animal horn. It is a sign of strength and power. See: Brown et al., *Hebrew and English Lexicon of the Old Testament*, 901–2; Harris et al., *Theological Wordbook of the Old Testament*, 815–816.

37. Perhaps as a mirror to the vain plotting of the wicked in Ps 2—a crucial starting point to the entire Psalter. See also footnote 36 above.

cut off the horns of the wicked, but the horns of the righteous will be lifted up." The latter is consistent with the imagery of gratitude that the psalm begins with. So we see God humbling the wicked and exalting the lowly—the reason for the psalmist's gratitude.[38]

In Ps 116, we find another cup raised—this time in the hand of the psalmist.[39] In response to God's goodness, the psalmist writes, "What shall I repay to the Lord for all his benefits to me? I will lift up the cup of salvation, and call upon the name of the Lord. I will pay my vows to the Lord in the presence of all his people!" (Ps 116:12–14 NASB). Surely this is the *alternative* cup to that which the wicked receive—a cup filled with God's salvation from our troubles—and an image of *tôḏâ*. We also raise a cup—one filled with *both* suffering and redemption—one containing God himself.

III: Properly Celebrating God's Blessings

Luke 17:11–19; Acts 2:17–21

Tôḏâ is found in the New Testament as well.[40] In this section, I will highlight two prominent examples: the gratitude of the Samarian leper (Luke 17:11–19) and the Eucharist—our essential act of *tôḏâ*.[41]

In Luke 17, we find Jesus and his disciples traveling between Samaria and Galilee on their way to Jerusalem. As they go, a group of people with leprosy come to them and, staying at a distance (Lev 13:45–46), cry out for mercy from Jesus, the "master." Luke uses *epistata* (Ἐπιστάτα) rather than *kyrios* (κύριος) or "Lord," for they do not recognize Jesus as God.

In response to their cry, Jesus instructs them to go and show themselves to the priests (Lev 14:1–32). Per the law, a priest will examine them. If the priest finds the person free of leprosy, they will perform a cleansing ceremony: the ritual of the birds. After that, the person may enter society, but he or she may not enter their home or worship for

---

38. See Mary's *Magnificat*, Luke 1:46–56, particularly vs. 53.

39. Orthodox Christians pray Pss 116 and 23 (115 and 22 in the Septuagint) before celebrating the Eucharist because of this connection. See: Mikitish and Herman, *Orthodox Christian Prayers*, 139–40. Both psalms are also popular as hymn texts.

40. Guthrie, *Theology as Thanksgiving*, 143–44.

41. Guthrie, *Theology as Thanksgiving*, 188–89.

a week.⁴² After that, they are free to enter into worship and give their thanks to God for the healing they have received.

On his way to Mount Gerazim, a Samaritan notices he has been healed.⁴³ We expect him to react by changing from a walk to a run to arrive at the temple as soon as possible and request an inspection.⁴⁴ He does not do this. Instead, we read, "Now one of them, when he saw that he had been healed, turned back, *glorifying God* with a loud voice, and he *fell on his face at [Jesus'] feet, giving thanks to him.*" (Luke 17:15–16 NRSVA) This is an extraordinary parallelism! The juxtaposition of glorifying *God* with giving thanks to *Jesus* is unmistakable. The praise and thanks that are due to *God* are also due to *Jesus*.⁴⁵ The "master" has become the "Lord" (*Epistata* [Ἐπιστάτα] to *Kyrios* [κύριος]). The one who stood at a distance now throws himself at Jesus' feet while the other nine go away.⁴⁶ As Paul before Ananias, the scales fall from his eyes and the Samaritan recognizes his God.

Jesus offers a peculiar response, asking, "'Were not ten made clean? But the other nine, where are they? Was none of them found to return and give praise to God except this foreigner?'" (Luke 17:18–19 NRSVA) Richard Hays suggests that Luke tends to "break the fourth wall." Luke lets us peek behind the screen to see the spiritual trends unfolding behind the drama.⁴⁷ I interpret this as Jesus addressing *us* as if to ask, "Do you see what has happened here? Do you understand what this Samaritan has recognized and why he acted this way?"

The Samaritan's actions demonstrate that he *did* recognize that the thanks and praise he owed to God—which could *only* be given at the temple before the incarnation—could be given by turning around and returning to the man who had healed him.⁴⁸ Instead of waiting to offer a *tôdâ* in the temple, he offers it to Jesus immediately. He does not think it over first. It is so deeply ingrained into him through his cultural identity

---

42. Ross, *Recalling the Hope of Glory*, 205.

43. Recall chapter 4, p. 105: he is not allowed to worship in Jerusalem after the temple was defiled just before Jesus' birth when Samaritans sneaked into the temple before Passover and scattered dead body parts throughout.

44. Guthrie, *Theology as Thanksgiving*, 10.

45. Kasper, *Mercy*, 113.

46. Others appear to have had similar recognitions about Jesus' identity, such as the woman in Luke 7:35–50. See: Bailey, *Jesus Through Middle Eastern Eyes*, 251, 258–59.

47. Hays, *Reading Backwards*, 54–55.

48. Remember that the temple is the place where God dwells on earth—the *only* place someone can go to fellowship with God properly.

that gratitude almost bursts out of him. Jesus accepts the man's gift—the only thing the Samaritan could offer—and sends him off in peace.

In such a culture, it would be foolish to assume that the institution of the Eucharist—the church's act of thanksgiving—arose in a vacuum.[49] While there is ongoing debate as to the full origins of the Eucharist, several traditions might be components.[50] Among these include the Passover meal, the sacrificial system (particularly for the forgiveness of sins), ratification of the covenant, the *tôdâ*, the scapegoat, and remembrance of Christ's crucifixion.[51] The Eucharist substitutes for many of the requirements of the law—forgiveness of sins, the New Exodus, assurance of our peace with God, and our offering of *gratitude*—hence the term "Eucharist," our "thanksgiving."[52]

Some believe the *tôdâ* is not part of the origin of the Eucharist. However, this is primarily due to the desire to find a *single* inspiration. As Daniel Block's interpretation of *multiple* origin points eliminates this need, I am comfortable accepting the *tôdâ* as *one* inspiration behind the Eucharist.[53]

How then does the *tôdâ* influence the Eucharist? Both combine the grain offering and the peace offering, both include the consumption of bread and wine, both are celebrated in community, and both emphasize overcoming a spiritual struggle by the intervention of God.[54] However, it is *Jesus* who is celebrating a *tôdâ*—not in remembrance of something

---

49. Gese, "Origin of the Lord's Supper," 117.

50. Löhr, "Eucharist and Jewish Ritual Meals," 468–83. He rejects the possibility of the *tôdâ* as the origin of the Eucharist. He points out that the *tôdâ* does not account for every aspect of the Last Supper and the resulting Eucharist, but he ignores the possibility that the Eucharist has multiple origins.

51. Block, *For the Glory of God*, 157–58; Ross, *Recalling the Hope of Glory*, 235–36, 391–96; Lindsay, "*Tôdâ* and Eucharist"; Löhr, "Eucharist and Jewish Ritual Meals," 468. Though I have read no argument to this effect to date, I believe that Yom Kippur—the Day of Atonement—is also a potential inspiration, particularly the scapegoat. The high priest would select an unblemished goat, place his hand on its head, and speak over it all of the sins of the people gathered. The goat would then be released into the wilderness to carry off the sins of the people. I believe one aspect of Jesus' crucifixion that must be recognized is that Jesus is *our* scapegoat. Instead of a goat, we receive God incarnate. Instead of carrying the sins of the people, he carries the sins of the world. Instead of carrying the sins into the wilderness, he carries them into death itself—note that Jesus is the one man who dies for the people (as per Caiaphas) and dies outside the city.

52. Ross, *Recalling the Hope of Glory*, 396–97; Leithart, *Gratitude*, 19; Pao, *Thanksgiving*, 15.

53. Block, *For the Glory of God*, 157–59.

54. Lindsay, "*Tôdâ* and Eucharist," 85–87.

CHAPTER 6: TO WHISPER A DOXOLOGY IN THE DARKNESS

in his *past* but rather in anticipation of the trial he will begin later that evening.[55] Our celebration of the Eucharist today is a recurring celebration with *Jesus* for what he has done—but it also reminds us that *we* have much to be thankful for too. We are permitted to celebrate God's *tôdâ* as our own. Alexander Schmemann writes:

> When man stands before the throne of God, when he has fulfilled all that God has given him to fulfill, when all sins are forgiven, all joy restored, then there is nothing else for him to do but to give thanks. Eucharist (thanksgiving) is the state of perfect man. Eucharist is the life of paradise. Eucharist is the only full and real response of man to God's creation, redemption and gift of heaven. But this perfect man who stands before God is *Christ*.[56]

The Eucharist is both Jesus' *tôdâ* and the church's *tôdâ*—our *tôdâ*.[57]

The New Testament recapitulates the feast of Pentecost too. Recall that Pentecost involves two opportunities for thanksgiving: The gift of first fruits and the opportunity for participation in the *tôdâ* ritual. Although the gift of the Holy Spirit outshines these elements, God reveals Pentecost as a celebration of our new life in the resurrected Christ—including the twofold acts of thanksgiving.

If the Eucharist was Jesus' *tôdâ*, then what were the first fruits of his harvest? Surely the first fruits of Jesus' harvest are his disciples—the men and women who followed him and handed on his teachings (John 17:6-8, 12). Thus, on Pentecost, we see Jesus' disciples offered (as if in a sacrifice) as Jesus' first fruits.[58] They are set on fire by the Holy Spirit yet do not burn: a "living sacrifice" (Dan 3; Acts 2:3; Rom 12:1).

Peter's speech is also noteworthy. He explains the strange events by quoting Joel 2:28-32.[59] However, Joel 2:28 does not read "in the last days," as Peter says, but "after this." Which raises the question, "After *what*?" Earlier in Joel 2, we find a list of the hardships Israel will endure (vs. 1-17), followed by a *turning point*. Joel's description reads:

---

55. Lindsay, "*Tôdâ* and Eucharist," 89-90.
56. Schmemann, *For the Life of the World*, 37-38.
57. Guthrie, *Theology as Thanksgiving*, 188-189.
58. Pao, *Thanksgiving*, 100-101.
59. Notice that Peter does *not* include vs. 32, which speaks of God's salvation *only* on Mount Zion. This is no longer true.

> Then the Lord will be zealous for his land, and will have compassion for his people. The Lord will answer and say to his people, "Behold, I am going to send you grain, new wine, and oil, and you will be satisfied *in full* with them; and I will never again make you a disgrace among the nations. . . . Do not fear, land; shout for joy and rejoice, for the Lord has done great things. Do not fear, animals of the field, for the pastures of the wilderness have turned green, for the tree has produced its fruit, the fig tree and the vine have yielded in full. So shout for joy, you sons of Zion, and rejoice in the Lord your God; for he has given you the early rain for *your* vindication. And he has brought down for you the rain, the early and latter rain as before. The threshing floors will be full of grain, and the vats will overflow with the new wine and oil. Then I will compensate you for the years that the swarming locust has eaten, the creeping locust, the stripping locust, and the gnawing locust—my great army which I sent among you. You will have plenty to eat and be satisfied, and you will praise the name of the Lord your God, who has dealt wondrously with you; then My people will never be put to shame. So you will know that I am in the midst of Israel, and that I am the Lord your God and there is no other; and My people will never be put to shame. (Joel 2:18–19, 21–27 NASB)

God will send grain, wine, and oil (appearing *twice*). The land and animals will celebrate *the harvest*. These promises are followed with the greater promise—that the Holy Spirit will be *poured out* on God's people, a promise that Peter declares is fulfilled on Pentecost. I cannot help but notice a similarity between the *rain* that is to be poured out for the nourishing of the harvest and the pouring out of the *Holy Spirit*—both to accept the disciples as Jesus' first fruits offering in fire and to nourish the work of the church seeking a new and greater harvest: to make disciples of all nations. To that end, some three thousand new followers of Jesus were baptized that day (Acts 2:41). This is the fruit of the first harvest of the *church*.[60]

Pentecost remains a celebration of God's bounty to us and an opportunity to give back to God from what we have received, but now God's bounty is the Holy Spirit, and the gifts we offer to God in gratitude are our *selves*. We also continue to participate in Jesus' *tôḏâ* offering—a celebration of his ministry and the fruits of that ministry: the founders of the church of which we are members two thousand years later.

---

60. Longman, *Immanuel in Our Place*, 191–96.

CHAPTER 6: TO WHISPER A DOXOLOGY IN THE DARKNESS   159

IV: Conclusion—Testimony and Generosity

Today we celebrate the Eucharist as our *tôḏâ*, but how else are we to give thanks to God? We should consider the ways in which the *tôḏâ* encouraged more specific acts of thanksgiving than the Eucharist does and how we might benefit from more specific acts of sharing in our communities. We may also practice *generosity* as the natural counterpart to gratitude. As we learn how to practice these, we will see how they help us combat bitterness.

The *tôḏâ* implicitly expects four things: (1) God *will respond* to our prayers and deliver us from our trouble (though not always in the way we expect; (2) therefore, we need to make our petitions known to God and then watch for his deliverance with *anticipation*; (3) when God inevitably delivers us from trials, we are *obligated* to share the story of God's deliverance *in community*, and (4) this story should be *personal*. Although the Eucharist incorporates these (as the Eucharist capitulates the entire sacrificial system), they are easy to miss. We must also learn a eucharistic *attitude*.

Therefore, we should engender a culture that anticipates God's action. Oliver O'Donovan writes, "That God is at work there is hardly a thesis to be questioned; it would not be the work of an omnipotent God to allow society simply to go its own way—if we can even imagine what that might mean."[61] I started to understand this during my graduate studies when I realized that I was *survival-oriented*. I assumed that God only cares *that* I arrive before him, not about *how* I arrive. Psalm 91:14–16 says, "Because he has loved me [God], I will save him; I will set him *securely* on high, because he has known my [God's] name. He will call upon me [God], and I will answer him; I will be with him in trouble; I will rescue him and honor him. I will satisfy him with a long life, and show him my [God's] salvation" (NASB). God promises these things to *us*. If we believe that God is not content with survival, that he wants us to *thrive*, then we need to act accordingly.

One way we could do this is to share *our* stories of God's deliverance with the community. Public testimony of gratitude is for the community as much as the one testifying.[62] This fulfills Paul's commandment

---

61. O'Donovan, *Entering into Rest*, 93. Deism is the "clock-maker" model of faith: God created a long time ago and set the world spinning, but he has not been involved with it since ancient times, see also: O'Donovan, *Entering into Rest*, 76.

62. DeSilva, *Hebrews*, 46.

to encourage one another (Eph 4:29; Heb 3:13; 10:25; 1 Thess 5:11).[63] Similar encouragement may be found in hagiography—the stories of the saints—and the Scriptures.[64] We could create space for public testimony, encourage one another in hardship, and seek out encouragement from our ancestors. This is also one of the few potential *values* I find in social media—the opportunity to receive encouragement from faithful Christians across the globe who might be suffering more than I am, to be able to pray for them and to bid their prayers on our behalf.[65]

In practical terms, public sharing should first reinforce the importance of regular celebration and participation in the Eucharist—our *tôdâ*. Leithart writes, "We must learn what it means to offer a continuous sacrifice of thanksgiving. Above all, the church must restore its ritual of gift and gratitude, the Eucharist, to its historically central place in worship, piety, and communal life, and Christians must learn how to practice a continuous Eucharist."[66] As practicing forgiveness through regular prayer and "baby steps" was the way to begin to forgive, participation in the Eucharist is the first step of learning gratitude. This is especially important for Protestant traditions that do not regularly celebrate the Eucharist or for believers concerned about receiving the Eucharist *too often*.

It would be difficult to share our blessings in public if we did not reflect on them in private. My family does this together during morning prayer (when we can all gather) by thinking back to the previous day and sharing things we were blessed by. We need not *feel* blessed; we merely recognize the good in the previous day. Another option is to keep a journal. Both of these options are summarized in the Ignatian practice of the daily examen.[67] This practice requires careful and prayerful examination of the previous day, asking God to reveal to us those things for which

---

63. O'Donovan, *Entering into Rest*, 77.

64. O'Donovan, *Entering into Rest*, 79–80; Pao, *Thanksgiving*, 37.

65. International stories should not replace local sharing. Local sharing should be the primary focus, given how much more personal it is to hear testimony from someone you can interact with physically. On this matter, I'm afraid I have to disagree with DeSilva, *Hebrews*, 96.

66. Leithart, *Gratitude*, 229.

67. Ignatius, *Spiritual Exercises of Saint Ignatius*, 50. The daily examen has been adapted for use under various circumstances (including particularly for gratitude) but originates primarily as a means of reviewing and discerning sin. A description of the adapted technique may be found here: Ignatian Spirituality, "Daily Examen," http://www.ignatianspirituality.com/ignatian-prayer/the-examen. I also recommend Thibodeaux, *Reimagining the Ignatian Examen*.

CHAPTER 6: TO WHISPER A DOXOLOGY IN THE DARKNESS

we should be thankful, those elements that moved us most deeply, and preparation for the day to come. Any of these would encourage greater awareness of God's blessings in our lives.

To share their blessings in public, some church traditions practice public testimony. Others might benefit from experimenting with the idea. An appropriate first step could be to encourage the sharing of blessings in small groups or Bible studies. This would provide opportunities for people to share their struggles and ask for prayer or share stories of their deliverance with the community. Alternatively, churches could create a physical or electronic list of prayers available to the community, such as a Google doc. A staff member would receive prayer requests for inclusion and manage the list. No details need to be included. Once delivered, parishioners could update their request with a written testimony describing God's salvation. The goal is to engender a community that practices *tôdâ* together.

Modern Christians might be wary of describing deliverance in terms of divine intervention. O'Donovan encourages us to understand this creatively: "To speak of our experience in thanksgiving is also to speak *interpretively*, since the . . . meaning of our experiences may not lie on the surface of our recollections, but may need to be drawn out by the discipline of thanksgiving."[68] We need not understand precisely *how* God has affected our deliverance, but we must assume God was involved. Above all, we must remember that God is *always* active in our lives for our good, no matter how grim the circumstances or how terrible our enemy. As Brennan Manning puts it, "To be grateful for an unanswered prayer, *to give thanks in a state of interior desolation*, to trust in the love of God in the face of the marvels, cruel circumstances, obscenities, and commonplaces of life is to whisper a doxology in darkness."[69]

Another element of the practice of gratitude is its natural counterpart: generosity. Generosity is the twin of gratitude, for "the spirit of true worship is gratitude, and generosity is the evidence of gratitude."[70] This should *especially* include the poor and needy. This is a crucial way to imitate God and learn from him.[71] This also helps satisfy the demands of justice:

---

68. O'Donovan, *Entering into Rest*, 80.
69. Manning, *Ruthless Trust*, 37, emphasis mine.
70. Ross, *Recalling the Hope of Glory*, 207.
71. Leithart, *Gratitude*, 60–61.

Christians reimagined the poor as "brothers" rather than distant "others," and thus in Christian giving, social lines were blurred as much as cosmic ones. The Old Testament characterized generosity to the poor in terms of justice rather than mercy. The just man gives generously, and the poor are not those who are materially bereft so much as the weak and vulnerable. Inspired by this Old Testament language, Christian leaders eventually pressed for structural and social changes on behalf of the poor. This definition of the Christian poor secured the triumph of Christianity in the cities of the Roman Empire because it implied that the church had to establish systematic justice rather than being satisfied with charitable relief.[72]

Though I must also be quick to point out that while we are required to give to the poor without restraint, we are *not* required to save them.[73] As Christ said, the poor will always be with us (Matt 26:11). Our generosity must last as long as the age.

Gratitude and generosity encourage us to love our enemies, but they also resist our bitterness. Gratitude is a counteragent to pride. Pao writes:

> In the constant act of thanksgiving, the relationship with God is nurtured. Through thanksgiving, the gracious acts are remembered and the life of a person is thereby changed. Thanksgiving then becomes an act of submission when the performance of such an act is not aimed at coercing God to act, but is a way to acknowledge him to be the Lord of all.

In this way, gratitude teaches us humility. We owe all we are and all we have to the creator, not to our creativity.

Generosity is a counteragent to materialism. St. Basil the Great wrote that the rich man who plans to tear down his barns is not hurting because he has too little space for his wealth but because he has too much wealth to begin with (Luke 12:13–21).[74] Better to store our wealth "in the stomachs of the poor."[75]

Both pride and materialism are forms of idolatry and sickness. Both are also as common in America today as sand on the shore. In order to be free from bitterness, we must reject them relentlessly. Pao clarifies:

---

72. Leithart, *Gratitude*, 81.

73. Leithart, *Gratitude*, 59; Volf, *Free of Charge*, 76–78. See also chapter 3, pp. 74–7, on justice and utopia. I will address this topic further in the following chapter.

74. Basil, *On Social Justice*, 59–61.

75. Basil, *On Social Justice*, 66.

When God is acknowledged as Lord of all, thanksgiving becomes a humbling act admitting the dependency of human existence. Modern psychologists have taught us that ingratitude is a sign of narcissism when a person is not able to acknowledge his or her need of others. In the words of Nancy McWilliams and Stanley Lependorf (1990: 444–445): "Gratitude seems to us to be an integral expression of our dependency on one another. To thank someone acknowledges our need to have been helped or enriched in the first place ... although those of us with predominantly narcissistic concerns may go through the motions of thanking, we frequently resist expressing whole-hearted appreciation, since that would acknowledge a previous insufficiency of some sort, an insult to the grandiose self." In biblical theology, the failure to acknowledge one's dependency upon the Creator is the root of all sins.[76]

Without gratitude and generosity, the risk of falling into idol-ology becomes greater.[77] Gratitude is our first defense against bitterness.

V: Testimony from Corrie ten Boom

It is for these reasons that Corrie ten Boom practiced gratitude. She was a Dutch Christian whose family hid Jews from the Nazis during WWII. She was arrested and survived imprisonment in the Ravensbrück concentration camp. Like Schindler, she is counted among the righteous of the nations. She is perhaps best known for the story of her encounter with one of the guards responsible for her sister Betsie's death. She shares how this man came to her after she had spoken at a church about the need to forgive our enemies. He thanked her for her kind words of encouragement and explained that he had become a Christian and repented of his complicity in the atrocities committed by the government. He explained that he had received forgiveness from Jesus but that he desperately wanted her forgiveness. She could only extend her hand and offer him the forgiveness he sought through force of will. She found in this decision that God granted her a measure of his love for the guard, and she had the blessing of sharing in God's righteous act of forgiveness.[78] This story

---

76. Pao, *Thanksgiving*, 35. See also: McWilliams and Lependorf, "Narcissistic Pathology of Everyday Life," 434–49.

77. Pao, *Thanksgiving*, 20, 35, 91–98, 153.

78. Ten Boom, *Clippings from my Notebook*, 93; Ten Boom, *Hiding Place*, 215.

encourages and challenges those who struggle to forgive our enemies. However, it does *not* occur without a foundation of gratitude.

When Corrie and Betsie had first arrived at Ravensbrück—the camp where Betsie would hand over her spirit—they were immediately faced with the hardships the camp would bring with it. For Corrie, her breaking point was the discovery that their barracks was infested with fleas. As a middle-aged woman, this was more than she could take. She asked Betsie how they would live in such a place as this. Betsie found their answer through prayer:

> "Corrie!" she said excitedly. "He's given us the answer! Before we asked, as he always does! In the Bible this morning. Where was it? Read that part again!" I glanced down the long dim aisle to make sure no guard was in sight, then drew the Bible from its pouch. "It was in First Thessalonians," I said. We were on our third complete reading of the New Testament since leaving Scheveningen. In the feeble light I turned the pages. "Here it is: "Comfort the frightened, help the weak, be patient with everyone. See that none of you repays evil for evil, but always seek to do good to one another and to all . . . .'" It seemed written expressly to Ravensbruck. "Go on," said Betsie. "That wasn't all." "Oh yes: ". . . to one another and to all. Rejoice always, pray constantly, give thanks in all circumstances; for this is the will of God in Christ Jesus—"That's it, Corrie! That's his answer. "Give thanks in all circumstances!'" That's what we can do. We can start right now to thank God for every single thing about this new barracks!"[79]

Corrie asked incredulously what they could possibly give thanks for in such a horrible place. However, as the sisters began to name their blessings, they found there was more to give thanks for than they had realized: they were still together, they had a Bible that had not been confiscated, and their barracks was full of women they could share their faith with. However, when Betsie continued to thank God for the fleas, Corrie interjected:

> "Betsie, there's no way even God can make me grateful for a flea." "'Give thanks in *all* circumstances,'" she quoted. "It doesn't say, 'in pleasant circumstances.' Fleas are part of this place where

---

79. Ten Boom, *Hiding Place*, 180. Probably citing 1 Thess 5:14–18.

CHAPTER 6: TO WHISPER A DOXOLOGY IN THE DARKNESS

God has put us." And so we stood between piers of bunks and gave thanks for fleas. But this time I was sure Betsie was wrong.[80]

I, for one, am with Corrie on this—we need not give thanks for the fleas. Even so, I am struck by the coincidence that Corrie and Betsie began their time in this place—a place that would rob Betsie of life and leave Corrie with deep psychological scars—with the practice of gratitude. This was more than a daily examen, but a sharing of blessings with the only community available and a creative effort to see God's goodness and provision even amid life's horrors. I am further struck that this act of gratitude would, in a sense, pave the way for Corrie to forgive one who served to make that place such a house of horrors in her future.

Lastly, I would like to offer a closing word from Leithart on gifts and gratitude. He writes:

> Jesus' "eschatology," his confidence about the future, plays a crucial role in his teaching on gifts and gratitude. For Jesus, the rewards of generosity are not to be sought from the recipients of favors, and they are not to be sought necessarily within time. There is a judgment to come, and at the judgment all the good deeds of the righteous will be rewarded, as all the deeds of the wicked will be punished. Be openhanded, be generous, Jesus can say: because the Father rewards at the last day. Within time, such gifts look like pure lines of altruistic self-sacrifice, but there is a time beyond time when all is repaid and restored. For Jesus, generosity is at its root an act of faith; one gives not because one sees where the return is coming from but because one trusts one's Father to see in secret and to reward, perhaps in the unseeable and unforeseeable future.[81]

I have never liked the idea that we must look to our eternal future for God's deliverance very much, but I have come to believe that our desire to find deliverance in the present is too narrow. To live our lives to the fullest, there *must* be an element of hope. For this reason, Paul wrote:

> I consider that the sufferings of this present time are not worth comparing with the glory about to be revealed to us. For the creation waits with eager longing for the revealing of the children of God; for the creation was subjected to futility, not of its own will but by the will of the one who subjected it, in hope that the creation itself will be set free from its bondage to decay and will

80. Ten Boom, *Hiding Place*, 181.
81. Leithart, *Gratitude*, 69.

obtain the freedom of the glory of the children of God. We know that the whole creation has been groaning in labour pains until now; and not only the creation, but we ourselves, who have the first fruits of the Spirit, groan inwardly while we wait for adoption, the redemption of our bodies. For in hope we were saved. Now hope that is seen is not hope. For who hopes for what is seen? But if we hope for what we do not see, we wait for it with patience. (Rom 8:18–25 NRSVA)[82]

Gratitude teaches us to look backward, but it also encourages us to look *forward*. This is the nature of hope, the subject of the next chapter.

---

82. See Ross, *Recalling the Hope of Glory*, 108; Volf, *Exclusion and Embrace*, 138; Kasper, *Mercy*, 127.

Chapter 7: **The Art of Losing Well**

Loving Our Enemies in Hope

> If we find ourselves with a desire that nothing in this world can satisfy, the most probable explanation is that we were made for another world. —C. S. Lewis[1]

I: Introduction

IN 1956 FIVE MISSIONARIES were killed while trying to bring the gospel to the people of the Waodani (then called the Auca or "savage killers") tribe in the jungles of Ecuador.[2] Despite the tragedy, the families of the missionaries (Rachel Saint and Elisabeth Elliot) continued their work. Today the Waodani (once considered the most dangerous and violent aboriginal people in the world) are Christians.[3] Their testimony today is "we acted badly, badly until they [the missionaries] brought us God's carvings [Scripture]. Now, seeing [God's] markings and following his trail, we live happily and in peace."[4]

This story is meaningful for our purposes because the missionaries believed the goal of bringing the gospel to the Waodani was worth giving their lives for. One of them, Jim Elliot, famously wrote, "He is

---

1. Lewis, *Mere Christianity*, 136–37.

2. Also frequently called the Waorani or Huorani.

3. Elliot, *Through Gates of Splendor*, 3; Saint, *End of the Spear*, xiv-xvi. I am oversimplifying the story for the sake of brevity. The conversion of the Waodani took years of sacrifice; see: Elliot, *Through Gates of Splendor*, 249, 262; Saint, *End of the Spear*, 2–5. For more information, see also: Elliot, *Shadow of the Almighty*.

4. Saint, *End of the Spear*, 59.

no fool who gives what he cannot keep to gain what he cannot lose."[5] The missionaries understood that giving up their lives (what we cannot keep) for the sake of the kingdom (what we cannot lose) is wise. Any earthly victories we achieve cannot add to God's eternal victory, and any earthly defeats we suffer cannot tarnish our hope of salvation. We can accept failures on earth because no amount of suffering, not even death, can diminish our joy.[6]

This is a stance for all of us and for all of life: we focus on our hope of glory, even in the face of great suffering and death. I call this "the Art of Losing Well" (*ALW*). Because we *know where we are going*, we can accept losses in the culture war gracefully and kindly, even when that might lead to great suffering and injustice.[7] This chapter will explore various components of *ALW*. I will examine how Dietrich Bonhoeffer taught *ALW*. I will illustrate how King David lived out *ALW*. I will meditate briefly on the Stigmata[8] and our response to suffering. I will incorporate into this what Miroslav Volf calls "the end of memory"—the means whereby we overcome our pain for forgiveness. I will conclude with a brief meditation on the *hope* God extends to us in Scripture of the coming kingdom. We know that our victory is certain; therefore, "Death, be not proud."[9]

II: The Art of Losing Well

Matt 5:38–48

In a situation of intractable conflict between the church and the world—one where only absolute victory or total defeat will end the conflict, where all positive options have been exhausted—the only recourse remaining to Christians is to accept temporary defeat.[10] History is replete with change,

---

5. Elliot, *Through Gates of Splendor*, 167.

6. Lewis, *Great Divorce*, 119.

7. This is similar to Glenn Tinder's "Prophetic Stance"; see: Tinder, *Political Meaning of Christianity*.

8. The scars from Jesus' crucifixion

9. Donne, "Holy Sonnets: Death Be Not Proud."

10. Some similar concepts have been presented in recent literature, such as Stanley, *Not in It to Win It*; Miller and Simon, *Truth Over Tribe*. I am going somewhat further than these by applying this concept to *all of life*, not just affective polarization. I cannot take full credit for this idea as I was inspired by my professor (Dr. Craig Gay) and fellow students (particularly Dafydd Russell-Jones) in a seminar on Christian political engagement that ran during the fall of 2017.

yet we know that Christ will come again to put all nations under his feet. Therefore, if we recognize that God has given us the freedom to *reject* his love and choose sin, we must honor how others choose to use this freedom. The decision to ignore rather than return an insult is *ALW*.[11]

In *The Cost of Discipleship*, Dietrich Bonhoeffer tackles the cost of loving our enemies as illustrated in the Beatitudes. He writes:

> At this point it becomes evident that when a Christian meets with injustice, he no longer clings to his rights and defends them at all costs. He is absolutely free from possessions and bound to Christ alone. Again, his witness to this exclusive adherence to Jesus creates the only workable basis for fellowship. . . . The only way to overcome evil is to let it run itself to a standstill because it does not find the resistance it is looking for. Resistance merely creates further evil and adds fuel to the flames. But when evil meets no opposition and encounters no obstacle but only patient endurance, its sting is drawn, and at last it meets an opponent which is more than its match.[12]

When being goaded into a fight, the appropriate response is to withdraw. So too, with sin.[13] This is especially important because "to triumph fully, evil needs two victories, not one. The first victory happens when an evil deed is perpetrated; the second victory, when evil is returned."[14]

Should we be tempted to object that our enemies are much too dangerous to justify such a response, Bonhoeffer continues:

> By our enemies Jesus means those who are quite intractable and utterly unresponsive to our love, who forgive us nothing when we forgive them all, who requite our love with hatred and our service with derision. . . . Be his enmity political or religious, he has nothing to expect from a follower of Jesus but unqualified love. . . . In [private and in public] we are disciples of Christ, or we are not Christians at all.[15]

---

11. See Matt 10:9–15; Chrysostom, "Resist Not Evil," 118.

12. Bonhoeffer, *Cost of Discipleship*, 157–58. See also: King, *Testament of Hope*, 17, 46, 63, 81, 84, 86, 144.

13. Simon Weil also sees this argument in the lives of the Cathars of Languedoc; see: Jacobs, *Year of Our Lord 1943*, 97–99; Weil, "Romanesque Renaissance," 44–54.

14. Volf, *End of Memory*, 9.

15. Bonhoeffer, *Discipleship*, 164–65.

We are commanded to love our enemies without exception. It does not matter whether they forgot your name or demand your crucifixion.[16] This can be practiced by none but followers of Jesus, for only we have the hope of the resurrection.[17]

Bonhoeffer raises an obvious question: how can we accept this from a man who conspired to assassinate Adolf Hitler? To understand this, we must investigate Bonhoeffer's writings. The phrase in Bonhoeffer's writing that is cited in support of violent activism reads "we are not simply to bandage the wounds of the victims beneath the wheel of injustice, we are to drive a spoke into the wheel itself."[18] Though urgent, to invoke this phrase is to floor the gas pedal. Bonhoeffer saw this as the last resort after all other options were exhausted.

For Bonhoeffer, society exists in two spheres: the church and state.[19] Both serve a unique and exclusive purpose. The purpose of the state is to preserve good in the world. The purpose of the church is to redeem sin in the world.[20] When church and state become too closely aligned or out of sync, the results are destructive. Too close and we have fascism, such as the crusades or Christian Nationalism. Too out of sync and we have communism, or what we might call Christian Globalism.[21]

When either occurs, the church must respond—though never with force. Michael DeJong summarizes Bonhoeffer's responses in six stages.[22]

---

16. Recall my discussion of enemies in chapter 4, pp. 92–4. We have to acknowledge the existence of our enemies before we can love them.

17. Bonhoeffer, *Discipleship*, 163; King, "Experiment in Love," 20.

18. Bonhoeffer, *Bonhoeffer Reader*, 374. See also: DeJong, *Bonhoeffer on Resistance*, 4. Bonhoeffer has been invoked in recent years by both conservative and liberal pundits to support their quest for victory through activism regarding their chosen culture war issue.

19. This accords with Abraham Kuyper's reformed theology of "Sphere Sovereignty."

20. DeJong, *Bonhoeffer on Resistance*, 30–36.

21. DeJong, *Bonhoeffer on Resistance*, 54. See also my discussion on the problem of seeking utopia in chapter 3, pp. 74–7, 80–1, as well as the limited commentary on how Marxism has been transformed to support contemporary social movements.

22. The first stage is to offer humanitarian aid to those oppressed by the government: DeJong, *Bonhoeffer on Resistance*, 63–64. The second for the church to establish programs to offer larger scale humanitarian aid: DeJong, *Bonhoeffer on Resistance*, 66–68. The third is preaching. This is not mere public speaking. Bonhoeffer taught that preaching had an incarnational power to cause the Gospel to be made manifest in the world—to make the *content* of the preaching into reality. This is the same power by which God *spoke creation into existence*: DeJong, *Bonhoeffer on Resistance*, 46–47; Rowley, *Worship in Ancient Israel*, 139, 141. This view is also held by Karl Barth and is present in the Orthodox Liturgy, see: Hart, "Word, the Words, and the Witness,"

Of these, the sixth and final stage is the only one that is relevant to this discussion. This stage, which Bonhoeffer struggled to define, allows faithful Christians to respond to injustice "through free independent action."[23] Five stages of activism should occur before anyone in the church considers violence—including offering humanitarian aid, preaching the gospel, public declarations of criticism by church leaders, and greater discipleship within the church.[24] Even then we should understand Bonhoeffer's sixth stage critically: when does this stage become relevant, what are its conditions, and are violent methods acceptable?

First, the last *two* phases (increased discipleship and free independent action) are *only* proper when the government is actively persecuting the church or murdering its citizens. As long as these are not taking place, violence is entirely unacceptable. Such governments have been exceedingly rare and are the only acceptable preconditions for Christian violence. For Bonhoeffer, such a state did not exist until 1936, when the confessing church stopped speaking in *statu confessionis*, which Bonhoeffer saw as betrayal.[25]

Second, the question of what constitutes acceptable free independent action is not entirely clear in Bonhoeffer's writing. Only three documents have ever been interpreted as connections between free and independent action and Bonhoeffer's conspiracy: "The State and the Church" (1941), "History and Good" (unpublished), and "After Ten Years" (1943). These

---

87, 102; Chrysostom, *Divine Liturgy*, 42. Before the reading of the gospel, the priest prays, "May God, through the prayers of the holy, glorious, and all-laudable Apostle and Evangelist N, enable you to proclaim the glad tidings with great power, *to the fulfillment of the gospel of his beloved Son*, our Lord Jesus Christ." Emphasis mine. The fourth is for church leaders to issue a public declaration of what they believe is right (*in statu confessionis* or "in a state of confessing"), highlight that the government has violated this belief, and that the church will not condone or endorse the government's actions. This must be done through ecumenical council, not individual speaking: DeJong, *Bonhoeffer on Resistance*, 71. An obvious issue that would fall under the category of *statu confessionis* is the divinity of Jesus. If the church were to compromise on this matter they would cease to be the church; it would be equivalent to theological suicide. A clear example of the church speaking in this manner during Bonhoeffer's life was "The Barmen Declaration" (Spring 1934); see: Sullivan, "After Ten Years," 31. Fifth is for the church to focus on discipling its members better so that they may live out the statement *in statu confessionis*: DeJong, *Bonhoeffer on Resistance*, 87, 122. A recent example is the model outlined in Rod Dreher's *The Benedict Option*; see: Dreher, *Benedict Option*, 12. Sixth and lastly is free independent action, See: DeJong, *Bonhoeffer on Resistance*, 142.

23. DeJong, *Bonhoeffer on Resistance*, 142.
24. See above footnote 22.
25. Sullivan, "'After Ten Years,'" 33.

documents do not use the language of free and independent action or offer explicit permission for persons to behave violently.[26] Even his initial writing in "The Church and the Jewish Question" suggests that he was not entirely sure whether the church was *allowed* to act politically or what form that might take. He argues that the church should never participate in direct political action but, thereafter, suggests that the church's responsibility to "seize the wheel" constitutes direct political action.[27] The essay has a strong character of a scholar working out their views *in situ*, as does his position paper on the church and state. He writes, "According to Scripture, there is no right to revolution, but there is a responsibility for all individuals to safeguard the purity of their offices and tasks in the polis."[28] This suggests *subversion* rather than the application of force.

Moreover, "After Ten Years," the essay that most strongly suggests violence, is not for the church. It is a private exhortation and encouragement for his co-conspirators.[29] Church leadership did not endorse their actions.[30] Bonhoeffer also writes that anyone who would participate in the kind of action in which he is participating should not be "outraged critics or opportunists, but must take [their] share of responsibility for the molding of history in every situation and at every moment, whether [they] are the victors or the vanquished."[31]

From this, we may conclude several principles for any political action the church takes. First, actions should be taken by the church as a *community* and not by individuals. Most forms of action Bonhoeffer listed occur within the church itself rather than in society.[32] We should also recognize that Bonhoeffer prioritizes action within the church rather than against the state. We must begin by removing the plank from our own eye (Matt 7:3–5). On a related note, we should recognize that our actions—including how we bind up the broken hearted—are our primary witness. We must do this *before* we criticize the government.

We should also recognize that our biggest problem today is our failure to resist through the first five methods (particularly preaching and

26. DeJong, *Bonhoeffer on Resistance*, 143.
27. Bonhoeffer, *Bonhoeffer Reader*, 373–75.
28. Bonhoeffer, *Bonhoeffer Reader*, 712–14.
29. Sullivan, "Bonhoeffer's Epidiectic Exhortation," 37.
30. Sullivan, "Bonhoeffer's Epidiectic Exhortation," 36.
31. Sullivan, "Bonhoeffer's Epidiectic Exhortation," 41.
32. DeJong, *Bonhoeffer on Resistance*, 120–22. Remember the discussion of individual and corporate action regarding sin in chapter 5, pp. 135–8.

discipleship in the church) rather than jumping straight to marches and protests. DeJong writes, "The thing that most clearly separates us from him is not that we prefer action and he prefers words. What really separates us [Christians from Bonhoeffer], I suspect, is our understanding of action. We associate action with our own deeds, while for Bonhoeffer the most fundamental action is God's word."[33] I believe Bonhoeffer was never quite sure what would constitute appropriate forms of independent action, so we should not judge him based on his conspiracy. He *was* sure that independent action should not be pursued until all other options have been exhausted or until all remaining options are equally evil.[34]

Bonhoeffer's choice to take direct action against Hitler demonstrates a breaking point. He could no longer live with himself without acting. Thus, his choice to *act* should not strike us as oddly as when he chose *not to act*. We have paid attention to Bonhoeffer's rebelliousness rather than his patience. Our responsibility to "bless, do good, and pray for [our] enemies without reserve and without respect of persons" is for *all* times.[35] To quote Rod Dreher, "'Bless those who persecute you,' Jesus taught. Vengeance is easier to resist if you have that mind-set."[36]

III: Hidden in the Rock

1 Sam 24–26; Pss 63; 142; 143

I want to look at King David as an exemplar of this mindset against vengeance. In Ps 63 David writes, "Oh God, you are my God; earnestly I seek you; my soul thirsts for you; my flesh faints for you, as in a dry and weary land where there is no water. So I have looked upon you in the sanctuary, beholding your power and glory. Because your steadfast love is better than life, my lips will praise you" (Ps 63:1–3 ESV). What an extraordinary declaration of David's love for God, but even more so when we understand the context!

David probably wrote this while he hid from Saul in the Judean Desert. In 1 Sam 24:1, we are told that David is in the En Gedi, an oasis on the

---

33. DeJong, *Bonhoeffer on Resistance*, 161–62.
34. Sullivan, "Bonhoeffer's Epidiectic Exhortation," 45.
35. Bonhoeffer, *Discipleship*, 133. This is almost certainly a reference to the Sermon on the Mount.
36. Dreher, *Live Not By Lies*, 193.

western edge of the Judean Desert near the Dead Sea.[37] The surrounding area is totally barren. The Dead Sea is so-called because it is a hypersaline lake with a salt content far higher than the ocean. Nothing lives there and the water is undrinkable. Average rainfall in the Judean Desert is roughly the same as the Arabian Desert. Temperatures fluctuate around 40°C (104°F), and the only way to find water is to search the caves and wadis. Between the heat and lack of water, the region is harsh. It truly is "a dry and weary land where there is no water."

Why is David fleeing Saul? David has been appointed king over Israel. However, before David can take the throne, Saul must abdicate the throne or die. Saul, though rejected by God (1 Sam 15), has been chasing David to kill him. Saul is paranoid and dangerous.[38] David, for his part, obeyed Saul as if he were Saul's son. David is married to Michal (Saul's daughter) and is an avowed friend of Jonathan (Saul's son).[39] David has been a powerful military leader and brought great victories to Saul, but now he is on the run with four hundred loyal soldiers.

God's promise that *David* will sit on the throne sounds like a pipe dream. In 1 Sam 27:1 we read, "Then David said to himself, 'Now I will perish one day by the hand of Saul. There is nothing better for me than to safely escape into the land of the Philistines. Then Saul will despair of searching for me anymore in all the territory of Israel, and I will escape from his hand'" (NASB).

Similar laments appear in the Psalms. In Ps 142, David cries to God from a cave, saying:

> I cry out with my voice to the Lord; with my voice I implore the Lord for compassion. I pour out my complaint before him; I declare my trouble before him. When my spirit felt weak within me, you knew my path. In the way where I walk they have hidden a trap for me. Look to the right and see; for there is no one who regards me favorably; there is no escape for me; no one cares for my soul. (Ps 142:1–4 NASB)

As if continuing this lament, David cries out to God for deliverance in Ps 143, saying, "For the enemy has persecuted my soul; he has crushed my life to the ground; he has made me dwell in dark places, like those who

---

37. Josephus disagrees with this interpretation, but I have chosen to accept the biblical testimony; see: Josephus, *Works of Josephus*, Ant. 6.12.4.

38. Saul tries to kill David thrice in 1 Sam 18–20.

39. Brueggemann, *First and Second Samuel*, 170.

have long been dead. Therefore my spirit feels weak within me; my heart is appalled within me. . . . I spread out my hands to You; my soul longs for You, like a weary land" (Ps 143:3–4, 6 NASB). The similarities between these two and Ps 63 should not be dismissed.

David believes he is living on borrowed time. He is a dead man walking.[40] He goes so far as to seek shelter in the land of his enemies, the Philistines.[41] David feels safer among them than among his own people in Israel. Under those circumstances, still he wrote in Ps 63, the love of God is *better than life*. The specter of death does not surpass the certainty of God's love. Even amid his suffering, David praises God.

This is the context where David chose to spare Saul's life in 1 Sam 24 and 26. Though it is possible David spared Saul's life twice, it is more likely that this singular incident had such an effect on those who heard it that the story was embellished over time until two structures came to be accepted.[42] The first account takes place in a cave (which accounts for the attribution in Ps 143 and the language in Pss 63, 142, and 143), and the second in the south of the desert amid Saul's camp. In the first account, David chooses to cut the "wing" of Saul's robe (symbolically cutting off Saul's manhood, thereby robbing him of descendants), and in the second, David steals the king's spear (a frequent symbol of Saul's power and fear) and his cup.[43] In both stories, David refers to Saul as "Father," and Saul is forced to respond by declaring David as his "Son."[44] Most importantly, however, both accounts have Saul acknowledge his inferiority to David in righteousness and in his right to the throne.[45]

Though our children most likely know about David from hearing the story of his victory over Goliath, the peak of David's goodness is not facing down a giant on the battlefield but skulking in the shadows of a cave while his enemy squats in the dank darkness taking a dump.[46]

---

40. Brueggeman, *First and Second Samuel*, 170.

41. This is after he has killed Goliath of Gath (1 Sam 17), brought to Saul one hundred Philistine foreskins as a dowry to marry Michal (1 Sam 18), and saved the town Keliah from an attack by the Philistines (1 Sam 23). See also Josephus, *Works of Josephus*, 166–67. Ant. 6.10.4.

42. Brueggemann, *First and Second Samuel*, 166.

43. Brueggeman, *First and Second Samuel*, 168, 184; Brueggemann, *David's Truth*, 28.

44. Brueggeman, *First and Second Samuel*, 171, 186.

45. Brueggeman, *First and Second Samuel*, 172–174, 187–188; Brueggemann, *David's Truth*, 10, 28–29.

46. Brueggeman, *David's Truth*, 28.

David's strength is not seen in the lives he has taken but in the life he spares.[47] David is kingly not because he is *just* but because he is *compassionate*—he chooses to *release* Saul's life and well-being to God rather than reach out and take it for himself.[48] This is the same character that Jesus displays at his trial before Pilate.[49] David spares Saul's life even though he is certain Saul will kill him in return. He does what is right and accepts the consequences.

We should also notice here how these two stories are not simply placed one after the other in the text but as bookends to a strange tale of David encountering a foolish and boorish man—Nabal. David comes to Nabal seeking charity. Though the rightful king of Israel, David comes to Nabal as a beggar looking for handouts. Nabal dismisses David, incurring his wrath. This time, David does *not* hold back but bids his men "lock n' load" to go take the wretch down (1 Sam 25:12).[50] If David was so eager to annihilate this man Nabal for insulting him, David's choice to spare Saul in chapters 24 and 26 should surprise us *more*.

Hearing that this calamity is about to come upon them, Nabal's wife, Abigail, goes to David to plead for mercy. Josephus's interpretation of their meeting is incredibly insightful. Abigail begs for leniency from David knowing *God* will avenge.[51] David responds by giving praise and thanks to *God*, not Abigail.[52] David follows the pattern of gratitude outlined in the previous chapter, and *both* attribute their actions to God.

We also see God's inevitable vengeance is brought upon Nabal's head mere days after David chooses to refrain from his act of revenge. The foolishness of Nabal is further reflected in the stories on either side,

---

47. Brueggeman, *David's Truth*, 48.

48. See chapters 4 and 5, especially pp. 119–122, 134.

49. Brueggeman, *David's Truth*, 29.

50. See also David's conduct in 2 Sam 16:5–14. In this section, David (now king and fleeing his son Absolom with his men) is cursed and pelted with stones by Shimei, a descendant of Saul. As with Saul, David refuses to retaliate against Shimei's insults, suggesting that Shimei might be following God's instructions. David demonstrates *ALW* years after his conflict with Saul through his refusal to defend himself against this treatment. This is particularly interesting given it immediately follows David's interaction with Ziba—steward of the house of Mephibosheth (another of Saul's descendants) whom David has honored and cared for. David blesses the house of Saul in one breath, and in the next is cursed by the house of Saul.

51. See chapter 4, pp. 108–111, there is one end for our enemies.

52. Brueggemann, *First and Second Samuel*, 180; Josephus, *Works of Josephus*, 174, Ant. 6.13.6–7. Recall chapter 6, pp. 148–9. See also Deut 32:35; Ps 94:1, Prov 25:22; Rom 12:20; Heb 10:30.

for in chapter 26:21, Saul acknowledges *himself* to have been a fool as well. Saul's foolish behavior reflects Nabal's one chapter prior—and now we know that the inevitable end that came upon Nabal also awaits Saul.[53] Our enemies need compassion more than we do.[54]

Though he is in the midst of this dry and weary land, living as a vagrant, and constantly thirsty, David instead turns his eyes to God and says, "Though I am physically thirsty from lack of water, my spiritual thirst for You is greater still." David has his eyes firmly fixed on God throughout these encounters. This enables him to give us a foretaste of Jesus' humble obedience before Pilate. So we see that God himself is willing to suffer on our behalf rather than strike us down and that he calls us to do the same for the salvation of our neighbors.

IV: Scars and Medals

John 20:24–29

David chose to spare Saul despite his conviction that he would die as a consequence. Allowing our enemies the occasional victory can have dire consequences. Sometimes our enemies will leave us with deep and lasting wounds, and practicing the *ALW* means we must choose to carry those wounds *without* seeking vengeance. How are we to do this and live? In this section, I will offer some theological insights into how we may carry and understand these burdens.[55]

I first encountered this idea in the Delirious? song "When All Around Has Fallen." The text echoes the Beatitudes:

> Blessed are those who are persecuted for righteousness's sake, for theirs is the kingdom of heaven. Blessed are you when people revile you and persecute you and utter all kinds of evil against you falsely on my account. Rejoice and be glad, for your reward is great in heaven, for in the same way they persecuted the prophets who were before you. (Matt 5:9–12 NRSVA)

In the midst of persecution we are called to rejoice because of the reward that waits for us. The marks of our suffering may remain, but that those

---

53. Brueggeman, *First and Second Samuel*, 187.

54. See chapter 4, pp. 148–9.

55. This is not intended to replace proper therapy. For anyone suffering from past or ongoing trauma, please seek out the services of a qualified therapist or other therapeutic literature. I recommend: Allender, *Healing Path*.

marks should become the source of rewards and honor and that *God should be the one giving them* is a wonder worth pondering.

One of my favorite Gospel stories is Thomas's encounter with the risen Jesus (John 20:24-29). When Thomas hears that Jesus has appeared to the disciples, he demands to see the physical evidence before he will believe. Yet, when Jesus comes before Thomas, there is not a single word of rebuke or condemnation for his unbelief. Instead, Jesus extends himself to Thomas and invites him to reach out and receive the proof he has asked for.

This is not exactly what *I* would have done in Jesus' shoes! If I were covered in stab wounds, I would not be so eager to have someone go sticking their blunt and dirty fingers in them! Peter Chrysologus reflected on this:

> Why Thomas, do you alone, a little too clever a sleuth for your own good, insist that only the wounds be brought forward in testimony to faith? . . . Do you think that no signs of his devotion and no evidence of the Lord's resurrection could be found unless you probed with your hands his inner organs that had been laid bare with such cruelty? Brothers, his devotion sought these things, his dedication demanded them so that in the future not even godlessness itself would doubt that the Lord had risen. But Thomas was curing not only the uncertainty of his own heart but also that of all human beings. . . . For the only reason the Lord had kept his wounds was to provide evidence of his resurrection.[56]

We see two things taking place here! First, Jesus confirms that Christians should not receive the testimony of his resurrection on faith alone. Thomas's skeptical demand for evidence is to be commended![57]

More striking to me is this image of Thomas "[probing] with [his] hands [Jesus'] inner organs that had been laid bare with such cruelty." Perhaps Jesus *allowed* Thomas to go through with his demand—to poke around inside Jesus' torso and poke his dirty fingers through the holes in Jesus' wrists. Not only that, but Jesus' resurrected body *still bears those scars* (Luke 20:31; 24:36; John 20:26)! So we sing rightly in Charles Wesley's hymn, "Those dear tokens of his passion still his dazzling body bears, cause of endless exultation to his ransomed worshipers. With

---

56. Chrysologus, "Reopening Old Wounds," 367-68; Hilary "Tolerate a Hidden Injury," 117-18.

57. Keck et al., *New Interpreter's Bible*, 849.

what rapture, with what rapture, with what rapture, gaze we on those glorious scars!"[58]

Brother Jerome applied this to our resurrection: "After the resurrection we shall have the same members that we now use, the same flesh and blood and bones, for it is not the nature of these that is condemned in the Holy Scripture but their works."[59] Augustine concluded further that this *must* be the glory of the saints of God in the resurrection:

> The love we bear for the blessed martyrs causes us—how, I do not know—to desire to see in the heavenly kingdom the marks that they received for the name of Christ. And possibly we shall see them. For this will not be a deformity but a mark of honor and will add luster to their appearance as well as a spiritual (if not a bodily) beauty.[60]

Those scars we bear because of our faith become medals of honor in the kingdom of God.[61] This honor is our *glory* even before the face of God.[62]

However, I find it doubtful that Jesus thought of his scars as "medals" when he had Thomas's stubby fingers prodding his spleen (though I suspect Jesus was beyond pain). Our own scars tend to ache *long after* the time we receive them, too. How then do we carry them? We may, of course, react as society recommends: lashing out in retaliation. We may follow the advice of R. T. Kendall's popular text on forgiveness and refuse even to speak of the incident we have suffered from.[63] I believe neither of these approaches is appropriate. To take vengeance does not heal the underlying wound and risks creating an escalating cycle of violence and bitterness. To ignore the wrong that has been done is neither just nor truthful. Instead, we must learn from Miroslav Volf what it means to remember *well*.

---

58. Charles Wesley, "Lo He Comes with Clouds Descending." See also the Edward Shilito poem "Jesus of the Scars": https://www.thegospelcoalition.org/blogs/justin-taylor/jesus-of-scars.

59. Brother Jerome, "Same Flesh but More Glorious," 367–68.

60. Augustine, "Will Martyrs Retain their Wounds," 367–68. Quote from *The City of God*, 22.19. See also: Chryssavgis, "Life in Abundance," 219.

61. Augustine does not apply this standard to *everyone*. He only applies it to those deemed "saints," that is, those who are outstanding in the kingdom of God. Even so, we should remember that even the least in the kingdom of God is, in some sense, a saint (albeit of lower standing). Insofar as this is true, we all have scars that we should bear like medals.

62. Lewis, *Weight of Glory*, 10.

63. Kendall, *Total Forgiveness*, 57–60.

It is not sufficient, claims Volf, to "never forget" the wrongs our enemies have done to us. It is not only that the memories shape us but that *we shape the memories*.[64] We naturally tend to play up our own virtues and exaggerate our enemies' failures when we remember past injustices. If we are to remember *well*, we must remember *all* that has passed. This includes the good in our enemy, and the wrongs we did to them without exaggeration.[65] This is important because, as our pain diminishes, it will color our memory of the event. We must allow the pain to continue to exist *alongside* our "sanitized" memory so that we do not hold our enemy guilty of things he or she has not done.[66]

Volf offers five principles for remembering rightly that are worth mentioning. First, we must recognize that our lives are neither accidental nor was God forced to bring us into being. Instead, we are each individually wrapped with love and care by our creator (Ps 139:13). Second, as I had to learn during my time in seminary, God does not place us here merely to "survive." He intends us to *thrive*. Third, God is not a distant observer of creation. He entered history, took for himself a body, and underwent the same suffering that we do on our behalf as evidence of his extreme love for every human soul. Fourth, the salvation God promised us is assured—though all appearances protest the contrary. Our suffering will not stall the coming of God's rule. Fifth and lastly, the scars we wear do not reflect who we are. God will ultimately expose all lies and injustices, punish wrongdoers, and honor the righteous who endure.[67] However, there is another element to our memories, one that is so extraordinary we can do no more than speculate or whisper of it.

In Dante's *Divine Comedy*, the intrepid Dante travels through the depths of hell, scales the heights of the mountain of purgatory, and stands prepared to ascend into the depths of heaven. Yet, before he can undertake this final journey, a vast stream stands before him. A woman (we presume Lady Wisdom) explains that it removes memory of sin (Lethe) and restores memory of good (Eunoe). Both must be tasted before we may ascend to heaven.[68] God knows that our pain *must* be healed for creation to be made whole. So Dante hypothesizes that we need to have our very *memories* redeemed. We must endure in this

64. Volf, *End of Memory*, 25.
65. Volf, *End of Memory*, 11.
66. This is work that is eased through sharing it with a therapist.
67. Volf, *End of Memory*, 43–44.
68. Volf, *End of Memory*, 135–36. See also: Dante, *Purgatorio*, 121–33.

hope: that we may someday recall the lessons and bear the marks of sin yet slough off the memory of pain that accompanies them. Without this, we cannot prepare to "climb unto the stars."[69]

V: Rejoice with Me in My Creation

Isa 2:1–4; 65:17–25; Rev 21

Tish Warren wrote that we do not suffer alone; God suffers with us through prayer.[70] Surely God does suffer with us, and I often find encouragement remembering that the God who cried to man, "Where are you?" (Gen 3:9) is also the man who cried to God, "Where are you?" (Matt 27:46; Mark 15:34).[71] God experienced the separation between heaven and earth from *both* sides. However, Lewis warned in *The Four Loves* that we must be wary of seeking earthly comfort in heaven, for heaven can give only heavenly comfort. In the long run there might be *no* earthly comfort.[72] I have come to believe that this "heavenly comfort"—the assurance of the blessing that awaits us—*must* be sought out if we are to survive (Pss 145–150, Rom 8:18).

This view of hope has largely disappeared from the church's social imaginary. Jürgen Moltmann explains this is "owing to the fact that Christian faith banished from its life the future hope by which it is upheld, and elevated the future to a beyond, or to eternity . . . hope emigrated as it were from the church and turned in one distorted form or another against the church."[73] More than this, hope requires a divided mindset: meditating on the ruin of the world now *and* the glory coming into the world.[74] We should not be surprised that hope has largely disappeared from the church, but we should seek to rekindle that memory.

This memory of hope appears throughout Scripture. John's Apocalypse vision is the most obvious, yet I would like to highlight Isaiah's

---

69. Volf, *End of Memory*, 135–36; Dante, *Purgatorio*, 142–45.

70. Warren, *Prayer in the Night*, 29–31.

71. This is not to suggest that the Trinity was in any real sense divided (neither the Father nor the Spirit abandoned the Son on the cross), but that Jesus—God the Son—*felt* as if it were. I suggest that Jesus' selection of Ps 22 was not merely a reference to an accepted cultural symbol of pain and suffering, but the clearest expression of how he felt on the cross.

72. Lewis, *Four Loves*, 139.

73. Moltmann, *Theology of Hope*, 15–16.

74. Moltmann, *Theology of Hope*, 91.

vision. Though Isaiah focuses primarily on the judgment coming upon Israel in their impending exile, small passages of hope appear unexpected in the midst of judgment. These passages include chapters 2:2–4, 11:6–9, 24:1–27:13 (the Apocalypse passages), and 65:17–25.

Isaiah begins with a bang: two visions of the future.[75] The first vision tells Israel and Judah that they have rebelled against God and that punishment is imminent and unavoidable. This is balanced by the second vision, which declares:

> Now it will come about that in the last days the mountain of the house of the Lord will be established as the chief of the mountains, and will be raised above the hills; and all the nations will stream to it. And many peoples will come and say, "Come, let's go up to the mountain of the Lord, to the house of the God of Jacob; so that he may teach us about his ways, and that we may walk in his paths." For the law will go out from Zion and the word of the Lord from Jerusalem. And he will judge between the nations, and will mediate for many peoples; and they will beat their swords into plowshares, and their spears into pruning knives. Nation will not lift up a sword against nation, and never again will they learn war. (Isa 2:2–4 NASB)

Micah 4:1–5 is nearly identical but appends, "Instead, each of them will sit under his vine and under his fig tree, with no one to make them afraid, because the mouth of the Lord of armies has spoken. Though all the peoples walk, each in the name of his god, as for us, we will walk in the name of the Lord our God forever and ever" (Micah 4:4–5 NASB). What are we to make of this?

The context suggests that these passages are the assurance of Israel's return from exile, but this is not the whole picture. The notion that there will be no war led the rabbinic interpreter Ibn Ezra to declare that this *must* point to something *beyond* Israel's inevitable return.[76] This is further indicated by Jesus' cryptic words to Nathanael in John 1:48, quoting Mic 4:4: "I saw you under the fig tree." Jesus seems to suggest two things—first, that he has seen Nathanael at prayer in the morning as evidence of his faith and that Jesus has seen Nathanael under his own fig tree *among the people of God at the end of days*. Nathanael's

---

75. We would typically expect a prophetic text to begin with the narrative of the prophet's divine calling. This is meant to establish the credentials of the text. It is unusual that *Isaiah* does not begin this way.

76. Ezra, *Commentary of Ibn Ezra*, 13–14.

declaration that Jesus is "the son of God" (John 1:49) bears witness to this. Micah's inclusion that the people of God will walk in the name of God "forever and ever" insists that the Isaiah passage speaks of something beyond Israel's return from exile.

Therefore, Isa 2 is an eschatological promise: *all nations* will dwell in the house of the Lord (Ps 23:6), in the lasting peace—the *shalom*—that comes only from God.[77] This peace is much more than the absence of conflict; it is the heart of God's salvation. Moltmann describes this as a state of "wholeness" or "rightness" that "bound up with the expectation of the lordship of God is the expectation that his people, mankind, and all that he has made will attain to salvation, peace, happiness, life—in a word, to what it was truly meant to be."[78] In Isa 11:6–9, *shalom* includes tamed animals—predators and prey will live together without fear of one another.[79] This, along with the image of the fig tree in Micah, carries echoes of the garden of Eden—of a return to our original vocation as God's stewards and a conclusion of the groaning of all creation (Rom 8:22). Yet the peak of Isaiah's eschatology is yet to come.

In chapter 65, Isaiah writes, "For behold, I create new heavens and a new earth; and the former things will not be remembered or come to mind. But be glad and rejoice forever in what I create; for behold, I create Jerusalem *for* rejoicing and her people *for* gladness" (Isa 65:17–18, NASB). I believe this is a mistranslation. While most Hebrew verb forms indicate their object, the form used in verse 18 for "rejoicing" and "gladness" does not.[80] So we *assume* that God is making Jerusalem so that *the people* might rejoice and be glad. However, if this is to be consistent with verses 17 and 19, which speak of *God's* action, then surely God is speaking about *his own joy*.[81] God does not exhort us to look forward to the coming kingdom "just *because*." He urges us to wait for the kingdom eagerly *because he does too*. We are not merely invited to share our sorrows with God but to share with God in his joy (Ps 104:31)!

77. Brueggemann, *Isaiah*, 24–25.
78. Moltmann, *Theology of Hope*, 216.
79. Brueggemann, *Isaiah*, 101–2; Seitz, *Isaiah 1–39*, 106–7.
80. Most verb forms indicate masculine or feminine, singular or plural, and first, second, or third person. The verbs here only indicate masculine or feminine and singular or plural. The verbs *gîlāh* and *māśôś* (גִּילָה and מָשׂוֹשׂ) indicate the imperative case. Without first, second, and third person, there is no way to determine with certainty whether the text is indicating God (first person) or his people (probably second person), see: Elliger and Rudolph, *Biblia Hebraica Stuttgartensia*, 776.
81. I have only found the passage translated this way in the RSV.

Chapter 65 is often mistakenly interpreted as a prefiguring of the millennial age of the reign of Christ *before* the last days. There are two reasons for this: the existence of death and the presence of sinners in this kingdom (vs. 20).[82] Though identifying chapter 65 as a prefiguring of the *millennial age* is one way to address these two issues, Jacques van Ruiten offers another. The Targum of Isa 65:20 reads: "No more shall there be a suckling that lives but a few days, or an old man who does not fill out his days, for a youth who sins shall be dying a hundred years old, and the sinner a hundred years old shall be expelled"(NASB).[83] Ruiten draws four conclusions. First, the main difference between Isa 65 and Rev 21 is that of "*untimely* death" rather than merely "death." Second, the parallel between the infant and the old man at the beginning of 65:20 creates a parallel with the sinner because they *will not* experience an untimely death whereas the sinner *will*. Thirdly, Ruiten points out that the tree of life is referenced in 65:22 of the Targum, which creates a bridge to Gen 1–3 and provides an assurance of life for the people of God in the face of the possibility of untimely death.[84] Fourth and finally, Ruiten notes that the author of Revelation must have drawn from somewhere other than Isa 65 to inspire an existence with God free from death, such as Isa 25:8.[85] Therefore, the author of Revelation clearly believes that Isa 25:8 and Isa 65:17–25 can be interpreted together without contradiction.[86]

Thus, chapter 65 affirms the promises of a new heaven and earth, peace between peoples, and the presence of God in our midst. It *also* assures us that the promise of eternal life offered by the tree of life in the garden will ultimately be fulfilled in the kingdom of God. However, the assurance of Isa 25:8—that the kingdom of God will be free from

---

82. Kaiser, *Isaiah 1–12*, 260.

83. Chilton, *Isaiah Targum*, 124–25. The Targum, the Aramaic translation of the Old Testament, is nearly identical to the typical English translation.

84. The Targum of Isa 65:22 reads: "They shall not build and others inhabit; they shall not plant and others eat; for like the days of *the tree of life* shall the days of my people be, and my chosen shall wear out the work of their hands." Chilton, *Isaiah Targum*, 124–25, emphasis mine. This also reinforces the connection between Gen 1–3 and Isa 2 and 11.

85. Van Ruiten suggests Isa 25:8, mainly due to the image of God wiping away all tears; an image that only appears in Isa 25:8, Jer 31:16, Ezek 24:16, and Ps 116:8, but that only occurs with similar grammar to Rev 21:4 in Isa 25:8. There is also the line that God "will swallow up death forever."

86. van Ruiten, "Intertextual Relationship," 503–8. See also: Beale, *Temple and the Church's Mission*, 24, 137, 221, 223, 310, 368, 375; Kaiser, *Preaching and Teaching the Last Things*, 155.

grief—hints that Lethe and Eunoe might be real. This does little to alleviate our pain in the present, but the church is responsible for emphasizing this truth, and her members must encourage one another. Though we must wait a lifetime, all pain will be redeemed, perhaps even our memories of pain. To paraphrase Aslan from Lewis's *The Lion, the Witch, and the Wardrobe*, even time will work backward.[87]

VI: Conclusion—Haven't Forgotten My Way Home

Paul writes in Rom 8:37 that "in all these things we '*hypernikōmen*'" (ὑπερνικῶμεν). That is, we "more-than-conquer"—we achieve an *overwhelming* victory. In what "things" are we "hyper-conquerors?" If we look back to verse 17, Paul describes us as "heirs" of God and Christ *if* or *as* we participate in Christ's sufferings. This is a *twofold* victory—receiving the kingdom of God as an inheritance *and* enduring our suffering. Moltmann writes:

> Resurrection and eternal life are the future that is promised, and thereby make obedience possible in the body. In all our acts we are sowing in hope. So, too, in love and obedience we are sowing for the future of the resurrection of the body. In obedience, those who have been quickened by the Spirit are on the way towards the quickening of the mortal body.[88]

There is no obedience—no endurance—without hope (Rom 5:3–5). So what does this hope look like?

Most importantly, hope accepts constant discomfort. Even if we are not suffering at *this* moment, we ought to be uneasy in the tension between what is and what will be.[89] Our hope necessitates a degree of discomfort because we are uncertain *when* it will be fulfilled (Matt 24:36). Another element of uncertainty is due to the chaos of history. Despite the optimistic viewpoint of modern culture, history does *not* progress on a steady incline toward perfection.[90] We are not constantly

---

87. Lewis, *Lion, the Witch, and the Wardrobe*, 133. In context, Aslan speaks of "death working backward," and I am confident we may interpret this as *all* death—including the deaths of our memories.

88. Moltmann, *Theology of Hope*, 212–13. Note that we should not masochistically seek out suffering.

89. Moltmann, *Theology of Hope*, 324.

90. My ever-optimistic spell check wanted to rewrite this sentence to read "History *has not progressed* . . . toward perfection *yet*." Although I agree with Dr. King that

improving on the successes of our forebears. History began in injustice and will end in justice, but the middle is ebb and flow, now improving, then declining. Hope must exist within this context.

We can *still* hope in God for two reasons. First, our success or failure as representatives does not constrain God. God nearly destroyed Israel at Mount Sinai and in the exile, but he, the Messiah, still came. Second, because our hope is ultimately in *God's* action, we have hope because God's "credit" is good. Though many of his promises still await fulfillment, God has shown himself to be reliable.[91] Hope doggedly persists in the belief that God is good *all the time.*

Practicing the *ALW* as an act of hope takes two forms: active and passive resistance. I will describe each of these in turn. As Michael Battle wrote, African Christianity has given us the best practices of active resistance.[92] Martin Luther King wrote of this kind of resistance on numerous occasions. In his essay "The Most Durable Power," King writes: "Honesty impels me to admit that [standing for justice] will require willingness to suffer and sacrifice. So don't despair if you are condemned and persecuted for righteousness' [sic] sake. . . . The end of life is to do the will of God, come what may."[93] We see him speaking here of *obedience to God's will* and that living in obedience to God's will means we must submit willingly to persecution—such as imprisonment. He also pointed out that this kind of resistance was practiced by Shadrach, Meshach, and Abednego, by the early Christians, and even Socrates.[94] From these descriptions, we have examples of what *ALW* looks like.

But lest we assume that active resistance is an easy path, let us remember that King insisted that *how* we protest matters as much as the cause for which we protest.[95] Everyone who participated in a protest with the SCLC was required to sign a contract in which they committed to conduct themselves according to certain principles and to attend

---

history ends with justice, I am not certain that the whole arc of history bends in that direction *consistently*. I think it is more accurate to say that whether the arc of history bends toward justice or not, it *will* end with justice. I think it is likely that this just ending will be as surprising an end as the second coming, which will arrive "as a thief in the night" (1 Thess 5:2). See also chapter 5, p. 126.

91. Moltmann, *Theology of Hope*, 103, 119.
92. Battle, "Penitence as Practiced," 330.
93. King, "Most Durable Power," 10.
94. King, "Letter from Birmingham Jail," 294.
95. King, "Nonviolence," 59.

workshops to prepare for any demonstration.[96] Most of the pledge had little to do with our external lives, or even how to protest, but with our *spiritual* lives. Without a healthy spiritual life, we cannot hope to practice *ALW*. King even said that "purification of the self" was the *third* stage of active resistance (following prayerful determination if injustice was present and attempting to negotiate) and necessarily preceded any concrete action.[97] Furthermore, this reinforces our need to act compassionately towards our enemies—even when we want to retaliate most.

The workshops King conducted are also essential to recognize. In an interview with Kenneth B. Clark, King was asked to explain more about these workshops. He explained, "We do a great deal in terms of teaching both the theoretical aspects of nonviolence as well as the practical application. We even have courses where we go through the experience of being roughed up and this kind of sociodrama has proved very helpful in preparing those who are engaged in demonstrations."[98] To practice *ALW* in times of active protest requires that we be prepared to be spit upon, insulted, "roughed up," and possibly imprisoned—and that we respond to each of these with compassion or, at the very least, silence. Such behavior is so unnatural to us that King required everyone to *practice* these behaviors in private before being called upon to do so in public. Such preparation is notably absent from our activism today.

If we are not prepared to respond this way when we speak out, then we would do better to avoid such engagements altogether. Those of us who are prepared to protest in this way or who can *become* prepared to protest in this way should do so prayerfully, humbly, with extensive practice, and with fear and trembling. Recall that liberation theology done poorly can

---

96. The pledge read: "I HEREBY PLEDGE MYSELF— MY PERSON AND BODY— TO THE NONVIOLENT MOVEMENT. THEREFORE I WILL KEEP THE FOLLOWING TEN COMMANDMENTS: (1) MEDITATE daily on the teachings and life of Jesus. (2) REMEMBER always that the nonviolent movement in Birmingham seeks justice and reconciliation—not victory. (3) WALK and TALK in the manner of love, for God is love. (4) PRAY daily to be used by God in order that all men might be free. (5) SACRIFICE personal wishes in order that all men might be free. (6) OBSERVE with both friend and foe the ordinary rules of courtesy. (7) SEEK to perform regular service for others and for the world. (8) REFRAIN from the violence of fist, tongue, or heart. (9) STRIVE to be good in spiritual and bodily health. (10) FOLLOW the directions of the movement and of the captain of a demonstration." King, "Why We Can't Wait," 537.

97. King, "Letter from Birmingham Jail," 290. This followed prayerful determination if injustice was present, and attempting to negotiate. King's stages of active resistance are similar to Bonhoeffer's, though not identical.

98. King, "Kenneth B. Clark Interview," 337. He continues to explain that this work was even required of the children.

be harmful. For those who are not prepared to do this, there should be no shame—and those who are zealous for a just society should be careful not to insist otherwise. However, when a community decides to protest, those who choose not to participate should pray for those who do.

For a sort of *passive* resistance, I turn to the example of the early church. It is a modern misconception that abortion is a recent development. We find even in the Didache an interpretation of the injunction against murder to include "you shall not murder a child by abortion, nor kill a child at birth."[99] Abortion has been a cause of Christian action since our founding 2,000 years ago. Rodney Stark has written extensively on how this activism took place.[100] There was no picketing outside of abortion clinics—there were no abortion clinics to picket.[101] There is no record of debates on the street and no "contact evangelism." Instead, the church engaged in a kind of *passive resistance* to the spirit of the age. This took two forms. First, Christians maintained a sort of parallel counterculture in which they firmly rejected the practice of abortion. Second, they took every opportunity to save children from infanticide through exposure. The practice was not to attempt to shame their neighbors into changing their ways but rather to offer an alternative through self-sacrifice, almost a sort of peaceful sabotage of the status quo. Less, "Don't kill your babies," and more, "If you don't want them, we'll take them!"

This should not be interpreted as a kind of quietism or withdrawal—it is not appropriate to abandon culture to the domain of Satan.[102] Instead, this is the choice to be salt and leaven within society. To this end, Dreher writes:

> Could it be that the best way to fight the flood is to . . . stop fighting the flood? That is, to quit piling up sandbags and to build an ark in which to shelter until the water recedes and we can put our feet on dry land again? Rather than wasting energy and resources fighting unwinnable political battles, we should instead work on building communities, institutions, and networks of resistance that can outwit, outlast, and eventually overcome the occupation. Fear not! We have been in a place like this before. In the first centuries of Christianity, the

---

99. "Didache."

100. For a thorough overview of the subject see: Stark, *Rise of Christianity*, 118–21.

101. Though there were public objections such as Minucius Felix's publication *Octavius*, see: Stark, *Rise of Christianity*, 118–21.

102. Moltmann, *Theology of Hope*, 218, 224.

early church survived and grew under Roman persecution and later after the collapse of the empire in the West. We latter-day Christians must learn from their example—and particularly from the example of Saint Benedict.[103]

Such passive activism aims to create and reinforce a faithful remnant within a culture that has turned to idol-ologies for their salvation—particularly to the government.[104] This is not withdrawal but the founding of resistance.[105]

It should also be recognized that passive resistance is not the same as political passivity. Even when engaging in passive resistance, Christians in democratic societies should continue to vote, write their representatives, and maintain a degree of political awareness. Passive resistance is primarily an alternative to active resistance for those not equipped to engage in active resistance. Yet both active and passive resistance forms should incorporate the *ALW*—whether accepting insult and imprisonment without objection or choosing to be a part of a countercultural resistance network.

VII: Testimony from Pastor Wang Yi

This is not only an ancient mode of resistance but a modern one as well. In December 2018, Pastor Wang Yi was arrested by the Chinese Communist Party for his leadership of an unauthorized house church and his criticism of party leadership. Upon his arrest, his church community released a pre-written statement explaining his actions that led to his arrest and describing how he intended to conduct himself when his arrest inevitably came. He wrote:

> I accept and respect the fact that this Communist regime has been allowed by God to rule temporarily. As the Lord's servant John Calvin said, wicked rulers are the judgment of God on a wicked people, the goal being to urge God's people to repent and

---

103. Dreher, *Benedict Option*, 12. Dreher's work is sometimes inaccurately interpreted as promoting fear and quietism, which is understandable given its pessimistic nature. See: Smith, "New Alarmism." A charitable interpretation would view Dreher's purpose as loving our neighbors enough to respect their freedom to dissent from Christian views. This is *ALW*. Thus, while we should take Dreher's perspective with a grain of salt, we should not reject it entirely.

104. Smith, *Awaiting the King*, 121.

105. Dreher, *Benedict Option*, 18. See also: Tinder, *Political Meaning of Christianity*.

> turn again toward him. For this reason, I am joyfully willing to submit myself to their enforcement of the law as though submitting to the discipline and training of the Lord. At the same time, I believe that this Communist regime's persecution against the church is a greatly wicked, unlawful action. As a pastor of a Christian church, I must denounce this wickedness openly and severely. The calling that I have received requires me to use non-violent methods to disobey those human laws that disobey the Bible and God. My Savior Christ also requires me to joyfully bear all costs for disobeying wicked laws. But this does not mean that my personal disobedience and the disobedience of the church is in any sense "fighting for rights" or political activism in the form of civil disobedience, because I do not have the intention of changing any institutions or laws of China. As a pastor, the only thing I care about is the disruption of man's sinful nature by this faithful disobedience and the testimony it bears for the cross of Christ. As a pastor, my disobedience is one part of the gospel commission. Christ's great commission requires of us great disobedience. The goal of disobedience is not to change the world but to testify about another world.[106]

Pastor Yi is describing the *ALW* here. Having decided to follow Jesus, he simultaneously disobeys the laws laid out by his government yet obediently accepts the consequences of those actions. He does this not out of a desire to change the law but in obedience to a higher law. He has allowed himself to be uncomfortable in society because his citizenship is of the kingdom. Because of this choice, he will be in prison until 2027.

Pastor Yi also explained why he is willing to accept such treatment without resistance. He continues:

> Those who lock me up will one day be locked up by angels. Those who interrogate me will finally be questioned and judged by Christ. When I think of this, the Lord fills me with a natural *compassion* and grief toward those who are attempting to and actively imprisoning me. Pray that the Lord would use me, that he would grant me patience and wisdom, that I might take the gospel to them. Separate me from my wife and children, ruin my reputation, destroy my life and my family—the authorities are capable of doing all of these things. However, no one in this

---

106. Yi, "My Declaration of Faithful Disobedience." The Chinese text of the letter was posted here: https://www.facebook.com/prayforearlyrain/posts/302174883736698. The document was originally drafted on September 21, 2018.

world can force me to renounce my faith; no one can make me change my life; and no one can raise me from the dead.[107]

We have our citizenship in another kingdom. It is in the cause of this kingdom that we will oppose the kingdom of Satan through quiet resistance, peaceful acts of sabotage, loving protest, accepting insult and imprisonment, and, if God so calls us, through death. Pastor Yi has his eyes firmly fixed on that kingdom to come, so though he appears to all the world to have been abandoned, this faithful disciple has not forgotten his way home (Ps 23:6).[108] Even so, Lord Jesus, quickly come![109]

---

107. Yi, "My Declaration of Faithful Disobedience." Emphasis mine. See also Martin Luther's hymn "A Mighty Fortress." Though this hymn text is often taken as an indictment of the Pope as the antichrist, there is a degree of ambiguity on this meaning even in the original. Though Pope Leo X probably deserves all the criticism he receives, equating him with the devil is extreme.

108. The interpretation of the last verse of Ps 23 has a text variant giving two possible meanings to the passage: "I will *dwell in* the house of the Lord," (*yāšab* יָשַׁב) or, "I will *return to* the house of the Lord," (*šûb* שׁוּב) The only time when a shepherd *follows* his or her flock (vs. 5) is when the flock is *returning home*. This is the translation I favor in this case.

109. "Come, Ye Thankful People, Come."

Chapter 8: **No Man Is an Island**

Loving Our Enemies Through Seasons of Bitterness

> Who, then, does not know that the human being is a tame and communal animal, and is neither solitary nor savage? For nothing is so proper to our nature as to share our lives with each other, and to need each other, and to love our own kind. As, therefore, the Lord himself granted us to receive the seeds beforehand, in accord with this he also seeks after the fruits, saying, "A new commandment I give you, that you love one another" [John 13:34].—Basil the Great[1]

I: Introduction

J. R. R. TOLKIEN's *The Hobbit* is something of an accidental commentary on Christian love. From Dwalin's arrival at the unexpected party of Bag-End,[2] through the celebrations at Lake Town where a cold prevented Bilbo from giving any speech more eloquent than "thag you very buch"[3] and finally to Bilbo's farewell declaration "if ever you are passing my way . . . don't wait to knock! Tea is at four; but any of you are welcome at any time,"[4] the story can be seen as a string of peculiar encounters—typically involving *some* kind of food. When we look at some of

---

1. Basil, *On the Human Condition*, 117.
2. Tolkien, *Hobbit*, 7.
3. Tolkien, *Hobbit*, 186.
4. Tolkien, *Hobbit*, 278.

these gatherings, however, we see that some are less hospitable than others, such as the troll's discussion of how best to cook the dwarves[5] or Bilbo learning "never laugh at live dragons,"[6] not every chance meeting goes as expected.

My favorite of these is with the skin-changer, Beorn. Gandalf the wizard entices the notoriously private man with the promise of a story, but as this story unfolds the size of Gandalf's party gradually . . . grows. The crafty old man tricks Beorn into accepting not just an old man and a tiny hobbit but also thirteen rugged and rowdy dwarves (who trickle in every few minutes in pairs) as house guests.[7] Beorn might be crafty, rugged, suspicious, and extremely dangerous, but although he is not particularly loveable (perhaps not even pleasant), he *is* loving. If the measure of love is showing hospitality to the loveless, we have much to learn from the bear-man.

Throughout this book, I have tried to offer a possible explanation for how American society has become so embittered in our politics—that we are experiencing a natural part of human society, albeit one that has been taken to the point of extreme intensity by social media networking and a smorgasbord of idol-ologies that have gradually replaced our religious affections. I have proposed that Nietzsche's model for an embittered society is the one that best fits our current circumstances and that Christians may weather this storm by recovering the practice of loving our enemies. I have offered four sub-practices for loving our enemies: extending compassion, seeking forgiveness, practicing gratitude, and engaging in the art of losing well by looking forward in hope. However, I have offered very few practical suggestions about love itself and have provided few recommendations for *how* to love our enemies. In this chapter, I will wrap up my study of the politics of bitterness by doing both of these things. In particular, I will be asking the question "what are people for?" and "what does it mean to love our enemies?" This will necessitate a return to the sociology with which we began. With this, we have come full circle.

---

5. Tolkien, *Hobbit*, 38–39.
6. Tolkien, *Hobbit*, 213–14.
7. Tolkien, *Hobbit*, 112–18.

II: Reclaiming Conversation

In his thought-provoking piece *Amusing Ourselves to Death,* Neil Postman wrote about the development of communications technology. His most cutting objection reads:

> Telegraphy did something that Morse did not forsee when he prophesied that telegraphy would make "one neighborhood of the whole country." ... [Henry David Thoreau remarked] that "We are in great haste to construct a magnetic telegraph from Maine to Texas; but Maine and Texas, it may be, have nothing important to communicate."[8]

The sharing of news became less about being informed and more about entertainment. Objective fact gave way to subjective opinion. However, telegraphy had nothing on the speed and efficiency of cable TV as entertainment and dissemination of information, and cable TV is being replaced by the apex predator of information technology: the internet. This predator consumes social interaction.

The internet has changed the face of conversation so completely that we now accept AI as a substitute conversation partner—such as with the rise of chatbots like Replika or AI girlfriends.[9] Such changes are likely a dialectic loop—we create technology to assist in day-to-day tasks, the technology reshapes our society as we adapt to the power it gives us, and we create new computer technologies shaped by the changes we have experienced.[10] To cite Ps 115:8, "Those who make [idols or idol-ologies] will become like them, *everyone* who trusts in them" (NASB).

Broadly speaking, the internet has produced four issues. First, the internet fulfills part of Postman's prophecy—we are amusing ourselves to death. This is manifest in our poor mental health. Second, the internet is causing a breakdown in family dynamics and hindering child communication development. Third, the internet has reduced our ability to deal with confrontation. Fourth, the internet is causing a breakdown in empathy, which is probably the cause of our inability to love. I will look briefly at each of these.

---

8. Postman, *Amusing Ourselves to Death,* 65, citing Thoreau, *Walden,* 36.

9. Carr, *Shallows,* 203–6; Turkle, *Alone Together,* 23–34; Oremus, "Google's AI Passed a Famous Test"; Yalalov, "ChatGPT Passes the Turing Test"; Brandon, "Why AI Girlfriends Will Be More Popular than you Think."

10. Carr, *Shallows,* 44. See also: McLuhan, *Understanding Media.*

CHAPTER 8: NO MAN IS AN ISLAND 195

First, on the issue of the internet as entertainment and a source of mental illness, Postman continues his discussion, saying:

> A man in Maine and a man in Texas could converse, but not about anything either of them knew or cared very much about. The telegraph may have made the country into "one neighborhood," but it was a peculiar one, populated by strangers who knew nothing but the most superficial facts about each other.[11]

Given the sheer volume of information the internet generates, this concern about conversation as entertainment ought to be self-evident. Conversation between a Mainer and a Texan may entertain and inform, but it is unlikely to lead to policy changes for either.

The internet can cause depression. Jean Twenge writes that teens no longer party. Why meet in person when they can Skype, play computer games, watch videos, read (if they so choose), and enjoy all the entertainment their devices provide?[12] However, this does not fulfill their emotional needs. Twenge's numbers indicate that teens who spend more time online are 50 percent more prone to depression, while those who socialize in person are 20 percent *less* prone. This has been correlated with Facebook use. Social media use also significantly increases suicide risk—merely three hours per day can lead to a 35 percent increase.[13]

This might be because overuse of technology leads to underdeveloped emotional skills.[14] This particularly encourages the illusion that well-adjusted people never experience negative emotions rather than the reality that negative emotions are normal and learning to cope is part of adulthood. Social media also decreases our ability to focus, suggesting that distraction and interruption are typical rather than vices to be resisted.[15] These risks are especially concerning given that nearly everyone—particularly teens and young adults—uses social media: a mere 3 percent of the population claims to use social media *rarely*.[16] We have accepted these effects almost without dissent.

---

11. Postman, *Amusing Ourselves to Death*, 67.
12. Twenge, *iGen*, 71.
13. For these stats and more, see Twenge, *iGen*, 71–89. Bullying on the playground at least affords the opportunity to practice confrontation and reconciliation. Cyberbullying, with its anonymous offenders, does not.
14. Turkle, *Reclaiming Conversation*, 40.
15. Turkle, *Reclaiming Conversation*, 41.
16. Twenge, *iGen*, 54–55.

Effects on family life are less severe but have more lasting consequences. With the rise in digital communication, families have begun to communicate through their devices.[17] Children like to "tune out" their parents.[18] Conversely, parents who use their devices for entertainment neglect their children.[19] Both patterns are detrimental to child development. Family conversation allows children to practice working through their negative emotions through conversing with people they trust. Because it promotes the development of empathy and emotional resilience, conversation is also valuable for teaching children how to handle bullying and abuse.[20] Though children are capable of adapting, misusing this period in a person's life still has lasting repercussions.[21]

Rising entertainment and declining family life lead to more negative interactions and fewer emotional skills to *handle* those problems.[22] Consequently, we are increasingly prone to view disagreement as a *threat* rather than an invitation to dialogue and relationship.[23] As Tom Nichols puts it, "The Internet is making us meaner, shorter-fused, and incapable of conducting discussions where anyone learns anything."[24] These trends have led to the rise of so-called "cancel culture," which Twenge has linked to the use of social media.[25] This is reflected in trends on college campuses:

> In 2017, 58% of college students said it is "important to be part of a campus community where I am not exposed to intolerant and offensive ideas." This statement was endorsed by 63% of very liberal students, but it's a view that is not confined to the left; almost half of very conservative students (45%) endorsed that statement, too.[26]

---

17. Turkle, *Reclaiming Conversation*, 112.
18. Twenge, *iGen*, 74–75.
19. Turkle, *Reclaiming Conversation*, 108.
20. Turkle, *Reclaiming Conversation*, 106; Twenge, *iGen*, 71–89.
21. Carr, *Shallows*, 34. This concern also applies to adults, who are less capable of adaptation than children.
22. We are already prone to seeing the world as a dangerous place; see chapter 1, pp. 7–9, on "Mean World Syndrome."
23. Twenge, *iGen*, 166–68.
24. Nichols, *Death of Expertise*, 111.
25. Nichols, *Death of Expertise*, 46–47. I understand cancel culture as the tendency to insist that people who share offensive opinions on the internet ought to be silenced online or even face real-world consequences such as termination of employment.
26. Lukianoff and Haidt, *Coddling*, 47–48. Notice again that an outgroup bias—indicative of *ressentiment*—is not isolated to one political view.

"Real people, with their unpredictable ways, can seem difficult to contend with after one has spent a stretch in simulation."[27] Social media use makes us unprepared to handle conversation. This is complicated by the necessity of empathy and the decline of empathy noted by Sherry Turkle.[28]

As *practice* is necessary for developing empathy, the *lack* of practice introduced by social media is a cause of empathy's decline. Turkle writes:

> Face-to-face conversation is the most human—and humanizing—thing we do. Fully present to one another, we learn to listen. It's where we develop the capacity for empathy. It's where we experience the joy of being heard, of being understood. And conversation advances self-reflection, the conversation with ourselves that are the cornerstone of early development and continue throughout life.[29]

Note the emphasis on face-to-face. Twenge writes that the most significant difference between younger and older generations today is that younger generations no longer interact face-to-face: "iGen teens are less likely to take part in every single face-to-face social activity measured across four data sets of three different age groups. . . . Instead, they are communicating electronically."[30] Twenge takes this issue somewhat further. She argues that the notion of "online together" is an oxymoron. We can interact online *or* we can be together. We cannot do both.[31]

Unfortunately, consistent conversation online reprograms our minds to perceive online interactions as normative.[32] Anything else starts to *feel* wrong. This is likely a significant contributor to our growing discomfort with face-to-face conversation. Along with this trend, we are growing more selfish and disinterested in supporting one another in community.[33] Turkle has also commented on this *feeling* of aversion to community:

27. Turkle, *Reclaiming Conversation*, 7.
28. Recall chapter 4, pp. 48–9, see also p. 8.
29. Turkle, *Reclaiming Conversation*, 3.
30. Twenge, *iGen*, 69, 75.
31. Twenge, *iGen*, 80.
32. Tweng, *iGen*, 89; Carr, *Shallows*, 120–21. See also: Heino et al., "Relationshopping," 427–447. This piece demonstrates that online dating encourages us to view other people as products to be consumed rather than persons to be loved. Rather than taking our "real world" social skills to the internet, we appear to be taking our internet social skills into the "real world."
33. Twenge, *iGen*, 176. See also: Twenge and Campbell, *Narcissism Epidemic*, 2, 19, 31, 108–11. See especially the chapter on social media.

> The essayist William Deresiewicz said that as our communities have atrophied, we have moved from living in actual communities to making efforts to feel as though we are living in them. So, when we talk about communities now, we have moved "from a relationship to a feeling." We have moved from *being* in a community to having a *sense* of community. Have we moved from empathy to a *sense* of empathy? From friendship to a *sense* of friendship?[34]

Cyberspace largely prevents offering material aid to others, which otherwise would invoke feelings of community. Thus, instead of serving others, we narcissistically expect others to feed our emotions, but we do not notice this shift because we do not *feel* any differently. Since we do not notice this shift, we do not recognize that we have ceased to practice empathy, and thus we love less.

I have already argued that social media *might* be a causal factor in the rise of political polarization.[35] However, when it comes to our mental and social health, scholars overwhelmingly agree that social media use harms both and consequently hinders our ability to love one another. Naturally, this will immediately affect our enemies—those we love *least*. This should lead us to ask a reciprocal question: assuming that our ability to love is declining, what is needed to *regain* it?

III: What Are People For?

To rebuild love is to rebuild empathy. To rebuild empathy means reestablishing patterns of face-to-face interaction, *particularly* during confrontation. Turkle writes:

> [When] face-to-face, you get to see that you have hurt the other person. The other person gets to see that you are upset. It is this realization that triggers the beginning of forgiveness. None of this happens with "I'm sorry," *hit send*. . . . A face-to-face apology is an occasion to practice empathic skills.[36]

This is important, but it only hints at the deeper reality of love. Rebuilding face-to-face conversation is merely a means to that end.

---

34. Turkle, *Reclaiming Conversation*, 173.

35. Twenge, *iGen*, 286. Twenge is quite willing to entertain this possibility—particularly that political apathy *and* political polarization share the internet as a root cause.

36. Turkle, *Reclaiming Conversation*, 31.

CHAPTER 8: NO MAN IS AN ISLAND

Turkle describes that end, saying, "To join in conversation is to imagine another mind, to empathize, and to enjoy gesture, humor, and irony in the medium of talk."[37] Nichols also notices this and comments:

> This strange combination of distance and intimacy [in social media] poisons conversation. Reasonable arguments require participants to be honest and well intentioned. Actual proximity builds trust and understanding. We are not just brains in a tank processing disparate pieces of data ... Distance and anonymity remove patience and presumptions of goodwill. Rapid access to information and the ability to speak without having to listen, combined with the "keyboard courage" that allows people to say things to each other electronically they would never say in person, kill conversation.[38]

This recognition of a *mind* is essential. We are not merely computers or "the ghost in the machine."[39] We rely on physical cues as much as verbal cues. Michael Polanyi's term *emergence* is instructive—the combination of our biological components gives rise to the *emergence* of a sentient entity—*more* than the sum of its parts. Simply understanding the interlocking parts is *not* enough to understand the whole person.[40]

I want to look briefly at what is involved with recognizing that a person possesses the quality of emergence. I believe two things hold us back: we struggle to comprehend systems of interaction where constituent components are intertwined rather than wholly inseparable, and we struggle to understand interaction with an utterly independent and unpredictable entity.

Peter Leithart writes that the challenge of understanding the *self* has been poisoned by Descartes's *cogito ergo sum*—"I think, therefore I am." We interact with our surroundings—we even come to depend on various tools as if they were extensions of our bodies—but we do not *become* our surroundings.[41] Leithart writes:

> I am different from the things around me, yet I'm also inseparably intertwined with them. The world isn't just outside; it's also inside. I'm not only outside the rest of the world; I'm in it. My

---

37. Turkle, *Reclaiming Conversation*, 105.
38. Nichols, *Death of Expertise*, 130.
39. Carr, *Shallows*, 172; Leithart, *Traces of the Trinity*, 3.
40. Polanyi, *Tacit Dimension*, 4–5, 35–37.
41. Polanyi, *Tacit Dimension*, 6–18, 29–33.

connection with the world is a Celtic knot. Inside and outside form a Möbius strip that folds back on itself.[42]

This duality also applies to our interactions with other human beings: "Humans connect to other humans at so basic a level that when we disconnect, our own souls shatter into a thousand little pieces."[43] This will be more noticeable with people we are more attached to, such as our parents, children, extended family members, close friends, and most especially our husband or wife.[44]

Another illustration of this may be found in speech theory. Kent Bach and Robert Harnish helpfully divided aspects of communication into three parts—illocution, locution, and perlocution. Illocution is the thought I construct in my head. Locution is the physical message conveying this thought through speech, body language, symbols, or written words. The recipient then perlocutes or interprets the message. A conversation is *two persons* taking turns being the sender or the receiver, locuting and perlocuting as appropriate.[45]

Though it is convenient to divide the conversation into these components, the words we choose cannot be separated from the thought by which they were chosen. Neither can we separate the act of interpretation from the medium we are interpreting. So conversation cannot be conceived of as mere links in a chain but rather as a continuous curve with discernible segments. For mathematicians, this is akin to the difference between a summation and an integral, between discrete numbers and a data stream. For the artist, this is the distinction between the color and the painting, the clay and the sculpture, or the note and the symphony. Understanding the constituent parts is important, but it is incomplete until those parts are *reconstituted*. We tacitly experience this as the *flow* of conversation.

---

42. Leithart, *Traces of the Trinity*, 4.

43. Leithart, *Traces of the Trinity*, 17.

44. Recall the distinction between interpersonal and intergroup relationships in chapter 2, p. 35. Interpersonal, or strong-tie relationships, derive their value from the connection itself. Intergroup, or weak-tie relationships, derive their value from how the relationship reinforces the plausibility of our religious affections. They are a component of our "Plausibility Structure." Therefore, the danger of breaking an intergroup relationship is not in losing a single relationship but losing *all* of them at once. Losing a single interpersonal relationship is nearly as damaging as losing all of our intergroup relationships.

45. Long, *Art of Biblical History*, 155–56. See also: Bach and Harnish, *Linguistic Communication and Speech Acts*.

Second is the challenge of understanding the existence of another *mind*. Walter Kasper writes, "Dialogue, rightly understood, presupposes a listening heart and reciprocal listening to each other."[46] As a somewhat antisocial individual myself, I struggle with this. No matter how I observe, listen, plan, and anticipate in conversation, I cannot control the outcome. I must do more than demand their reception; I must also be receptive. This creates a sort of social dance in which we mutually accommodate each other. The adage that you connect by "putting yourself out there" is a lie, plain and simple. If I put myself "out there," I am making myself available for connections, but the others "out there" need to reciprocate:

> The Christian existentialist Gabriel Marcel argued that instead of considering others as inconveniences, we should welcome them with expectant "availability." Availability is "the aptitude to give oneself to anything which offers, and to bind oneself by the gift. . . . It means to transform mere circumstances into 'opportunities,' we might even say favours [*sic*], thus participating in the shaping of our own destiny and marking it with our seal." Availability means accepting unexpected situations not only as gifts for me but also as opportunities to imprint myself on the other who intrudes. . . . In a word, availability is love, and it is a love to others within one's immediate circle that opens out beyond the circle in "absolute availability." Not only my chosen others like my wife or husband, not only the close but unchosen loved ones like parents and children—not only those, but also strangers on the street, the beggar on the sidewalk, the enraged customer on the phone, the demanding boss, the resistant employee, the recalcitrant violinist, all are enclosed in the circle of my availability.[47]

So the nature of love itself—a mutual indwelling and interpenetration—is the nature of Love himself: the one triune God presented to us by his incarnate son, Jesus Christ. To love requires that we *practice* availability.

Practicing availability entails risk, but the alternative is far worse. To quote C. S. Lewis:

> To love at all is to be vulnerable. Love anything and your heart will be wrung and possibly broken. If you want to make sure of keeping it intact you must give it to no one, not even an animal. Wrap it carefully round with hobbies and little luxuries; avoid

---

46. Kasper, *Mercy*, 162–63.
47. Leithart, *Traces of the Trinity*, 102, 103.

all entanglements. Lock it up safe in the casket or coffin of your selfishness. But in that casket, safe, dark, motionless, airless, it will change. It will not be broken; it will become unbreakable, impenetrable, irredeemable.[48]

Given that the alternative is worse, we must choose to embrace availability even with its risks.

Availability involves three risks. First, we risk becoming a monster by taking away another person's uniqueness, to try to consume or subsume them:

> To love truly, one must not only move ecstatically out from himself to dwell in another, must not only open up a home in himself for the beloved, but must do so in a way that preserves the irreducible *otherness* of the beloved. Lovers penetrate one another only when they do not eradicate the individuality that makes their love possible. Love must *in*gest without *di*gesting the other.[49]

Availability, in this sense, entails risking the opportunity to sin.[50]

There is the opposite risk of being consumed by the other person. This is particularly damaging when the other is asking that I share in their pain:

> Painful as it may be, this psychological occupation of our souls by other people should not be shaken off. Our openness to their habitation in our minds, memories, imaginations is an act of love. We make ourselves, our very souls available to them. We become vulnerable to their fears, which become our fears; their worries and anxieties become ours. We bear their burdens in the deepest part of our psyche. And thus, painfully, our souls are enlarged.[51]

This can be a learning experience (as Leithart says), but this can *also* become a matter of inappropriate or insufficient boundary setting.[52] Such behavior should be addressed before it foments bitterness.

The third risk is failing to see the other as a person I must respect and care for. Though this is similar to the first risk, this goes beyond

---

48. Lewis, *Four Loves*, 121
49. Lewis, *Four Loves*, 46.
50. Lewis, *Four Loves*, 121.
51. Leithart, *Traces of the Trinity*, 104.
52. Cloud and Townsend, *Boundaries*, 51–54, 133.

being simply overbearing. This is not manipulation but apathy. This is not simply defacing but destroying:

> Not surprisingly, the self-enclosed person is hostile to interruption, to the demands and claims of others. We meet "what is not part of the self-generated (and self-generating) project [i.e., myself] with refusal or a sense of defeat." If I can't turn another person to my own purposes, that person is a roadblock, something to be run over and plowed under.[53]

Though this behavior can *seem* intentional, Hanlon's Razor should be applied here: never ascribe to malice that which can be equally explained by ignorance or stupidity. Even so, it remains a deeply sinful act, and it can lead to people shunning the sinner to avoid becoming the next victim.

To be *available* is to allow relationships to be *emergent*. We fail this when we come into a relationship with a *purpose* in mind for this person and refuse to relinquish control. When we do this, we are at risk of a sort of soft murder. We might deprive the person of *vitality* and relegate them to the status of a machine. To treat another person in this manner is to force them into a sort of living death—one that they can only escape by abandoning the relationship. To recognize that a person is an emergent entity is to recognize that they need things from me. Relationships cannot be formed from a pre-existing blueprint; instead, we must "start tinkering about" and see what surprises may be discovered. The relationship itself must be allowed to *emerge*.

Availability encapsulates my entire argument thus far. In addition to promoting empathy (or compassion), availability and forgiveness are linked. Without availability we view others as machines who need not apologize or forgive. To be available—to look for the humanity in others—requires us to forgive and seek forgiveness. Healthy Christian community is not a community where people never hurt one another or disagree. It is a community where people forgive.

Availability is also essential for the art of losing well. We may "turn the other cheek" or destroy the other by coercing them into the identity *we* have prepared for them. Sadly, availability also means allowing them the freedom to *reject* love, or even God's plans—but we should always be humble enough to recognize that *only God* knows who we are intended to be.

---

53. Leithart, *Traces of the Trinity*, 101.

We need to "re-humanize" people. Social media makes us forget that people are *people*. People are not nice, predictable, neat, or comfortable. If we expect a person to fulfill us as quickly and as easily as our phone apps do, we are in for disappointment.[54] The payoff, however, is that biological relationships are significantly more fulfilling than their artificial counterparts.[55]

Moreover, we need to remember that the value of a person goes far beyond the physical. The intended purpose of the person is not utilitarian but symbolic, for we are all made to imitate Christ (Rom 8:29).[56] C. S. Lewis wrote that the promises in Scripture include that at the last we shall be *like* Christ, and we shall have *glory*.[57] To be like Christ and to receive glory goes beyond the promise of *shalom*.[58] We shall stand before our creator and miraculously (and in proportion to how we have run the race), God will grant us the likeness of Jesus. This is the identity that God *delights* to create in us, one that creates *delight* in ourselves and brings *delight* to all of creation.[59]

This reality of what people are for must inform every part of our lives together. That I or others around me might become like this is a solemn and delightful burden. It is, as Lewis puts it, our "Weight of Glory:"

> It may be possible for each to think too much of his own potential glory hereafter; it is hardly possible for him to think too often or too deeply about that of his neighbour. The load, or weight, or burden of my neighbour's glory should be laid daily on my back, a load so heavy that only humility can carry it, and the backs of the proud will be broken. It is a serious thing to live in a society of possible gods and goddesses, to remember that the dullest and most uninteresting person you talk to may one day be a creature which, if you saw it now, you would be strongly tempted to worship, or else a horror and a corruption such as you now meet, if at all, only in a nightmare. All day long we are, in some degree, helping each other to one or other of these destinations. It is in the light of these overwhelming possibilities, it is with the awe and the circumspection proper to them, that we should conduct all our dealings with one another, all

---

54. Turkle, *Reclaiming Conversation*, 323.
55. Turkle, *Reclaiming Conversation*, 3, 12, 109–110, 174–175, 180, 297.
56. Ross, *Recalling the Hope of Glory*, 29.
57. Lewis, "Weight of Glory," 10.
58. Lewis, "Weight of Glory," 10; Moltmann, *Theology of Hope*, 216.
59. Lewis, "Weight of Glory," 13.

friendships, all loves, all play, all politics. There are no ordinary people. You have never talked to a mere mortal.[60]

People—even our enemies—are *for glory*. We owe them respect that is similar in essence to the respect we owe to God. Not, as Martin Buber puts it, "I and you" but "I and Thou."[61] We must not merely see people through the eyes of God but *God behind the eyes of others*.[62] People are living icons of Christ.

IV: Loving Our Enemies

To quote Jesus' disciples, "Who then can be saved?" (Luke 18:26). Can we love like this? Boris Bobrinskoy responds, "It is not easy to speak of the love for enemies. To speak of it, one must live it, and who of us can say that he or she lives this commandment of the Lord: 'Love your enemies, and pray for those who persecute you' (Matt 5:44 NRSVA)?"[63] We love them by seeking their flourishing.[64] This must be learned gradually. However, two approaches may be considered.

The first involves methods of improving our relationship skills.[65] Stephen Worchel has suggested several ways to do so. Worchel encourages improving our conflict management skills. We may begin by seeking an appropriate balance of communication and silence. We need to talk through our problems, but too much talk creates fatigue so we should take the occasional break. These conversations should be face-to-face whenever possible.[66] In situations involving group conflict, appointing representatives can be beneficial and reduce chaos.

---

60. Lewis, "Weight of Glory," 18–19.

61. Buber, *I and Thou*, 56–61, 69, 84, 89–95.

62. Bobrinskoy, *Compassion of the Father*, 28. This is *not* to be understood in the same manner as the Hindu greeting "namaste"—"I acknowledge the god within you." Persons are not themselves gods, no matter how much their deified state might appear as such. Rather, this is acknowledging that we all carry the image of *one* god who is above all and in all. See also: Bandura, "Social Cognitive Theory," 105.

63. Bobrinskoy, *Compassion of the Father*, 67.

64. Lewis, "*Storge*," in *Four Loves*, 16:58. See also "*Agape*" in the same collection: 13:20. This definition is heavily implied though not entirely explicit.

65. Therapeutic techniques include cognitive behavioral therapy, dialectical behavior therapy, and acceptance and commitment therapy. Lukianoff and Haidt, *Coddling*, 36–37. See chapter 1, p. 19.

66. Turkle, *Reclaiming Conversation*, 34; Twenge, *iGen*, 299.

Worchel also argues that identifying a common enemy or common cause has proven to be more effective than pure dialogue. Common-cause solutions are preferable, as common-enemy solutions tend to exacerbate conflict.[67] Dr. Martin Luther King suggested that race relations could be improved by engaging white and black communities in the cause of combating poverty. Specifically, he suggested that public welfare programs be constructed to address poverty by constructing and repairing infrastructure. Though more of these projects would naturally occur within black communities, they would create opportunities for white and black people to work *together* on a problem that affected *both*.[68] Such solutions ought to be pursued.

The second approach is to reduce the influence of social media on our lives. We can make a significant difference by approaching how we parent our children differently. Jean Twenge recommends that elementary school children be given no electronic devices, middle school children be given a dumbphone, and smartphones be given to high school students only.[69] As children have a noticeable lack of self-control, it is up to parents to help their children to learn that such devices are *tools* before they are toys. We can help to model this by choosing to *avoid* using the internet or software to solve problems whenever possible.[70]

Turkle suggests many ways to reduce our reliance on social media. In her words, "We don't want to discard social media, but we may want to rewrite our social contract with it."[71] We can begin by recognizing that this problem does not stem from a lack of self-control. The draw of technology must be respected. We are not addicts, but we *are* vulnerable.

Consequently, we should have a clear plan in mind for when it is acceptable for us to use these tools and for how long. This can be as simple as deciding to limit our time or as complex as creating a sort of

---

67. Worchel, "Cooperation and the Reduction of Intergroup Conflict," 263–64; Lukianoff and Haidt, *Coddling*, 267. See also: Sherif, "Superordinate Goals in the Reduction," 261. Common-enemy solutions cause two warring tribes to make peace but only in order to compete against a *third* tribe. Although this third tribe could be conceptual (such as coming together to combat world hunger), such a focus could eventually lead to the rise of *ressentiment* if the shared campaign is not successful. Moreover, there is not guarantee that the two previously warring tribes will not simply return to their conflict once their shared campaign is concluded. See chapter 1, pp. 20–1.

68. King, *Testament of Hope*, 476–77, 600–602, 614–17.

69. Twenge, *iGen*, 291–293.

70. Turkle, *Reclaiming Conversation*, 324.

71. Turkle, *Reclaiming Conversation*, 330.

"written contract" for ourselves, whatever method makes it easiest for *me* to remember how I have decided to conduct myself.[72] On the other hand, we should also have a clear plan in mind for when we will *not* use these tools and what we will fill that time with instead. This should include creating space for silence and creativity, especially if these are challenging. The goal is to learn to embrace boredom as an opportunity to daydream and reflect rather than as an invitation to play with your phone.[73] This can be further assisted by seeking out hobbies that involve "physical stuff," such as arts and crafts or athletics.[74]

Next, we should approach our conversations intentionally. Families should schedule times to connect with one another and talk about their hopes, fears, and upcoming activities. These times should have a strict prohibition on technology placed over them. If the "phone magnetism" is too strong, they should be stored in another room.[75] We should also take time to reflect on these interactions and our relationships in general. Who are the people we find ourselves interacting with the most? What works well within those relationships, and what could be improved? We should be especially aware of *our* faults, not others'. These are good opportunities to empathize—take a moment to slow down, catch your breath, and ask where your family members are hurting, fearful, or angry and what they are trying to create.[76]

We should also remember that the sheer volume of data on the internet generates content without context—it creates a sort of "white noise" that entertains rather than informs. Postman writes:

> You may get a sense of what is meant by context-free information by asking yourself the following question: How often does it occur that information provided you on morning radio or television, or in the morning newspaper, causes you to alter your plans for the day, or to take some action you would not otherwise have taken, or provides insight into some problem you are required to solve? . . . You may get a sense of what this means by asking yourself another series of questions: What steps do

---

72. I further encourage finding an accountability partner or spiritual father for guidance.

73. Turkle, *Reclaiming Conversation*, 319, 322. This can be a good opportunity to practice the Ignatian Examen; see chapter 6, p. 160n67.

74. Turkle, *Reclaiming Conversation*, 320.

75. Turkle, *Reclaiming Conversation*, 320.

76. Turkle, *Reclaiming Conversation*, 325. Recall chapter 2, pp. 33–8, on Social Identity Theory.

you plan to take to reduce the conflict in the Middle East? Or the rates of inflation, crime and unemployment? What are your plans for preserving the environment or reducing the risk of nuclear war? What do you plan to do about NATO, OPEC, the CIA, affirmative action, and the monstrous treatment of the Baha'is in Iran? I shall take the liberty of answering for you: You plan to do nothing about them.[77]

Postman is being hyperbolic, and his claim is out of date, but he has a point. Before taking to our keyboard, we should fact-check the issue, and we should recognize that our comment will only influence this particular conversation online. I apply a ten-minute limit to my replies in comment threads. If I cannot craft an appropriate response within that time, I delete what I have written and move on.

We should also take Postman's questions about significant geopolitics seriously. We can vote for change, but unless we are on-site, we cannot interact with *people*. Jürgen Moltmann argues:

> The Christian ethic is . . . reduced to the "ethical demand" to accept one's self and take responsibility for the world in general. But it is no longer able to give any pertinent ethical instructions for the ordering of social and political life. Christian love accordingly quits the realm of justice and of the social order. It is a thing that comes about in each several event of spontaneous co-humanity, in the I-thou relationship which is immediate and not objectively mediated. Justice, social order and political righteousness, once they have been rendered so void, must then be understood positivistically as pure organization, as matters of power and law. . . . Our "neighbour" comes on the scene only in personal encounter.[78]

There is a great deal to be said about how we deal with people groups or people at a distance. However, when the day is over, I am not *available* to these people to love them in any way. When I obsess over matters of power and law, I abandon opportunities to love the people God has placed *before me today*. We long for kingdom work, but what we get is mostly quotidian.[79] Although Turkle says, "Life is not a problem looking for a quick fix. Life is a conversation and you need places to have it. *The virtual provides*

---

77. Postman, *Amusing Ourselves to Death*, 68.

78. Moltmann, *Theology of Hope*, 313–14. Notice the reference to Martin Buber.

79. For encouragement in this, see: Norris, *Acedia and Me*; Norris, *Quotidian Mysteries*; and Harrison Warren, *Liturgy of the Ordinary*.

us with more spaces for these conversations and these are enriching," (and she is correct) these virtual spaces have their limits.[80] They demand too much, too fast, and with faceless persons. Such conversations should not be discarded, but before we engage one we should ask *what can be done here and now* as well as *what should be done out there eventually*, and we should notice the gap between the two. Rinse, repeat.

V: Conclusions—Practicing Love, Enduring Bitterness

As my study on bitterness concludes, I would like to summarize the preceding chapters. This is how we may seek justice without being consumed by bitterness. Perhaps the most common theme has been that we *must know our limits*. Justice activism conducted in bitterness is worse than weak justice activism or none. When we fall into the trap of bitterness, avoiding the cause might be appropriate. At the very least, we must set healthy boundaries. We cannot spend all our time immersed in the issues; we need to break from them and rest.

Loving our enemies requires striving to see their individuality and extending empathy at all times (chapter 4). We must listen before we speak. I have included prayers to prime us for this in the appendix. We need to maintain this subtext within activism—particularly remembering that we are called to imitate Jesus, not to avenge ourselves. Out of compassion we need to ask, "What is causing your pain and fear?" Looking for the *root cause* behind our enemy's behavior communicates to them that we value the *person*, not just the issue at hand, and demonstrates that we are not indifferent to the needs of others—and we might come to see our own flaws more clearly.

Compassion requires that we acknowledge the sins of our tribe. White supremacy is more historically prevalent, but black supremacy is currently accepted if not endorsed. As the Jews are the root yet the gentiles are grafted in, there is no room to boast (Rom 11:11–24). Misogyny is more historically prevalent, but misandry is currently accepted if not endorsed. There is no Jew nor Greek but all are one in Christ Jesus (Gal 3:28). Bigotry against homosexuals is more historically prevalent, but the rise of LGBT self-identification looks like a social contagion—peer

---

80. Turkle, *Reclaiming Conversation*, 331.

pressure into "being gay" or "being trans." We must love without competing for the moral high ground.

Compassion is the foundation of forgiveness or *releasing* our enemy from his or her sins against us (chapter 5). This entails reframing our enemy's actions, or it may start with the *decision* to forgive and work out the pain later.[81] However, to release our enemies from their sins, we must first remember that we are *commanded* to do this and that we ourselves require release from *our* sins.

Having greater concern for the practice of formal confession may facilitate this. Simply calling ourselves "sinners" only abstracts the issue—we must remember that our sins are concrete and ongoing, requiring us to identify them. The work of forgiveness—of release—begins small. We release sins that are easy to release. We release people whom we love. By going through the motions first, we practice for when it gets hard. Therefore, we should pray for our enemies at least weekly.[82]

The command to forgive means we repent of our sins too. This can cause discomfort, especially when our enemies are unrepentant. We need to anticipate this, particularly through boundary setting. This does not constitute real forgiveness, nor should it discount the future possibility of forgiveness, but it gives us the space to heal. Though this helps us, it is *more* important for our enemies.

Forgiveness is aided by maintaining a practice of gratitude (chapter 6). We must abide in the belief that every good thing is a gift from God. In particular, we ought to reclaim the *tôḏâ* ritual. When in trouble, we need to (1) Ask God for deliverance, believing that he *will* deliver, (2) anticipate God's deliverance, and (3) when God delivers, we need to testify to God's work in person. Churches could hold regular community events that invite testimony or through sharing prayers through an internet forum or email chains. We can supplement this with readings from hagiography for our edification and encouragement. Since the *tôḏâ* has been subsumed into the Eucharist we should *not* be lax in celebrating it as our corporate act of gratitude.[83]

The act of public testimony should be supplemented with private reflection. This practice has existed in the church from antiquity as the daily examen. This can be done in prayer, supported by journaling.

81. See chapter 5, p. 139, on the REACH and Enright models.
82. See Appendix A for some suggestions.
83. I do not see this as the sole reason why we should participate in the Eucharist on a regular basis.

When reflecting, we should ask, "Where was God at work in my life today? What things am I grateful for?"

Gratitude is also expressed through generosity. We should be willing to lend without interest and to give lavishly. Though this practice of giving is reinforced through tithing, we should also give charitably to those in need.[84] This should be done *locally* when possible—particularly by providing specific needs directly rather than giving money when asked. It can also be done through giving to charitable organizations. Our giving ought to be *more* than simply giving money as well—we have time and skills that can be offered to our neighbors and the church.

Lastly, we must come to terms with the possibility that our activism could fail (chapter 7). If so, we must be prepared to accept that loss graciously rather than resort to force. We should learn to live with our discomfort in the world. It is a reminder that we are waiting for something *more*—for the kingdom of God to be revealed among us in all its fullness. This hope transcends any earthly pain we might suffer and is *worth* the pain. There truly is *life* after death.

Without a firm foundation in faith, affirmed through daily prayer, reading Scripture, regular participation worship and sacrament, and fellowship, we cannot resist the world. Rod Dreher's recommendations in *The Benedict Option* should be taken seriously, though we should guard against defeatism and quietism.

Accepting loss is painful. We need to strive to redeem our memories of suffering. We should not deny suffering nor should we should diminish its severity, but we should make every effort not to embellish it. We should resist adopting a victim mentality. Instead, we should share our suffering with God and practice gratitude. We do not suffer needlessly or alone.

Even so, we must continue to resist evil and advocate for those in need. However, we must remember the *purpose* of advocacy—loving our neighbor rather than defeating evil. David Kinnaman says, "We have become famous for what we oppose, rather than who we are for."[85] This needs to change. We have an extraordinary model of this in Dr. King's contract for activism and preparatory workshops. Contemporary activism lacks these practices, and their absence is glaring.

---

84. Although a 10 percent tithe was required, the total value of the gifts required of Israel would amount to approximately 25 percent.

85. Twenge, *iGen*, 140. See also: Kinnaman et al., *unChristian*.

We can also resist evil passively. Like the early church, we can choose to be a subversive presence in the world to show how things could be *better*. We can also take action insofar as we are able to reduce injustice for others through our vocation. We ought to conduct our lives this way as a matter of course, but we should also recognize that this is *not* insufficient. It merely falls short of the profound social change that we might prefer—change that happens rarely and typically through violence.

Though I fear we are living in a time when the bitterness of our activism is a more serious problem than the injustice we protest, I return to these words by John Donne:

> No man is an island, entire of itself.
>
> Each is a piece of the continent, a part of the main.
>
> If a clod be washed away by the sea, Europe is the less.
>
> As well as if a promontory were.
>
> As well as if a manor of thine own or of thine friend's were.
>
> Each man's death diminishes me, for I am involved in mankind.
>
> Therefore, send not to know, for whom the bell tolls, it tolls for thee.[86]

Our shared humanity is the essential cause of our bitterness. We are sinful in our failures, and even our attempts to *redress* those failures can lead to greater sin. Yet as much as our humanity is the cause, it is also our way through. It is not our salvation. Salvation comes from God alone. Yet even God shares in our humanity. Therefore, "Beloved, let us love one another, because love is from God; everyone who loves is born of God and knows God. Whoever does not love does not know God, for God is love." (1 John 4:7–8 NRSVA) Yes, even when thirteen dwarves show up on your doorstep unannounced.

---

86. Donne, "For Whom the Bell Tolls/No Man Is an Island."

Conclusion

> Blessed is the man who has learnt to love all men equally.
> —Maximus the Confessor[1]

I'M VISITING WITH MY father's side of the family today. We're celebrating Thanksgiving a few days early so that my uncle and his family can travel out to Ohio from Idaho. It is now nearly twenty days since Donald Trump was elected to the White House for a second term in an overwhelming victory. The country is experiencing a sense of anticipation, as if profound change is on the horizon. Some anticipate with dread, others with hope. Some have even suggested that the era of "woke politics" is over and that we are finally returning to normalcy. As ever, I remain skeptical. However, although I cannot say what precisely the future holds, neither can I deny that we are living through moments of transition.

Yet, the promise of a new heaven and a new earth remains just as immanent. Poor Paul probably believed he would not die before the coming of the kingdom, such was his belief in Jesus' immanent return. No doubt he was (and perhaps still is) surprised that God's plan has taken so long to unfold. Except, his belief was right. God's return truly is immanent, whether it comes this year or in a thousand years. We do not hope in vain, and as dark as history has become, we can remain confident that God will not permit us to utterly self-destruct, annihilating the Creator's creation and us along with it.

For this reason, Paul also exhorted the church to *encourage one another*. We're not meant to live this life alone. Wendell Berry wrote:

---

1. Maximus, *Selected Writings*, 37.

> Good work finds the way between pride and despair. It graces with health. It heals with grace. It preserves the given so that it remains a gift. By it we lose loneliness: we clasp the hands of those who go before us, and the hands of those who come after us; we enter the little circle of each other's arms, and the larger circle of lovers whose hands are joined in a dance, and the larger circle of all creatures, passing in and out of life, who move also in a dance, to a music so subtle and vast that no ear hears it except in fragments.[2]

As love for our enemies might answer our bitterness towards one another, love is also how we endure. We endure by our love for one another, by our love for those gone before us in faith, and by the love poured out on us through the Holy Spirit whom God has given to us (Rom 5:5). If we forget this, we are nothing (1 Cor 13:2). If we cannot love one another, we cannot hope to love our enemies. If we can neither love one another nor receive God's love, then truly our faith and our hope are garbage.

Therefore, fellow pilgrims, whether we are hopeful or fearful of the future, let us soldier on. Let us love one another. Let us love God's word and meditate on it day by day. Above all, let us love God and fellowship with him in prayer. I freely admit, my understanding of love is incomplete at best. What I do know is that God's love truly does make things better. Even when it doesn't feel like it.

> So we do not lose heart. Even though our outer nature is wasting away, our inner nature is being renewed day by day. For this slight momentary affliction is preparing us for an eternal weight of glory beyond all measure, because we look not at what can be seen but at what cannot be seen; for what can be seen is temporary, but what cannot be seen is eternal. (2 Cor 4:16–18 NRSVA)

---

2. Berry, *What Are People For*, 10.

Appendix

THESE PRAYERS MAY BE used as written or as inspiration for your own prayers. I have used these myself and found them especially useful when struggling to love others (especially in conflict circumstances) or to forgive my enemies.

Prayers for our Enemies:

To be prayed together—

For Those Whom You Have Wronged:
Lord, I pray to thee on behalf of all whom I, a sinner, have sorrowed, offended, or insulted, in word, deed, or thought, with knowledge or in ignorance: do not abandon them, but, in thy mercy, help them and save them. Amen

For Enemies and Those Who Grieve You:
I pray thee, Lord, especially for those who have offended me in any way, or have sorrowed me, or done me some other evil: Do not punish them on account of me, a sinner, but instead pour out thy grace upon them. Amen

To be prayed before partaking in the Eucharist—

A Prayer of St. John Damascene:
Grant mercy, O Lord, to them that hate me, or oppose me, or wrong me, or slander me, so that none of them may suffer any evil in any way—whether in this present age or in the age to come—on account of me, an unclean sinner. Cleanse them instead by thy mercy and protect them, O Good One, by thy grace. Amen

To be prayed in any time that pride causes us to think ourselves wholly good and our enemies wholly evil; but especially to be prayed during Advent, Lent, or other seasons of repentance—

> *The Prayer of St. Ephraim:*
> O Lord and Master of my life, give me not a spirit of sloth, despair, lust of power, and idle talk. But give rather a spirit of chastity, humility, patience, and love to thy servant. Yea, O Lord and King, grant me to see my own transgressions, and not to judge my brother: for blessed art thou unto ages of ages. Amen

Prayers taken from:

Mikitish and Herman, *Orthodox Christian Prayers*, 71, 111, 156.

Prayer of Francis of Assisi

To be prayed when in an argument that is unavoidable, or before such an argument—

> Lord, make me an instrument of your peace.
>
> Where there is hatred, let me sow love;
> where there is injury, pardon;
> where there is doubt, faith;
> where there is despair, hope;
> where there is darkness, light;
> and where there is sadness, joy.
>
> O Divine Master, grant that I may not so much seek
> to be consoled as to console;
> to be understood as to understand;
> to be loved as to love.
> For it is in giving that we receive;
> it is in pardoning that we are pardoned;
> and it is in dying that we are born to eternal life.
>
> Amen.

St. Francis of Assisi, first published in *La Clochette*, Dec. 1912. Details unknown. https://www.archspm.org/faith-and-discipleship/prayer/catholic-prayers/st-francis-of-assisi-make-me-an-instrument-of-your-peace.

Bibliography

Acampora, Christa Davis, ed. *Nietzsche's "On the Genealogy of Morals": Critical Essays*. Lanham, MD: Rowman & Littlefield, 2006.
Adachi, Paul J. C., et al. "From Outgroups to Allied Forces: Effect of Intergroup Cooperation in Violent and Nonviolent Video Games on Boosting Favorable Outgroup Attitudes." *Journal of Experimental Psychology: General* 145.3 (2016) 259–65.
Adams, Douglas. *The Ultimate Hitchhiker's Guide to the Galaxy*. New York: Del Ray, 2002.
Alcott, Hunt, et al. "The Welfare Effects of Social Media." *American Economic Review* 110.3 (2020) 629–76.
Alighieri, Dante. *Purgatorio*. In *The Divine Comedy*. Translated and edited by Allen Mandelbaum. New York: Alfred A. Knopf, 1986.
Allender, Dan B. *The Healing Path: How the Hurts in Your Past Can Lead You to a More Abundant Life*. Colorado Springs: Waterbrook, 1999.
Ambrose. "On the Cross, Christ Prays for His Slanderers." In *Luke* by Arthur A. Just Jr., edited by Thomas C. Oden, 3:108. Ancient Christian Commentary on Scripture: New Testament. Downers Grove, IL: IVP, 1998.
Andersen, Margaret L., and Patricia Hill Collins (eds.). *Race, Class, and Gender: An Anthology*. 9th ed. Boston: Cengage Learning, 2015.
Anderson, Ashley, et al. "The 'Nasty Effect': Online Incivility and Risk Perceptions of Emerging Technologies." *Journal of Computer-Mediated Communication* 19 (2014) 373–87.
Anderson, Benedict. *Imagined Communities: Reflections on the Origin and Spread of Nationalism*. First Indian Reprint. Jaipur: Rawat, 2015.
Arendt, Hannah. *Eichmann in Jerusalem: A Report on the Banality of Evil 1963*. New York: Penguin, 2006.
Arnett, Jeffery, and Lene Jensen. "A Congregation of One: Individualized Religious Beliefs Among Emerging Adults." *Journal of Adolescent Research* 17.5 (2002) 451–67.
Athanasius of Alexandria. *On the Incarnation: De Incarnatione Verbi Dei*. Translated by John Behr. Foreword by C. S. Lewis. Popular Patristics. Crestwood, NY: St. Vladimir's Seminary Press, 2011.

Augustine. "Will Martyrs Retain Their Wounds?" In *John 11–12* by Joel C. Elowski, edited by Thomas C. Oden, 4b:371. Ancient Christian Commentary on Scripture: New Testament. Downers Grove, IL: IVP, 1998.

Bach, Kent, and Robert M. Harnish. *Linguistic Communication and Speech Acts.* Cambridge, MA: MIT Press, 1982.

Backstrom, Lars, et al. "Four Degrees of Separation." *Proceedings of the 4th Annual ACM Web Science Conference* (2012) 33–42. https://arxiv.org/abs/1111.4570.

Baider, Fabienne. "'Go to Hell Fucking Faggots, May You Die!': Framing the LGBT Subject in Online Comments." *Łódź Papers in Pragmatics* 14.1 (2018): 69–92.

Bail, Chris. *Breaking the Social Media Prism: How to Make Our Platforms Less Polarizing.* Princeton, NJ: Princeton University Press, 2021.

Bail, Christopher A., et al. "Exposure to Opposing Views on Social Media Can Increase Political Polarization." *Proceedings of the National Academy of Sciences* 115.37 (2018) 9216–221.

Bailey, Kenneth. *The Cross and the Prodigal: Luke 15 Through the Eyes of Middle Eastern Peasants.* Revised and expanded ed. Downers Grove, IL: IVP, 2005.

———. *Jesus Through Middle Eastern Eyes: Cultural Studies in the Gospels.* Downers Grove, IL: IVP, 2008.

———. *Paul Through Mediterranean Eyes: Cultural Studies in 1 Corinthians.* Grand Rapids: IVP Academic, 2011.

Bakshy, Eytan, et al. "Exposure to Ideologically Diverse News and Opinion on Facebook." *Science* 348.6239 (2015) 1130–32.

Baldassarri, Delia, and Barum Park. "Was There a Culture War? Partisan Polarization and Secular Trends in US Public Opinion." *Journal of Politics* 82.3 (2020) 809–27.

Bandura, Albert. "Social Cognitive Theory of Mass Communication." In *Media Effects: Advances in Theory and Research,* 3rd ed, edited by Bryant Jennings and Mary Beth Oliver, 94–124. New York: Routledge, 2009.

———. *Social Foundations of Thought and Action: A Social Cognitive Theory.* Englewood Cliffs, NJ: Prentice-Hall, 1986.

———. *Social Learning Theory.* Englewood Cliffs, NJ: Prentice Hall, 1977.

Banks, Antoine, et al. "#PolarizedFeeds: Three Experiments on Polarization, Framing, and Social Media." *International Journal of Press/Politics* 26.3 (2021) 609–34.

Barberá, Pablo. "How Social Media Reduces Mass Political Polarization: Evidence from Germany, Spain, and the US." Job Market Paper, New York University, 2014.

———. "Social Media, Echo Chambers, and Political Polarization." In *Social Media and Democracy,* edited by Nathaniel Persily and Joshua A. Tucker, 34–55. Cambridge, MA: Cambridge University Press, 2020.

———. "Tweeting from Left to Right: Is Online Political Communication More Than an Echo Chamber?" *Psychological Science* 26.10 (2015) 1531–42.

———., et al. "Social Media, Political Polarization, and Political Disinformation: A Review of the Scientific Literature." *SSRN Electronic Journal* (2018). DOI: 10.2139/ssrn.3144139.

Barnes, Julian. *Nothing to Be Frightened Of.* New York, NY: Knopf, 2008.

Barnidge, Matthew. "Exposure to Political Disagreement in Social Media Versus Face-to-Face and Anonymous Online Settings." *Political Communication* 34.2 (2017) 302–21.

———. "The Role of News in Promoting Political Disagreement on Social Media." *Computers in Human Behavior* 52 (Nov. 2015) 211–18.

———. "Social Affect and Political Disagreement on Social Media." *Social Media + Society* (Jul.-Sep. 2018) 1–12.

———., et al. "Networks and Selective Avoidance: How Social Media Networks Influence Unfriending and Other Avoidance Behaviors." *Social Science Computer Review* (2022) 1–22.

Bar-Tal, Daniel, et al. "A Sense of Self-Perceived Collective Victimhood in Intractable Conflicts." *International Review of the Red Cross* 91.874 (2009) 229–58.

Basil the Great. *On the Human Condition.* Translated by Nona Verna Harrison. Edited by John Behr and Augustine Casiday. Popular Patristics. Crestwood, NY: St. Vladimir's Seminary Press, 2005.

———. *On Social Justice.* Translated by C. Paul Schroeder. Popular Patristics. Crestwood, NY: St. Vladimir's Seminary Press, 2009.

Battle, Michael. "Penitence as Practiced in African/African American Christian Spirituality." In *Repentance in Christian Theology,* edited by Mark J. Boda and Gordon T. Smith, 329–46. Collegeville, MN: Liturgical, 2006.

Baumeister, Roy F. "The Victim Role, Grudge Theory, and Two Dimensions of Forgiveness." In *Dimensions of Forgiveness: Psychological Research and Theological Perspectives,* edited by Everett L. Worthington, Jr., 79–106. Philadelphia: Templeton Foundation, 1998.

Bautch, Richard J. "May Your Eyes Be Open and Your Ears Attentive: A Study of Penance and Penitence in the Writings." In *Repentance in Christian Theology,* edited by Mark J. Boda and Gordon T. Smith, 67–86. Collegeville, MN: Liturgical, 2006.

Beale, G. K. *The Temple and the Church's Mission: A Biblical Theology of the Dwelling Place of God.* New Studies in Biblical Theology. Series editor D. A. Carson. Downers Grove, IL: IVP, 2004.

Beam, Michael, et al. "Facebook News and (De)Polarization: Reinforcing Spirals in the 2016 US Election." *Information, Communication & Society* 21 (2018) 1–19.

Berger, Peter L. *A Rumor of Angels: Modern Society and the Rediscovery of the Supernatural.* Garden City, NY: Doubleday and Company, 1970.

———. *The Many Altars of Modernity: Toward a Paradigm for Religion in a Pluralist Age.* Boston: De Gruyter, 2014.

———. *The Sacred Canopy: Elements of a Sociological Theory of Religion.* New York: Anchor, 1967.

———., and Thomas Luckmann. *The Social Construction of Reality: A Treatise in the Sociology of Knowledge.* Garden City, NY: Anchor, 1966.

Bergin, A. E. "Three Contributions of a Spiritual Perspective to Counseling, Psychotherapy, and Behavior Change." *Counseling and Values* 33 (1988) 21–32.

Berkowitz, Leonard. "Aggressive Humors as a Stimulus to Aggressive Responses." *Journal of Personality and Social Psychology* 16.4 (1970) 710–17.

———. "Some Effects of Thoughts on Anti- and Prosocial Influences of Media Events: A Cognitive-Neoassociation Analysis." *Psychology Bulletin* 95.3 (1984) 410–27.

Bergland, Christopher. "How Has News Changed Over the Past 30 Years? A 28-Year Analysis Shows That Reporting Has Become More Subjective Since 1989." *Psychology Today,* May 19, 2019. https://www.psychologytoday.com/us/blog/the-athletes-way/201905/how-has-news-changed-over-the-past-30-years.

Berry, Wendell. *What Are People For?: Essays by Wendell Berry.* San Francisco: North Point, 1990.

Bhattacharya, Sanmitra, et al. "Perceptions of Presidential Candidates' Personalities in Twitter." *Journal of the Association for Information Science and Technology* 67.2 (2016) 249–67.

Bittner, Rüdiger. "Ressentiment." In *Nietzsche, Genealogy, Morality: Essays on Nietzsche's Genealogy of Morals*, edited by Amélie Okensberg Rorty and Richard Schacht, 127–38. Philosophical Traditions. Berkeley: University of California Press, 1994.

Block, Daniel. *For the Glory of God: Recovering a Biblical Theology of Worship*. Grand Rapids: Baker, 2014.

Bobrinskoy, Boris. *The Compassion of the Father*. Translated by Anthony P. Gythiel. Crestwood, NY: St. Vladimir's Seminary Press, 2003.

Boda, Mark J. "Renewal in Heart, Word, and Deed: Repentance in the Torah." In *Repentance in Christian Theology*, edited by Mark J. Boda and Gordon T. Smith, 3–24. Collegeville, MN: Liturgical, 2006.

———., and Gordon T. Smith, eds. *Repentance in Christian Theology*. Collegeville, MN: Liturgical Press, 2006.

Boersma, Hans. *Heavenly Participation: The Weaving of a Sacramental Tapestry*. Grand Rapids: Eerdmans, 2011.

Bollhagen, James. *Ecclesiastes*. Edited by Dean O. Wenthe et al. Concordia Commentary: A Theological Exposition of Sacred Scripture. St. Louis: Concordia, 2011.

Bonhoeffer, Dietrich. *The Bonhoeffer Reader*. Edited by Clifford J. Green and Michael P. DeJonge. Minneapolis: Fortress, 2013.

———. *The Cost of Discipleship*. Translated by Chr. Kaiser Verlag, R. H. Fuller, and Irmgard Booth. Revised and abridged ed. London: SCM, 1959.

———. "Thy Kingdom Come! The Prayer of the Church-Community for God's Kingdom on Earth." In *The Bonhoeffer Reader*, edited by Clifford J. Green and Michael P. DeJonge, 341–57. Minneapolis: Fortress, 2013.

Boulianne, Shelley, et al. "Right Wing Populism, Social Media and Echo Chambers in Western Democracies." *New Media and Society* 22.4 (2020) 683–99.

Bourdieu, Pierre. "The Forms of Capital." In *Handbook of Theory and Research for the Sociology of Education*, edited by John G. Richardson, 46–58. New York: Greenwood, 1946.

Boxell, Levi, et al. "Greater Internet Use Is Not Associated with Faster Growth in Political Polarization Among US Demographic Groups." *Proceedings of the National Academy of Sciences of the United States of America* 114.40 (2017) 10612–17.

Boyd, James. "Nixon's Southern Strategy: 'It's All in the Charts.'" *New York Times*, May 17, 1970.

Bozdag, Cigdem. "Managing Diverse Online Networks in the Context of Polarization: Understanding How We Grow Apart on Social Media." *Social Media + Society* (Oct.–Dec. 2020) 1–13.

Brady, William J., et al. "Attentional Capture Helps Explain Why Moral and Emotional Content Go Viral." *Journal of Experimental Psychology General* 149 (2019) 746–56.

———. "Emotion Shapes the Diffusion of Moralized Content in Social Networks." *Proceedings of the National Academy of Sciences of the United States of America* 114 (2017) 7313–18.

Brandon, Marianne. "Why AI Girlfriends Will Be More Popular Than You Think: Meet the Latest Iteration of AI Companions." *Psychology Today*, Jan. 21, 2024. https://www.psychologytoday.com/us/blog/the-future-of-intimacy/202401/why-ai-girlfriends-will-be-more-popular-than-you-think.

Brewer, Marilynn B. "The Social Self: On Being the Same and Different at the Same Time." *Personality and Social Psychology Bulletin* 17.5 (1991) 475–82.

Brother Jerome. "The Same Flesh, But More Glorious." In *John 11–12* by Joel C. Elowsk, edited by Thomas C. Oden, 4b:371. Ancient Christian Commentary on Scripture: New Testament. Downers Grove, IL: IVP, 1998.

Brown, Francis, S. R. Driver, and C. A. Briggs, eds. *Hebrew and English Lexicon of the Old Testament: With an Appendix Containing the Biblical Aramaic*. Translated by Edward Robinson. Oxford: Clarendon, 1906.

Brueggemann, Walter. *David's Truth in Israel's Imagination and Memory*. 2nd ed. Minneapolis: Augsburg Fortress, 2002.

———. *First and Second Samuel*. Interpretation Bible Commentary. Louisville: Westminster John Knox, 1990.

———. *Isaiah 1–39*. Edited by Patrick D. Miller and David L. Bartlett. Westminster Bible Companion. Vol. 13. Louisville: Westminster John Knox, 1998.

———. "The Summons to New Life: A Reflection." In *Repentance in Christian Theology*, edited by Mark J. Boda and Gordon T. Smith, 347–70. Collegeville, MN: Liturgical, 2006.

Bryant, Jennings, and Dolf Zillman. "Using Television to Alleviate Boredom and Stress: Selective Exposure as a Function of Induced Excitational States." *Journal of Broadcasting* 28.1 (1984) 1–20.

———., and Mary Beth Oliver, eds. *Media Effects: Advances in Theory and Research*. 3rd ed. New York: Routledge, 2009.

Buber, Martin. *I and Thou*. Translated by Walter Kaufmann. New York: Touchstone, 1970.

Bullivant, Stephen. *Nonverts: The Making of Ex-Christian America*. New York: Oxford University Press, 2022.

Busselle, Rick. "Television Exposure, Parents' Precautionary Warnings, and Young Adults' Perceptions of Crime." *Communication Research* 30.5 (2003) 530–56.

———., and Helena Bilandzic. "Fictionality and Perceived Realism in Experiencing Stories: A Model of Narrative Comprehension and Engagement." *Communication Theory* 18.2 (2008) 255–80.

Calice, Mihaila M. "Polarized Platforms?: How Partisanship Shapes Perceptions of 'Algorithmic News Bias.'" *New Media and Society* (2021) 1–22.

Campbell, Donald T. *Ethnocentric and Other Altruistic Motives*. Lincoln: University of Nebraska Press, 1965.

Campbell, Scott W., and Rich Ling. "Effects of Mobile Communication: Revolutions in an Evolving Field." In *Media Effects: Advances in Theory and Research*, 4th ed., edited by Mary Beth Oliver, Arthur A. Raney, and Jennings Bryant, 389–404. New York: Routledge, 2019.

Card, Orson Scott. *Ender's Game*. Author's definitive edition. New York: Tor, 1991.

———. *Speaker for the Dead*. New York: Tor, 1986.

Carr, Nicholas. *The Shallows: What the Internet Is Doing to Our Brains*. New York: W. W. Norton, 2010.

Carrette, Jeremy, and Tim Dowley. "Critical Theory and Religion." In *Introduction to World Religions: Third Edition*, edited by Christopher Partridge, 28–31. Minneapolis: 1517 Media, 2018.

Cartwright, Dorwin. "Some Principles of Mass Persuasion." *Human Relations* 2 (1949) 253–67.

Carson, D. A. *Love in Hard Places*. Wheaton, IL: Crossway, 2002.

Casili, Antonio A., and Paola Tubaro. "Social Media Censorship in Times of Political Unrest: A Social Simulation Experiment with the UK Riots." *Bulletin de Méthodologie Sociologique* 115 (2012) 5–20.

Cate, Curtis. *Friedrich Nietzsche*. Woodstock, NY: Overlook, 2005.

Cehajic, Sabina, and Rupert Brown. "Silencing the Past: Effects of Intergroup Contact on Acknowledgment of In-group Responsibility." *Social Psychological and Personality Science* 1.2 (2009) 190–96. http://dx.doi.org/10.1177/1948550609359088.

―――., et al. "Forgive and Forget? Antecedents and Consequences of Intergroup Forgiveness in Bosnia and Herzegovina." *Political Psychology* 29.3 (2008) 351–67. http://dx.doi.org/10.1111/ j.1467-9221.2008.00634.x.

Ceron, Andrea. "Internet, News, and Political Trust: The Difference Between Social Media and Online Media Outlets." *Journal of Computer-Mediated Communication* 20.5 (2015) 487–503.

Chaitin, Julia, and Shoshana Steinberg. "You Should Know Better: Expressions of Empathy and Disregard Among Victims of Massive Social Trauma." *Journal of Aggression, Maltreatment & Trauma* 17.12 (2008) 197–226. http://dx.doi.org/10.1080/ 10926770802344851.

Chang, Chingching. "Motivated Processing: How People Perceive News Covering Novel or Contradictory Health Research Findings." *Science Communication* 37 (2015) 602–34.

Chilton, Bruce D. *The Isaiah Targum: Introduction, Translation, Apparatus and Notes*. Edited by Keven Cathcart et al. Translated by Bruce D. Chilton. Aramaic Bible. Vol. 11. Wilmington, DE: Michael Glazier, 1987.

Choi, Doo-Hun, and Donghee Shin. "Exploring Political Compromise in the New Media Environment: The Interaction Effects of Social Media Use and the Big Five Personality Traits." *Personality and Individual Differences* 106 (2017) 163–71.

Chrysologus, Peter. "Reopening Old Wounds." In *John 11–12* by Joel C. Elowski, edited by Thomas C. Oden, 4b:367–68. Ancient Christian Commentary on Scripture: New Testament. Downers Grove, IL: IVP, 1998.

Chrysostom, John. "Homily 61.4." In *Matthew 14–28* by Manilo Simonetti, edited by Thomas C. Oden, 1b:87–88. Ancient Christian Commentary on Scripture: New Testament. Downers Grove, IL: IVP, 1998.

―――. "In Ascensionem Christi." English translation in Edith M. Humphrey, "Reclaiming All Paul's Rs: Apostolic Atonement by Way of Some Eastern Fathers." In *One God, One People, One Future: Essays in Honour of N. T. Wright*, edited by John Anthony Dunne and Eric Lewellen, 421–39. London: SPCK, 2018.

―――. *The Divine Liturgy According to St. John Chrysostom with Appendicies*. 2nd ed. South Canaan, PA: St. Tikhon's Seminary Press, 1977.

―――. "Praying Daily for Forgiveness." In *Matthew 1–13* by Manilo Simonetti, edited by Thomas C. Oden, 1a:136. Ancient Christian Commentary on Scripture: New Testament. Downers Grove, IL: IVP, 1998.

―――. "Resist Not Evil." In *Matthew 1–13* by Manilo Simonetti, edited by Thomas C. Oden, 1a:118. Ancient Christian Commentary on Scripture: New Testament. Downers Grove, IL: IVP, 1998.

Chryssavgis, John. "Life in Abundance: Eastern Orthodox Perspectives on Repentance and Confession." In *Repentance in Christian Theology*, edited by Mark J. Boda and Gordon T. Smith, 211–230. Collegeville, MN: Liturgical, 2006.

Cloud, Henry, and John Townsend. *Boundaries: When to Say Yes, How to Say No to Take Control of Your Life*. Grand Rapids: Zondervan, 1992.

Chung, Adrienne, and Michael D. Slater. "Reducing Stigma and Out-Grow Distinctions Through Perspective-Taking in Narratives." *Journal of Communication* 63.5 (2013). DOI: 10.1111/jcom.12050.

Cikara, Mina, and Jay Van Bavel. "The Neuroscience of Intergroup Relations: An Integrative Review." *Perspectives on Psychological Science* 9.3 (2014) 245–74.

Cimino, Richard P., and Don Lattin. *Shopping for Faith: American Religion in the New Millennium*. San Francisco: Jossey-Bass, 1998.

Cinelli, Matteo, et al. "The Echo Chamber Effect on Social Media." *Proceedings of the National Academy of Sciences* 118.9 (2021) https://doi.org/10.1073/pnas.2023301118.

Clinton, Hillary (@HillaryClinton). "George Floyd's family and community deserved for his killer to be held accountable . . ." Tweet, Apr. 20, 2021, 5:13 PM. https://twitter.com/HillaryClinton/status/1384616338002366468.

Cohen, Jonathan, et al. "Media Identity and the Self." In *Media Effects: Advances in Theory and Research*. Edited by Mary Beth Oliver et al. 4th ed. 179–94 (New York: Routledge, 2020).

"Come, Ye Thankful People, Come." Text by Henry Alford (1844). Harmony "St. Georges of Windsor" by George J. Elvey (1856). https://hymnary.org/text/come_ye_thankful_people_come.

Comello, Maria Leonora. "William James on 'Possible Selves': Implications for Studying Identity in Communication Contexts." *Communication Theory* 19.3 (2009) 337–50.

Cone, James H. *Black Theology and Black Power*. Maryknoll, NY: Orbis, 1969.

———. *A Black Theology of Liberation*. Maryknoll, NY: Orbis, 1970.

———. *The Cross and the Lynching Tree*. Maryknoll, NY: Orbis, 2011.

Constantinou, Eugenia Scarvelis. *Thinking Orthodox: Understanding and Acquiring the Orthodox Christian Mind*. Chesterton, IN: Ancient Faith, 2020.

Content Team. "Post Hoc Ergo Propter Hoc." Legaldictionary.net, Sep. 25, 2016. https://legaldictionary.net/post-hoc-ergo-propter-hoc.

Cosner, Lewis. "Introduction." In *Ressentiment* by Max Scheler, edited by Lewis A. Coser, translated by William W. Holdheim. New York: Schocken, 1972.

Countryman, L. William. *Forgiven and Forgiving*. Harrisburg, PA: Morehouse, 1998.

Crenshaw, Kimberlé, et al., eds. *Critical Race Theory: The Key Writings That Formed the Movement*. New York: New Press, 1996.

Cronin, Jane. "Book Review: *Frenemies: How Social Media Polarizes America*." *Convergence* 26.3 (2019) 700–701.

Cunningham, B. B. "The Will to Forgive: A Pastoral Theological View of Forgiving." *Journal of Pastoral Care* 39 (1985) 141–49.

Cyprian. "Asking Pardon Daily." In *Matthew 1–13* by Manilo Simonetti, edited by Thomas C. Oden, 1a:136. Ancient Christian Commentary on Scripture: New Testament. Downers Grove, IL: IVP, 1998.

Cyril of Alexandria. "Jesus Gives to His Church the Power to Heal and Forgive." In *Luke* by Arthur A. Just, Jr., edited by Thomas C. Oden, 3:93–94. Ancient Christian Commentary on Scripture: New Testament. Downers Grove, IL: IVP, 1998.

———. "To Forgive Sins Is to Imitate God." In *Luke* by Arthur A. Just, Jr., edited by Thomas C. Oden, 3:188. Ancient Christian Commentary on Scripture: New Testament. Downers Grove, IL: IVP, 1998.

Dawn, Marva. *Reaching Out Without Dumbing Down: A Theology of Worship for this Urgent Time*. Grand Rapids: Eerdmans, 1995.
DeCort, Andrew D. *Bonhoeffer's New Beginning: Ethics After Devastation*. London: Lexington, 2018.
DeJonge, Michael P. *Bonhoeffer on Resistance: The Word Against the Wheel*. Oxford: Oxford University Press, 2018.
Deleuze, Gilles. *Nietzsche and Philosophy*. Translated by Hugh Tomlinson. New York: Columbia University Press, 1983.
Delirious?. "When All Around Has Fallen." By Martin Smith. Track 3 on *Cutting Edge Fore* by Delirious?. Produced by Andy Piercy. Furious?, 1995. CD.
Demerath, N. J., III. "Cultural Victory and Organizational Defeat in the Paradoxical Decline of Liberal Protestantism." *Journal for the Scientific Study of Religion* 34.4 (1995) 458–69.
Dempsey, Carol J. "Turn Back, O People: Repentance in the Latter Prophets." In *Repentance in Christian Theology*, edited by Mark J. Boda and Gordon T. Smith, 47–66. Collegeville, MN: Liturgical, 2006.
DeSilva, David A. *Hebrews: Grace and Gratitude*. Nashville: Abingdon Press, 2020.
Devine, Patricia. "Stereotypes and Prejudice: Their Automatic and Controlled Components." *Journal of Personality and Social Psychology* 56.1 (1989) 5–18.
Didache. *Legacyicons.com*, Apr. 21, 2023. https://legacyicons.com/content/didache.pdf.
Donath, Judith, and Danah Boyd. "Public Displays of Connection." *BT Technology Journal* 22.4 (2004) 71–82.
Donne, John. "For Whom the Bell Tolls/No Man Is an Island." https://allpoetry.com/for-whom-the-bell-tolls.
———. "Holy Sonnets: Death Be Not Proud." https://www.poetryfoundation.org/poems/44107/holy-sonnets-death-be-not-proud.
Doob, Leonard. *Propaganda, Its Psychology and Technique*. New York: Holt, 1935.
Dreher, Rod. *The Benedict Option: A Strategy for Christians in a Post-Christian World*. New York: Penguin House, 2017.
———. "'Despair,' 'Alarmism,' & the Benedict Option." *American Conservative*, Mar. 17, 2017.
———. *Live Not by Lies: A Manual for Christian Dissidents*. New York: Sentinel, 2020.
Druckman, James, and Jeremy Levy. "Affective Polarization in the American Public." Northwestern Institute for Policy Research, May 17, 2021. https://www.ipr.northwestern.edu/documents/working-papers/2021/wp-21-27.pdf.
Dubois, Elizabeth, and Grant Blank. "The Echo Chamber is Overstated: The Moderating Effect of Political Interest and Diverse Media." *Information, Communication & Society* 21 (2018) 729–45.
Dühring, Eugen. *Cursus der Philosophie als streng wissenschaftlicher—Weltanschauung und Lebensgestaltung*. Leipzig: L. Heimann's Verlag, 1875.
Durkheim, Emile. *The Elementary Forms of the Religious Life*. Translated by K. E. Fields. New York: Free, 1995.
Eady, Gregory, et al. "How Many People Live in Political Bubbles on Social Media?: Evidence From Linked Survey and Twitter Data." *SAGE Open* 9.1 (2019) 1–21.
Eck, Diana. *A New Religious America: How a "Christian Country" Has Become the World's Most Religiously Diverse Nation*. New York: HarperCollins, 2001.
Edunov, Sergey, et al. "Three and a Half Degrees of Separation." Meta Research, Feb. 4, 2016. https://research.facebook.com/blog/2016/2/three-and-a-half-degrees-of-separation.

Elgat, Guy. "How Smart (and Just) is *Ressentiment?*" *Journal of Nietzsche Studies* 47.2 (2016) 247–55.

———. "Nietzsche on the Genealogy of Universal Moral Justice." *History of Philosophy Quarterly* 33.2 (2016) 155–77.

———. *Nietzsche's Psychology of Ressentiment: Revenge and Justice in* On the Genealogy of Morals. Routledge Studies in Nineteenth-Century Philosophy. New York: Routledge, 2017.

———. "Slave Revolt, Deflated Self-Deception." *British Journal for the History of Philosophy* 23.3 (2015) 524–44.

———. "Why Friedrich Nietzsche Is the Darling of the Far Left and the Far Right." *Tablet Magazine*, May 8, 2017. https://www.tabletmag.com/sections/arts-letters/articles/nietzsche-left-right.

Elliger, Karl, and Willhelm Rudolph, eds. *Biblia Hebraica Stuttgartensia*. 5th ed. Stuttgart: Deutsche Bibelgesellschaft, 2015.

Elliot, Elisabeth. *The Shadow of the Almighty: Life and Testament of Jim Elliot*. San Francisco: Harper Collins, 1989.

———. *Through Gates of Splendor*. Carol Stream, IL: Tyndale, 1956.

Ellul, Jacques. *Propaganda: The Formation of Men's Attitudes*. Translated by Konrad Kellen and Jean Lerner. New York: Vintage, 1973.

Elowsky, Joel C. *John 1–10*. Ancient Christian Commentary on Scripture: New Testament 4a. Edited by Thomas C. Oden. Downers Grove, IL: IVP, 1998.

———. *John 11–21*. Ancient Christian Commentary on Scripture: New Testament 4b. Edited by Thomas C. Oden. Downers Grove, IL: IVP, 1998.

Emden, Christian J. *Nietzsche on Language, Consciousness, and the Body*. Champaign, IL: University of Illinois Press, 2005.

Engels, Jeremy. *The Politics of Resentment: A Genealogy*. University Park, PA: Penn State University Press, 2015.

Enright, Robert D., and Catherine T. Coyle. "Researching the Process Model of Forgiveness Within Psychological Interventions." In *Dimensions of Forgiveness: Psychological Research and Theological Perspectives*, edited by Everett L. Worthington Jr., 139–62. Philadelphia: Templeton Foundation, 1998.

Episcopal Church. *The Book of Common Prayer: And Administration of the Sacraments and Other Rites and Ceremonies of the Church Together with the Psalter or Psalms of David*. New York: Seabury, 1977.

Ermida, Isabel. "'Get the Snip—and a Job!': Disagreement, Impoliteness and Conflicting Identities on the Internet." *Token: A Journal of English Linguistics* 6 (2017) 205–47. https://token.ujk.edu.pl/wp-content/uploads/8_Token_6_I_Ermida.pdf.

Esser, Frank. "History of Media Effects." In *The International Encyclopedia of Communication*, edited by W. Donsbach, 2891–96. London: Blackwell, 2008.

Ezra, Ibn. *The Commentary of Ibn Ezra on Isaiah*. Translated by M. Friedländer. New York: Philip Feldheim, 1873.

Farley, Lawrence R. *The Gospel of John: Beholding the Glory*. Orthodox Bible Study Companion. Munster, IN: Conciliar, 2006.

Farrell, Warren. *The Myth of Male Power: Why Men Are the Disposable Sex*. Berkeley: Berkeley Trade, 1993.

———., and John Gray. *The Boy Crisis: Why Our Boys Are Struggling and What We Can Do About it*. Dallas: BenBella, 2019.

Fazio, Russell. "Multiple Processes by Which Attitudes Guide Behavior: The MODE Model as an Integrative Framework." In *Advances in Experimental Social Psychology*, edited by Mark Zanna, 75–109. Vol 23. New York: Academic, 1990.

Finkel, Eli J., et al. "Political Sectarianism in America." *Science* 370.6516 (2020) 533–36.

Fisher, Gene A., and Kyum Koo Chon. "Durkheim and the Social Construction of Emotions." *Social Psychology Quarterly* 52.1: Special Issue: Sentiments, Affect and Emotion (1989) 1–9.

Fletcher, Richard, et al. "How Polarized Are Online and Offline News Audiences?: A Comparative Analysis of Twelve Countries." *International Journal of Press/Politics* 25.2 (2020) 169–95.

———., and Rasmus Kleis Nielson. "Are News Audiences Increasingly Fragmented?: A Cross-National Comparative Analysis of Cross-Platform News Audience Fragmentation and Duplication." *Journal of Communication* 67.4 (2017) 476–98.

Foot, Philippa. "Nietzsche's Immoralism." In *Nietzsche, Genealogy, Morality: Essays on Nietzsche's Genealogy of Morals*, edited by Amélie Okensberg Rorty and Richard Schacht, 3–14. Philisophical Traditions series. Berkeley: University of California Press, 1994.

Francis of Assisi. "Make Me an Instrument of Your Peace." https://www.archspm.org/faith-and-discipleship/prayer/catholic-prayers/st-francis-of-assisi-make-me-an-instrument-of-your-peace.

Frankl, Viktor E. *Man's Search for Meaning*. Translated by Isle Lasch. 1st ed. Boston: Beacon, 2006.

Freedman, Suzanna, and Robert D. Enright. "Forgiveness as Intervention with Incest Survivors." *Journal of Consulting and Clinical Psychology* 64.5 (1996) 983–92.

Fretheim, Terence E. "Repentance in the Former Prophets." In *Repentance in Christian Theology*, edited by Mark J. Boda and Gordon T. Smith, 24–46. Collegeville, MN: Liturgical, 2006.

Fry, Prem S. "Religious Involvement, Spirituality and Personal Meaning for Life: Existential Predictors of Psychological Wellbeing in Community-Residing and Institutional Care Elders." *Aging and Mental Health* 4.4 (2000) 689–718.

Gabay, Rahav, et al. "The Tendency for Interpersonal Victimhood: The Personality Construct and Its Consequences." *Personality and Individual Differences* 165 (2020) 1–43. https://doi.org/10.1016/j.paid.2020.110134.

Gaertner, Samuel L. "The Common Ingroup Identity Model: Recategorization and the Reduction of Intergroup Bias." *European Review of Social Psychology* 4.1 (1993) 1–26.

———., and John F. Dovidio. *Reducing Inter-Group Bias: The Common In-Group Identity Model*. Hove, UK: Psychology, 2012.

———. "Reducing Intergroup Bias: The Common Ingroup Identity Model." In *Handbook of Theories of Social Psychology*, edited by Paul A. M. Van Lange, et al., 2:439–57. Thousand Oaks, CA: Sage, 2012.

Garfield, James B. *Follow My Leader*. London: Puffin, 1994.

Garimella, Kiran, and Ingmar Weber. "A Long-Term Analysis of Polarization on Twitter (ICWSM 2017)." In *Proceedings of the Eleventh International AAAI Conference on Web and Social Media* (2017). https://ingmarweber.de/wp-content/uploads/2017/05/A-Long-Term-Analysis-of-Polarization-on-Twitter.pdf.

Garrett, Robert K., et al. "Implications of Pro- and Counterattitudinal Information Exposure for Affective Polarization." *Human Communication Research* 40.3 (2014) 309–32.

Gay, Craig M. *The Way of the (Modern) World: Or, Why It's Tempting to Live As If God Doesn't Exist*. Grand Rapids: Eerdmans, 1998.

Gearhart, Sherice, and Weiwu Zhang. "Gay Bullying and Online Opinion Expression: Testing Spiral of Silence in the Social Media Environment." *Social Science Computer Review* 32.1 (2014) 18–36.

Geertz, Clifford. "Ethos, World-View and the Analysis of Sacred Symbols." *Antioch Review* 17.4 (1957) 421–37.

Geertz, Lovink. "What Is the Social in Social Media?" In *Art in the Global Present*, edited by Nikos Papastergiadis and Victoria Lynn, 97–111. London: Ubiquity, 2019.

Gerbner, George. "The Structure and Process of Television Program Content Regulation in the U.S." In *Television and Social Behavior, Content and Control*, edited by George Comstock and Eli Rubinstein, 1:386–414. Washington, DC: U.S. Government Printing Office, 1972.

———. "Toward 'Cultural Indicators': The Analysis of Mass Mediated Message Systems." *AV Communication Review* 17.2 (1969) 137–48.

Gerbner George, et al. "The "Mainstreaming" of America: Violence Profile No. 11." *Journal of Communication* 30.3 (1980) 10–29.

———., and Larry Gross. "Living with Television: The Violence Profile." *Journal of Communication* 26.2 (1976) 173–99.

Gese, Harmut. "The Origin of the Lord's Supper." In *Essays on Biblical Theology*, 117–40. Minneapolis: Fortress, 1981.

Gharib, Hoda, and Meghan Boler. "Narratives in America: The Connection Between Affective Polarization and Victimhood in the 2020 US Election." *AoIR Selected Papers of Internet Research 2021*. https://doi.org/10.5210/spir.v2021i0.12169.

Girard, René. "Dionysius Versus the Crucified." *Modern Language Notes* 99.4 (1984) 816–35.

———. *Il risentimento*. Edited by Stefano Tomelleri. Milan: Raffaello Cortina, 1999.

Goidel, Robert, et al. "The Impact of Television on Perceptions of Juvenile Crime." *Journal of Broadcasting and Electronic Media* 50.1 (2006) 119–39.

Goldberg, Herb. *The Hazards of Being Male: Surviving the Myth of Masculine Privilege*. Fairlawn, OH: Signet, 1976.

Goldingay, John. *Psalms. Baker Commentary on the Old Testament: Wisdom and Psalms 2*. Edited by Tremper Longman III. Grand Rapids: Baker Academic, 2007.

González-Bailón, Sandra. "Book Review: *Frenemies: How Social Media Polarizes America*, by Jaime E. Settle." *Journalism and Mass-Communication Quarterly* 97.4 (2020) 1178–80.

Graham, Jesse, et. al. "Moral Foundations Theory: The Pragmatic Validity of Moral Pluralism." *Advances in Experimental Social Psychology* 47 (Dec. 2012) 55–130.

Green, Donald, et al. *Partisan Hearts and Minds: Political Parties and the Social Identities of Voters*. New Haven: Yale University Press, 2002.

Green, Melanie C., and Timothy C. Brock. "The Role of Transportation in the Persuasiveness of Public Narrative." *Journal of Personality and Social Psychology* 79.5 (2000) 701–21.

———. "In the Mind's Eye: Transportation-Imagery Model of Narrative Persuasion." In *Narrative Impact: Social and Cognitive Foundations*, edited by Melanie C. Green, Jeffrey J. Strange, and Timothy C. Brock, 315–42. Mahwah, NJ: Lawrence Erlbaum Associates, 2002.

Greenwald, Anthony, and Mahzarin Banaji. "Implicit Social Cognition: Attitudes, Self-Esteem, and Stereotypes." *Psychological Review* 102.1 (1995) 4–27.

Gregory of Nyssa. *On Virginity.* Translated by William Moore. Philadelphia: Dalcassian, 2018.

Griswold, Charles. *Forgiveness: A Philosophical Exploration.* Cambridge: Cambridge University Press, 2007.

Gross, Kimberly, and Sean Aday. "The Scary World in Your Living Room and Neighborhood: Using Local Broadcast News, Neighborhood Crime Raters, and Personal Experience to Test Agenda-Setting and Cultivation." *Journal of Communication* 53.3 (2003) 411–26.

Guthrie, Harvey H. *Theology as Thanksgiving: From Israel's Psalms to the Church's Eucharist.* New York: Seabury, 1981.

Gutiérrez, Gustavo. *Theology of Liberation.* New York: Orbis, 1988.

Haidt, Jonathan. *The Righteous Mind: Why Good People Are Divided by Politics and Religion.* New York: Vintage, 2012.

———., and Craig Joseph. "Intuitive Ethics: How Innately Prepared Intuitions Generate Culturally Variable Virtues." *Daedalus* (Fall 2004) 55–66.

———., and Craig Joseph. "The Moral Mind: How 5 Sets of Innate Intuitions Guide the Development of Many Culture-Specific Virtues, and Perhaps Even Modules." In *The Innate Mind*, edited by Peter Carruthers, Stephen Laurence, and Stephen Stich, 367–91. Foundations of the Future 3. Oxford: Oxford University Press, 2007.

———., and Jesse Graham. "Planet of the Durkheimians, Where Community, Authority, and Sacredness are Foundations of Morality." In *Social and Psychological Bases of Ideology and System Justification*, edited by John T. Jost, Aaron C. Kay, and Hulda Thórisdóttir, 371–401. Oxford: Oxford University Press, 2009.

———., and Jesse Graham. "When Morality Opposes Justice: Conservatives Have Moral Intuitions that Liberals May Not Recognize." *Social Justice Research* 20.1 (2007) 98–116.

Hampton, K. N., et al. "Social Media and the 'Spiral of Silence.'" Pew Research Center, August 26, 2014. https://www.pewresearch.org/internet/2014/08/26/social-media-and-the-spiral-of-silence.

Harber, Kent, and Dov Cohen. "The Emotional Broadcaster Theory of Social Sharing." *Journal of Language and Social Psychology* 24.4 (2005) 382–400.

Haren, Tal Orion, et al. "The Normalization of Hatred: Identity, Affective Polarization, and Dehumanization on Facebook in the Context of Intractable Political Conflict." *Social Media + Society* (Apr.–Jun. 2020) 1–10.

Harris, Joshua. "Strong Enough to Be Wrong." TEDTalks. https://www.ted.com/talks/joshua_harris_strong_enough_to_be_wrong/transcript.

Harris, R. Laird, Gleason L. Archer Jr., and Bruce K. Waltke, eds. *Theological Wordbook of the Old Testament.* 2nd ed. Chicago: Moody Bible Institute, 1981.

Harris, Tristan. "Our Brains Are No Match for Our Technology." *New York Times*, Dec. 5, 2019. https://www.nytimes.com/2019/12/05/opinion/digital-technology-brain.html.

———. "How Better Tech Could Protect Us from Distraction." TED Talks. https://www.ted.com/talks/tristan_harris_how_better_tech_could_protect_us_from_distraction.

———. "How a Handful of Tech Companies Control Billions of Minds Every Day." TED Talks. https://www.ted.com/talks/tristan_harris_how_a_handful_of_tech_companies_control_billions_of_minds_every_day.

Harrison Warren, Tish. *Liturgy of the Ordinary: Sacred Practices in Everyday Life*. Grand Rapids: IVP, 2016.

———. *Prayer in the Night: For Those Who Work, or Watch, or Weep*. Woollahra, New South Wales: ReadHowYouWant, 2021.

———. "We Worship with the Magi, Not MAGA." *Christianity Today*, Jan. 7 2021. https://www.christianitytoday.com/2021/01/trump-capitol-mob-election-politics-magi-not-maga.

Hart, P. Sol, et al. "Public Attention to Science and Political News and Support for Climate Change Mitigation." *Nature Climate Change* 5.6 (2015) 541–45.

Hart, Trevor. "The Word, the Words, and the Witness: Proclamation as Divine and Human Reality in the Theology of Karl Barth." *Tyndale Bulletin* 46.1 (1995) 81–102.

Harvard, William C., ed. *The Changing Politics of the South*. Baton Rouge, LA: Louisiana State University Press, 1972.

Hawkins, Robert, and Suzanne Pingree. "Television's Influence on Social Reality." In *Television and Behavior: Ten Years of Scientific Progress and Implications for the 80s, Vol. II: Technical Review*, 224–247. Edited by David Pearl, Lorraine Bouthilet, and Joyce Lazar. Rockville, MD: National Institute of Mental Health, 1982.

Hays, Richard B. *Reading Backwards: Figural Christology and the Fourfold Gospel Witness*. Waco, TX: Baylor University Press, 2014.

Heino, Rebecca D., et al. "Relationshopping: Investigating the Market Metaphor in Online Dating." *Journal of Social and Personal Relationships* 27.4 (2010) 427–47. DOI: 10.1177/0265407510361614.

Helfand, David. *A Survival Guide to the Misinformation Age: Scientific Habits of Mind*. New York: Columbia University Press, 2016.

Heltzel, Gordon, and Kristin Lauren. "Polarization in America: Two Possible Futures." *Current Opinion in Behavior Sciences* 34 (2020) 179–84.

Herklus, Rosamond. "Forgive Our Sins as We Forgive." In *The New English Hymnal*. Edited by George Timms. Norwich: Canterbury Press, 1986.

Herman, Judith Lewis. "Justice from the Victim's Perspective." Violence Against Women 11.5 (May 2005) 571–602. DOI: https://doi.org/10.1177/1077801205274450.

Hick, Jon. *An Interpretation of Religion: Human Responses to the Transcendent*. New Haven: Yale University Press, 1989.

———. "The Next Step Beyond Dialogue." In *the Myth of Religious Superiority: A Multifaith Exploration*, edited by Paul F. Knitter, 3–12. Maryknoll, NY: Orbis, 2005.

Hicks, Stephen. *Explaining Postmodernism: Skepticism and Socialism from Rousseau to Foucault*. Phoenix: Scholarly, 2004.

Hilary. "Tolerate a Hidden Injury as a Witness to Future Judgment." In *Matthew 1–13* by Manilo Simonetti, edited by Thomas C. Oden, 1a:117–18. Ancient Christian Commentary on Scripture: New Testament. Downers Grove, IL: IVP, 1998.

Hoff Sommers, Christina. *The War Against Boys: How Misguided Policies Are Harming Our Young Men*. New York: Simon and Schuster, 2015.

Holbert, Robert Lance, et al. "Fear, Authority, and Justice: Crime-Related TV Viewing and Endorsements of Capital Punishment and Gun Ownership." *Journalism and Mass Communication Quarterly* 81.2 (2004) 343–63.

Holbrook, Andrew, and Timothy Hill. "Agenda-Setting and Priming in Prime Time Television: Crime Dramas as Political Cues." *Political Communication* 22.3 (2005) 277–95.

hooks, bell. *Feminism is For Everybody*. 2nd ed. New York: Routledge, 2014.

Horwitz, Robert B. "Politics as Victimhood, Victimhood as Politics." *Journal of Policy History* 30.3 (2018) 552–74.

Hovland, Carl, et al. *Communication and Persuasion*. New Haven: Yale University Press, 1953.

Humble, Malcolm. "Heinrich Mann and Arold Zweig: Left-Wing Nietzscheans?" *Journal of Nietzsche Studies* 13 (1997) 40–52. http://www.jstor.org/stable/20717668.

Humphrey, Edith M. *Further Up and Further In: Orthodox Conversations with C. S. Lewis on Scripture and Theology*. Yonkers, NY: St. Vladimir's Seminary Press, 2017.

———. *Grand Entrance: Worship on Earth as in Heaven*. Grand Rapids: Brazos, 2011.

———. "And I Shall Heal Them: Repentance, Turning, and Penitence in the Johannine Writings." In *Repentance in Christian Theology*, edited by Mark J. Boda and Gordon T. Smith, 105–26. Collegeville, MN: Liturgical, 2006.

Humprecht, Edda, et al. "Hostile Emotions in New Comments: A Cross-National Analysis of Facebook Discussions." *Social Media + Society* (Jan.–Mar. 2020) 1–12.

Hunter, James Davison. *The Death of Character: Moral Education in an Age Without Good or Evil*. New York: Basic, 2001.

———. *Evangelicalism: The Coming Generation*. Chicago: University of Chicago Press, 1987.

———. *To Change the World: The Irony, Tragedy, and Possibility of Christianity in the Late Modern World*. Oxford: Oxford University Press, 2010.

Hwang, Jerry. *Hosea: God's Reconciliation with His Estranged Household*. Series Editor Daniel I. Block. Zondervan Exegetical Commentary on the Old Testament: A Discourse Analysis of the Hebrew Bible. Grand Rapids: Zondervan Academic, 2021.

Hyman, Herbert, and Paul Sheatsley. "Some Reasons Why Information Campaigns Fail." *Public Opinion Quarterly* 11 (1947) 412–23.

Ignatius of Loyola. *The Spiritual Exercises of Saint Ignatius of Loyola*. Translated by W. H. Longridge. 4th ed. London: A. R. Mowbray and Co., 1950.

Irvuzumugabe, Eric, and Tracey D. Lawrence. *My Father, Maker of the Trees: How I Survived Rwandan Genocide*. Grand Rapids: Baker, 2009.

Iyengar, Shanto. "The Home as a Political Fortress: Family Agreement in an Era of Polarization." *The Journal of Politics* 80.4 (2018) 1326–1338.

———., et al. "Affect, not Ideology: a Social Identity Perspective on Polarization." *Public Opinion Quarterly* 76, no. 1 (2012) 405–31.

———., "The Origins and Consequences of Affective Polarization in the United States." *Annual Review of Political Science* 22.1 (2019) 129–46.

———., and Kyu S. Hahn. "Red Media, Blue Media: Evidence of Ideological Selectivity in Media Use." *Journal of Communication* 59.1 (2009) 19–39.

———., and Masha Krupenkin. "The Strengthening of Partisan Affect." *Political Psychology* 39 (2018) 201–18.

———., and Sean J. Westwood. "Fear and Loathing Across Party Lines: New Evidence on Group Polarization." *American Journal of Political Science* 59.3 (2015) 690–707.

Jackson, Jay W., and Verlin B. Hinsz. "Group Dynamics and the U.S. Capitol Insurrection: An Introduction to the Special Issue." *APA* 26.3 (2022) 169–77.

Jacobs, Alan. *The Year of Our Lord 1943: Christian Humanism in an Age of Crisis*. New York: Oxford University Press, 2018.

Jamieson, Kathleen Hall, and Joseph N. Capella. *Echo Chamber: Rush Limbaugh and the Conservative Media Establishment*. Oxford: Oxford University Press, 2008.

Jastrow Jr., Morris. *A Gentle Cynic: Being a Translation of the Book of Koheleth, Commonly Known As Ecclesiastes*. Philadelphia: J. B. Lippincott, 1919.

Jaye, Cassie, dir. *The Red Pill*. El Segundo, CA: Gravitas Ventures, 2017.

Jenkins, Jack. "Top Catholic Bishop Calls Social Justice Movements 'Pseudo-Religion.'" *Washington Post*, Nov. 5, 2021. https://www.washingtonpost.com/religion/2021/11/05/catholic-bishop-gomez-social-justice.

John, Nicholas A., and Noam Gal. "'He's Got His Own Sea': Political Facebook Unfriending in the Personal Public Space." *International Journal of Communication* 12 (2018) 2971–88.

John Paul II (Pope). "Dives in Misericordia: Encyclical on the Mercy of God." Nov. 30, 1980. Section IV:12. https://www.vatican.va/content/john-paul-ii/en/encyclicals/documents/hf_jp-ii_enc_30111980_dives-in-misericordia.html.

Jones, Terry, and Terry Gilliam. *Monty Python and the Holy Grail*. United States: Cinema 5 Distributing, 1975.

Josephus Flavius. *The Works of Josephus*. Translated by William Whiston. New updated edition, complete and unabridged. Peabody, MA: Hendrickson, 1987.

Jung, Carl Gustav. *The Archetypes and the Collective Unconscious*. Vol. 9, Part 1. Edited by Gerhard Adler. Translated by R. F. C. Hull. Collected Works of C. G. Jung. Princeton, NJ: Princeton University Press, 1981.

Junger, Sebastian. *Tribe: On Homecoming and Belonging*. 1st ed. New York: Twelve, 2016.

Just, Arthur A., Jr. *Luke*. Edited by Thomas C. Oden. Ancient Christian Commentary on Scripture: New Testament 3. Downers Grove, IL: IVP, 1998.

Kaiser, Otto. *Isaiah 1–12*. Translated by John Bowden. Old Testament Library. Series editor Peter Ackroyd, et al. 2nd ed. Philadelphia: Westminster, 1983.

Kaiser, Walter C., Jr. *Preaching and Teaching the Last Things: Eschatology for the Life of the Church*. Grand Rapids: Baker, 2011.

Kalsen, Kevin. "Letter from a Chinese Jail: My Declaration of Faithful Disobedience." *Anglican Ink*, Dec. 18, 2018. https://anglican.ink/2018/12/18/letter-from-a-chinese-jail-my-declaration-of-faithful-disobedience/.

Kasper, Walter. *Mercy: The Essence of the Gospel and the Key to Christian Life*. Translated by William Madges. New York: Paulist, 2014.

Kates, Naama. *Incel Podcast*. Produced by Crawlspace Media.

Kaufmann, Walter. *Nietzsche*. New York: Meridian, 1956.

Kaylor, Brian. "Likes, Retweets, and Polarization." *Review and Expositor* 116.2 (2019) 183–92.

Kearney, Michael W. "Analyzing Change in Network Polarization." *New Media & Society* 21.6 (2019) 1380–1402.

Keck, Leander et al, ed. *The Gospel of Luke, the Gospel of John*. New Interpreter's Bible: A Commentary in Twelve Volumes 9. Nashville: Abingdon Press, 1995.

Kellner, Douglas. "The Trump Horror Show Through Nietzschean Perspectives." In *Nietzsche and Critical Social Theory: Affirmation, Animosity, and Ambiguity*, edited by Christine A. Payne and Michael James Roberts, 60–72. Studies in Critical Social Sciences 154. Leiden: Brill, 2019.

Kelly, Casey Ryan. "Donald J. Trump and the Rhetoric of *Ressentiment*." *Quarterly Journal of Speech* 106.1 (Dec. 20, 2019) 2–24. https://doi.org/10.1080/00335630.2019.1698756.

Kelman, Herbert C. "Reconciliation from a Social-Psychological Perspective." In *The Social Psychology of Inter-Group Reconciliation: From Violent Conflict to Peaceful Coexistence*. Edited by Arie Nadler, Thomas E. Malloy, and Jeffery D. Fisher, 15–37. 1st ed. Oxford: Oxford University Press, 2008.

Kendal, R. T. *Total Forgiveness*. Rev. ed. Lake Mary, FL: Charisma House, 2007.

Kenski, Kate, et al. "Lying, Liars, and Lies: Incivility in 2016 Presidential Candidate and Campaign Tweets During the Invisible Primary." *American Behavioral Scientist* 62 (2018) 286–99.

Kidner, Derek. *Psalms 73–150: A Commentary on Books III–V of the Psalms*. London: IVP, 1975.

Kim, Yonghwan. "The Contribution of Social Network Sites to Exposure to Political Difference: The Relationships Among SNSs, Online Political Messaging, and Exposure to Cross-Cutting Perspectives." *Computers in Human Behavior* 27.2 (2011) 971–77.

———. "Does Disagreement Mitigate Polarization?: How Selective Exposure and Disagreement Affect Political Polarization." *Journalism and Mass Communication Quarterly* 92.4 (2015) 915–37.

———., et al. "Influence of Social Media Use on Discussion Network Heterogeneity and Civic Engagement: The Moderating Role of Personality Traits." *Journal of Communication* 63 (2013) 498–516.

King, Martin Luther, Jr. *A Call to Conscience: The Landmark Speeches of Dr. Martin Luther King Jr.* Edited by Clayborne Carson and Kris Shepard. New York: Grand Publishing Central, 2001.

———. "The American Dream." In *A Testament of Hope: The Essential Writings and Speeches of Martin Luther King, Jr.*, edited by James M. Washington, 208–216. New York: Grand Publishing Central, 2001.

———. "The Current Crisis in Race Relations." In *A Testament of Hope: The Essential Writings and Speeches of Martin Luther King Jr.*, edited by James M. Washington, 85–90. San Francisco, CA: HarperOne, 1986.

———. "Draft of Chapter III, 'On Being a Good Neighbor.'" *King Institute* (Jul. 1962–Mar. 1963). https://kinginstitute.stanford.edu/king-papers/documents/draft-chapter-iii-being-good-neighbor.

———. "The Ethical Demands for Integration." In *A Testament of Hope: The Essential Writings and Speeches of Martin Luther King, Jr.*, edited by James M. Washington, 117–35. New York: Grand Publishing Central, 2001.

———. "An Experiment in Love." In *A Testament of Hope: The Essential Writings and Speeches of Martin Luther King, Jr.*, edited by James M. Washington, 16–20. New York: Grand Publishing Central, 2001.

———. "Facing the Challenge of a New Age." In *A Testament of Hope: The Essential Writings and Speeches of Martin Luther King, Jr.*, edited by James M. Washington, 135–44. New York: Grand Publishing Central, 2001.

———. "Give Us the Ballot—We Will Transform the South." In *A Testament of Hope: The Essential Writings and Speeches of Martin Luther King, Jr.*, edited by James M. Washington, 197–200. New York: Grand Publishing Central, 2001.

———. "I've Been to the Mountaintop." In *A Call to Conscience: The Landmark Speeches of Dr. Martin Luther King Jr.*, edited by Clayborne Carson and Kris Shepard, 201–23. New York: Grand Publishing Central, 2001.

———. "*Playboy* Interview: Martin Luther King, Jr." In *A Testament of Hope: The Essential Writings and Speeches of Martin Luther King, Jr.*, edited by James M. Washington, 340–77. New York: Grand Publishing Central, 2001.

———. "Kenneth B. Clark Interview." In *A Testament of Hope: The Essential Writings and Speeches of Martin Luther King, Jr.*, edited by James M. Washington, 331–39. New York: Grand Publishing Central, 2001.

———. "Letter from Birmingham Jail." In *A Testament of Hope: The Essential Writings and Speeches of Martin Luther King, Jr.*, edited by James M. Washington, 289–302. New York: Grand Publishing Central, 2001.

———. "Nonviolence: The Only Road to Freedom." In *A Testament of Hope: The Essential Writings and Speeches of Martin Luther King, Jr.*, edited by James M. Washington, 54–61. New York: Grand Publishing Central, 2001.

———. "The Most Durable Power." In *A Testament of Hope: The Essential Writings and Speeches of Martin Luther King, Jr.*, edited by James M. Washington, 10–11. New York: Grand Publishing Central, 2001.

———. *A Testament of Hope: The Essential Writings and Speeches of Martin Luther King, Jr.*, edited by James M. Washington. San Francisco: HarperOne, 1986.

———. "The Trumpet of Conscience." In *A Testament of Hope: The Essential Writings and Speeches of Martin Luther King, Jr.*, edited by James M. Washington, 634–56. New York: Grand Publishing Central, 2001.

———. "Why We Can't Wait." In *A Testament of Hope: The Essential Writings and Speeches of Martin Luther King, Jr.*, edited by James M. Washington, 518–54. New York: Grand Publishing Central, 2001.

Kinnaman, David, et al. *unChristian: What a New Generation Really Thinks About Christianity . . . and Why It Matters.* Grand Rapids: Baker, 2012.

———., and Aly Hawkins. *You Lost Me: Why Young Christians Are Leaving Church . . . and Rethinking Faith.* Grand Rapids: Baker Academic, 2011.

Kittler, Friedrich A. *Gramophone, Film, Typewriter.* Stanford, CA: Stanford University Press, 1999.

Klapper, Joseph. *The Effects of Mass Communication.* Glencoe, IL: Free, 1960.

Klar, Samara, Yanna Krupnikov, and John Barry Ryan. "Polarized, or Sick of Politics?" *New York Times*, April 12, 2019. https://www.nytimes.com/2019/04/12/opinion/polarization-politics-democrats-republicans.html.

Klar, Yechiel, et al. "In the Aftermath of Historical Trauma: Perceived Moral Obligations of Current Group Members," in *The Social Psychology of Collective Victimhood*, edited by Johanna Ray Vollhardt, 208–28. New York: Oxford University Press, 2020.

———. "The 'Never Again' State of Israel: The Emergence of the Holocaust as a Core Feature of Israeli Identity and Its Four Incongruent Voices." *Journal of Social Issues* 69.1 (2013) 125–43.

Klinger-Vilenchik, Neta, et al. "Interpretive Polarization Across Platforms: How Political Disagreement Develops Over Time on Facebook, Twitter, and WhatsApp." *Social Media + Society* (Jul.–Sep. 2020) 1–13.

Knobel, Peter S. "The Targum of Qohelet." In *The Targums of Job, Proverbs, Qohelet.* Edited by Kevin Cathcart, Michael Maher, and Martin McNamara. Aramaic Bible 15. Collegeville, MN: Liturgical, 1991.

Knobloch-Westerwick, Silvia. "The Selective Exposure Self- and Affect-Management (SESAM) Model: Applications in the Realms of Race, Politics, and Health." *Communication Research* 42.7 (2015) 959–85.

———., et al. "Media Choice and Selective Exposure." In *Media Effects: Advances in Theory and Research*, 4th ed., edited by Mary Beth Oliver, Arthur A. Raney, and Jennings Bryant, 146–162. New York: Routledge, 2019.

Kruger, Justin, and David Dunning. "Unskilled and Unaware of It: How Difficulties in Recognizing One's Own Incompetence Lead to Inflated Self-Assessments." *Journal of Personality and Social Psychology* 77.6 (1999) 1121–34.

Krueger, Thomas. *Qoheleth*. Edited by Kalue Blatzer. Translated by O. C. Dean, Jr. Minneapolis: Fortress, 2004.

Kuijpers, Moniek M., et al. "Towards a New Understanding of Absorbing Reading Experiences." In *Narrative Absorption*, edited by Frank Hakemulder, et al, 11–27. Linguistic Approaches to Literature. Amsterdam: John Benjamins, 2017.

Kwon, K. Hazel, et al. "Social Network Influence on Online Behavioral Choices: Exploring Group Formation on Social Network Sites." *American Behavioral Scientist* 58.10 (2014) 1345–60.

Lang, Annie. "Discipline in Crisis?: The Shifting Paradigm of Mass Communication Research." *Communication Theory* 23.1 (2013) 10–14. DOI: 10.1111/comt.12000.

Langford, Joe, and Pauline Rose Clance. "The Imposter Phenomenon: Recent Research Findings Regarding Dynamics, Personality and Family Patterns and Their Implications for Treatment." *Psychotherapy* Volume 30.3 (Fall 1993) 495–501.

Lanier, Jaron. *Dawn of the New Everything: Encounters with Reality and Virtual Reality.* New York: Henry Colt and Co., 2017.

———. *Ten Arguments for Deleting Your Social Media Accounts Right Now.* New York: Picador, 2018.

———. *Who Owns the Future?* New York: Simon and Schuster, 2013.

———. *You Are Not a Gadget: A Manifesto.* New York: Alfred A. Knopf, 2010.

Lansdall-Welfare, Tom, et al. *Change-point Analysis of the Public Mood in UK Twitter During the Brexit Referendum.* Paper presented at the 2016 IEEE International Conference on Data Mining in Politics Workshop (DMIP), 434–39. DOI: 10.1109/ICDMW.2016.0068.

Lasswell, Harold W. *Propaganda Techniques in the World War.* New York: Peter Smith, 1927.

Lee, Francis L. F. "Impact of Social Media on Opinion Polarization in Varying Times." *Communication and the Public* 1.1 (2016) 56–71.

Lee, J. K. "Social Media, Network Heterogeneity, and Opinion Polarization." *Journal of Communication* 64.4 (2014) 702–22.

Lee, Jiyoung, and Yunjung Choi. "Effects of Network Heterogeneity on Social Media and Opinion Polarization Among South Koreans: Focusing on Fear and Political Orientation." *International Communication Gazette* 82.6 (2020) 119–39.

Lee, Morgan. "Christian Nationalism Is Worse Than You Think." *Christianity Today* 13 (Jan. 2021). https://www.christianitytoday.com/podcasts/quick-to-listen/christian-nationalism-capitol-riots-trump-podcast.

Legge, Matthew. "Victimhood Is Tearing Us Apart: Here's What the Evidence Says About the Impact of Feeling Like a Victim." *Psychology Today*, Feb. 10, 2022. https://www.psychologytoday.com/us/blog/are-we-done-fighting/202202/victimhood-is-tearing-us-apart.
Leithart, Peter J. *Gratitude: An Intellectual History*. Waco, TX: Baylor University Press, 2014.
———. *Traces of the Trinity: Signs of God in Creation and Human Experience*. Grand Rapids: Brazos, 2015.
Lelkes, Yphtach. "Mass Polarization: Manifestations and Measurements." *Public Opinion Quarterly* 80 (2016) 392–410.
———, et al. "The Hostile Audience: The Effect of Access to Broadband Internet on Partisan Affect." *American Journal of Political Science* 61.1 (2017) 5–20.
Lerner, Melvin J. *The Belief in a Just World: A Fundamental Delusion*. New York: Springer, 1980.
Leung, Dennis K. K., and Francis L. F. Lee. "Cultivating an Active Online Counterpublic: Examining Usage and Political Impact of Internet Alternative Media." *International Journal of Press/Politics* 19.3 (2014) 340–59.
Levendusky, Matthew S. *How Partisan Media Polarize America*. Chicago: University of Chicago Press, 2013.
———. "Why Do Partisan Media Polarize Viewers?" *American Journal of Political Science* 57 (2013) 611–23.
———, and Neil Malhotra. "(Mis)perceptions of Partisan Polarization in the American Public." *Public Opinion Quarterly* 80.S1 (2016) 378–91.
Levenson, Michael. "A Psychiatrist Invited to Yale Spoke of Fantasies of Shooting White People." *New York Times*, Jun. 6 2021. https://www.nytimes.com/2021/06/06/nyregion/yale-psychiatrist-aruna-khilanani.html?searchResultPosition=1.
Levinson, Bradley A. U. *Beyond Critique: Exploring Critical Social Theories and Education*. 1st ed. New York: Routledge, 2011.
Levitsky, Steven, and Daniel Ziblatt. *How Democracies Die*. New York: Crown, 2018.
Levy, Robin. "Social Media, News Consumption, and Polarization: Evidence from a Field Experiment." *American Economic Review* 111.3 (2021) 831–70.
Lewis, C. S. *The Abolition of Man*. New York: MacMillan, 1947.
———. *The Four Loves*. New York: Harvest, 1960.
———. *The Great Divorce*. New York: MacMillan, 1978.
———. *Mere Christianity*. New York: HarperOne, 2001.
———. *The Reading Life: The Joy of Seeing New Worlds Through Others' Eyes*. Edited by David C. Downing and Michael G. Maudlin. New York: HarperCollins, 2019.
———. *Reflections on the Psalms*. London: Fontana, 1958.
———. *The Screwtape Letters*. UK: William Collins Sons and Co., 1979.
———. *Til' We Have Faces*. Boston: Houghton Mifflin Harcourt, 2012.
———. *The Lion, The Witch, and the Wardrobe*. Chronicles of Narnia 1. New York: MacMillan, 1950.
———. *The Weight of Glory: And Other Addresses*. Edited by Walter Hooper. Revised and expanded edition. New York: MacMillan, 1980.
Ley, David J. "The Culture of Victimhood: Hoaxes, Trigger Warnings, and Trauma-Informed Care." *Psychology Today*, Jun. 28, 2014. https://www.psychologytoday.com/us/blog/women-who-stray/201406/the-culture-victimhood.

Lin, Carolyn A. "Effects of the Internet." In *Media Effects: Advances in Theory and Research*, 3rd ed., edited by Bryant Jennings and Mary Beth Oliver, 567–91. New York: Routledge, 2009.

Lindsay, Dennis R. "*Tôḏâ* and Eucharist: The Celebration of the Lord's Supper as a 'Thank Offering' in the Early Church." *Restoration Quarterly* 39.2 (1997) 83–100.

Lindsey, James. *Race Marxism: The Truth About Critical Race Theory and Praxis*. Independently Published: New Discourses, 2022.

———., and Helen Pluckrose. *Cynical Theories: How Activist Scholarship Made Everything About Race, Gender, and Identity—and Why This Harms Everybody*. Independently Published: New Discourses, 2020.

———., and Mike Nayna. "Postmodern Religion and the Faith of Social Justice." *New Discourses*, Jun. 18, 2020. https://newdiscourses.com/2020/06/postmodern-religion-faith-social-justice.

Lipka, Michael, and Claire Gecewicz. "More Americans Now Say They're Spiritual but Not Religious." *Pew Research*, Sep. 6, 2017. https://www.pewresearch.org/short-reads/2017/09/06/more-americans-now-say-theyre-spiritual-but-not-religious.

Lippmann, Walter. *Public Opinion*. New York: Macmillan, 1992.

Löhr, Hermut. "The Eucharist and Jewish Ritual Meals: The Case of the Tôḏâ." *Early Christianity* 7.4 (2016) 468–83.

Lohr, Steve. "Troubled Banks and the Role of the Press." *New York Times*, Feb. 19, 1991. A33.

Long, Phillip V. *The Art of Biblical History*. Grand Rapids: Zondervan, 1994.

Longman, Tremper, III. *Immanuel in Our Place: Seeing Christ in Israel's Worship*. Edited by Tremper Longman, III, and J. Allen Groves. Gospel According to the Old Testament. Phillipsburg, NJ: P&R, 2001.

Lord, Charles, et al. "Biased Assimilation and Attitude Polarization: The Effects of Prior Theories on Subsequently-Considered Evidence." *Journal of Personality and Social Psychology* 37.11 (1979) 2098–109.

Louw, Johannes P., and Eugene A. Nida, ed. *Greek-English Lexicon of the New Testament Based on Semantic Domains*. 1st ed. New York: United Bible Societies, 1988.

Love, Nancy S. "Epistemology and Exchange: Marx, Nietzsche, and Critical Theory." *New German Critique* 41: Special Issue on the Critiques of the Enlightenment (Spring–Summer, 1987), 71–94. https://www.jstor.org/stable/488276.

Lukianoff, Greg, and Jonathan Haidt. *The Coddling of the American Mind: How Good Intentions and Bad Ideas are Setting up a Generation for Failure*. New York: Penguin Random House, 2018.

Macdonald, Bradley J. "Critical Theory." In *The Encyclopedia of Political Thought*, edited by M. T. Gibbons. Hoboken, NJ: John Wiley & Sons, 2014. https://doi.org/10.1002/9781118474396.wbept0226.

Macionis, John J. *Society: The Basics*. 10th ed. Upper Saddle River, NJ: Pearson Education, 2009.

Mackie, Diane, et al. "Intergroup Emotions: Explaining Offensive Action Tendencies in an Intergroup Context." *Journal of Personality and Social Psychology* 79.4 (2000) 602–16.

Manning, Brennan. *Ruthless Trust: The Ragamuffin's Path to God*. New York: HarperOne, 2000.

Mar, Raymond A., and Keith Oatley. "The Function of Fiction is the Abstraction and Simulation of Social Experience." *Perspectives on Psychological Science* 3.3 (2008) 173–92.

———., et al. "Exploring the Link Between Reading Fiction and Empathy: Ruling Out Individual Differences and Examining Outcomes." *Communications* 34 (2009) 407–28.

Martin, Joanne. "Moving Beyond Just Forgive: Recovering Biblical Values of Repentance and Community in Pastoral Discussions of Interpersonal Forgiveness and Reconciliation." Master's Thesis, Ambridge, PA: Trinity Episcopal School for Ministry, 2012. BT738.27 .M37 2012.

Martinez, Rudy. "Your DNA is an Abomination." Sybil.com, Nov. 25, 2017. https://web.archive.org/web/20190307020248/https://www.sybiljournal.com/work-2/2018/11/12/your-dna-is-an-abomination-by-rudy-martinez.

Marty, Martin E. "The Ethos of Christian Forgiveness." In *Dimensions of Forgiveness: Psychological Research and Theological Perspectives*, edited by Everett L. Worthington Jr., 9–28. Philadelphia: Templeton Foundation, 1998.

Mason, Lilliana. "I Disrespectfully Agree: The Differential of Partisan Sorting on Social and Issue Polarization." *American Journal of Political Science* 59.1 (2015) 128–45.

———. *Uncivil Agreement: How Politics Became Our Identity*. Chicago: University of Chicago Press, 2018.

Matuszewski, Paweł Michał, and Gabriella Szabó. "Are Echo Chambers Based on Partisanship?: Twitter and Political Polarity in Poland and Hungary." *Social Media + Society* 5.2 (2019) 1–14.

Maximus the Confessor. *Maximus the Confessor: Selected Writings*. Translated by George C. Berthold. Classics of Western Spirituality. Mahwah, NY: Paulist, 1985.

Mayo, Maria. *The Limits of Forgiveness: Case Studies in the Distortion of a Biblical Ideal*. Minneapolis: Fortress, 2015.

McAdams, Dan P., and Michelle Albaugh. "The Redemptive Self, Generativity, and American Christians at Midlife: Explorations of the Life Stories of Evangelical and Mainline Protestants." In *Autobiography and the Psychological Study of Religious Lives*, edited by Jacob A. Belzen and Antoon Geels, 255–86. Boston: Brill, 2008.

McCarty, Nolan. *Polarization: What Everyone Needs to Know*. Oxford: Oxford University Press, 2019.

McClure, Paul K. "Faith and Facebook in a Pluralistic Age: The Effects of Social Networking Sites on the Religious Beliefs of Emerging Adults." *Sociological Perspectives* 59.4 (2016) 818–34.

McCombs, Maxwell, and Amy Reynolds. "How the News Shapes Our Civic Agenda." In *Media Effects: Advances in Theory and Research*, 3rd ed., edited by Bryant Jennings and Mary Beth Oliver, 1–16. New York: Routledge, 2009.

———., and Donald Shaw. "The Agenda-Setting Function of Mass Media." *Public Opinion Quarterly* 36.2 (1972) 176–87.

McCullough, Michael E., et al. "Interpersonal Forgiving in Close Relationships." *Journal of Personality and Social Psychology* 73.2 (1997) 321–336.

McGilchrist, Iain. *The Master and his Emissary: The Divided Brain and the Making of the Western World*. New Haven: Yale University Press, 2009.

McGuire, William J. "The Myth of Massive Media Impact: Savagings and Salvagings." In *Public Communication and Behavior*, edited by G. Comstock, 1:173–257. New York: Academic, 1986.

McLuhan, Marshall. *Understanding Media: The Extensions of Man.* New York: MIT Press, 1994.
McWilliams, Nancy, and Stanley Lependorf. "Narcissistic Pathology of Everyday Life." *Contemporary Psychoanalysis* 26 (1990) 434–49.
Melville, Herman. *Moby Dick: Illustrated.* Timeless Tales. 1st ed. La Jolla, CA: Positive, 2024.
Mert, Moral. "The Bipolar Voter: On the Effects of Actual and Perceived Party Polarization on Voter Turnout in European Multiparty Democracies." *Political Behavior* 39.4 (2017) 935–65.
Mert, Moral, and Robin E. Best. "On the Relationship Between Party Polarization and Citizen Polarization." *Party Politics* 29.2 (2022) 1–19.
Merton, Thomas. "Social Structure and Anomie." *American Sociological Review* 3.5 (Oct. 1938) 672–82.
Mikitish, Priest John, and Hieromonk Herman, eds. *Orthodox Christian Prayers.* 2nd indent. South Canaan, PA: St. Tikhon's Monastery Press, 2019.
Miller, James. "Some Implications of Nietzsche's Thought for Marxism." *Telos* 37 (Fall 1978) 22–41.
Miller, Paul D. *The Religion of American Greatness: What's Wrong with Christian Nationalism.* Grand Rapids: IVP Academic, 2022.
———. "What Is Christian Nationalism?" *Christianity Today*, Feb. 3, 2021. https://www.christianitytoday.com/2021/02/what-is-christian-nationalism.
Mills, Charles Wright. *The Power Elite.* New York: Oxford University Press, 2000.
———. *The Sociological Imagination.* 40th anniversary edition. New York: Oxford University Press, 2000.
Minow, Martha. *Between Vengeance and Forgiveness: Facing History After Genocide and Mass Violence.* Boston: Beacon, 1998.
Misiano, Christopher, dir. *The West Wing.* Season 7, Episode 8. "Undecideds." Written by Deborah Cahn. Created by Aaron Sorkin. Aired Dec. 4, 2005. NBC.
Moltmann, Jürgen. *The Crucified God.* 40th anniversary edition. Minneapolis: Fortress, 2015.
———. *Theology of Hope: On the Ground and Implications of a Christian Eschatology.* Grand Rapids: Fortress, 1993.
Morgan, Michael, et al. "Growing Up With Television: Cultivation Processes." In *Media Effects: Advances in Theory and Research*, 3rd ed., edited by Bryant Jennings and Mary Beth Oliver, 34–49. New York: Routledge, 2009.
Moule, C. F. D. *Forgiveness and Reconciliation: And Other New Testament Themes.* London: SPCK, 1998.
Mouw, Richard J. *Uncommon Decency: Christian Civility in an Uncivil World.* Downers Grove, IL: IVP, 2010.
Mowinckel, Sigmund. *The Psalms in Israel's Worship.* Translated by D. R. Ap-Thomas. Two Volumes in One. Grand Rapids: Eerdmans, 2004.
Muddiman, Ashley, and Natalie J. Stroud. "News Values, Cognitive Biases, and Partisan Incivility in Comment Sections." *Journal of Communication* 67 (2017) 586–609.
Murphy, Jeffrie G. *Getting Even: Forgiveness and Its Limits.* New York: Oxford University Press, 2003.
Murphy, Jeffrie G., and Jean Hampton. *Forgiveness and Mercy.* Cambridge: Cambridge University Press, 1988.
Murphy, Reg. *The Southern Strategy.* New York: Scribner, 1971.

Mutz, Diana, and Jeffery J. Mondak. "The Workplace as a Context for Cross-Cutting Political Discourse." *Journal of Politics* 68.1 (2006) 140–55.
Nestle, Erwin. *Novum Testamentum Graece*. 26th ed. Edited by Barbara Aland, et al. Stuttgart: Deutsche Bibelgesellschaft, 1979.
Nabi, Robin L. "Media and Emotion." In *Media Effects: Advances in Theory and Research*, 4th ed., edited by Mary Beth Oliver, Arthur A. Raney, and Jennings Bryant, 163–78. New York: Routledge, 2019.
Nave, Guy Dale, Jr. "Repent, for the Kingdom of God is at Hand: Repentance in the Synoptic Gospels and Acts." In *Repentance in Christian Theology*, edited by Mark J. Boda and Gordon T. Smith, 87–104. Collegeville, MN: Liturgical, 2006.
Newbigen, Leslie. *The Gospel in a Pluralist Society*. Grand Rapids: Eerdmans, 1989.
———. *The Open Secret*. Revised ed. Grand Rapids: Eerdmans, 1995.
Newport, Frank. "More U.S. Protestants Have No Specific Denominational Identity." *Gallup*, Jul. 18, 2017. https://news.gallup.com/poll/214208/protestants-no-specific-denominational-identity.aspx.
Nguyen, C Thi. "Echo Chambers and Epistemic Bubbles." *Episteme* 17.2 (2020) 141–61.
Nichols, Tom. *The Death of Expertise: The Campaign Against Established Knowledge and Why It Matters*. New York: Oxford University Press, 2017.
Niebuhr, Reinhold. *An Interpretation of Christian Ethics*. Louisville: Westminster John Knox, 2013.
———. *Moral Man and Immoral Society: A Study in Ethics and Politics*. Louisville: Westminster John Knox, 2001.
Nier, Jason A., et al. "Changing Interracial Evaluations and Behavior: The Effects of a Common Group Identity." *Group Processes and Intergroup Relations* 4 (2001) 299–316.
Nietzsche, Friedrich. *Beyond Good and Evil*. Translated by Helen Zimmern. Introduction by Willard Huntington Wright. New York: Boni and Liverlight, 1917.
———. *The Gay Science: With a Prelude in German Rhymes and an Appendix of Songs*. Edited by Bernard Williams. Translated by Josefine Nauckhoff and Adrian Del Caro. Cambridge Texts in the History of Philosophy. Cambridge: Cambridge University Press, 2001.
———. *On the Genealogy of Morals*. Translated by Douglas Smith. Oxford: Oxford University Press, 1996.
———. *Thus Spoke Zarathustra: A Book for Everyone and No One*. Translated by R. J. Hollingdale. London: Penguin Classics, 1969.
Nisbet, Erik C., et al. "The Partisan Brain: How Dissonant Science Messages Lead Conservatives and Liberals to (Dis)Trust Science." *ANNALS of the American Academy of Political and Social Science* 658.1 (2015) 36–66.
Noor, Masi, et al. "Precursors and Mediators of Intergroup Reconciliation in Northern Ireland: A New Model." *British Journal of Social Psychology* 47.3 (2008) 481–95.
Nordbrand, Maria. "Affective Polarization in the Digital Age: Testing the Direction of the Relationship Between Social Media and User's Feelings for Out-Group Parties." *New Media and Society* (Sep. 2021) 1–20.
Norris, Kathleen. *Acedia and Me: A Marriage, Monks, and a Writer's Life*. New York: Riverhead, 2008.
———. *The Quotidian Mysteries: Laundry, Liturgy, and Women's Work*. Mahwah, NJ: Paulist, 1998.

Northrup, Terrel A. "The Dynamic of Identity in Personal and Social Conflict." In *Intractable Conflicts and their Transformation*, edited by Louise Kriesberg, Terrell A. Northrup, and Stuart J. Thorson, 55–82. Syracuse, NY: Syracuse University Press, 1989.

North, Joanna. "Wrongdoing and Forgiveness." *Philosophy* 62.242 (1987) 499–508.

Nouwen, Henri J. M. *The Wounded Healer*. New York: Doubleday, 1972.

Novatian, "One with the Father." In *John 1–10* by Joel C. Elowsky, edited by Thomas C. Oden, 4a:358. Ancient Christian Commentary on Scripture: New Testament. Downers Grove, IL: IVP, 1998.

Nussbaum, Martha C. *Anger and Forgiveness*. Oxford: Oxford University Press, 2016.

———. *The Monarchy of Fear: A Philosopher Looks at Our Political Crisis*. New York: Simon and Schuster, 2018.

———. "Pity and Mercy: Nietzsche's Stoicism." In *Nietzsche, Genealogy, Morality: Essays on Nietzsche's Genealogy of Morals*, edited by Richard Schacht, 139–67. Berkeley: University of California Press, 1994.

Nyíri, J. C. "Thinking with a Word Processor." In *Philosophy and the Cognitive Sciences*, edited by R. Casati, 63–74. Vienna: Hölder-Pichler-Tempesky, 1994.

Ocasio-Cortez, Alexandra (@AOC). "That a Family Had to Lose a Son . . ." Tweet, Apr. 20, 2021, 6:09 PM. https://twitter.com/AOC/status/1384630276593180674.

O'Connor, Flannery. *Mystery and Manners*. New York: Farrar, Straus, & Giroux, 1969.

O'Donovan, Oliver. *Entering into Rest*. Ethics as Theology 3. Grand Rapids: Eerdmans, 2017.

Oatley, Keith, "Fiction: Stimulation of Social Worlds." *Trends in Cognitive Sciences* 20.8 (2016) 618–28.

Oden, Thomas C., and Christopher A. Hall. *Mark*. Edited by Thomas C. Oden. Ancient Christian Commentary on Scripture: The New Testament 2. Downers Grove, IL: IVP, 1998.

Ogden, Graham. *Qoheleth*. 1st ed. Sheffield: Sheffield Academic, 1987.

———. *Qoheleth*. 2nd ed. Sheffield: Sheffield Academic, 2007.

Oliver, Mary Beth, Arthur A. Raney, and Jennings Bryant, eds. *Media Effects: Advances in Theory and Research*. 4th ed. New York: Routledge, 2019.

Oremus, Will. "Google's AI Passed a Famous Test—And Showed How the Test is Broken." *Washington Post*, June 17, 2022. https://www.washingtonpost.com/technology/2022/06/17/google-ai-lamda-turing-test.

Orlowski, Jeff, dir. *The Social Dilemma*. Netflix, 2020.

Orsi, Robert A. "Introduction: Crossing the City Line." In *Gods of the City: Religion and the American Urban Landscape*. Edited by Robert A. Orsi. Bloomington: Indiana University Press, 1999.

Orwell, George. *Animal Farm*. Introduction by Julian Symons. New York: Everyman's Library, 1993.

Ott, Brian L., and Greg Dickinson. *The Twitter Presidency: Donald J. Trump and the Politics of White Rage*. New York: Routledge, 2019.

Pao, David W. *Thanksgiving: An Investigation of a Pauline Theme*. Edited by D. A. Carson. New Studies in Biblical Theology. Downers Grove, IL: IVP, 2002.

Park, Crystal L., et al. "Why Religion? Meaning as Motivation." In *APA Handbook of Psychology, Religion, and Spirituality, Vol. 1: Context, Theory, and Research*, edited by Kenneth I. Pargament, Julie J. Exline, and James W. Jones, 157–71. Washington, DC: American Psychological Association, 2013.

Payne, Christine A., and Michael James Roberts, eds. *Nietzsche and Critical Social Theory: Affirmation, Animosity, Ambiguity*. Leiden: Brill, 2020.

Pecora, Vincent P. "Nietzsche, Genealogy, Critical Theory." *New German Critique* 53 (Spring–Summer 1991) 104–30.

Penwell, Stewart. "Josephus on Samaritan Origins." The Bible and Interpretation—University of Arizona (Oct. 2019). https://bibleinterp.arizona.edu/articles/josephus-samaritan-origins.

Pesce, Nicole Lyn. "'Accountability . . . but Not Justice': AOC, Pelosi, Zuckerberg and Other Leaders React to Chauvin Verdict." *MarketWatch*, Apr. 21, 2021. https://www.msn.com/en-us/news/politics/accountability-%E2%80%A6-but-not-justice-aoc-pelosi-zuckerberg-and-other-leaders-react-to-chauvin-verdict/ar-BB1fRYFU.

Peters, John Durham. "Institutional Opportunities for Intellectual History in Communication Studies." In *The History of Media and Communication Research*, edited by David.W. Park and Jefferson Pooley, 143–152. New York: Peter Lang, 2008.

———. *Speaking into the Air: A History of the Idea of Communication*. Chicago: University of Chicago Press, 1999.

Peterson, David. *Engaging with God: A Biblical Theology of Worship*. Downers Grove, IL: IVP Academic, 1992.

Peterson, Eugene. *Eat This Book: A Conversation on the Art of Spiritual Reading*. Grand Rapids: Eerdmans, 2006.

Petty, Richard E., et al. "Mass Media Attitude Change: Implications of the Elaboration Likelihood Model of Persuasion." In *Media Effects: Advances in Theory and Research*, 3rd ed., edited by Bryant Jennings and Mary Beth Oliver, 125–64. New York: Routledge, 2009.

Pew Research Center. "Large Majority of the Public Views Prosecution of Capitol Rioters as 'Very Important.'" Mar. 18, 2021. https://www.pewresearch.org/politics/2021/03/18/large-majority-of-the-public-views-prosecution-of-capitol-rioters-as-very-important.

Philo. *The Works of Philo*. Translated by C. D. Yonge. Complete and unabridged, new updated version. Peabody, MA: Hendrickson, 1993.

Pinker, Aaron. "The Oppressed in Qohelet 4:1." *Vetus Testamentum* 61 (2011) 393–405.

Polanyi, Michael. *Personal Knowledge: Towards a Post-Critical Philosophy*. Chicago: University of Chicago Press, 2015.

———. *The Tacit Dimension*. Chicago: University of Chicago Press, 1966.

———., and Harry Prosch. *Meaning*. Chicago: University of Chicago Press, 1977.

Polus, Sarah. "Ocasio-Cortez: Chauvin 'Verdict Is Not a Substitute for Policy Change.'" *The Hill*, Apr. 20, 2021. https://thehill.com/homenews/house/549357-ocasio-cortez-chauvin-verdict-is-not-a-substitute-for-policy-change.

Porter, Stanley E. "Penitence and Repentance in the Epistles." In *Repentance in Christian Theology*, edited by Mark J. Boda and Gordon T. Smith, 127–52. Collegeville, MN: Liturgical, 2006.

Postman, Neil. *Amusing Ourselves to Death: Public Discourse in the Age of Show Business*. 20th anniversary edition. London: Penguin, 2005.

———. *Technopoly: The Surrender of Culture to Technology*. London: Vintage, 1993.

Powers, Shawn, and Mohammed el-Nawawy. "Al-Jazeera English and Global News Networks: Clash of Civilizations or Cross-Cultural Dialogue?" *War, Media & Conflict* 2.3 (2009) 263–84.

Preston, Jesse, and Daniel M. Wegner. "Ideal Agency: The Perception of Self as the Origin of Action." In *On Building, Defending, and Regulating the Self: A Psychological Perspective*, edited by Abraham Tesser, Joanne Wood, and Deiderik Stapel, 103–26. New York: Taylor & Francis, 2005.

———., et al. "Principles of Religious Prosociality: A Review and Reformulation." *Social and Personality Psychology Compass* 4.8 (2010) 574–90.

Provan, Iain. *The NIV Application Commentary: From Biblical Text to Contemporary Life*. Edited by Terry Much. NIV Application Commentary. Grand Rapids: Zondervan, 2001.

Putnam, Robert D. *Bowling Alone: The Collapse and Revival of American Community*. New York: Simon and Schuster, 2001.

———., and David E. Campbell. *American Grace: How Religion Divides and Unites Us*. New York: Simon and Schuster, 2012.

Pütz, Peter. "Nietzsche and Critical Theory." *Telos* 50 (Winter 1981–82) 103–14.

Quattrociocci, Walter, et al. "Echo Chambers on Facebook." *SSRN Electronic Journal*. 2016. https://papers.ssrn.com/sol3/papers.cfm?abstract_id=2795110.

Ranulf, Svend. *Moral Indignation and Middle Class Psychology*. Introduction by Harold D. Lasswell. New York: Schocken, 1964.

Redlawsk, David P., et al. "The Affective Tipping Point: Do Motivated Reasoners Ever 'Get it?'" *Political Psychology* 31.4 (2010) 563–93.

Reed, Phil. "Are Echo Chambers a Threat to Intellectual Freedom?" *Psychology Today*, March 30, 2019. https://www.psychologytoday.com/us/blog/digital-world-real-world/201903/are-echo-chambers-threat-intellectual-freedom.

Remley, William. *The Philosophical Foundation of Alt-Right Politics and Ressentiment*. London: Rowman and Littlefield, 2019.

Rhode, Deborah L. "Feminist Critical Theories." *Stanford Law Review* 42.3 (Feb. 1990) 617–38.

Rogowski, Jon C., and Joseph L. Sutherland. "How Ideology Fuels Affective Polarization." *Political Behavior* 38.2 (2016) 485–508.

Rojas, Hernando. "Egocentric Publics and Perceptions of the Worlds Around Us." In *New Technologies and Civic Engagement: New Agendas in Communication*, edited by Homero Gil de Zúñiga, 93–102. Abingdon: Routledge, 2015.

———., et al. "Patterns of Media Use, Conversation and Perceived Political Polarization in 10 Countries." Paper presented at the annual meeting of the World Association for Public Opinion Research, Hong Kong, June 14–16, 2012.

Roof, Wade Clark. *Spiritual Marketplace: Baby Boomers and the Remaking of American Religion*. Princeton, NJ: Princeton University Press, 1999.

Ross, Allen P. *Recalling the Hope of Glory: Biblical Worship from the Garden to the New Creation*. Grand Rapids: Kregel Academic, 2006.

Rowe, Ian. "Deliberation 2.0: Comparing the Deliberative Quality of Online News User Comments Across Platforms." *Journal of Broadcasting & Electronic Media* 59.4 (2015) 539–55.

Rowley, H. H. *Worship in Ancient Israel: Its Forms and Meaning*. Eugene, OR: Wipf & Stock, 2010.

Ruiz, Carlos D., and Thomas Nilsson. "Disinformation and Echo Chambers: How Disinformation Circulates on Social Media Through Identity-Driven Controversies." *Journal of Public Policy and Marketing* (2022) 18–35.
Saint, Steve. *End of the Spear*. Carol Stream, IL: Salt River, 2006.
Sanders, Bernie (@SenSanders). "The jury's verdict delivers accountability for Derek Chauvin . . ." Tweet, Apr. 20, 2021, 5:20 PM. https://twitter.com/SenSanders/status/1384618108980244481.
Schacht, Richard, ed. *Nietzsche, Genealogy, Morality: Essays on Nietzsche's Genealogy of Morals*. Edited by Amélie Okensberg Rorty. Philosophical Traditions. Berkeley: University of California Press, 1994.
Scheler, Max. *Ressentiment*. Edited by Lewis A. Coser. Translated by William W. Holdheim. New York: Schocken, 1972.
Schmemann, Alexander. *For the Life of the World: Sacraments and Orthodoxy*. Crestwood, NY: St. Vladimir's Seminary Press, 1973.
Schopenhaur, Arthur. *The Basis of Morality*. Translated by Arthur Brodrick Bullock. London: Sonnenschein, 1903.
Schori-Eyal, Noa, et al. "The Shadows of the Past: Effects of Historical Group Trauma on Current Intergroup Conflicts." *Personality and Social Psychology Bulletin* 43.4 (2017) 1–17.
———. "Perpetual Ingroup Victimhood as a Distorted Lens: Effects on Attribution and Categorization." *European Journal of Social Psychology* 47.2 (2017) 180–94.
Sears, David, and Richard Whitney. *Political Persuasion*. Morristown, NH: General Learning, 1973.
———., and Rick Kosterman. "Mass Media and Political Persuasion." In *Persuasion: Psychological Insights and Perspectives*, edited by Timothy Brock and Sharron Shavitt, 251–78. Needham Heights, MA: Allyn & Bacon, 1994.
Segarra, Lisa Marie. "Read What Pope Francis Said About Power and Humility at Surprise TED Talk." *Time*, Apr. 26, 2017. https://time.com/4755663/pope-francis-ted-talk-transcript/.
Seitz, Christopher R. *Isaiah 1–39*. Paperback ed. Interpretation: A Biblical Commentary for Teaching and Preaching. Louisville: Westminster John Knox, 2012.
Settle, Jamie E. *Frenemies: How Social Media Polarizes America*. Cambridge: Cambridge University Press, 2018.
Shakespeare, William. *The Merchant of Venice*. Edited by John Russell Brown. Reprint Edition. Cambridge, MA: Harvard University Press, 1959.
———. *The Tragedy of King Lear*. Edited by Alfred Harbage. Baltimore: Penguin, 1958.
Shanahan, James, and Michael Morgan. *Television and Its Viewers: Cultivation Theory and Research*. Cambridge, MA: Cambridge University Press, 1999.
Shapiro, Gary. "Translating, Repeating, Naming: Foucalt, Derrida, and the Genealogy of Morals." In *Nietzsche's "On the Genealogy of Morals": Critical Essays*, edited by Christa Davis Acampora, 233–44. Lanham, MD: Rowman & Littlefield, 2006.
Shehata, Adam, and Jesper Strömbäck. "Not (Yet) a New Era of Minimal Effects: A Study of Agenda Setting at the Aggregate and Individual Levels." *International Journal of Press/Politics* 18.2 (2013) 234–55.
Sherif, Muzafer. "Superordinate Goals in the Reduction of Intergroup Conflict: An Experimental Evaluation." In *The Social Psychology of Intergroup Relations*, edited by William G. Austin and Stephen Worchel, 257–61. Monterey, CA: Brooks/Cole Publishing, 1979.

———., and Carolyn Sherif. *Groups in Harmony and Tension: An Integration of Studies of Intergroup Relations*. New York: Harper and Brothers, 1953.

———., et al. *The Robbers Cave Experiment: Intergroup Conflict and Cooperation*. Middletown, CT: Wesleyan University Press, 1988.

Shnabel, Nurit, et al. "When Suffering Begets Suffering: The Psychology of Competitive Victimhood Between Adversarial Groups in Violent Conflicts." *Personality and Social Psychology Review* 16 (2012) 351–74.

———. "Overcoming Competitive Victimhood and Facilitating Forgiveness Through Re-Categorization into a Common Victim or Perpetrator Identity." *Journal of Experimental Social Psychology* 49.5 (2013) 867–77.

Shori-Eyal, et al. "Three Layers of Collective Victimhood: Effects of Multileveled Victimhood on Intergroup Conflicts in the Israeli-Arab Context." *Journal of Applied Social Psychology* 44.12 (2014) 778–94. http://dx.doi.org/10.1111/jasp.12268.

Shriver, Donald W., Jr. *An Ethic for Enemies: Forgiveness in Politics*. New York: Oxford University Press, 1995.

Shrum, L. J. "Assessing the Social Influence of Television: A Social Cognition Perspective on Cultivation Effects." *Communication Research* 22.4 (1995) 402–29.

———. "The Implications for Survey Method for Measuring Cultivation Effects." *Human Communication Research* 33.1 (2007) 64–80.

———. Shrum, L. J. "Media Consumption and Perceptions of Social Reality: Effects and Underlying Processes." In *Media Effects: Advances in Theory and Research*, 3rd ed., edited by Bryant Jennings and Mary Beth Oliver, 50–73. New York: Routledge, 2009.

———. "The Relationship of Television Viewing with Attitude Strength and Extremity: Implications for the Cultivation Effect." *Media Psychology* 1.1 (1999) 3–25.

———. "The Role of Source Confusion in Cultivation Effects May Depend on Processing Strategy: A Comment on Mares (1996)." *Human Communication Research* 24.2 (1997) 349–58.

Signorielli, Nancy. "Selective Television Viewing: A Limited Possibility." *Journal of Communication* 36.3 (1986) 64–76.

———. "Television's Mean and Dangerous World: A Continuation of the Cultural Indicators Perspective." In *Cultivation Analysis: New Directions in Media Effects Research*, edited by Nancy Signorielli and Michael Morgan, 85–106. Newbury Park, CA: Sage, 1990.

Simas, Elizabeth N., et al. "How Empathetic Concern Fuels Political Polarization." *American Political Science Review* 114.1 (2020) 258–69.

Simonetti, Manlio. *Matthew 1–13*. Edited by Thomas C. Oden. Ancient Christian Commentary on Scripture: New Testament 1a. Downers Grove, IL: IVP, 1998.

———. *Matthew 14–28*. Edited by Thomas C. Oden. Ancient Christian Commentary on Scripture: New Testament 1b. Downers Grove, IL: IVP, 1998.

Skoric, Marko M., et al. "What Predicts Selective Avoidance on Social Media?: A Study of Political Unfriending in Hong Kong and Taiwan." *American Behavioral Scientist* 62.8 (2018) 1097–1115.

Slater, Michael D., et al. "Temporarily Expanding the Boundaries of the Self: Motivations for Entering the Story World and Implications for Narrative Effects." *Journal of Communication* 64.3 (2014) 439–55.

Smedes, Lewis B. *Forgive and Forget: Healing the Hurts We Don't Deserve*. San Francisco: Harper and Row, 1984.

Smith, Christian, et al. *Lost in Transition: The Dark Side of Emerging Adulthood*. New York: Oxford University Press, 2011.

———., and Melinda Lundquist Denton. *Soul Searching: The Religious and Spiritual Lives of American Teenagers*. Oxford: Oxford University Press, 2005.

———., and Patricia Snell. *Souls in Transition: The Religious and Spiritual Lives of Emerging Adults*. Oxford: Oxford University Press, 2009.

Smith, Douglas. "Introduction." In *The Genealogy of Morality* by Friedrich Nietzsche. Translated by Douglas Smith. Oxford: Oxford University Press, 1996.

Smith, Gordon T. "The Penitential: An Evangelical Perspective." In *Repentance in Christian Theology*, edited by Mark J. Boda and Gordon T. Smith, 267–86. Collegeville, MN: Liturgical, 2006.

Smith, James K. A. *Awaiting the King: Reforming Public Theology*. Cultural Liturgies 3. Grand Rapids: Baker Academic, 2017.

———. *Desiring the Kingdom: Worship, Worldview, and Cultural Formation*. Cultural Liturgies 1. Grand Rapids: Baker Academic, 2009.

———. *How (Not) to Be Secular: Reading Charles Taylor*. Grand Rapids: Eerdmans, 2014.

———. *Imagining the Kingdom: How Worship Works*. Cultural Liturgies 2. Grand Rapids: Baker Academic, 2013.

———. "The New Alarmism: How Some Christians Are Stoking Fear Rather Than Hope." *Washington Post*, Mar. 10, 2017.

———. *You Are What You Love: The Spiritual Power of Habit*. Grand Rapids: Brazos, 2016.

Solomon, Robert C. "One Hundred Years of *Ressentiment*: Nietzsche's Genealogy of Morals." In *Nietzsche, Genealogy, Morality: Essays on Nietzsche's Genealogy of Morals*, edited by Amélie Okensberg Rorty and Richard Schacht, 95–126. Philosophical Traditions. Berkeley: University of California Press, 1994.

———. *A Passion for Justice: Emotions and the Origins of the Social Contract*. Lanham, MD: Rowman and Littlefield, 1995.

Solzhenitsyn, Aleksandr I. *A World Split Apart*. New York: Harper and Row, 1978.

———. *The Gulag Archipelago, 1918–2008: An Experiment in Literary Investigation*. Edited by Edward E. Ericson Jr. Translated by Thomas P. Whitney and Harry Willets. Foreword by Anne Applebaum. Abridged ed. New York: Harper Perennial, 2007.

Sophrony, St. Archimandrite. *Starets Silouan, Moine du Mont-Athos*. Edited by Présence. Translated by Rosemary Edmunds. New York: St. Vladimir's Seminary Press, 1999.

Spangenberg, Izak. "Psalm 73 and the Book of Qoeleth." *OTE* 29.1 (2016) 161.

Stanley, Andy. *Not in It to Win It: Why Choosing Sides Sidelines the Church*. Grand Rapids: Zondervan, 2022.

Stark, Rodney. *The Rise of Christianity: How the Obscure, Marginal Jesus Movement Became the Dominant Religious Force in the Western World in a Few Centuries*. Princeton, NJ: Princeton University Press, 1996.

Steiglitz, Stefan, and Linh Dang-Xuan. "Emotion and Information Diffusion in Social Media—Sentiment of Microblogs and Sharing Behavior." *Journal of Management Information Systems* 29 (2013) 217–48.

Stroud, Natalie Jomini. *Niche News: The Politics of News Choice.* Oxford: Oxford University Press, 2011.

———. "Polarization and Partisan Selective Exposure." *Journal of Communication* 60.3 (2010) 556–76.

Stukal, Denis, et al. "Detecting Bots on Russian Political Twitter." *Big Data* 5.4 (2017) 310–24.

Suk, Jiyoun, et al. "The More You Know, the Less You Like: A Comparative Study of How News and Political Conversation Shape Political Knowledge and Affective Polarization." *Communication and the Public* 7.1 (2022) 40–56.

Sullivan, Dale L. "'After Ten Years': Dietrich Bonhoeffer's Epidiectic Exhortation to Responsible Action." *Journal of Communication and Religion* 26.1 (2003) 28–50.

Sumner, William Graham. *Folkways: A Study of the Sociological Importance of Usages, Manners, Customs, Mores, and Morals.* Reprint. Seattle: Createspace, 2014.

Sunstein, Cass R. *#Republic: Divided Democracy in the Age of Social Media.* Princeton, NJ: Princeton University Press, 2017.

———. *Republic.com.* Princeton, NJ: Princeton University Press, 2001.

———. *Republic.com 2.0.* Princeton, NJ: Princeton University Press, 2007.

Swedeberg, Richard. *Tocqueville's Political Commentary.* Princeton, NJ: Princeton University Press, 2009.

Sykes, Charles J. *A Nation of Victims: The Decay of the American Character.* New York: St. Martin's, 1992.

Taber, Charles S., et al. "The Motivated Processing of Political Arguments." *Political Behavior* 31.2 (2009) 137–55.

———., and Milton Lodge. "Motivated Skepticism in the Evaluation of Political Beliefs." *American Journal of Political Science* 50.3 (2006) 755–69.

Tajfel, Henri. *Differentiation Between Social Groups: Studies in the Social Psychology of Intergroup Relations.* London: Academic, 1978.

———., and John Turner. "An Integrative Theory of Intergroup Conflict." In *The Social Psychology of Intergroup Relations*, edited by William G. Austin and Steven Worchel, 33–48. Monterey, CA: Brooks Cole, 1979.

Tal-Or, Nurit, and Yariv Tsfati. "When Arabs and Jews Watch TV Together: The Joint Effect of the Content and Context of Communication on Reducing Prejudice." *Journal of Communication* 66.4 (2016) 646–68.

Tate, Marvin E. *Psalms 51–100.* Edited by David Hubbard, et al. Word Biblical Commentary 20. Dallas: Word, 1990.

Taylor, Charles. *Modern Social Imaginaries.* Durham, NC: Duke University Press, 2004.

———. *Multiculturalism and "The Politics of Recognition."* Princeton, NJ: Princeton University Press, 1992.

———. *A Secular Age.* Cambridge, MA: Belknap, 2007.

———. *Sources of the Self: Making of the Modern Identity.* Cambridge, MA: Harvard University Press, 1989.

Taylor, Vincent. *Forgiveness and Reconciliation: A Study in New Testament Theology.* London: MacMillan, 1956.

Ten Boom, Corrie. *Clippings from My Notebook.* Nashville: Thomas Nelson, 1982.

———. *The Hiding Place.* Carmel, NY: Guideposts, 1971.

Thaler, Richard H., and Cass R. Sunstein. *Nudge: Improving Decisions About Health, Wealth, and Happiness.* New Haven: Yale University Press, 2008.

Thibodeaux SJ, Fr. Mark. *Reimagining the Ignatian Examen: Fresh Ways to Pray from Your Day.* Chicago: Loyola Press, 2014.

Tinder, Glenn. *The Political Meaning of Christianity: The Prophetic Stance: An Interpretation.* Reprint ed. New York: HarperCollins, 1991.

Tisby, Jemar. *The Color of Compromise: The Truth about the American Church's Complicity in Racism.* Grand Rapids: Zondervan, 2019.

———. "White Christians, Do Not Cheapen the Hug and Message of Forgiveness from Botham Jean's Brother." *Washington Post*, Oct. 3, 2019: https://www.washingtonpost.com/religion/2019/10/03/white-christians-do-not-cheapen-hug-message-forgiveness-botham-jeans-brother/.

Tocqueville, Alexis de. *Democracy in America.* Edited by Francis Bowen. Translated by Henry Reeve. Two Volumes Bound as One, Dover Thrift Editions. Minneola, NY: Dover, 2017.

Tolkien, J. R. R. *The Hobbit.* Illustrations by Alan Lee. New York: Houghton Mifflin, 1997.

Tolman, Edward. "Cognitive Maps in Rats and Men." *Psychological Review* 55 (1948) 189–208.

Tomelleri, Stefano. *Ressentiment: Reflections on Mimetic Desire and Society.* Edited by William A. Johnson. Kindle Edition. East Lansing, MI: Michigan State University Press, 2015.

Törnberg, Petter, et al. "Modeling the Emergence of Affective Polarization in the Social Media Society." *PLoS ONE* 16.10 (2021) 1–17.

Trilling, Damian. "Two Different Debates?: Investigating the Relationship Between a Political Debate on TV and Simultaneous Comments on Twitter." *Social Science Computer Review* 33.3 (2014) 259–76.

Trueman, Carl. *The Rise and Triumph of the Modern Self: Cultural Amnesia, Expressive Individualism, and the Road to Sexual Revolution.* Wheaton, IL: Crossway, 2020.

Tsfati, Yariv, et al. "Exposure to Ideological News and Perceived Opinion Climate: Testing the Media Effects Component of Spiral-of-Silence in a Fragmented Media Landscape." *International Journal of Press/Politics* 19.1 (2014) 3–23.

———., and Nathan Walter. "The World of News and Politics." In *Media Effects: Advances in Theory and Research*, 4th ed., edited by Mary Beth Oliver, Arthur A. Raney, and Jennings Bryant, 36–50. New York: Routledge, 2019.

Tucker, Joshua A., et al. *Social Media, Political Polarization, and Political Disinformation: A Review of the Scientific Literature.* Mar. 2018. http://hewlett.org/wp-content/uploads/2018/03/Social-Media-Political-Polarization-and-Political-Disinformation-Literature-Review.pdf.

Turkle, Sherry. *Alone Together: Why We Expect More from Technology and Less from Each Other.* 3rd ed. New York: Basic, 2017.

———. *Reclaiming Conversation: The Power of Talk in a Digital Age.* New York: Penguin, 2015.

———. "The Tethered Self: Technology Reinvents Intimacy and Solitude." *Continuing Higher Education Review* 75 (2011) 28–31.

Tutu, Desmond. *No Future Without Forgiveness.* New York: Doubleday, 1999.

Twenge, Jean M. *iGen: Why Today's Super-Connected Kids Are Growing Up Less Rebellious, More Tolerant, Less Happy—and Completely Unprepared for Adulthood and What That Means for the Rest of Us.* New York: Atria, 2017.

Twenge, Jean M., et al. "Age, Period, and Cohort Trends in Mood Disorder Indicators and Suicide-Related Outcomes in a Nationally Representative Dataset, 2005–2017." *Journal of Abnormal Psychology* 128.3 (2019) 185–99.

———., et al. "Generational and Time Period Differences in American Adolescents' Religious Orientation, 1966-2014." *PLoS One* 10.5 (May 11, 2015): e0121454. doi: 10.1371/journal.pone.0121454. Erratum in: *PLoS One* 14.8 (Aug. 15, 2019) e022 1441. doi: 10.1371/journal.pone.0221441.

———. "Underestimating Digital Media Harm." *Nature Human Behavior* 4 (2020) 346–48.

———. "Increases in Depressive Symptoms, Suicide-Related Outcomes, and Suicide Rates Among US Adolescents After 2010 and Links to Increased New Media Screen Time." *Clinical Psychological Science* 6.1 (2018) 3–17.

———., and W. Keith Campbell. "Media Use Is Linked to Lower Psychological Well-Being: Evidence from Three Datasets." *Psychiatric Quarterly* 90.2 (2019) 311–31.

———. *The Narcissism Epidemic: Living in the Age of Entitlement*. New York: Free, 2009.

Ugander, Johan, et al. "The Anatomy of the Facebook Social Graph." 2011. https://arxiv.org/abs/1111.4503.

Unknown. "You Tear Yourself Apart by Hating." In *Matthew 1–13* by Manilo Simonetti, edited by Thomas C. Oden, 1a:120. Ancient Christian Commentary on Scripture: New Testament. Downers Grove, IL: IVP, 1998.

Vaccari, Christian, et al. "Social Media and Political Communication. A Survey of Twitter Users During the 2013 Italian General Election." *Rivista italiana di scienza politica* 43.3 (2013) 381–410.

Valkenburg, Patti M., and Mary Beth Oliver. "Media Effects Theories: An Overview." In *Media Effects: Advances in Theory and Research*, 4th ed., edited by Mary Beth Oliver, Arthur A. Raney, and Jennings Bryant, 16–35. New York: Routledge, 2019.

Vallone, Robert P., et al. "The Hostile Media Phenomenon: Biased Perception and Perceptions of Media Bias in Coverage of the Beirut Massacre." *Journal of Personality and Social Psychology* 49.3 (1985) 577–85.

van de Loo, Stephanie. *Versöhnungsarbeit: Kriterien, theologischer Rahmen, Praxisperspektiven*. Stuttgart: Kohlhammer, 2009.

Van den Bulck, Jan. "Research Note: The Relationship Between Television Fiction and Fear of Crime." *European Journal of Communication* 19.2 (2004) 239–48.

van Ruiten, Jacques. "The Intertextual Relationship Between Isaiah 65,17–20 and Revelation 21,1–5." *Estudios Bíblicos* 51.4 (1993) 473–510.

Van Swol, Lyn, et al. "The Banality of Extremism: The Role of Group Dynamics and Communication of Norms in Polarization on January 6." *APA* 26.3 (2022) 239–51.

Vicario, Del, et al. "The Spreading of Misinformation Online." *Proceedings of the National Academy of Sciences* 113.3 (2016) 554–59.

Volf, Miroslav. *The End of Memory: Remembering Rightly in a Violent World*. Grand Rapids: Eerdmans, 2006.

———. *Exclusion and Embrace: A Theological Exploration of Identity, Otherness, and Reconciliation*. Nashville: Abingdon, 1996.

———. *Free of Charge: Giving and Forgiving in a Culture Stripped of Grace*. Grand Rapids: Zondervan, 2005.

Vollhardt, Johanna Ray, ed. *The Social Psychology of Collective Victimhood*. New York: Oxford University Press, 2020.

Vollhardt, Johanna R., and Rezarta Bilali. "The Role of Inclusive and Exclusive Victim Consciousness in Predicting Intergroup Attitudes: Findings from Rwanda, Burundi, and DRC." *Political Psychology* 36 (2014) 489–506. http://dx.doi.org/10.1111/pops.12174.

Vorderer, Peter, et al. "A History of Media Effects Research Traditions." In *Media Effects: Advances in Theory and Research*, 4th ed., edited by Mary Beth Oliver, Arthur A. Raney, and Jennings Bryant. New York: Routledge, 2019.

Vries, Maya de, et al. "Like a Bridge Over Troubled Water: Using Facebook to Mobilize Solidarity Among East Jerusalem Palestinians During the 2014 War in Gaza." *International Journal of Communication* 9 (2015) 2622–49.

Wachowskis. *The Matrix*. Written and Directed by the Wachowskis. Warner Brothers, 1999.

Wakefield, Mary. "The Dangerous Pleasure of Hating Men." *Spectator*. Nov. 13, 2021. https://www.spectator.co.uk/article/the-dangerous-pleasure-of-hating-men.

Walters, Suzanna Danuta. "Why Can't We Hate Men?" *Washington Post*, Jun. 8, 2018.

Watkin, Christopher. *Biblical Critical Theory: How the Bible's Unfolding Story Makes Sense of Modern Life and Culture*. Grand Rapids: Zondervan Academic, 2022.

Webster, James G. "The Myth of Partisan Selective Exposure: A Portrait of the Online Political News Audience." *Social Media & Society* 3.3 (2017) 1–13.

Webster, James G., and Thomas B. Ksiazek. "The Dynamics of Audience Fragmentation: Public Attention in an Age of Digital Media." Journal of Communication 62.1 (2012) 39–56.

Webster, Steven W., and Alan I. Abramowitz. "The Ideological Foundations of Affective Polarization in the US Electorate." *American Politics Research* 45.4 (2017) 621–47.

Weil, Simone. "The Romanesque Renaissance." In *Selected Essays, 1934–1943: Historical, Political, and Moral Writings*, translated by Richard Rees, 44–54. Eugene, OR: Wipf & Stock, 2015.

Wells, Chris, et al. "When We Stop Talking Politics: The Maintenance and Closing of Conversation in Contentious Times." *Journal of Communication* 67 (2017) 131–57.

Wesley, Charles. "Lo He Comes with Clouds Descending." Hymnary.org. https://hymnary.org/text/lo_he_comes_with_clouds_descending_once.

Whitehead, Andrew L., and Samuel L. Perry, *Taking America Back for God: Christian Nationalism in the United States*. Oxford: Oxford University Press, 2020.

Whyte, Max. "The Uses and Abuses of Nietzsche in the Third Reich: Alfred Baeumler's 'Heroic Realism.'" *Journal of Contemporary History* 43.2 (2008) 171–94. http://www.jstor.org/stable/30036502.

Wigram, George V. *The Englishman's Greek Concordance of the New Testament: Coded with Strong's Concordance Numbers*. Peabody, MA: Hendrickson, 1996.

Williams, Dmitir, and Marko Skoric. "Internet Fantasy Violence: A Test of Aggression in an Online Game." *Communication Monographs* 72.2 (2005) 217–33.

Wilson, Catherine. "Darwin and Nietzsche: Selection, Evolution, and Morality." *Journal of Nietzsche Studies* 44.2 (2013) 354–70. https://doi.org/10.5325/jnietstud.44.2.0354.

Wilson, Timothy, et al. "A Model of Dual Attitudes." *Psychological Review* 107.1 (2000) 101–26.

Wohl, Michael, and Nyla R. Branscombe. "Forgiveness and Collective Guilt Assignment to Historical Perpetrator Groups Depend on Level of Social Category Inclusiveness." *Journal of Personality and Social Psychology* 88 (2005) 288–303.

Wojcieszak, Magdalena, et al. "No Polarization from Partisan News: Over-Time Evidence from Trace Data." *International Journal of Press/Politics* 28.3 (2021). https://doi.org/10.1177/19401612211047194.

———. "Partisan News and Political Participation: Exploring Mediated Relationships." *Political Communication* 33.2 (2015) 1–20.

Wolfe, Alan. *Moral Freedom: The Search for Virtue in a World of Choice.* New York: Norton, 2001.

Wolleback, Dag, et al. "Anger, Fear, and Echo Chambers: The Emotional Basis for Online Behavior." *Social Media + Society* 5.2 (2019) 1–14.

Worchel, Stephen. "Cooperation and the Reduction of Intergroup Conflict: Some Determining Factors." In *The Social Psychology of Intergroup Relations*, edited by William G. Austin and Stephen Worchel, 262–73. Monterey, CA: Brooks/Cole Publishing, 1979.

Worthington, Everett L., Jr. "The Pyramid Model of Forgiveness: Some Interdisciplinary Speculations About Unforgiveness and the Promotion of Forgiveness." In *Dimensions of Forgiveness: Psychological Research and Theological Perspectives*, edited by Everett L. Worthington Jr., 107–38. Philadelphia: Templeton Foundation, 1998.

Wright, N. T. *The New Testament and the People of God.* Christian Origins and the Question of God 1. Minneapolis: Fortress, 1992.

Wuthnow, Robert. *After Heaven: Spirituality in America Since the 1950s.* New ed. Berkeley: University of California Press, 1998.

———. *After the Baby Boomers: How Twenty- and Thirty-somethings Are Shaping the Future of American Religion.* Princeton, NJ: Princeton University Press, 2010.

———. *America and the Challenges of Religious Diversity.* Princeton, NJ: Princeton University Press, 2007.

———. *American Mythos: Why Our Best Efforts to Be a Better Nation Fall Short.* Princeton, NJ: Princeton University Press, 2009.

———. *The Left Behind: Decline and Rage in Small-Town America.* Princeton, NJ: Princeton University Press, 2018.

———. *Meaning and Moral Order: Explorations in Cultural Analysis.* Berkeley and Los Angeles, CA: University of California Press, 1987.

Yalalov, Damir. "ChatGPT Passes the Turing Test." *Metaverse Post*, Dec. 8 2022. https://www.mpost.io/chatgpt-passes-the-turing-test.

Yancey, George, and Ashlee Quosigk. *One Faith No Longer: The Transformation of Christianity in Red and Blue America.* New York: New York University Press, 2021.

Yardi, Sarita, and Danah Boyd. "Dynamic Debates: An Analysis of Group Polarization Over Time on Twitter." *Bulletin of Science, Technology, & Society* 30.5 (2010) 316–27.

Verdeja, Ernesto. *Unchopping a Tree: Reconciliation in the Aftermath of Political Violence.* Philadelphia: Temple University Press, 2009.

Yi, Wang. "My Declaration of Faithful Disobedience." *China Partnership*, Dec. 12, 2018. Translated by Amy, Brent Pinkall, and the China Partnership Translation Team. https://www.chinapartnership.org/blog/2018/12/my-declaration-of-faithful-disobedience.

Yovel, Yirmiyahu. "Nietzsche, the Jews, and *Ressentiment*." In *Nietzsche, Genealogy, Morality: Essays on Nietzsche's Genealogy of Morals*, edited by Amélie Okensberg Rorty and Richard Schacht, 214–36. Philisophical Traditions. Berkeley: University of California Press, 1994.

Zaller, John. "Information, Values, and Opinion." *American Political Science Review* 85.4 (1991) 1215–37.

Zhang, Xinzhi, et al. "The Political Consequences of Disagreement: The Filtering of Communication Networks in a Polarized Political Context." *Social Media + Society* (Jul.–Sep. 2022) 1–14.

Ziegele, Marc, et al. "Linking News Value Theory with Online Deliberation: How News Factors and Illustration Factors in News Articles Affect the Deliberative Quality of User Discussions in SNS' Comment Sections." *Communication Research* (Sep. 2018) 1–31.

Zillman, Dolf. "Mood Management Through Communication Choices." *American Behavioral Scientist* 31.3 (1988) 327–40.

General Index

A.I., 13, 16, 23, 28n151, 48n67, 194
Abortion, 188.
Anger, xiii, 59, 68–70, 80–86, 98, 105;
    and justice, 71, 73, 172; and
    revenge, 63, 90, 93–94, 101;
    and social media, 9–10, 19, 26,
    77–78; belongs to god, 110,
    142–43; love instead of, 107,
    112–13, 115, 120–21, 147n3,
    168–70, 207. *See also:* Bitterness;
    Ressentiment
Anomy, 40, 46–49, 51–52, 53n99,
    55–56, 120–21, 198n35. *See also:*
    Bitterness; *Ressentiment*; Social
    Identity Theory (SIT); Suffering
Art of Losing Well (*ALW*), The, xvii,
    167–91, 203; active resistance,
    170–73, 186–88, 187n96;
    bearing suffering, 169, 177–81,
    185–86, 187; Bonhoeffer on,
    169–70, 187; King David and,
    174–76; passive resistance,
    76n87, 188–89, 211–12; what is
    the *ALW*, 168–69, 189–91. *See*
    also: Hope; Solutions; Suffering
Asaph, 91, 108–110, 111, 113, 121n28,
    147n3, 153
Availability, 201–4, 208. *See also:*
    Community; Emergence; Love

Bitterness, xi–xiii, xiv, xvi–xvii, 57, 58–
    62, 63n29, 65–66, 94, 119, 153;
    America and, 84–88, 193; and
    justice, 71, 76, 101, 209, 212; and
    ressentiment, 36n20, 58–62, 65–
    66, 81, 84–88, 121n24, 121n25,
    131, 134, 179, 212; common
    cause solutions to, 15, 20–21,
    112, 206; eliminating bitterness,
    78n95, 90–92, 108–111, 112–13,
    142, 147, 153, 162–63, 202,
    209, 212; social media and, 2,
    6, 9–10,16, 21, 26–27, 27–30 ,
    112–13; to compassion, 78n95,
    90–92, 108–111, 112–13; to
    forgiveness, 115–16, 119,
    122, 124, 127–28, 131, 134,
    143–45; to gratitude, 147,
    159, 162–63, *See also:* Anger;
    Compassion; Forgiveness;
    Grudge Theory; Polarization;
    Politics; *Ressentiment*; Revenge;
    Solutions; Suffering; Victimhood
    Psychology
Bonhoeffer, Dietrich, 126, 168, 169–73,
    187n97 ; Stages of Resistance,
    170n22, 170–72

Christian, xiii–xiv, xvi; and ALW, 168–71, 178–79, 186, 188–89, 189–91; and bitterness, 57, 84–88, 134; and feminism, 44n51; and forgiveness, 129, 134, 137, 141, 143–45; and gratitude, 148–49, 160–66; and hope, 178–79, 181, 183–85, 189–91; and justice, 71–72, 74n74, 76, 100–102, 162, 173, 208; and love, 93, 111–14, 192–93, 201, 203–5, 208; and Nietzsche, 59–61, 64, 66–70; globalism, 170; in America, 44n51, 49–54, 84–88, 170, 173, 178; Nationalism, 63n29, 85, 170 See also: Globalism; Love; Nationalism; Religion
Chrysostom, Saint John, 133, 170n22
Cognitive Behavioral Therapy (CBT), 18–19, 65n37, 66n41, 73n72, 205n65; internal/external locus of control, 18, 62n27, 66. See also: Anomy; Media Effects Models; Psychotherapy; Suffering
Common-Enemy Model, 15, 206
Community, 126, 135–38, 135n100, 140, 159–60, 192–212; children in, 194, 196; interaction, 195–97, 198–200, 201, 205–9; risks of, 201–3. See also: Listening; Group Identity; Love; Social Identity Theory (SIT)
Compassion, xvii, 20, 70, 89–114, 117, 170–71; as justice, 95, 102, 111, 137, 169, 172; for Zacchaeus, 98–100; god's compassion; 94–96, 98–99, 102, 154, 180–81, 181, 183, 183; how to be compassionate, 92, 99, 107–8, 110, 112–14, 126, 172, 205; lack of, 10–11, 16–19, 101, 107–8; why compassion, 91–92, 95–96, 111–12, 117. See also: Bitterness; Empathy; Solutions
Confession, 109, 113, 126, 141, 210. See also: Forgiveness
Critical Theory, See: Marxism

Cross, The, 69, 91, 95, 116, 129–34, 138, 140, 142, 181n71, 189–90; and atonement, 126, 131–34, 136, 140; and Eucharist, 156–57, 156n51
Cross-Cutting, See: Echo Chambers
Cultivation Theory, 6–10, 16, 18n90, 22, 27, 40n36, 62n24, 83; Mean-World Syndrome, 7–9

Daily Examen, 160, 160n67, 165, 207n73, 210–11, See also: Listening; Journaling; Solutions
Dante, 58, 180–81
David, King of Israel, 173–77, and Nabal, 176
Democrat, 10, 11, 15, 28, 38, 80, 83–84
Don Giovanni, 109

Echo Chambers, See: Media Effects
Egocentric Publics, See: Social Imaginary
Emergence, 197, 199–201, 203–4. See also: Availability; Love
Emotional Broadcaster Theory, See: Media Effects Models
Empathy, 15, 18, 48, 75n84, 86n132, 110–12, 171, 173, 194, 196–97, 203. See also: Compassion; Holbrooke
Ender's Game, 91–92
Enemies, xiii, xvii, 17–18, 37–38, 55, 59, 62–66, 103–7, 173–77; and social media, 17–18, 77–80; compassion for; 67, 90, 91–96, 96–98, 99, 100n46, 102, 108–110, 111–14, 126, 133, 145n138, 180, 187, 197–98, 209; end of, 100, 108–9, 110n91, 112; forgiving 116–17, 119–20, 122, 128–29, 132–34, 138, 143, 145, 163–64, 180, 210; loving, 59, 69, 87–88, 90, 91–92, 96–98, 102, 107, 111–14, 138–43, 146–47, 153, 162, 169–70, 173, 180, 193, 197–98, 204, 205–9, 209–212, 214; victimhood, 17–18, 37–38, 63–65, 82–83, 119n15, 138,

144, 173–75, 180; who are our enemies, 30, 42, 63, 65–66, 82–87, 93–94, 96– 97, 100, 108–9, 153, 161–62, 169, 173, 199, 201; Zacchaeus, 98–99, 137–38; *See also:* Group Identity; Polarization; *Ressentiment*; Victimhood Psychology

Eschaton, 75–77, 87, 100, 108–9, 110n91, 165, 181–85, 191

Eucharist, 100n46, 147, 149n14, 153–54, 158, 159–60, 210; origins of, 156–57

Facebook, *See:* Social Media

Fear, 8–9, 62, 65, 86, 92, 112–13, 189n103, 209. *See also:* Anger, Bitterness

Feminism, xi–xiii, 44n51, 63n29, 80, 83–84, 124, 138, *See also:* Men's Advocacy

Follow My Leader, 58–59, 80

Forgiveness, xvii, 115–45, 150; and the Cross, 129–34, 140, 142; Enright Model, 120, 139, 210n81; how to, 118–20, 122, 127–28, 134, 140–43, 203; meaning of, 118–20, 122, 138; REACH Model, 139, 210n81; reconciliation, 116, 122–24, 126, 134, 134n83, 135, 138, 140–41, 143; release, 116, 122–24, 126–29, 130–34; reparations, 116, 121, 125, 135–38; repentance, 99n41, 116, 122–29, 130, 134; three parties, 130–31, 148. *See also:* Bitterness; Compassion; Justice; Liberation Theology; Revenge; Solutions; Suffering

Framing, *See:* Social Imaginary

Frankfurt School, The, *See:* Marxism

Generosity, 149, 151, 161–62; gifts, 147–49; god's, 148, 150, 183–85, 186. *See also:* Bitterness; Gratitude; Solutions

Globalism, 57n113, 85–87, 170

Good Samaritan, The, 106–7. *See also:* Samaritans

Gratitude, xvii; 146–66; what is gratitude, 147–49; given to god, 150–53, 155, 159–61. *See also:* Bitterness; Generosity; Solutions

Group Identity, 10, 15, 17–19, 45, 54–57, 63, 151–52, 172, 208–9. *See also:* Social Identity Theory (SIT); Social Imaginary; Tribe

Grudge Theory, 120–21

Harvest, 151–52, 157, 158; Rogation Sunday, 146. *See also:* Pentecost

Hate, *See:* Anger; Bitterness; *Ressentiment*

Hobbit, The, 192–93, 212

Holbrooke School, 48, 75n94. *See also:* Empathy

Holocaust, The, 18, 21, 60n5, 115–16, 138, 144, 170–73

Hope, xvii, 88; in eternity, 76n87, 110n91, 147, 165–66, 168, 170, 180–81, 181–85, 185–87, 189–91, 193, 204–5, 211–12, 213–14; in the near future, 29, 40, 114, 143–44, 147, 159, 174–75, 180, 186–87, 213–14. *See also:* Art of Losing Well, The (*ALW*); Eschaton; Solutions

"I and Thou," 92, 107, 111–12, 205, 208

Idol-ology, 32, 44–45, 50, 55–56, 70n56, 100–101, 163, 189, 193, 194. *See also:* Idolatry

Idolatry, 70, 77, 135–37, 162, 194, *See also:* Idol-ology; Sacrifice

Imagination, 32–33, 39, 63–66, 70, 71n62, 78, 107, 113–14, 145, 159, 162, 199, 202; reimagine, 159, 162. *See also:* Social Identity Theory (SIT); Social Imaginary

In-Group, *See:* Group Identity

Internet, 2–6, 9, 20, 28–30, 38, 47–49, 51, 54–55, 77–80, 83, 194–98, 199, 206–8, 210. *See also:* Social Media

Irvuzumugabe, Erik, *See:* Testimonies

Israel; ancient, 31, 76n87, 87, 103–6, 107, 110, 127–29, 133, 136–37, 149n15, 151–52, 157–58, 173–75, 182, 186; modern, 18, 20, 34, 101n47. *See also:* Symbol

Joseph the Patriarch, 116–17, 127–28, 138

Journaling, 160–61, 210. *See also:* Listening

Justice, xv, xvii, 55–56, 59, 70, 71–77, 71n62, 94, 99n42, 116, 124n41, 126, 140; and Zacchaeus, 98–100; becomes mercy, 95, 102, 120–21, 134, 137; god as arbiter of, 76–77, 87, 100, 108–9, 110, 133, 145n138, 165, 182, 185–86; just-world hypothesis, 9, 18n90, 56; lex talionis, 94n15; nature of, 71–77, 123–24; risk of overcorrection, 72–73, 101, 128, 145n138. *See also:* Bitterness; Liberation Theology; King, Martin Luther; Polarization; Politics; Power; Race; *Ressentiment*; Revenge; Sin; Solutions; Suffering; Tocqueville Paradox; Victimhood Psychology

King, Martin Luther, 89–91; Activism of, 186–87, 197n96, 206, 211; and compassion, 90, 106–7, 111–12, 114; and Ressentiment, 65n40, 101, 101n47, 111; contract, 187n96; The Good Samaritan, 106–7. *See also:* Compassion, Justice

Liberation Theology, 99–102, 99n42, 125–27, 130, 138n111, 145n138, 162, 187, 208–9. *See also:* Justice; Politics

Listening, 30, 48–49, 90–91, 111, 144, 197, 199, 200–201, 204–5, 207–8, 209. *See also:* Journaling

Love, 59, 68–69, 43–45, 91, 179, 185, 193, 198, 201–2, 204; for enemies, 70, 88, 90, 92–94, 101–2, 111–12, 138, 147, 162, 168–70, 198–205, 205–212; for neighbors, 70, 75–76, 90–91, 92, 112, 141–42, 192, 198, 200–201, 205, 212; humanizing, 20–21, 30, 92–94, 99n42, 101, 107, 111–12, 117, 170n16, 197–98, 197n32, 198–200, 201, 204; of god for us, 69, 88, 94–96, 102, 110, 129, 131, 142, 161, 173–75, 180, 201, 203; for god, 125, 137, 159, 161, 173–75. *See also:* Availability; Emergence; Solutions

Maccabean Martyrs, 104n66, 133
Machiavellianism, 40n36, 71, 76
Malaises of Modernity, 40. *See also:* Anomy
Marx, Karl, 59, 61, 80–81
Marxism, xv, 59, 61, 75n82, 79n97, 80–81, 87, 101, 170n21
Mass Society, 78–79. *See also:* Tocqueville Paradox
McLuhan, Marshall, 3–4, 8n32, 29, 194n10
Media Effects, 1–30; and polarization 12–16; and victimhood psychology, 19–20; echo chambers 6, 13, 16, 19, 21–27, 46–47, study of, xvi, 2, 3–5, *See also:* Cultivation Theory; Internet; Media Effects Models; Social Media
Media Effects Models, 4, 5, 13n66; agenda setting theory, 4, 27n147; emotional broadcaster theory, 19–20, 78n93; mood management theory, 22; nudge theory, 13, 22, 28; SESAM, 22, 26n143, 43n50; social cognitive theory, 27n147, 78n95, 205n62; spiral of silence, 26. *See also:* Cognitive Behavioral Therapy; Cultivation Theory; Echo Chambers; McLuhan, Marshall; Moral Foundations Theory; Polarization; Psychotherapy;

Tocqueville Paradox;
  Victimhood Psychology
Memory, 19n99, 112–13, 119, 126–27,
  128, 140, 142–43, 151–52, 159–
  61, 168, 179–81
Men's Advocacy, xii, *See also:* Feminism
Mercy, 92n8, *See also:* Compassion;
  Empathy
Mimetics, 32n6, 62–63, 65, 68,
  70, 82n111, 84, 97; and
  Ressentiment, 61n10, 62–65, 70,
  71n60, 74, 75–76, 82n111
Monty Python, 2, 30, 103n57
Mood Management Theory, *See:* Media
  Effects Models
Moral Foundations Theory, 14–15,
  72, 73n72, 82n115. *See also:*
  Cognitive Behavioral Therapy
  (CBT)

Nationalism, 57n113, 85–87, 170
News, 4, 9, 24–25, 194–95, 207–8;
  news media, 4, 12, 20, 25, 194;
  newspaper, 4, 77. *See also:* Media
  Effects; Social Media
Nietzsche, Friedrich, xi, xv–xvii, 1,
  9n35, 59–88, 129, 147n3,
  193; *Also Sprach Zarathustra*,
  59–60, 67; and America, 83–87;
  aristocratic/slave morality,
  60–64, 69; the parable of the
  madman, 60n5, 66–67; pathos
  of distance, 60–61; revolution
  in morals, 37, 55, 59, 61, 64, 70,
  172. *See also:* Bitterness; Justice;
  Marxism; Politics; *Ressentiment*;
  Suffering
Nudge Theory, *See:* Media Effects
  Models

Operation Auca, 167–68

Paradox; god's compassion, 94–96;
  god's forgetting, 119n12; god's
  suffering, 94–86, 142n126,
  177–79, 181, 181n71. *See also:*
  Imagination; Memory
Pentecost, 151–52, 157–58. *See also:*
  Eucharist
Peterson, Eugene, 44

Pluralism, 42, 50, 55
Polarization, 6, 10–16, 17, 21, 22, 23,
  24–26, 37n28, 38, 43n50, 46–47,
  59, 82–83, 112n98; affective,
  10–11, 12, 15, 16, 24, 26, 32,
  34, 37, 79, 168n10, 198; false,
  10, 47; perceived, 10–11, 13,
  14, 17, 23, 26, 29, 63–64. *See
  also:* Bitterness; Media Effects;
  Politics; *Ressentiment*; Solutions;
  Suffering; Victimhood
  Psychology
Politics, xiii, xv–xvi, 4, 20, 23, 25, 32,
  34n13, 38, 44, 49, 71, 76n87,
  78–79, 80–86, 93, 102, 103–5,
  169, 193, 204–5, 213; 2016
  Presidential Election, xiii, 9, 20,
  48, 56, 85n128, 93; and media,
  4, 9–10, 10–16, 23–24, 26,
  37–38, 74–75, 79, 198, 206–7;
  and religion, 32, 33–34, 38,
  43n50, 44, 49, 54, 57, 84–85,
  85n128, 87, 93, 103–6, 135–38;
  movements of, 10, 15, 61,
  74–76, 82–87, 80–81, 111,
  138n107, 145n138, 196n26;
  political action, 54, 56, 61, 71,
  93, 100–101, 106, 111, 126,
  145n138, 168n7, 170n22, 170–
  73, 186–89, 190, 206, 208, 211;
  shifting, 11. *See also:* Democrat;
  Feminism; Justice; News; Power;
  Race; Republican; Revenge;
  Solutions; Tocqueville, Alexis
  de; Tocqueville Paradox
Poor, The, 56, 69, 87, 92, 96–102,
  98n35–36, 152, 152n30, 161–62.
  See also: Justice; Power; Race
Power, xiv, xvii; of enemies, 18, 36–37,
  60–66, 62n27, 71, 83–84, 96–97,
  96n25, 100, 169, 174–75, 208;
  of god, 42, 89, 92, 95–96, 150,
  170n22, 173–75; of media, 3, 5,
  8, 75n84, 77, 194; of ourselves,
  15, 18, 34, 36–37, 63–64, 92,
  100, 208; powerlessness, 18,
  36–37, 61, 64, 66, 77–79, 80,
  84, 86–87, 113, 120–21, 201–2.
  See also: Nietzsche, Friedrich;
  Politics; *Ressentiment*

Prayer, 122n29, 131, 133, 142–43, 151, 159–61, 164, 181, 187, 210–11, 214, 215–16

Pseudo-Environment, *See:* Social Imaginary

Psychotherapy, 19, 65–66, 73, 139, 177n55, 180n66, 205; REACH Model, 139, 210n81; Enright Model, 120, 139, 210n81. *See also:* Cognitive Behavioral Therapy (CBT); Solutions; Suffering

Race, xiii, 21, 63n28, 71, 74–75, 80, 84, 86, 89–90, 111, 138, 143–45, 145n138, 206, 209; Battle on, 143; King on, 90, 101n47107, 111, 206; Tutu on, 117, 135n100, 138, 140–41, 143. *See also:* Bitterness; Enemies; Justice; Love; Poor, the; Power; *Ressentiment*

Radio, 3–4, 29, 207. *See also:* Media Effects; Social Media

Relationships, *See:* Community; Love; Tribe

Religion (Sociological), xvi, 2, 6, 32, 34, 40–45, 46, 49–54, 54–57, 66–67, 82, 84–85, 86–87; decline of, 52–53; Demerath, 52–53; Plausibility Structure, 45–48, 200n44. *See also:* Christian; Social Identity Theory (SIT); Social Imaginary

Republican, 10, 12, 15, 28, 38, 81, 85–86

Ressentiment, 9, 10, 16–19, 37, 58–88, 90, 94, 101n48, 109, 109n89, 109n90, 111, 115, 119–21, 142, 147n3, 196n26, 206n67; and christianity, 67–70, 100–101, 109, 147n3; and justice, 60n9, 71–76, 100–101, 126–28; and media, 74–75, 77–80; definition, 61–66; in politics, 74–76, 82–87, 101n48, 196n26. *See also:* Anger; Bitterness; Nietzsche, Friedrich; Polarization; Victimhood Psychology

Resurrection, 67, 95, 131n76, 132, 157, 168, 170, 175, 178–79, 184, 185, 191, 211. *See also:* Eschaton

Revenge, 16–19, 58–59, 163n29, 62–66, 70, 72, 73, 74n77, 76, 77–79, 80, 84, 87, 90, 97, 109, 115, 119, 121, 123, 127–28, 143, 173, 176–77, 179, 209. *See also:* Justice

Rwandan Genocide, *See:* Testimonies

Sacrifice, 57, 125n49, 156–57, 160, 186, 187n96; dedication offering, 126, 150; guilt offering, 125, 150; peace offering, 150; ritual of the birds, 154; scapegoat, 156; thank offering, 149n14, 150, 153n33; todah, 150–51, 152, 154–55, 156–57, 158, 159–61; sin offering, 125, 150. *See Also:* Sin; Solutions; Symbol; Worship

Salvation, *See:* Cross, The; Eschaton; Forgiveness; Hope

Samaritans, 91, 102–7, 154–56. *See also:* Good Samaritan, The

Schindler's List, *See:* Holocaust, The

SESAM, *See:* Media Effects Models

Sin, 57, 69–70, 94, 96, 113, 118–19, 124n40, 127–28, 129, 131, 147, 163, 169, 180–81, 190, 202, 212; corporate, 100, 117, 129, 133, 135–38, 141–42, 144, 145n138, 172n32, 209, 212; enemies, 94, 99, 100n46, 101, 127–29, 130, 136, 144, 203, 210; intergenerational, *See:* "Sour Grapes;" personal, 100n46, 117, 125–26, 130, 131–34, 139–42, 160n67, 202–3, 210; salvation from, 100n43, 112, 119n12, 129, 130, 131n76, 131–34, 141, 147, 150, 156n51, 156–57, 170, 180–81, 184, 210; unforgiveable, 132, 142n129. *See also:* Enemies; Forgiveness; Sacrifice; Solutions; Suffering

Smartphone, 23, 28, 48, 195–97, 206, 207

Social Media, xv, xvii, 1, 2, 9, 12–14, 16–21, 22–23, 24, 26, 27–30, 31, 33, 38, 46–47, 59, 77–80, 194–98, 206–9; Bail, Chris, 13n62, 21, 24, 25, 26n145, 47n64; Facebook, 12, 45, 48, 195; Instagram, 27, 75; Lanier, Jaron, 28, 48n68; Mason, Lilliana, 10, 11n46, 37, 47n63; Settle, Jamie, 10n39, 11–12, 27; Sunstein, Cass, 13, 22–23, 28n151; Twitter (X), 12, 12n58, 13, 59, 66, 77–80; harm from, 194–98. *See also:* Bitterness; Internet; Media Effects Models; Politics; Social Identity Theory (SIT); Social Imaginary; Solutions; Suffering.\

Social Identity Theory (SIT), 2, 14, 26n145, 32–38, 54–57, 59, 61n14, 151–52, 181, 196, 207–9

Social Imaginary, 2, 6, 7, 28, 31–32, 39, 43, 46; *cosmos*, 32, 40–41, 46, 55, 59; egocentric publics, 23; framing, 6, 7; *nomos*, 32, 39–41, 46, 54–55, 59; pseudo-environment, 4, 8, 39; story, 3, 5n17, 6, 17, 28–29, 32, 32n6, 37, 39–40, 44n51, 54, 59, 62, 64, 67, 89–90, 105–6, 126, 151–52, 159–60, 175–76, 185n90; *telos*, 7, 32–33, 39–44, 40n37, 40n39, 43n50, 54–55, 59, 60n5, 203–5. *See also:* Community; Imagination; Social Identity Theory (SIT); Tribe

Social Ties (Strong/Weak), 23–24, 35, 39, 49, 200n44

Solutions, 3, 20–21, 24, 74–77, 88, 92–94, 101–2, 107, 110–14, 117, 125, 138–43, 147, 159–62, 168–70, 185–89, 198–205, 205–212

"Sour Grapes," 9, 135–39. *See also:* Sin

Speech Theory, 200

Spiral of Silence Theory, *See:* Media Effects Models

Stigmata, *See:* Suffering

Strong Ties, *See:* Social Ties

Suffering, xv, 9, 19n99, 60–66, 72–75, 78, 82–87, 92, 94–95, 97, 108, 113, 128, 142, 177–81, 185; and justice, 14n72, 72–73, 108–9, 126–27; David's, 173–75; depression, 49–52, 79, 112, 195–97, 206; of children, 195–97; of our enemies, 96–98, 108–110; of god, 94–96, 140, 142n126, 181; scars, 177–79; stigmata, 178–79. *See also:* Anomy; Bitterness; Enemies; Poor, The; Psychotherapy; Revenge; Sin; Solutions; Victimhood Psychology

Sukkoth, *See:* Pentecost

Symbol, xvi, 2, 3n8, 7, 32, 32n6, 33, 42n45, 46, 65, 126, 147, 150, 152–53, 175, 181n71, 200, 204; of Judaism, 105–6. *See also:* Imagination; Social Imaginary

Syncretism, 50–54, 55, 84; The Nova Effect, 55. *See also:* Religion; Social Imaginary

Television, 3, 4, 6–8, 29, 44, 50, 54, 194, 207. *See also:* Media Effects; Social Media

Telos, *See:* Social Imaginary

Ten Boom, Corrie, 115, *See:* Testimonies

Testimonies; Irzuvumugabe, Eric, xiv, 143–45; Ten Boom, Corrie, 163–66; Yi, Pastor Wang, 189–91

Todah, *See:* Sacrifice

Tocqueville, Alexis de, 11n49, 36–37, 78–79

Tocqueville Paradox, 11, 36–37, 75n83, 88n136

Tribe, 10n38, 29–30, 35–38, 45, 54, 60–65, 83, 136, 141n123, 209. *See also:* Community; Group Identity; Social Identity Theory (SIT)

Trump, Donald, xiii, 20n105, 85–86, 93, 213. *See also:* Bitterness; Enemies; Politics; *Ressentiment*

Twitter (X), *See:* Social Media

Victimhood Psychology, 6, 10, 16–21, 22, 29, 36, 38, 57, 59, 62n26, 63, 71, 82–84, 85–86, 90, 101n47, 119n15, 121, 124, 138, 140, 143–45, 211; and politics, 20–21, 38, 59, 63, 71, 82–84, 90, 119n15, 138, 140, 170; PIVO, 17–19; TIV, 18. *See also:* Bitterness; Polarization; Politics; Power; *Ressentiment*; Social Identity Theory (SIT); Solutions; Suffering

Weak Ties, *See:* Social Ties
West Wing, The, 89–90, 111
Worship, xiv, 32, 107, 110n92, 126, 134, 149n14, 150–51, 152–55, 157, 160–61, 173, 178–79, 211; temple, 104–7, 109, 155. *See also:* Idolatry; Sacrifice

Yi, Pastor Wang, *See:* Testimonies
Young Adults, 49–54, 79, 141, 195–98

"Zero Sum" 10, 17, 37, 82

Ancient Document Index

Josephus

Ant. 6.10.4	175
Ant. 6.12.4	174
Ant. 6.13.6–7	176
Ant. 8.12.5	103
Ant. 9.14.1–3	103
Ant. 10.9.7	103
Ant. 11.4.3	104
Ant. 11.8.2–5	104
Ant. 12.5.3–5	104
Ant. 13.3.4	104
Ant. 14.4.2–4	105
Ant. 18.2.2	105

Philo

IX. 70	100
XIX. 136	100
XXXIV. 176–82	98
XLII. 231	100

Genesis

1–3	184, 184n84
3:9	181
4:10	95
18:1–16	150n22
37:28	127
43–45	127
43:30	128
45:2	128
50:15–21	127

Exodus

16	152
20:5–6	137n105
20:17	106n74
21:24	74n74
22:21	150n22
32	135
32:7, 11–14, 30–32	136
34:6–7	137n105
34:22	151n27

Leviticus

2–7	150–54
4–7	125
5:2	105n68
13:45–46	154
14:1–32	154
19:17–18	150n22
19:18	74n77
23	152n28
23:9–14	151n27
23:22	152n30

Numbers

5:2	105n68
14:18–19	137n105
19:11–16	105n68
25	136n101
29:12–40	151n27

Deuteronomy

4:25–26	70n56
4:31	137n105
5:9–10	137
6:4–10	31n2
7:9–10	137n105
8:19–20	70n56
10:19	150
11:18–21	31n2
23:7	101n47
26	150–54, 151n28
26:5–10	151–52
26:12	152
31:20	70n56
32:35	74n77, 176n52
32:45–47	31n2

Joshua

4:20	106n74
7	136, 136n101
21:43–45	103n61
22	136n101

Judges

1:2	103n61

1 Samuel

15	174
17	175n41
18	175n41
18–20	174n38
23	175n41
24–26	173–77
24:1	173
25:12	176
27:1	174

1 Kings

16:24	103

2 Kings

17:18	136
17:24–41	103
22–23:30	137
23:26–27	137
23:27	136
25:1–26	103

2 Chronicles

34–35	137

Ezra

4	104n62
10	136

Job

	108, 108n83, 137

Psalms

1	108–110
1:6	109
2	108–110, 153n37
2:9	109
3	108n84
7:17	151n24
8:2	60n6
18	152n33
22	122n29, 143, 181n71
23	154n39, 191n108
23:6	183, 191
28:1–5, 6–9	151n24
30	150–54, 152–53, 152, 152n33
30:5	137n105
30:6	153
30:10	153
32	152n33
35	108–110
37	152n33
37:1–2	108–9
37:11	60n6

37:35-36	108	145-50	181
40	152n33	149	108-110
41	109	149:6-7	87n134
49:7-8, 15	149n14	149:6-9	74n77, 109
50:9-13	148		
63	173-77, 175		

Proverbs

20:22	74n77
25:22	176n52

63:1-3	173
65	152n33
66	152n33
73	91, 108-110, 143, 150-54, 152n33, 153

Ecclesiastes

1:14	57n115
4	110
4:1	91, 96, 108
4:1-12	86-102, 97-98
7	110
10:20	77n90

73:3-12	108
73:16-19	108
73:21-22	109
73:22	113, 147n3
75	150-54, 153, 152n33
75:5	153
75:8	153
75:10	153-54

Isaiah

2:1-4	181-85, 182-83, 184n84
11:6-9	182, 183, 184n84
24:1-27:13	182
25:8	184, 184n85
40:2	131
49:15-16	32n3
53	133n87
55:6-7	131
65:17-18	74n77, 183
65:20	184
65:22	184n84
65:17-25	181-85, 182, 184

86:5	137n105
88	109, 109n86
91:14-16	159
92	150-54, 152n33
94:1	176n52
103:8-9	137n105
104:31	183
107	152n33
112:9	149
115:4-8	44n52
115:8	194
116	150-54, 152n33, 153, 154, 154n39
116:8	184n85
116:12-14	154
118	151n25, 152n33
127:5	93
130:8, 12	119n12
136	152n33
137	109, 109n86
138	152n33
139:13	180
142	173-77, 175
142:1-4	174
143	173-77, 175
143:3-4, 6	174-75

Jeremiah

12:1	108n83
12:7-17	109
25:5-6	70n56
31:16	184n85
31:29-30	9n34, 137
31:34	119n12, 131
32:18	137n105
35:15	70n56
49:12	153n35

Ezekiel

18:1–4	9n34, 137
18:23	94
24:16	184n85
33:11	94
36:25–32	131

Daniel

3	157
9	136

Joel

2:13	137n105
2:18–19; 21–27	158
2:28–32	157

Jonah

3:4	103n57
4:2	137n105

Micah

4:1–5	182
7:18–19	119n12, 137n105

4 Esdras

15:4–5, 22–25	109n85

Wisdom

2	62n22

1 Maccabees

1:10–53	104n66

2 Maccabees

7:5–38	133

Matthew

5:5	60n6, 61n16
5:9–12	177
5:38–48	168–73
5:38, 44	93
5:38–46	118
5:44	205
6:9–15	116, 118, 129–34, 130n67
6:12	130
7:1–5	140
7:3–5	172
9:2–8	118
10:9–15	169n11
12:32	118
10:9–15	169n11
18	123n37, 130, 189
18:15–17	118, 129–34
18:15–35	116
18:18–35	118
18:21	130
18:23–35	130
23:37–39	32n3
24:36	185
25:31–46	71n59
26:11	162
26:38, 42	132
27:46	181

Mark

2:1–12	118
3:28–30	118
11:25	118
14:36	132
15:34	181

Luke

1:46–56	154n38
1:77–78	96
3:13–14	98n36
5:17–26	118
5:32	94
6:37–38	118
7:36–50	150n22, 155n46
7:36–59	118

10:25–37	102–7	
10:37	107	
11:2–4	129–34, 116, 118, 130n37	
11:4	130	
12:8–10	118	
12:13–21	162	
15:11–32	125	
17:3–4	118, 129	
17:11–19	106n75, 154–58	
17:15–16	155	
17:18–19	155	
18:26	205	
18:35–19:10	96–102, 98	
18:40–43	99	
19:1–10	xiv, 91	
19:2–3	99	
19:41–44	32n3	
20:31	178	
22:43	132	
23:34	129–34, 116–17, 118, 132, 132n78	
24:36	178	

John

1:4	110
1:29	133
1:48	182
1:49	183
4:1–42	106n75
5:19, 30	132n84
6:38	132n84
6:68	91
8:28	132n84
8:58	132n82
9:2	137
9:4	132n82
10:10	132n82
12:49–50	132n82
13:34	192
14:10	132n82
17:6–8, 12	157
20:23	141n124
20:24–29	177–81, 178
20:26	178

Acts

2:3	157
2:17–21	154–58
2:41	158
4:32–35	149

Romans

1:21, 28–32	147, 147n3
1:23	147n3
5:3–5	185
5:5	214
5:6–8	117, 129, 131
5:8	112
6	100n43
8:18	181
8:18–25	166
8:22	183
8:29	204
8:37	185
11:11–24	209
12:1	157
12:19	74n77
12:20	176n52

1 Corinthians

1:25	69
13:2	214
15:12–19	67

2 Corinthians

4:16–18	214
12:5–9	60n6

Galatians

3	133n88
3:28	209

Ephesians

4:26	121
4:29	160
6:10–13	87
6:12	92

Philippians

3:18–19	134
4:4–6	147
4:8	32n4

Colossians

3:12–14	129n62

1 Thessalonians

5:2	185n90
5:11	160
5:14–18	164
5:16–18	147

Hebrews

2:17	133n87
3:13	160
8:12	119n12
10:25	160
10:30	176n52

James

1:17	148
3:9–12	68
2:13	102n53
4:7	87
4:1–2, 7–8	70
4:1–12	62n22
5:1–11	62n22

1 Peter

5:8	70, 70n56

1 John

1:5	94n18
4:7–8	94n18, 212
4:18	92

Revelation

21	181–85, 184
21:4	74n77, 184n85
21–22	74n77

www.ingramcontent.com/pod-product-compliance
Lightning Source LLC
Chambersburg PA
CBHW071933240426
43668CB00038B/1561